Jane Warre

Crossing: Language and Ethnicity Among Adolescents

Real Language Series

General Editors:
Jennifer Coates, Roehampton Institute, London,
Jenny Cheshire, Universities of Fribourg and Neuchâtel,
and
Euan Reid, Institute of Education, University of London

Titles published in the series:

Crossing:
Language and Ethnicity
Among Adolescents

Ben Rampton

LONGMAN
London and New York

Longman Group Limited,
Longman House, Burnt Mill,
Harlow, Essex CM20 2JE, England
and Associated Companies throughout the world.

Published in the United States of America
by Longman Publishing, New York

© Longman Group Limited 1995

First published 1995

ISBN 0 582 217903 CSD
ISBN 0 582 217911 PPR

British Library Cataloguing-in-Publication Data

A catalogue record for this book is
available from the British Library

Library of Congress Cataloging-in-Publication Data

Rampton, Ben
    Crossing: language and ethnicity among adolescents / Ben Rampton.
        p.   cm. – (Real language series)
    Includes bibliographical references and index.
    ISBN 0-582-21790-3. – ISBN 0-582-21791-1 (pbk.)
    1. Code switching (Linguistics)–Great Britain.
2. Sociolinguistics–Great Britain. 3. Languages in contact–Great
Britain. 4. Youth–Great Britain–Language. 5. Language and
education–Great Britain. I. Title. II. Series.
P115.3.R36   1995
306.4'4'0941–dc20   94-29266
                                                                  CIP

Set by 8 in 10/12pt Sabon
Produced by Longman Singapore Publishers (Pte) Ltd.
Printed in Singapore

Contents

Transcription symbols and conventions

Prosody

ˎ	low fall	'	high stress
ˏ	low rise	ˌ	low stress
ˋ	high fall	"	very high stress
ˊ	high rise	͵	very low stress
ˇ	fall rise	⌐	pitch register shift upwards
ˏˋ	rise fall	∟	pitch register shift downwards
		↑	extra pitch height

Segmental phonetics

[ ] IPA phonetic transcription (revised to 1979)

The sounds of the phonetic symbols used in transcription can be roughly glossed as follows:

Vowels

[ɪ]   as in 'kit' [kɪt]
[i]   as in 'fleece' (but shorter) [fliːs]
[e]   as in 'dress' [dɹes]
[ɛ]   as in French 'père'
[æ]   as in 'trap' [tɹæp]
[a]   as in French 'patte' [pat]
[ɑ]   as in 'start' (but shorter) [stɑːt]
[ʌ]   as in 'strut' [stɹʌt]
[ɒ]   as in 'lot' [lɒt]

[ɔ]   as in 'north' (but shorter) [nɔːθ]
[o]   as in French 'eau'
[ʊ]   as in 'foot' [fʊt]
[u]   as in 'goose' (but shorter) [guːs]
[ə]   as in '<u>a</u>bout', 'upp<u>er</u>' [əbaʊt]
[ɜ]   as in 'nurse' (but shorter) [nɜːs]
[eɪ]   as in 'face' [feɪs]
[aɪ]   as in 'price' [pɹaɪs]
[ɔɪ]   as in 'choice' [tʃɔɪs]
[ɪə]   as in 'near' [nɪə]
[ɛə]   as in 'square' [skwɛə]
[ʊə]   as in 'cure' [kjʊə]
[əʊ]   as in 'goat' [gəʊt]
[aʊ]   as in 'mouth' [maʊθ]

Consonants

[p]   as in 'pea' [piː]
[b]   as in 'bee' [biː]
[t]   as in 'toe' [təʊ]
[ʈ]   like [t], but with the tip of the tongue curled back (retroflexed)
[ʇ]   voiceless alveolar click, the sound often made in disappointment, or, used twice, with disapproval
[d]   as in 'doe' [dəʊ]
[ɖ]   like [d], but with the tip of the tongue retroflexed
[k]   as in 'cap' [kæp]
[g]   as in 'gap' [gæp]
[x]   as in Scottish 'loch' [lɒx]
[f]   as in 'fat' [fæt]
[v]   as in 'vat' [væt]
[θ]   as in 'thing' [θɪŋ]
[ð]   as in 'this' [ðɪs]
[s]   as in 'sip' [sɪp]
[ʂ]   like [s], but with the tip of the tongue retroflexed
[z]   as in 'zip' [zɪp]
[ʃ]   as in 'ship' [ʃɪp]
[ʒ]   as in 'measure' [meʒə]
[h]   as in 'hat' [hæt]
[ʔ]   glottal stop, as in Cockney 'butter' [bʌʔə]

[m] as in 'map' [mæp]
[n] as in 'nap' [næp]
[ɳ] like [n], but with the tip of the tongue retroflexed
[ŋ] as in 'hang' [haŋ]
[l] as in 'led' [led]
[ɭ] like [l], but with the tip of the tongue retroflexed
[ɫ] as in 'table' [teɪbɫ]
[ɹ] as in 'red' [ɹed]
[ɽ] like [ɹ], but with the tip of the tongue retroflexed
[ɾ] like [ɹ], but with the tongue tip tapping once against the teeth ridge (sometimes used in English 'very')
[j] as in 'yet' [jet]
[w] as in 'wet' [wet]
[ʧ] as in 'chin' [ʧɪn]
[ʤ] as in 'gin' [ʤɪn]

Conversational features

[overlapping turns

= two utterances closely connected without a noticeable overlap, or different parts of a single speaker's turn
(.) pause of less than one second
(1.5) approximate length of pause in seconds
l. lenis (quiet) enunciation
f. fortis (loud) enunciation
CAPITALS fortis (loud enunciation)
(( )) 'stage directions'
( ) speech inaudible
(text) speech hard to discern, analyst guess
Bold instance of crossing of central interest in discussion

Informant backgrounds

The ethnic background of informants is indicated as follows:

AC = Afro-Caribbean
An = white Anglo
Ba = Bangladeshi

In = Indian
Pa = Pakistani

(Classifying informants in terms of ethnic background raises some of the problems discussed in Chapter 1.2. The use of classifications such as these is discussed in Chapter 1, note 3.)

F   = Female
M   = Male

THE INTERNATIONAL PHONETIC ALPHABET

		Bilabial	Labiodental	Dental, Alveolar, or Post-alveolar	Retroflex	Palato-alveolar
CONSONANTS (pulmonic air-stream mechanism)	Nasal	m	ɱ	n	ŋ	
	Plosive	p b		t d	ʈ ɖ	
	(Median) Fricative	ɸ β	f v	θ ð s z	ʂ ʐ	ʃ ʒ
	(Median) Approximant		ʋ	ɹ	ɻ	
	Lateral Fricative			ɬ ɮ		
	Lateral (Approximant)			l	ɭ	
	Trill			r		
	Tap or Flap			ɾ	ɽ	
CONSONANTS (non-pulmonic air-stream)	Ejective	p'		t'		
	Implosive	ɓ		ɗ		
	(Median) Click	ʘ		ʇ ʗ		
	Lateral Click			ʖ		

DIACRITICS

ₒ	Voiceless n̥ d̥	ˌ or .	Raised e˔, ẹ, e̝ w	
ˬ	Voiced s̬ ṭ	˓ or .	Lowered e˕, ẹ, e̞ ʁ	
ʰ	Aspirated tʰ	+	Advanced u+, u̟	
‥	Breathy-voiced b̤ a̤	- or ‒	Retracted i̠, i-, t̠	
̩	Dental t̪	‥	Centralized ë	
̫	Labialized t̫	~	Nasalized ã	
̬	Palatalized t̬	ɹ, ɾ, ʁ	r-colout̫rf a˞	

Velarized or Pharyngealized ɫ, ɬ : Long ɑː

Syllabic n̩ l̩ · Half-long ɑ·

^ or ˌ Simultaneous sf (but see ˘ Non-syllabic u̯
also under the heading´ ˒ More rounded ɔ˒
Affricates) ˓ Less rounded y˓
‒‒‒ Creaky voice

OTHER SYMBOLS

ɕ, ʑ	Alveolo-palatal fricatives
ʃ, ʒ	Palatalized ʃ, ʒ
ɼ	Alveolar fricative trill
ɺ	Alveolar lateral flap
ɧ	Simultaneous ʃ and x
ʃˢ	Variety of ʃ resembling s, etc.
ɪ	= ɩ
ʊ	= ɷ
ɜ	= Variety of ə
ɚ	= r-coloured ə

(Revised to 1979)

Palatal	Velar	Uvular	Labial-Palatal	Labial-Velar	Pharyngeal	Glottal
ɲ	ŋ	N				
c ɟ	k g	q G		k͡p g͡b		ʔ
ç j	x ɣ	χ ʁ		ʍ	ħ ʕ	h ɦ
j	ɰ		ɥ	w		
ʎ						
		ʀ				
		ʀ				
	k'					
	ɠ					

		VOWELS			STRESS, TONE (PITCH)

Front		Back			Front	Back	
i	ɨ	ɯ	*Close*	y	ʉ	u	
ɪ				Y		ɤ	
e		ɣ	*Half-close*	ø		o	
ə					θ		
ɛ	ʌ		*Half-open*	œ		ɔ	
æ ɐ							
a	ɑ		*Open*	Œ		ɒ	

Unrounded   *Rounded*

STRESS, TONE (PITCH)

' stress placed at beginning of stressed syllable: , secondary stress: ⁻ high level pitch, high tone: ˍ low level: ´ high rising: ˌ low rising: ` high falling: ˏ low falling: ^ rise-fall: ˜ fall-rise.

AFFRICATES can be written as digraphs, as ligatures, or with slur marks; thus ts, tʃ, dʒ: ʦ, ʧ, ʤ: t͡s t͡ʃ d͡ʒ. c, ɟ may occasionally be used for tʃ , dʒ.

Author's acknowledgements

This book has taken a long time to complete. It would have been impossible without the young people who acted as informants. They made fieldwork the high point of the research process, and I have a very great debt to them. I would also like to thank their teachers and youth leaders. I hope I can be forgiven for using pseudonyms when I refer to them.

Though they may not recognise it in the end product, there have also been a number of other people who have taken time to improve my understanding of the social and linguistic processes that I try to describe: Chris Brumfit, Jill Bourne, Debbie Cameron, Paul Drew, Liz Frazer, Penny Harvey, Roger Hewitt, Dick Hudson, Eric Kellerman, David Langford, Bob Le Page, Iris Lincoln, Derek Lincoln, Carol Pfaff, Kay Richardson, Celia Roberts, Mukul Saxena, Peter Skehan and Mike Stubbs. I am also grateful to Liz Frazer, Euan Reid and Jennifer Coates, whose detailed comments on earlier drafts have made the final text much more readable and to the staff at Longman for their considerable efficiency and help.

Financial support for the work has been provided by the Economic and Social Research Council (a doctoral studentship and a project grant – No. 00232390), the British Association of Applied Linguistics (a grant for equipment), and the Leverhulme Trust (a Research Fellowship). I would like to thank all three.

Words can never properly acknowledge the extent of my debt to the inspiration and support of Joan, Tony and Amelia Rampton.

Publisher's acknowledgements

We are grateful to the following for permission to reproduce copyright material:

Association of Caribbean Studies for adapted extracts from 'Coughing up Five' by L Back in *Journal of Caribbean Studies* 6.2, 1988; Blackwell Publishers for extracts from *Forms of Talk* by E Goffman, *Language in the Inner City* by W Labov; British Sociological Association Publications Ltd & the author for extracts adapted from 'Political Ritual and Social Integration' by S Lukes in *Sociology* Volume 9, No 2, May 1975; Cambridge University Press & the author for an extracts from *White Talk, Black Talk* by R Hewitt; Cambridge University Press for extracts & adapted extracts from *Language, Gender and Sex in Comparative Perspective* by M & G Goodwin 1987, *Bilinguality and Bilingualism* by J Hamers & M Blanc 1989, *Acts of Identity* by R LePage & A Keller-Tabouret 1985, 'Ten Hypotheses for the Analysis of the New Movements' by A Melucci in *Contemporary Italian Sociology* (ed. D Pinto) 1981, 'Agreeing & disagreeing with assessments' by A Pomeratz in *Structures of Social Action* (eds. M Atkinson & J Heritage) 1984, *Rethinking Symbolism* by D Sperber 1975, *Communicative Methodology in Language Teaching* by C Brumfit 1984, 'Today There is no Respect' by J Hill in *Pragmatics* 2/3 1992, *Discourse Strategies* by J Gumperz 1982, 'Introduction' by J Gumperz & J Cook-Gumperz in *Language and Social Identity* (ed. J Gumperz) 1982; European Science Foundation for extracts & adapted extracts from 'Bilingualism in/as socialisation' by J Auer in *Papers for the*

Sympsoium on Code-Switching in Bilingual Studies. 1991; The Controller of Her Majesty's Stationery Office for extracts & adapted extracts from *CMND 9453 – Education for All* D.E.S. 1985, *English for Ages 5 to 16* D.E.S. 1989; International Thomson Publishing Services for extracts & adapted extracts from 'Subcultures, Cultures & Class' by J Clarke, S Hall, T Jefferson, B Roberts in *Resistance through Rituals* (ed. S Hall, T. Jefferson) 1976, *There Ain't No Black in the Union Jack* by P Gilroy, pubd. Hutchison 1987; Manchester University Press, for an extract adapted from *Te Kalela Dance* by J C Mitchell; Mouton de Gruyter for extracts & adapted extracts from 'A Conversation analytic approach to Code-switching in transfer' by J Auer in *Codeswitching* (ed. M Heller) 1988, 'Caught in a well of words' by J Cook-Gumprez & W Corsaro in *Children's Words & Children's Language* (ed. J Cook Gumperz, W Corsaro, J Streech) 1986, 'Communicative functions of phobic communion' in *Organisation of Behaviour in Face to Face Interaction* (ed. A Kendon, R Harris & M Key) 1975; New School for Social Research for extracts from 'The Symbolic Challenge of Contemporary Movements' by A Melucci in *Social Research 52.4* 1985; Open University Press for extracts adapted from 'Bhangra 1984–8' in *Black Music in Britain* by Banerji & Bauman (ed. P Oliver) 1990; Penguin Books Ltd/ Gillian Sankoff, Executrix of the Ervin Goffman Will for an extract adapted from *Interaction Ritual: Essays on Face to Face Behaviour* by Erving Goffman (Allen Lane The Penguin Press, 1972) copyright © Erving Goffman, 1967; Penguin Books Ltd/Harper Collins Inc. for extracts from *Relations in Public: Microstudies of the Public Order* by Erving Goffman (Allen Lane The Penguin Press, 1971) copyright © Erving Goffman, publ. Basic Books Inc; PAJ Publications (a division of the Performing Arts Journal)/Johns Hopkins University Press for extracts & adapted extracts from *From Ritual to Theatre* by Victor Turner. 1974; Routledge for extracts & adapted extracts from 'Religion & Ritual' in *The Social Science Encyclopedia* (eds. A Kuper, J Kuper) publ. Routledge & Kegan Paul 1985, Hobson Jobson by H Yule & A Burnell, publ. Routledge & Kegan Paul 1985, *The Dialogics of Critique* by M Gardiner, 1992; Seminar Press Ltd for extracts & adapted extracts from *Marxism and the Philosophy of Language* by V Volosinov (trans. L Matejka & J R Titunik) 1973; Taylor &

Francis for an extract adapted from *Investigating Classroom Talk* by A Edwards & D Westgate, pubd. Falmer 1987; Texas A & M University Press for extracts & adapted extracts from *The Dialogic Imagination* by M Bakhtin (trans. C Emerson, M Holquist); University of Arizona Press for extracts & adapted extracts from *Speaking Mexicano* by J Hill & K Hill. 1986; University of Minnesota Press for extracts & adapted extracts from *Problems in Dostoevsky's Poetics* (trans. C Emerson) Copyright © 1984 University of Minnesota Press; Verso/New Left Books for an adapted extract from *Walter Benjamin: Or Toward A Revolutionary Criticism* by T Eagleton:

We have unfortunately been unable to trace the copyright holders of 'Play & Ritual' in *Its a Funny Thing Humour* by D Handleman and *Racism & Popular Culture: A Cultural Studies Approach* by P. Cohen, and would appreciate any information which would enable us to do so.

For
Amelia
Joan and Tony

Part I

Preliminaries

1 *Introduction: Language, ethnicity and youth in late industrial Britain*

During a game of badminton:

Chris ((to Peter)):	what you doing
Peter:	PLAYING BADMINTON
Chris:	could have fooled me
Rich.:	go on you serve
Peter:	((in Indian English)): **ONE NIL**
Imran:	love- love one
	(adapted from Extract III.8 in Chapter 6)

During detention:

Ms J:	I'll be back in a second with my lunch
Asif:	NO dat's sad man. I had to miss my play right, I've gotta go
	(2.5)
	((Ms J must now have left the room))
Asif ((Creole influenced)):	**llunch** you don't need no lunch **not'n grow** anyway ((laughs))
Alan:	((laughs))
Asif:	have you eat your lunch Alan
	(adapted from Extract II.17 in Chapter 5)

Listening to Panjabi music during breaktime:

Sally ((calling out)):	OH LORRAINE EH LORRAINE HAS IT GOT **KENOO MINOO** ON it
?:	you want the other side
Anon A:	it's got ((singing)) **holle holle**
Sally ((sings)):	**o kennoo mennoo** I love-
Gurmit:	oh that
	(adapted from Extract IV.6 in Chapter 10)

Concentrating on exchanges such as these, this book studies sociolinguistic processes in multiracial urban youth culture. It draws on ethnographic research into adolescent friendship groups in one neighbourhood in the South Midlands of England, and it focuses on 'language crossing' – the use of Panjabi by young people of Anglo and Afro-Caribbean descent, the use of Creole by Anglos and Panjabis, and the use of stylised Indian English by all three. Although linguistic interchange of this kind has been very little researched, it plays an important role in the negotiation of social identity, and serves as a rich point of entry for analysis of the connections between language, ethnic relations, youth culture and the experience of social change.

Due to the diversity of their ethnic backgrounds, the adolescents in this study differed a good deal in their knowledge of neighbourhood languages. In addition, Panjabi, Creole and Indian English had each been the subject of considerable controversy in race politics. But running contrary to potentially divisive pressures such as these, adolescents often seemed to renegotiate the relationship between language and group membership in the course of spontaneous multiracial recreation. How far, and in what ways, were intricate processes of language sharing and exchange turning the resources originally associated with separate ethnic inheritances towards the enunciation of interethnic youth, class and neighbourhood community?

It can be very difficult to obtain accurate reports of these delicate processes, or to simulate them outside the context of spontaneous peer group interaction. But they can be investigated using the methodologies of ethnographic sociolinguistics (Hymes 1972a, 1972b; Gumperz 1982), combining close attention to the situations, activities and social relationships that promote language crossing, with detailed analysis of the spontaneous discourse in which it occurs.

1.1 Starting points in sociolinguistics and sociology

In a variety of ways, Roger Hewitt's book *White Talk, Black Talk* (1986) acts as a central point of departure. Looking closely at adolescent social life in playgrounds, streets and youth clubs in South London, Hewitt provides an ethnographic description of the different ways in which white adolescents developed the use of

English-based Caribbean Creole in their interactions with white and black peers. In principle, young people of Caribbean descent were generally opposed to what they regarded as an unjustifiable expropriation of one of the vital resources of their ethnic inheritance, and Hewitt explains this opposition in terms of Creole's major symbolic role in the political struggle against race oppression, locally, nationally and indeed internationally as well. Despite this however, certain minimal uses of Creole by whites were quite widely acceptable to black adolescents, and within the relative privacy of interracial friendship, some white youngsters actually used Creole quite extensively. In describing the delicate processes through which these adolescents managed to gain access to Creole, Hewitt provides a detailed view of the ways in which adolescents provisionally renegotiated the political significance that wider patterns of race stratification had for them.

For sociolinguistics, Hewitt's study is significant both in its sustained attention to the politics of interactional language use, and in its comprehensive description of a type of linguistic practice that has received very little attention in the literature. But it is also important as a sociological contribution to the study of race and youth.

Over the last 20 years in Britain, the social relations of young people of different ethnic backgrounds have been researched from a number of perspectives. The links between race, peer relations and school have been studied quite extensively in education, psychology and social psychology,[1] but within these disciplines the emerging descriptions have frequently been limited by at least three factors. First, because the importance of ethnic group membership usually varies a great deal from one interactional situation to another, there are problems of validity for methods built around a fairly brief encounter between researcher and informant (e.g. sociometry and attitude testing). Secondly, adolescents (and indeed adults) often express their group identifications in inexplicit, non-propositional ways, for example through style, activity and accent, and so some of the most important ethnic processes can be missed in studies that rely on the answers given in questionnaires and interviews (Willis 1977: 122; Hewitt 1986: 7–8). Thirdly, research in these traditions is usually very limited in what it can say about the ways in which adolescents actually negotiate ethnic difference in interaction with one another (cf. Milner 1983: 125; Tomlinson 1983: 126; Hewitt 1986: 2).

During the 1970s and early 1980s there were also a number of ethnographic studies of school and peer group culture which attended to ethnicity (e.g. Pearson 1976; Taylor 1976; Robins and Cohen 1978; Troyna 1978; Pryce 1979; Kitwood and Borrill 1980; Wright 1984). These generally presented a fuller picture of the youth cultural milieux influencing group relations, but they were overwhelmingly concerned with providing a description of particular ethnic groups: what actually happened in the arena of intergroup contact was seldom empirically addressed. It is only more recently that a number of studies of youth have centred their attention on cross-ethnic interaction itself, and have located this within a broader context of political and economic relations (Gilroy 1987; Gilroy and Lawrence 1988; Jones 1988; Back 1993). Hewitt's research comes as a front-runner among these more recent studies, and it is unique in its demonstration of the central role that language plays in adolescent negotiations of race and ethnic difference.

In the chapters that follow, I shall frequently refer back to Hewitt's research. My own work includes analyses of Creole use among adolescents of non-Caribbean descent, it attends to roughly the same historical period and, in a number of respects, my fieldwork methods directly replicated Hewitt's. As with other forms of ethnography, critics often accuse linguistic ethnography of a-theoretical butterfly collecting – 'descriptive fieldwork . . . at the expense of comparative analysis' (Philipsen and Carbaugh 1986: 387; Fasold 1990: 60–2; also Hammersley 1987, 1992). Taking note of this, my own study attempts to contribute to a properly cumulative, comparative ethnography of communication (Hymes 1980), and in part, it is through cross-reference to the South London research that I try to do so. In addition, theoretical aspirations are also assisted by the availability of other, more exclusively sociological studies of the socio-cultural terrain that Hewitt describes, and among these, Paul Gilroy's book *There Ain't No Black in the Union Jack* (1987) is especially helpful.

Gilroy's book is a detailed cultural history of ethnic relations in Britain from the 1970s to the mid-1980s, focusing on dominant mass media discourses, municipal antiracist campaigns, antiracist popular movements, and expressive youth culture. These analyses are set in a framework of sociological theory that is much more explicit than Hewitt's, and because (a) it provides an important cultural and political map of contemporary Britain, and because (b)

I shall draw on several of its key notions quite frequently, it is worth taking a little time to summarise some of its central arguments.

1.2 Competing grounds for political solidarity

Gilroy pays particular attention to the relationship between race and class: he recognises that the unequal social and material relationships generated around work are important, but rejects any idea that these have an exclusive role in social structuring. Workplace relations and the conflict between capital and labour are no longer central in the subjective experience of inequality: less than 30 per cent of the United Kingdom workforce is now engaged in manufacturing; there is mass unemployment and substantial regional inequality; race solidarity often cross-cuts formal economic divisions; feminist analyses reveal major structural inequalities at home. In view of the many kinds of discrimination that exist outside the workplace, it is no longer possible to regard class alone as an adequate basis for political organisation:

> What is the working class today? What gender is it? What colour is it? How in the light of its obvious segmentation, is it to be unified? Is this unification still possible or even desirable? . . . The complex experiential chemistry of class, 'race' and gender . . . yields an important reminder of the limitations of analysis based exclusively on a narrow conception of class. (Gilroy 1987: 19)

Gilroy offers no definitive answer to the questions he poses. But he does provide a detailed account of the way in which different kinds of solidarity compete to replace class as central points for political affiliation. For my research, two are particularly important.

One strand can be found in the discourses of nation that feature in formal politics and the mass media. Here with increasing force, an ethnically exclusive idea of British culture and nationhood is put forward as a central basis for political solidarity. With the late industrial crisis in the political representation of the working-class movement, people in subordinate material and economic positions are increasingly invited to conceptualise their political situation in terms of nation and ethnicity. Discourses about nation are involved in some of the most obvious forms of racism. But at the same time, there is also a shift away from crude efforts to define nationhood in terms of biological race, towards a view of nationhood in terms of 'culture' and 'way of life'.

This shift accommodates more subtle forms of racism and it finds expression in more respectable political circles. When nationality is understood as 'culture' rather than as biological descent, the boundaries around national belonging become more permeable, there is some scope for assimilation, and there is no longer such an obvious contradiction of the fundamental liberal view that people should be judged by their conduct rather than by their birth. Even so, this new approach continues to have much the same kind of impact as discourses which invoke biological definitions of 'race'. This is because it is grounded in a narrow interpretation of 'culture'.

'Cultures' are seen as a set of discrete, homogeneous and fairly static ethnic essences, and these ethnic essences are regarded as serving as the central influence in shaping a person's character. Gilroy calls this perspective 'ethnic absolutism' (1987: ch. 2). It gives to ethnicity an exclusive emphasis which hides all the other social categories which individuals belong to (categories defined in terms of age, gender, sexual orientation, residence, occupation, interests, style, activity, role, and so on). It obscures the fact that individuals form complicated and often contradictory patterns of solidarity and opposition across a *range* of category memberships. And the emphasis on one aspect of identity to the exclusion of all others permits the straightforward division of people into simple dichotomous groups, a division supported by the spurious and idealised notion of unitary 'Britishness'. The possibility of conversion from non-British to British remains, but ethnic absolutism means that any activity showing the traces of non-British roots can be read for signs of disloyalty rather than, for example, as an effort to articulate complex experience in a way that might make sense of life in Britain for a highly heterogeneous population.[2] Gilroy argues that in concrete terms, from about 1976, one of the effects of this discursive shift towards a culturalist definition of Britishness has been to draw black cultural and recreational institutions (for example clubs and social events) into sharp public focus, casting them as the alien catalysts of social disruption in British life. These have become the target for heavy police surveillance, as well as a primary site of political confrontation (Gilroy 1987: ch. 3).

This cultural definition of Britishness has, then, been one

influential and reactionary effort to generate new forms of late industrial solidarity – it makes itself very evident in the press and public media, it is 'ethnically absolutist', equating nation with culture and then culture with ethnicity, and it has coordinated with increased state surveillance of black recreational institutions. Differing from this in almost every respect, Gilroy then draws attention to the political sensibilities emerging from within mixed communities in inner city areas. He suggests that as a potential point of orientation in the organisation of (radical) collective action, experiences of multiracial urban community actually compete with discourses of 'Britishness', and in an attempt to define the character of this kind of alternative political solidarity, he draws on the theory of 'new social movements' (Gilroy 1987: ch. 6; also Melucci 1980, 1981, 1985, 1988; Touraine 1981, 1985).

Gilroy's analysis of urban communities as social movements is more tentative than his analysis of the dominant race and nation discourses, and he also suggests that a more robust radical politics can be identified in black music and the modes of consumption most closely associated with it (1987: ch. 5). Nevertheless, there is a great deal of relevance for my own work in the way in which Gilroy discusses social movements.

A social movement – for example, the women's or the peace movement – is neither simply a pressure group, nor is it a 'peripheral phenomenon of deviation or outright conflict' (Touraine 1981: 94). Far from being 'exceptional or dramatic events, social movements lie permanently at the heart of social life' (p. 29), and this is reflected in Gilroy's phrase 'interpretive community'. Seen as interpretive communities, social movements

> are not ready made agents for structural change, but rather 'symptoms of resistance to domination'. They have their roots in a radical sense of powerlessness and though their resistances may have important effects on cities and societies, they are best understood as defensive organisations which are unlikely to be able to make the transition to more stable forms of politics (Gilroy 1987: 231)

Social movements are ensembles of causes, and rather than seeking to conquer political power or state apparatuses, their objective is 'the control of a field of autonomy or independance *vis-à-vis* the system' (p. 226).

Their goals involve the transformation of new modes of subordination located outside the immediate processes of production and
consequently require the reappropriation of space, time, and of
relationships between individuals in their day to day lives . . . 'The
defense of identity, continuity and predictability of personal experience is beginning to constitute the substance of new conflicts'
(Melucci 1980) . . . advanced capitalism has developed a 'capacity
for intervention and transformation which extends beyond the
natural environment and exerts an influence on social systems, on
interpersonal relations and on the very structure of the individual'
(Melucci 1980: 218; Gilroy 1987: 224, 225)

Political action usually focuses on the immediate conditions in
which exploitation and domination are experienced, and in this
context, face-to-face interaction becomes a potentially important
arena for action and analysis. In fact, with its connotations of
mass political mobilisation, the term 'social movement' can be a
little misleading. To bring out the importance of relatively small-
scale local processes, Melucci suggests the phrase 'movement
networks' to describe the most common situation:

The normal situation of today's 'movement' is a network of small
groups submerged in everyday life which require a personal
involvement in experiencing and practicing cultural innovation.
They emerge only on specific issues, as for instance the big mobilisations for peace, for abortion, against nuclear policy . . . [But for
much of the time, movements are 'latent'.] Latency allows people to
experience directly new cultural models – changes in the system of
meanings – which are very often opposed to the dominant social
codes: the meaning of sexual differences, time and space, relationship to nature, to the body and so on. Latency creates new cultural
codes and makes individuals practice them . . . [Movements leave
latency and become visible w]hen small groups emerge to confront
a political authority on a specific issue, . . . demonstrat[ing] opposition to the logic underlying decision making with regard to public
policy. (Melucci 1985: 800–1)

In Gilroy's analysis, the symbolic repertoire of black expressive
culture plays a central role articulating opposition to 'dominant
social codes', and more generally, urban social movements are
often unified by the rituals and symbols associated with community, where it is the 'multi-accentuality' and 'malleability' of such

symbols that constitute their value:

> The idea of a social movement as an interpretive community should
> not lead to an undifferentiated monadical view of the group from
> which it wins support. Sharing a common body of symbols created
> around notions of 'race', ethnicity or locality, common history or
> identity does not dictate the sharing of the plural meanings which
> may become attached to those symbols and cluster around them.
> Community is as much about difference as it is about similarity.
> (Gilroy 1987: 235)

It is clear, then, that as points of political orientation to replace
the discourses of class, there is a sharp contradiction and a continuing conflict between an active sense of urban community on the
one hand, and on the other, absolutist discourses of race and
nation. Discourses of race and nation have their roots in constituencies remote from the experience of inner city life. They merge the
inner city with images of crime, danger and alienation (Gilroy
1987: ch. 3), and in the representation of urban riots, they filter out
the facts of white participation and instead talk only of black youth
criminality. In contrast, an active sense of urban community is
generated locally, and neighbourhood serves as a symbolic resource
articulating a diverse range of local interests. At local level, the ethnic absolutism and the culturalist definitions of nation disseminated
through the mass media are experienced as a set of disabling racist
images, which continually threaten to insert themselves into the
interpersonal relations of everyday life (Gilroy 1987: 234, 235;
Hewitt 1986: 236; Jones 1988: 177), and here, if anything, urban
riots are regarded as major events reclaiming neighbourhood from
the intrusion of a state surveillance which persistently transgresses
the norms of decent conduct (1987: chs 3 and 6).

A full treatment of absolutist discourses, social movements and
the tension between them would require a much more comprehensive account of macro-social organisation than I can provide in
this study. Nevertheless, these concepts serve as important points
of background orientation, and in much of what follows, I shall
try to situate multiracial adolescent language use in the terrain
where these forms of solidarity conflict.

In fact Gilroy's analysis is compatible with sociolinguistics in
other ways. It treats 'race' (and indeed 'class') as a socio-cultural

construct, a contextually contingent interpretive device shaping a range of often conflicting actions at interpersonal, local and national levels (Gilroy 1987: 17, 27, 38; cf. e.g. Gumperz 1982: 99). And although language itself figures only occasionally, Gilroy's account provides a clear rationale for the political import-ance of linguistic and cultural phenomena. Where the economic relations of class are seen as the single most important axis of stratification, the political significance of culture has often been played down. This has happened, for example, within the soci-ology of youth subculture: 'There is no "subcultural career" for the working-class lad, no "solution" in the subcultural milieu for problems posed in the key structuring experiences of the class . . . Subcultures . . . "solve", but in an imaginary way, problems which at the concrete material level remain unresolved' (Clarke et al 1976: 47–8). The same occurs in linguistics. In discussion of lan-guage and gender, Cameron notes:

> a change in linguistic practice is not just a reflection of some more fundamental social change: it is, itself, a social change. Anti-feminists are fond of observing that eliminating generic masculine pronouns does not secure equal pay. Indeed it does not – whoever said it would? Eliminating generic masculine pronouns precisely eliminates generic masculine pronouns. And in so doing it changes the reper-toire of social meanings and choices available to social actors. In the words of [one observer], it 'constitutes a restructuring of at least one aspect of one social relationship'. (Cameron 1990: 90)

Though they are undoubtedly still important, politics involves more than economic class relations.

So, in their analyses of the complicated dialectic between race, class, language and multiracial community, Hewitt and Gilroy provide the most important initial bearings for the present study. In what ways can my analysis claim to be distinctive? In due course, a number of differences will emerge, but two are particu-larly clear at the outset.

1.3 Distinctive concerns in the present study

One of the most significant differences between my work and the research of Hewitt, Gilroy and closely related authors lies in its attention to adolescents of South Asian descent. Although they sometimes make passing reference to young Asians, sociological discussions of interethnic youth culture have been overwhelmingly concerned with the relationship between white and black.[3] Furthermore, to date, sociological descriptions suggest that in some areas Asians are not only excluded from this multiracial dynamic, but that they are also the object of shared black and white hostility (Cohen 1972: 29; Hewitt 1986: 195, 216–8; Jones 1988: 217–9; Back 1992: 29; Centre for Multicultural Education 1992: 37). In contrast, my own work was based in a neighbourhood where young Asians played a major role in multiracial youth culture, just at the time when a form of popular music with Panjabi roots was starting to achieve some national celebrity (bhangra). As a result, my research is able to add an important corrective to the growing sociological literature on multiracial youth culture. In terms of sociolinguistic analysis, this also means that Hewitt's micropolitical analyses of Creole are extended to Panjabi and Indian English.[4]

I also give fuller attention to language education issues (though cf. Gilroy and Lawrence 1988; Hewitt 1989). School corridors, dinner halls and playgrounds serve as settings in many of my empirical analyses; educational responses to cultural and linguistic diversity feature quite often in my interpretations of the significance of language crossing (especially in Part II); and as a whole, this study has implications for language policy discussion that are drawn out in Part V. Language education obviously involves far more than technical pedagogic issues, and over the last 30 years in Britain, language and race in education has been a major focus for conflict between central government, local government, educational professionals, parents, pupils and the 'general public' (each of these constituencies itself embracing a range of frequently conflicting positions). Questions about equality of opportunity, cultural pluralism, racism, social cohesion and social justice have featured as significantly as issues of teaching method in the discourse of language educationalists, and in race politics more generally, language in education has frequently been a central concern.[5]

In this debate, there has been a great deal of concern with the impact that different forms of linguistic provision are likely to have on interethnic relations among youth (e.g. DES 1985: ch. 7; DES 1988: 43; DES 1989: 10.12). But despite widespread sociolinguistic recognition of the peer group's role as a key socialising agency (Bernstein 1960, 1975; Hudson 1980; Romaine 1984), with the exception of Hewitt, there has been a dearth of ethnographic research into language and ethnic relations in pupil peer groups. In the fairly extensive British literature on young ethnic minority bilinguals and bidialectals,[6] some research has focused on attitudes, relations and language use with age-mates, but like many other British studies, these have entailed neither prolonged first-hand contact with informants in the field, nor close analysis of the details of cross-ethnic adolescent interaction. A number of educational studies have used observational methods to describe peer group interaction in the classroom,[7] and a few have also observed behaviour in the playground. But their perspective has been pedagogic rather than sociolinguistic or sociological. One of this book's aims is to make up for some of this deficiency, and to enable debate about language education to refer to a more firmly grounded base of research on multilingual peer group interaction (see also Rampton 1988, 1992).

With these sociolinguistic, sociological and educational coordinates for my own research in place, it is now possible to formulate the central questions guiding it. These are, primarily,

1. How do outgroup uses of Panjabi, Indian English and Creole relate to the shifting and contested relationship between race and class in late industrial Britain?
2. How far and in what ways can language crossing practices be construed as a form of everyday cultural politics?

Also,

3. What implications do they have for educational discussions that are often oblivious to the cultural activities of the youth that they target?

These questions also mean that in more purely sociolinguistic terms, I shall also be asking:

4. What is language crossing? As a discursive strategy, how is it to be characterised? For the purposes of initial description, we can take it as the use of language varieties associated with social or ethnic groups that the speaker does not normally 'belong' to,

but in due course, crossing will need to be systematically situated among other pragmatic phenomena.

To address these questions, it will be necessary to attend to several different levels of social organisation, some micro and some macro. I shall briefly refer to these in the next section, and provide some general theoretical comment on the relationship between them.

1.4 Descriptive and theoretical concepts

Verbal interaction will be the central object of empirical attention in this study (from Chapter 3 onwards). In the course of its examination, four broad dimensions of linguistic and socio-cultural organisation will be taken into consideration:

1. *Language use*: The pragmatic and symbolic meanings of Creole, Panjabi and Indian English, particularly when these are used by people who neither have linguistic 'ownership rights', nor normally speak these languages.
2. *Interaction structures and processes*: The kinds of phenomena extensively explored by Ervin Goffman – different speech and listening roles, the ways in which participants arrange themselves, access one another and distribute their attention both in verbal and non-verbal conduct, and the concern with moral propriety which suffuses every gathering and interaction.[8]
3. *Institutional organisation*: Interpersonal networks; institutional domains; and activity types as 'culturally recognised units of interaction that are identifiable by constraints on (a) goals, (b) roles activated in the activity, (c) interactional structure, and (to some extent) (d) participants and settings' (Brown and Fraser 1979: 40).
4. *Participants' knowledge specifically as this relates to ethnic groups*: People's ideas and feelings about ethnic groups, their attributes, their positions in society, their prestige, their interrelationships, its legitimacy and so forth.

A fuller introductory discussion of these analytic dimensions is given in Appendix I. Here though, it is important to be explicit about my (fairly unremarkable) social constructionist assumptions about the relationships between knowledge and action that operate across these four descriptive levels. This will clarify some of the ways in which interpersonal conduct can be linked up with widespread social change. Social change is centrally at issue in the first and second of the guiding questions outlined in the previous section, and discussion of it will also lead into a few observations on the notion of ritual.

The assumption is that understanding and activity exist in a close dialectical relationship. People's social evaluations and classifications are shaped through their experiences of interaction. Equally, in combination with inferencing, processes of classification play a crucial role in getting action to make sense. Classifications channel participation in further activity, and are themselves embodied, endorsed or reshaped as action develops. A person's knowledge is idiosyncratic to quite an extent, but it generally becomes fairly extensively synchronised with other people's through experiences in which participants coordinate the action to which their cognitive and emotional understandings give shape (though this certainly does not mean that individuals agree with one another at every point: individuals can vary a great deal in their commitment to the provisional consensus established in an interaction, and more generally, network analysis serves as a valuable tool for tracing the breaks and continuities in the social distribution of these understandings).

In language, the dialectical relationship between knowledge and action is extensively recognised in functional and sociolinguistics (e.g. Halliday 1985), as indeed is idiosyncrasy (Hudson 1980: 12; LePage 1980: 1–2). Though speech events have been most frequently described as objective practices, their cognitive representation is directly entailed in Hymes' notion of communicative competence (1972b) and it is foregrounded in Levinson's account of activity types as sets of 'inferential schemata' (1979). And though domains may summarise objective regularities of conduct, they only do so because people operate with them as socio-cognitive constructs that 'guide them through the infinite encounters of daily interaction' (Fishman 1972: 51). Of course classifications and evaluations refer across a far larger array of entities than these, but the first point here is that both our knowledge and our interaction play an important role in continuously reproducing central features of what one can loosely call 'social structure'. Sapir puts it in the following terms:

> It is obvious that for the building up of society, its units and sub-divisions, and the understandings which prevail between its members, some processes of communication are needed. While we often speak of society as though it were a static structure defined by tradition, it is, in the more intimate sense, nothing of the kind, but a highly intricate network of partial or complete understandings between members of organisational units of every degree of size and complexity, ranging from a pair of lovers or a family to a league of nations or that ever increasing portion of humanity which can be reached by the press through all its transnational ramifications. It is only apparently a static sum of social institutions: actually it is being reanimated or creatively reaffirmed from day to day by particular acts of a communicative nature which obtain among individuals participating in it. (Sapir 1931 [1949]: 104; also e.g. Heritage 1984: ch. 7)

The second point is that although there are obviously limits to what individual actors can achieve – as is often said, social reality may be a human product but it faces humans like a coercive force – there are implications in this for the ways in which interactional experience connects with social change. This second point needs a little elaboration.

In making sense of the world around us, we rely quite extensively on the assumption that things generally run together in predictable clusters. Much of the time we operate with the expectation that particular sounds, words, objects, topics, ways of speaking, interaction structures, roles, situations, and so on combine with one another in predictable ways, and these expectations about likely cooccurrence relationships make it much easier for us to process the endless flux of sensory data in which we are immersed. Beyond that, these routinised expectations constitute much of our everyday, commonsense knowledge of social reality.

Obviously, for a huge number of reasons (unfamiliarity, ignorance, rhetorical purpose, and so forth), people often encounter pieces of talk and action that fall outside the boundaries of what they normally expect, and they frequently cope with these without too much difficulty. Frequently, these contradictions and interruptions of normal expectancy are highly diverse, differing from encounter to encounter. But on occasion, customary assumptions about rather fundamental relationships between elements of the social world can be destabilised quite generally. This is what happens in the case of major social contestation. During such periods, conservative reaction often emphatically reaffirms the assumptions that have been dominant hitherto, but elsewhere, people find that they can no longer depend confidently on their routine presuppositions. In fact, it would be mistaken to suggest that this destabilisation of tacit understandings stems only from larger outside forces. In their daily conduct and communication, individuals can themselves undermine taken-for-granted realities and try to establish new conventions and assumptions where old ones no longer seem tenable. Their success is achieving this will depend on a number of factors.

Bourdieu has broadly comparable processes in mind when he talks of 'heretical discourse'. But he stresses the complex collective political task involved in establishing alternative definitions of reality:

> Heretical discourse must not only help to sever the adherence to the world of common sense by publicly proclaiming a break with the ordinary order, it must also produce a new common sense and integrate within it the previously tacit or repressed practices and experiences of an entire group, investing them with the legitimacy conferred by public expression and collective recognition. (Bourdieu [1981] 1990: 129)

Alternative orders/conceptions of social reality need to be given enduring institutionalised status, and Bourdieu goes on to consider the way these can be publicly sanctioned through symbolism, dramatisation and ceremony.

This discussion about interpersonal and collective conduct affirming or disrupting taken-for-granted reality can be tied to Gilroy's account of dispute about the meaning of race and ethnicity. There is a prima facie case for suggesting that in contemporary Britain, race/ethnicity constitutes precisely one of those sociocognitive categorisations on which interactional consensus can now no longer be assumed, and that it has become the site of intensive contestation, as different interests struggle to redefine its meaning.

In much of what follows, I shall use a broadly focused discourse analysis (drawing on the four analytic dimensions outlined above) to consider the ways in which race and ethnicity are asserted, questioned and contested in daily adolescent language crossing. Taking up the cues provided by Gilroy and Bourdieu, I shall also pay particular attention to the *ritual* aspects of adolescent activity.

Prototypically, ritual can be defined as formulaic conduct that displays an orientation to issues of respect for social order and that emerges from some sense of the (actual or potential) problematicity of social relations. Typically, ritual gives a more prominent role to symbols than to propositional expression, it elicits a marked emotional response, it creates an increased feeling of collectivity between at least some of the participants, and it is itself subject to comment and sanctions. The empirical forms that ritual takes are in fact very varied. The considerable sociological and anthropological literatures on the topic make it clear that ritual action can be serious or playful, lengthy or fleeting; it can occur in large gatherings or two-person encounters; it can strengthen feelings of either similarity or difference; and its meanings are intricately tied to the particular symbols it employs. In fact, because of the many different forms in which it has been described, ritual recommends itself as a 'sensitising' rather than as a 'definitive concept' for the present study, suggesting 'directions along which to look' rather than 'prescriptions of what to see' (Blumer 1969: 148). In what follows, different aspects of ritual will be introduced stage by stage, closely tied to particular pieces of data.

Even so, it is worth taking a brief glance at ritual's potential relevance to the social field that is being sketched out here. Whether in religious ceremony, in greetings or apologies, ritual action is intricately associated with problematic moments in the flow of social life, occasions when habitual assumptions about commonsense reality and normal social relations loosen their hold. For this reason alone, one might expect to find a lot of ritual activity in circumstances where fundamental socio-cognitive categories have become the focus of uncertainty and dispute. But the value of ideas about ritual reaches further. In their analysis of initiation rites in agrarian society, anthropologists have often identified a central period of transition, and during this, initiands occupy neither their former nor their future statuses. This 'liminal' period *outside* normal social structure is invested with great risk and promise, and Victor Turner extends this concept to the kinds of activity that occur in contemporary urban recreation (1974). Appropriating this for analysis of the dynamics of race and ethnicity, we will be able to investigate actions which create, sustain, terminate or simply occupy these liminal periods outside dominant social structure. Focusing on moments such as these, it will be possible to examine adolescent attempts to escape, resist or affirm the racial orderings that threaten to dominate their everyday experience.

Perhaps it is also worth noting that ritual seldom figures in sociolinguistics textbooks, and that in the sociolinguistics of contemporary urban society, ritual is most generally understood either as routine (e.g. Coulmas 1981a) or as politeness (Brown and Levinson [1978] 1987). While both of these may fall within its ambit, neither carries the concept as far as it can go: 'routine', for example, ignores ritual's creative potential, and 'politeness' neglects its role in subversion. In contrast, all of these aspects will feature in the discussions that ensue.

Leaving the issue of ritual temporarily to one side, this is an opportune moment to give a more precise description of this study's subdisciplinary position within sociolinguistics itself.

1.5 Siting within sociolinguistics

The most sustained effort to integrate all four of the descriptive dimensions that I shall attend to – language, interaction structures, institutional organisation and knowledge about social groups – can be found in the tradition of 'interpretive' or 'interactional sociolinguistics' associated with John Gumperz (e.g. Erickson and Shultz 1982; Gumperz 1982; Gumperz and Cook-Gumperz 1982; Chick 1985; Cook-Gumperz 1986). In fact, there is interactional sociolinguistic work that examines communication between Anglos, Afro-Caribbeans and South Asians in contemporary Britain (e.g. Gumperz et al., 1979; Furnborough et al., 1982; Gumperz 1982a, 1982b; Roberts and Simonot 1987; Roberts et al., 1992). But though this study is loosely comparable in its interest in the interaction of social identities with the micro-processes of talk, in many ways its empirical portrait of 'cross-cultural communication' contrasts very sharply with all of these analyses.

Interactional sociolinguistic studies of interethnic communication in Britain have been generally concerned

1. with workplace interactions involving adults, who
2. have been brought up both inside and outside Britain, who
3. are unfamiliar with one another, and who
4. occupy different positions of institutional power.

The gist of these studies is to show how,

5. despite initial good will, hidden differences in participants' communicative resources disrupt
6. straight discussion, generate negative social categorisations, and
7. result in the reproduction of racism.

In contrast, my concern is

a) with the recreational interaction of
b) British-born adolescents, who
c) know each other well, and
d) whose institutional positions are roughly similar.

These young people

e) recognise and even exaggerate the differences in their communicative repertoires
f) in a set of stylised and often playful interactions that up to a point at least,
g) constitute a form of antiracism.

The approach taken in previous studies has much to offer. They generally examine sites where interactional discourse and institutional processes come together – interviews, advice sessions, committee meetings – and by analysing face-to-face processes that result in decisions that critically affect a person's access to knowledge or material resources, they have revealed dimensions of discrimination that have been unrecognised hitherto. These studies also contest legitimating official ideologies that blame the victim, and challenge, for example, language teaching orthodoxies by stressing the inadequate social and communicative practices of monolinguals in authority.

Nevertheless, even though they are no longer seen as exclusively responsible for their own failure, there is no fundamental break with the 'blacks as victims' idea that Gilroy identifies as a cornerstone in the discourses of racism (1987: 11; on this issue in cross-cultural training, see Roberts et al. 1992: 33, 121). Specifically surveying interactional sociolinguistics, Singh et al. (1988) pick up on this, and they also argue that interactional sociolinguistic studies of 'cross-cultural' communication have been too concerned with language as an instrument for assimilation to the demands of capitalist bureaucracy. They suggest that rather than studying 'joyless [managerial] formalisms', ethnic resistance needs to be recognised and 'understood in light of the human sense for the joyfulness of speech' (1987: 45). There is much in this to key with Hewitt and Gilroy's analyses. The account of communicative practice in stratified multiracial settings can be usefully extended to include a few of the phenomena listed in (a) to (g) above.

This is probably sufficient as an introduction to the descriptive and theoretical angle on language, youth and race that I shall be adopting. In this chapter, two further tasks of preliminary clarification are still required: first a summary of my empirical methods; secondly, a brief introduction to the town, neighbourhood and networks where the research was set.

1.6 Fieldwork, methods and the database

The research draws on two periods of fieldwork – one year in 1984, and a second in 1987. There were a few differences in my data collection procedures during these two periods, but radio-microphone recording, interviewing, and participant observation featured centrally in both. The main methods that I used can be summarised as follows (Appendix II contains a fuller account):

1. *Radio-microphone recordings* of recreational activity at a youth club and during free time at school. In 1984, radio-microphones were given out to 23 informants, producing about 45 hours of data; in 1987, 37 informants were involved, resulting in approximately 100 hours of data.
2. *Interviews* focusing on language and adolescent social life. In 1987, 35 informants participated in the language interview,

and 39 in the one that addressed social issues. Interviewing in 1984 involved 23 informants.

3. *Participant observation* as a voluntary worker at the local youth club – about 40 evenings during the 1984 fieldwork, and about 50 evenings during 1987.
4. *Local translation and commentary* on all recordings of Panjabi. As my own proficiency is very limited, in 1987 two 17 year-old bilinguals from the locality translated and commented on all the examples of Panjabi recorded on radio-microphone during 1984 and 1987 (about 500 extracts).

The most relevant differences between fieldwork procedures in 1984 and 1987 were as follows:

5. *Retrospective discussion* with participants of extracts selected from the radio-microphone recordings. I did this during 1987 with 33 informants.
6. *Discussions of findings from the 1984 research*. In 1987, I discussed the findings from fieldwork in 1984 with about 25 young people, 18 of whom had been informants during the earlier research.

In 1984, I approached Southleigh Middle School to make contact with four youngsters who I already knew. Thereafter, informants were recruited through friendship networks. In 1984, this resulted in a sample of 23 informants, comprising two boys of Caribbean descent, one of mixed Caribbean/Anglo parentage, three Anglo, seven Indian and 10 Pakistani. There were no female informants at this stage, partly due to statistical analysis that had been originally planned.[9] In 1987, a total of 64 13–16 year-old adolescents – virtually all now attending the local upper school – were recorded in at least one of the elicitation contexts in which I was a participant (procedures (2) to (6)): 12 were Afro-Caribbean (7M 5F), 2 were mixed Caribbean/Anglo (1M 1F), 14 Anglo (9M 5F), 3 Bangladeshi (M), 18 Indian (10M 8F), 1 mixed Indian/Anglo (F), 12 Pakistani (10M 2F). A core of 34 of these were tape recorded in at least three of the 1987 elicitation contexts, and of this core, 14 had acted as informants during the 1984 fieldwork. Eighteen informants in 1987 lived outside Ashmead, and most of them had gone to lower and middle schools outside the neighbourhood. The rest had been at Ashmead's Southleigh Middle School with the 1984 informants. It was originally planned that the 1987 sample should be balanced in terms of gender, but because the youth club was more heavily frequented by boys, the eventual ratio of males to females was about two to one.

The analysis of language crossing that follows is based on about 68 episodes in which non-Panjabis used Panjabi (59 taped and 9 observed), about 160 exchanges involving stylised Asian English (SAE) (40 observed, 120 taped), and more than 250 episodes where I detected a clear Creole influence in the speech of whites and Asians. Two limitations need to be emphasised here.

First, my purpose in giving these figures is (a) to show that language crossing was not a freak occurrence – a molehill isn't being built into a mountain; and (b) to give the very roughest idea of the comparative frequency of different kinds of crossing. However, it is impossible to use these figures in any precise quantification. This would require a much more systematic specification of linguistic units than anything I have used here.[10] In addition, the quality of the recorded data varies: good recordings can be used for a range of analytic purposes, but poor ones may be much more limited in the useability of the information they provide. This means that the size of the empirical base itself varies, according to the question being asked.

Secondly, the data on Creole crossing has not been as intensively analysed as the extracts involving Panjabi and SAE. They have been comprehensively scrutinised at the level of analysis traditionally associated with the ethnography of communication – participants, topics, events and so forth – but because of their quantity, only a small proportion has been transcribed closely enough to allow detailed commentary on interaction structures and processes. So in this regard, generalisations about language crossing in Creole are more impressionistic than they are about Panjabi and stylised Indian English.

In spite of this, the combination of methods used in fieldwork provides quite a sound basis for establishing the authenticity of a lot of the data: working in one extended peer group meant that there were a great many cross-references in what adolescents talked about, and several sources and kinds of data can be brought to bear in the analysis of particular linguistic practices.

There is also some scope for longitudinal investigation of developments in language crossing over time. In addition, Hewitt's use of radio-microphones and participant observation served as a model for my own, and so as I have already suggested, there are good opportunities for cumulative comparison with other studies.

Although interactional conduct is the major focus of this study, an understanding of the local setting will often be important, and so it is now worth turning to a sketch of this.

1.7 The town, the neighbourhood and networks

The town

Stoneford (not its real name) is situated in the South Midlands of England, and it has a population of about 100,000. Although substantial immigration from expatriate Anglo communities and from other parts of the UK dates from the latter part of the last century, migration from overseas was particularly significant after the Second World War. This began with refugees and political exiles from Poland, the Baltic States, the Ukraine, Croatian, Slovenia and Serbia. From the early 1950s, wage earners started to arrive from Italy, and from 1958 onwards, this was followed by substantial immigration from the West Indies, from India and from Pakistan. As these became established, many of their close dependants came over to join them, although immigration laws introduced from the mid-1960s to the early 1970s increasingly restricted migration from the New Commonwealth. After 1972, those to arrive came chiefly from Bangladesh and East Africa. In 1979, figures produced by the local education authority reported that 31 per cent of its pupils were from ethnic minorities (6 per cent of Afro-Caribbean extraction, 10 per cent Indian, 8 per cent Italian, 2 per cent Pakistani, 5 per cent other). In some lower schools, minority ethnic children represented less than 5 per cent of the school roll, while in others they constituted between 70 per cent and 90 per cent.

Generally speaking, racial discrimination and minority ethnic disadvantage were fairly well entrenched in housing, employment and local government. At the same time, there was also a degree of stratification between settling groups, with Italians and Indians prospering more than Afro-Caribbeans and Pakistanis, and

Bangladeshis in the worst position of all. Nevertheless, the housing stock in Stoneford was better than in many inner city areas, and the rate of unemployment had been consistently below the national average. So there was not the same intensity of material and economic deprivation that could be found in major conurbations during this period. Neither did it appear to match them in the extent of racist violence. After the urban riots in 1981, there was some disturbance in two or three inner areas of Stoneford, but these were relatively minor. In comparison with other towns, the consensus among my informants was that Stoneford was a 'quiet' place, and even rather 'boring'.

The neighbourhood

The neighbourhood that I shall call 'Ashmead' is a geographically well-defined area on the edge of Stoneford. Three-quarters of its housing was constructed between 1875 and 1914 (mainly two–three bedroomed terraced houses), and in 1976, it accounted for one-third of all Stoneford's 'high stress' housing. Ashmead was the most ethnically mixed of the main areas of minority settlement in Stoneford, and it contained specialised retail and grocery shops catering for local Anglos, Caribbeans, Italians, Indians and Pakistanis. When I conducted my fieldwork at Southleigh, the area's state middle school, the pupils were 9 per cent Afro-Caribbean, 20 per cent Anglo, 12 per cent Bangladeshi, 28 per cent Indian, 28 per cent Pakistani and 0.7 per cent Italian (virtually all local children of Italian descent went to the Roman Catholic schools nearby).

Elsewhere in the town, attitudes towards Ashmead were predominantly negative, showing signs of being influenced by dominant discourses of race such as those outlined in section 1.2. My own informants were aware that the area had an unwarranted reputation for crime, and that jokes about visitors 'needing a passport' were common. A number of Asian and Afro-Caribbean informants reported experiences of racist aggression when they left Ashmead and went into the centre of town, and during my fieldwork, a visit by Ashmead youth club to a club in one of the villages nearby ended in violent confrontation. The neighbourhood's multiracial, predominantly working-class character was at the centre of local debate when falling pupil numbers in the town forced the local education authority to close one of its upper schools. Initially, Ashmead's Newton Upper was chosen for the axe.

In the event, Ashmead residents and Newton staff successfully mobilised to prevent this, and here and in other contexts, there was a strong sense of local identity among my informants – 'Remember, AM always wins', 'the AM boys', 'the latest from AM'. Even so, this was not a seamless social unity, and divisions of ethnicity, class, religion, caste and residential area were evident in varying ways among different sectors of the local population. To get a preliminary picture of how some of these differences affected the adolescents I studied, it is worth summarising the findings of some network analysis.

Local adolescent friendship networks

Only discourse analysis will show what particular social divisions actually meant to local youngsters, and how they managed them in interaction. Even so, network analysis provides a rough but useful view of the extent to which adolescents with different ethnic backgrounds associated with one another on a regular and friendly basis.

Both among the 11–13-year-old boys that I studied at Southleigh Middle, and among the 13–16-year-old males and females at Newton Upper, there was a general tendency to associate with peers who were of the same sex and ethnic background (cf. also Davey 1983; Thomas 1984).[11] In 1987, I most closely observed about 15 friendship clusters, and in about nine or 10 of these, one ethnic group could be said to predominate. A number of informants themselves said that people tended to hang around with others from the same background, and adolescents often referred to ethnicity when identifying different network groupings (as being Indian, black, Pakistani and so forth). Indeed several informants who participated in more mixed clusters felt that these were unusual, and even rather fragile:

> you know you're expected to be either white and stick around with white girls, or black and stick around with black girls, or be Indian and stick around with Indians, but I'm the sort of Indian girl that goes with everybody. ((Anita, Indian background, 15 years old))

> you can sort of tell that when they get older, most people don't hang around with black people ... if they're whites they hang

around with white people, and if they're coloureds they hang around with coloured people . . . I think it's probably going to happen to most of the people in this school who hang around with white people, it already is happening really . . . Hopefully I'll still be hanging around with coloured people but I dunno, I think we might split, I'm not sure. ((Ian, Anglo background, 15; abbreviated transcription))

So ethnic descent was clearly an important organising principle in the associative networks of local adolescents. Even so, in comparison with home and the adult community, school and peer recreation were still important sites for ethnic *mixing*. In 1984, no one associated exclusively with co-ethnics, and while most friendship cliques were *predominantly* co-ethnic in 1987, only a small proportion were exclusively so. In fact, patterns of interethnic friendship interacted with gender and neighbourhood residence in quite complex ways.

Although there were one or two notable exceptions, youngsters of Bangladeshi descent were generally excluded from mixed and other-ethnic friendship clusters. There were a lot of friendships between Indian and Pakistani youngsters, though it was much more common for boys of Indian and Pakistani descent to go around with Caribbeans or Anglos than it was for Indian and Pakistani girls. There were other striking sex differences. White boys only participated in cliques with Afro-Caribbeans or Asians if they lived in the same area (or had done until recently). In contrast, neighbourhood co-residence seemed less important for white girls. In fact, although local patterns can vary and change quite rapidly (Hewitt 1986: 42, 91–2; Jones 1988: 136), in this neighbourhood the only cross-ethnic dating involved white girls, and in my sample, they tended to live in a different area from the boys they went out with. Neighbourhood co-residence did not seem to be as important as a criterion for cluster membership for black or Asian young people either. In fact for some, the move to a school with a larger catchment area led to the consolidation of ethnic networks (cf. Thompson 1974: 247).

It is also important to recognise the extensive general sociability that occurred in large, polyethnic, mixed sex crowds. School provided a number of sites for this kind of wider socialising. Lessons were one important setting: 'when you get to know friends in lessons, you can mess about'; 'I know a lot of others – Leela, Marina and Julie – but I don't hang around with them out of lessons'; 'I reckon more goes on in lessons than there does in six weeks holiday'. Dinner queues and breaktimes were others, and outside school, many adolescents congregated in large groups in parks and youth clubs. The social field that each of these sites made available were of course constrained in a number of different ways. In lessons, participants were grouped according to an idea of academic ability, which was not random in the way it intersected with race. Dinner queues only brought together pupils from the same year group. Unofficial social zoning of the upper school playground meant that you couldn't meet a full cross-section of the pupil population if you hung around only in one place. And at the local youth club you would be much more likely to encounter Pakistani, Anglo and Indian boys than girls, Afro-Caribbeans, Bangladeshis or Italians. Nevertheless, it was within larger gatherings of this kind that male–female relationships were formed and it was here that network clusters came together, defined themselves, and sometimes changed their membership. And though to differing degrees, many of these bigger gatherings were multi-ethnic.

Investigation of local adolescent networks suggests, then, that a shared ethnic background was of major significance in friendship formation. Even so, its force was far from absolute. In fact, this combination of influential co-ethnicity on the one hand, and on the other, a substantial amount of movement across the boundaries of ethnic in-group membership, would appear to be a central feature of the terrain in which language crossing took root as an important symbolic practice.

However, because it has been framed primarily in terms of contact and liking, this account of interethnic friendship has had little to say about race stratification. Stereotypes about ethnic groups and their inferiority have been identified as active principles in the allocation of material resources in Stoneford generally, but the effects of race hierarchisation were much more pervasive than this. The ways in which local adolescents themselves recognised and negotiated social division of this kind could focus on a number of different practices, but language crossing played an especially obvious role in this process. This will start to emerge in the next chapter, which provides a preliminary outline of the ways in which adolescents themselves reported on this practice. But before then, it is important to say just a few words about the organisation of this book.

1.8 The chapters that follow

Writing one text about three varieties – four if you include the local multiracial vernacular – presents certain organisational challenges. If it was structured around theoretical themes, the book would run the risk of obscuring or collapsing important empirical differences in the way each variety was used. Since language crossing is a relatively new area for sociolinguistic research, it is important not to underestimate the value of trying to make a descriptive contribution to 'the ethnographic record'. On the other hand, although it might be more adequate descriptively, taking each variety separately could result in some rather weary plodding backwards and forwards over the same theoretical terrain. In the end, I have aimed for a compromise, which at least gives a fair impression of the inductive processes that led to the relatively 'grounded' theoretical perspectives which the book proposes. More specifically, its organisation is as follows.

The main empirical analyses are grouped together into three central sections, each one describing a different situational context. In order, these contexts are: *adolescent interaction with adults, informal peer–peer interaction* and *interaction focused around performance art.* Each of these entailed different institutional role relationships, and they also often differed in the prestige that they accorded to the languages at issue here.

Within each of these three settings, Creole, Panjabi and stylised Asian English are introduced in separate chapters. This means that the book itself develops through a process of cumulative comparison: initially, crossings in Panjabi, Creole and Asian English are compared *within* each of the three broad contexts, but gradually, similarities and differences *across* contexts also become clear. Usually – though not always – in Parts II, III, and IV, the largest part of each chapter is relatively descriptive, looking at the situated use of a particular out-group variety more or less in its own terms. But of course, these descriptions themselves necessarily draw on wider analytic frameworks, and they also invariably invite a number of theoretical extrapolations about language crossing itself. And so the later parts of each chapter are usually more theoretical, and the more general points they address are flagged up in the subtitles attached to each one. In fact, the theoretical interpretations themselves build up and in trying to account for language crossing as a phenomenon, certain key ideas are progressively elaborated (concerning for example, resistance, ritual, polyphony, and the relationship between macro and micro). In the last part of the book, much of this is drawn together. There is an attempt to provide a clear statement about code-crossing's character both as a sociolinguistic practice and as a form of everyday cultural politics. In the very last chapter, I discuss some of the wider educational implications of a mode of language use that has either been neglected, or conceptualised in ways that obscure its social and political significance.

Before starting on the empirical interactional analyses, it is useful to consider what adolescents themselves had to say about language crossing.

Notes

1. For useful surveys, see Taylor 1981 and Taylor and Hegarty 1985.
2. In fact, it is not only in reactionary discourse about the British way of life that Gilroy detects the influence of ethnic absolutism: despite their being radically opposed on a number of others grounds, it also operates within municipal antiracist discourse (1987: 143) and in certain forms of black cultural nationalism which rely on 'mystical and essentialist ideas of a transcendental blackness' (1987: 65).
3. It is important to say a word in explanation of my use of terms like 'Asian', 'Anglo', 'Afro-Caribbean', and so on, since both ethnic labelling and ethnicity itself are highly problematic processes. All my informants were British, and the labels I use generally describe the countries or regions that their parents or grandparents come from. In line with a lot of local practice, my use of the term 'black' generally excludes young people of Asian descent, though in recognition of their *in*clusion in the term in certain political discourses, I often use 'Afro-Caribbean' to designate black adolescents with family links to countries in the Caribbean. The danger with all these labels is that they invite ethnic absolutist interpretations, which run directly contrary to my central concern with processes of social redefinition. This risk, though, seems unavoidable, since the research is itself located in a period when biological descent and domestic upbringing – basic terms in absolutism – compete alongside (for example) class position

and neighbourhood residence as active factors in people's ongoing negotiations of social identity. Indeed, to obscure racial categorisation would be to deprive the research of its central analytic interest. The only safeguard against absolutism can be to underline the fact that 'race', 'ethnicity' and indeed 'inheritance' are themselves social constructions that are continuously negotiated through processes of social interaction (this point is discussed at greater length in Chapters 11.6, 13.4, 13.6–13.7 below).

4. In an analysis of the people who used them as a part of their ordinary speech, the terms 'Creole', 'Panjabi' and 'Indian' or 'Asian English' would be very clumsy, clustering a number of varieties which both the speakers themselves and professional linguists might well want to distinguish (on variation among speakers with roots in the Caribbean, cf. e.g. Sebba 1986, 1993; Hewitt 1986: 102–4; on speakers with links to Pakistan and Northern India, see Shackle 1979, Fitzpatrick 1987, Linguistic Minorities Project (LMP) 1985). But in their informally acquired use among members of ethnic outgroups, these differences were generally unimportant (the special case of the interface between Creole and local vernacular English is discussed in Chapters 5.5 and 5.6). Occasionally with 'Asian English', an imitation closely following on the utterance of a particular ESL (English as a second language) speaker might achieve a degree of verisimilitude that would allow one to identify it as a copy of, for example, specifically Bengali English. But this was very rare and it does not warrant the introduction of linguistic subdivisions into the secondary stylisations that are of central concern here.

5. There have been, for example, repeated scares about linguistic diversity and educational standards (cf. e.g. Rose et al. 1969; Halstead 1988: ch. 3); government frequently invokes Standard English as a key symbol of national culture to legitimate its centralisation of the curriculum, sometimes with acute electoral timing (Cameron and Bourne 1988; Rampton, et al. 1988); and in fact, the possibility that government policies on parental choice might lead to ethnically segregated schools has sometimes been justified in the right-wing press by 'horror' stories about white children learning Asian languages at school (cf. e.g. *The Sun*, 7.5.87). The interweaving of sociolinguistic and political issues is enormously complex in this educational debate, and schooling is clearly a major institutional target for discourses of ethnic absolutism, as well as being the focus of minority ethnic and urban community campaigns (cf. e.g. Halstead 1988 on the Honeyford affair). For some further discussion, see Chapter 13.

6. Mercer et al. 1979; Ganguly 1980; Rosen and Burgess 1980; Sutcliffe 1982; Miller 1983; LMP 1983, 1985; Sebba 1986. For research on

attitudes, relations and language use with agemates, see, e.g. Durojaiye 1971, Dickinson et al. 1975, Agnihotri 1979, Smith 1979, Edwards 1986.

7. Hester and Wight 1977; Brown 1979; Wiles 1981; Coates 1985. Lucas 1972, Payne 1985 and Clarke et al. 1985: ch. 13 carried out some playground observation.

8. It is chiefly in its more detailed attention to the 'interaction order' that the analytic focus of my study differs from Hewitt's.

9. In the original design for my PhD, I planned to conduct a statistical analysis of language variation in the manner of Labov 1972a, LePage 1980 and Milroy 1980. With ethnicity alone as the independant variable, I needed a minimum of 20 informants (five of Afro-Caribbean descent, five Anglo, five Indian, five Pakistani). To introduce gender as a variable, I would have had to double my sample size. Given the rather elaborate methodology I was trying to develop, this would not have been practicable (cf. Rampton 1989, 1992).

10. In view of the thin and shifting line that separated it from local multiracial vernacular speech, this would be a particularly complex with Creole (cf. Sebba 1993: Appendix 1; Hewitt 1986; also Chapter 5).

11. Full details of the 1984 networks are contained in Rampton 1987a.

2 *Local Reports of Language Crossing*

This chapter introduces language crossing by way of informant reports. It is intended as a preliminary sketch map, and it provides an outline of issues which are taken up in much greater detail in the analyses of spontaneous interaction contained in the three central parts of this book.

In sequence, this chapter takes interview accounts of crossing in Creole, Panjabi and Indian English, and with each variety, it addresses the following questions: what kinds of people were and were not regarded as being involved in crossing? In what contexts? What attributes were they thought to project in their use of out-group varieties? And how were they evaluated? As the account progresses, I shall take space to build up a comparative overview, giving an indication of the way informants discerned similarities and differences in the kinds of symbolic meaning offered by these three language varieties. This cumulative process will also make it easier to achieve another of this chapter's aims, which is to start tying language crossing back to the specific historical setting of race and class relations portrayed in Chapter 1.

In fact, the comparison process can begin immediately, taking Hewitt's research in South London in the late 1970s and early 1980s as the starting point.

2.1 Reports of interracial Creole

Hewitt's research emphasised the central role that race stratification played in the dynamics of adolescent Creole use, and it serves as an important initial reference point. In Hewitt's interview discussions with black informants, two issues were especially apparent which

> clearly located Creole as a cultural resource or marker of ethnicity within a *specific* historical/economic frame. These were that white creole use was regarded (a) as derisive parody, and hence as an assertion of white superiority, and (b) as a further white appropriation of one of the sources of power – 'It seems as if they are stealing our language' (1986: 162)

However, 'despite the generalised hostility to white Creole use, the practice is acceptable in the case of particular white friends' (1986: 162).

My sample of black adolescents was much smaller than Hewitt's,[1] but there were some similarities in their responses. There was one report of Creole being used in hostile mockery, and generally, Afro-Caribbean responses were unenthusiastic. But while it was quite frequently said that out-group users of Creole were stereotyping, 'stupid', 'silly' and should 'stick to their own language', there was no mention of the expropriation of language as a resource of power:

Extract I.1

Participants: Cyril [15 AC M], Paul [15 AC M], David [15 AC M], BR [30+ An M].
Setting: 1987. Interview. [Simplified and abbreviated transcription]

Cyril: well, there're, there are some people who act black, which isn't wrong, it's just that . . . the way how they do it . . . I mean . . . if they act black that means that they think that everybody, or every black person sort of acts like that, so they

Paul: stereotype

Cyril: go around to some people talking like that. They probably don't mean to sort of offend, but it's just that

Paul: it does
((.....))

Cyril: them two, they don't don't mean to offend as I said, but they're just silly really, 'cos they should act normal, as themselves

Indeed, these black informants sometimes found out-group Creole quite amusing, and in contrast to the South London situation, Creole crossing was often associated with (a) quite widely recognised *groups* of adolescents that (b) the respondents *did not* have a particularly close relationship with – in Hewitt's account, it was only the usage of exceptional *individuals* that was deemed acceptable, and such usage was generally negotiated through 'private conspiracies' and in the 'privacy of close friend-ship' (1986: 163, 165):

Extract I.2

Participants: Martha, Hazel [15 AC F], BR
Setting: Ashmead 1987. M and H are listening to recordings of their interaction a few days before. Jagdish and Jeets are Indian boys, and Asif and Kazim are Pakistani. 'Kukabin' is a nonsense Creole pastiche. [Simplified transcription]

BR:	who do you think, which white or Asian person do you think knows it best around here
Martha:	Jamaican? I've heard Jagdish . . . think Jeets or one of them
Hazel:	yeh one of them lot, one of Asif and them
Martha:	yeh they speak Jamaican quite good
Hazel:	((laughs))
BR:	like what, like what
Hazel:	they make you laugh
BR:	((referring to the recording)) we have an example on here of Kazim saying 'kukabin'
M and H:	((loud laughter))

For their part, a substantial number of informants of Asian and Anglo descent said that they used Creole quite frequently, and that black peers didn't usually disapprove. They generally recognised that white and Asian uses of Creole were potentially disrespectful and offensive, but that there would be no problems if this was done with an understanding of certain constraints: in the presence of a black person who didn't know or like them, other-ethnic Creole should be avoided – otherwise it would be challenged. In addition, white and Asian informants often emphasised that they didn't use Creole seriously, only joking and mucking about.

In certain respects, these reports from white and Asian inform-ants also tune quite closely with Hewitt's findings. In the South London study, 'joking' uses of Creole were much more common than serious ones, as well as being less likely to elicit black

disapproval (1986: 170ff). There was also substantial correspondence with Hewitt's account of the connotations that peer group
Creole had for white (and indeed often for black) adolescents.
Informants of Asian and Anglo descent variously thought it tough,
cool and good to use, and associated it with argument, abuse,
assertiveness, verbal resourcefulness and opposition to authority.
Participation in this kind of Creole crossing was also generally
regarded as more common among males, though some girls were
mentioned in the interviews I conducted, and several female
informants reported using it themselves (again cf. Hewitt 1986:
141).

It was noticeable in Ashmead that far from being a matter of
ephemeral fashion, a number of non-Afro-Caribbean boys
regarded these non-serious uses of Creole as locally rooted and as
something of a tradition for them:

> Zaffar [15 Pa M]: all of us you know Asian guys, we can use it well
> you see, cos we've all been talk ... you know speaking it since
> Southleigh second years

Extract I.3

Participants: Manwar [14 Pa M], Faizal [14 Pa M], Billy [14 An
M], BR
Setting: 1987 interview. Barbara is a white girl whose use of black
expressions was noted by several informants. [Simplified and abbreviated transcription]

Manwar: here Faizal, Barbara goes to me 'laters' – I was cracking
   up man ((laughs)) – 'who you saying that to!'
 Faizal: 'laters'!
   ((......))
  BR: do you do you use some ((black expressions)) at all?
   M: yeh but ( )
   F: yeh we do sometimes, but we've been doing it for a long
    time anyway

The 1984 recordings, made about three years earlier, confirm
these reports, and once again there is a degree of ressemblance to
what Hewitt found (1986: 150). But at the same time, systematic
differences persist. In young whites' early familiarity with Creole,
Hewitt again emphasises the importance of close association with
black friends (1986: 158, 164, also 53, 85, 88; and Jones 1988:

129–30). In contrast, in spite of its being something that 'we've been doing . . . for a long time', it was clear from the 1984 field-work that in Ashmead, this kind of Creole use was not linked to any particularly close involvement or strong identification with black age-mates. In 1984, the two or three black boys in Manwar, Faizal and Zaffar's friendship circle used very little Creole, and were referred to as sources comparatively rarely. At that time, black female classmates, other Asian friends, older brothers and the mass media were much more widely cited as models. Even now, none of these boys were part of primarily Afro-Caribbean friendship groups, they did not attend the social events where they said Creole was used most (parties, blues dances), and they were sometimes critical of activities which they associated with black youth culture.

In addition to these long-standing but relatively autonomous appropriations, there was however another commonly reported strand of out-group Creole use, which did appear to involve close identification and involvement with black friendship groups. Here informants often mentioned a young person of Bangladeshi descent, who ran a sound system with a substantial black follow-ing, as well as several white girls who came to Newton Upper School from smarter areas outside. These were often described as 'acting black' or 'thinking they're black', and in the sample of the informants that I interviewed, opinions were sometimes more strongly opposed to crossing than before (though this was by no means always the case). My own fieldwork contact with crossers of this kind was generally only passing and rather indirect, and I was unable to study the way in which these adolescents negotiated access to this type of Creole use in any detail. However, it was clear that in its spread across the adolescent population, there was something very similar to the broad distinction that Hewitt's informants made between joking uses of Creole on the one hand, and serious ones on the other (1986: 170).

Summarising this preliminary view of out-group Creole use, it is evident that in a number of respects, there was a good deal of sim-ilarity to Hewitt's account of the situation in South London several years earlier: Creole had connotations of toughness, the potential offensiveness of its other-ethnic use was recognised, for some it had become established before their teens, a distinction was made between joking and serious uses, and there appeared to be exponents of both. But there were also some significant differences: black informants did not mention expropriation, their objections to out-group Creole seemed to be a bit more relaxed, its use was accepted to a greater extent outside the context of intimate friendship, and indeed, it was outside the context of intimate friendship that Creole had originally become established among many relatively accepted other-ethnic users. What could account for these differences?

Up to a point, these differences could be related to a change in the forms of black music that were most popular during the periods when the fieldwork for these pieces of research was conducted. In the situation that Hewitt describes, Rastafari and reggae were major forces in the immediate history of black youth culture, 'elaborating the connections between Creole and political relations' (1986: 110). Even so, Hewitt writes,

> [t]he balance between Jamaican and North American cultural orientations were at a pivotal point during my fieldwork period. In the very early 1980s, the strongest input was closely associated with reggae music. At the same time, the American influence was effected through Black American soul music. Soul, it was often said, was a black musical form but one equated with black and white social mixing, while reggae was a music essentially for black people (1986: 100)

Since the early 1980s, there had been a major shift in favour of North American forms (cf. Gilroy 1987: 187–97; Hebdige 1987: chs 13–17; Jones 1988: 55, 143), and in 1987, this was reflected among black, Anglo and Asian informants, who in interviews almost invariably mentioned soul, funk, and hip hop before reggae. Though black performers remained preeminent within it, hip hop's frame of reference was also urban American rather than Caribbean, and it was more open to Hispanic, white and Asian participation (Gilroy 1987: 190, 217; Jones 1988: 139, 218). With this shift, some important external support for the political meaning of Creole receded, and a specifically Afro-Caribbean inheritance became less important in the access it granted to the most prestigious forms of expressive youth culture.

Another important factor contributing to the difference between Hewitt's findings and my own appeared to be more local. In the schools where my research was conducted, South Asians formed the largest section of the pupil population: the figures for Southleigh were given in Chapter 1.7, and at Newton Upper, 30 per cent were Anglo, 8–9 per cent were Afro-Caribbean while Asians constituted about 50 per cent. More generally, informants frequently described Ashmead as a mainly Asian neighbourhood; the youth club which a lot of black youngsters frequented lay *outside* Ashmead in the centre of town; there were no white 'posses' in the locality; and talking of the ways in which Asians used 'ghetto-blasters' (very large portable tape-recorders) to play Indian music, one black informant reckoned that 'the Asians just do stuff like that just cos nobody's going to criticise them because . . . this area is mostly Asian'. In Hewitt's analysis of adolescent race relations, in 'Area B' black predominance and power at street level played an important part shaping white acceptance of black youth (Hewitt 1986: 80, 90–1; also Jones 1988: 219). Something of the same process seemed to occur in Ashmead, only here South Asians were dominant, and part of the impact was on attitudes to out-group Creole use.

In fact, reports about relatively uncontroversial joking uses of Creole mentioned Asians as a group and Asian individuals much more often than whites.[2] References to *unacceptable* joking uses occasionally alluded to whites but not Asians, and as well as some of the females in my sample, it tended to be Anglos from outside the area who played down their use of Creole, or said they didn't use it at all. This suggested some kind of special relationship between young people of Caribbean and Asian descent, and this was further indicated in reports of language 'exchange':

Extract I.4

Participants: Martha, Hazel [both AC F 15], BR
Setting: 1987 interview. Martha is talking about Asif and his friends [Simplified and abbreviated transcription]

    Martha: they learn ((Creole)) quite quick – you say something, first thing you say in English ((lessons)), by the end of the lesson you hear them saying it again, pass it on like that
      Hazel: yeh ((. . .))
    Martha: if you say something, they might say it and it sort of sticks in their head and they carry on saying it . . . They

             might forget about it and then it might come back to
             them.

        BR: is it that they kind of catch you saying something or
             that you actually teach them

Martha: no

  Hazel: no, they catch it

Martha: but they sometimes try to teach us Indian,

  Hazel: yeh ((laughs))

Martha: bad words

        BR: and do you learn them

Martha: yeh ((laughs))

  Hazel: try to

Martha: ((laughs)) ((. . .))

        BR: like what things do they teach you

Martha: I can't really remember now. It's funny when they're
             around us, I sort of like . . . copy them but I don't
             know

  Hazel: I can't remember them

Indeed, this parity in access to ethnically specific linguistic
resources extended beyond reciprocal language learning or teaching to the (generally good humoured) exchange of abuse:

Extract I.5

Participants: Mohan [15 In M], [Jagdish 15 In M], BR
Setting: 1987 interview. Mohan and Jagdish are talking about
interactions with black peers. 'Raas klaat' is a term of abuse in
Creole. [Simplified transcription]

  Mohan: we sometimes we just say you're a 'raas klaat' and all
           this

Jagdish: yeh yeh stuff like that . . . they even know some Panjabi
           words as well

Extract I.6

Participants: Andrew [14 AC M], Darren [15 AC M], BR
Setting: 1987 interview. Getting 'blown' means being shamed or
made a fool of. 'teri maadi' is Panjabi abuse. [Simplified transcrip-
tion]

  Andrew: suppose a ((Indian)) girl's getting rude now she's speak-
           ing Indian . . . probably that's when we'll use it
           ((Panjabi))

Darren:	yeh man
BR:	right okay
Andrew:	see we might be just getting blown and we don't even know about it
Darren:	exactly
Andrew:	in Indian innit, so you know, we have to sort of attack in an Indian word – that 'teri madi', and putting in a ragamuffin tune into it – 'raas klaat you chat bout there'

These reports also start to suggest the way in which in interaction, Creole and Panjabi could be used in very close proximity.

2.2 Interracial Panjabi

Knowledge of Panjabi was reported to be quite widespread among adolescents of Caribbean and Anglo descent – over 30 individuals were specified in 1987, and this was spread fairly evenly over males and females, blacks and whites.[3] Several black youngsters said that some knowledge of Panjabi was the inevitable consequence of long residence in the area, and according to Asian informants, white and black uses of Panjabi were generally linked to familiarity with Indian and Pakistani peers:

> if they're our friends, we teach them it

> most of them do really, who hang around with us lot, you see, they all know one word I bet you

> it's mostly the boys . . . um I think most . . . popular boys. . . . yeh right, who are not Asian, who get a lot of swear words because they get them all off their Asian friends

On occasion, Indian and Pakistani informants saw attempts to use Panjabi as intrusive and derisory, and in turn, their own use of it could sometimes be seen as aggressively exclusive by white and black youngsters. But accounts of hostile Panjabi were comparatively rare. A number of bilinguals explicitly denied the suggestion that Panjabi crossing was disrespectful, and attitudes were generally quite enthusiastic:

Extract I.7

Participants: Sukhbir [15 In M], Asif [15 Pa M], BR
Setting: 1987 interview. Timms is an Anglo whose Panjabi swearing vocabulary was quite renowned. Jonesie is also Anglo. [Simplified transcription]

Sukhbir: no it's quite good, it's impressive, ain't it, if they learn it

BR: yes well I think it is

Sukhbir: I think it is as well

BR: but sometimes it might happen ( ) some people thought they were you know, taking the piss or anything, does that happen at all or not?

Sukhbir: if they can talk it right, they're obviously interested in us, innit, so they won't take the piss

Asif: yeh like Timms, he's alright he is

Sukhbir: cos if they, if they . . . the type of people take the piss wouldn't like us innit, they wouldn't be interested to learn anyway, innit

Asif: yeh like Jonesie, he's a piss-taker

It was invariably reported that Anglo and Afro-Caribbean knowledge of Panjabi was very limited. References were made to the way in which black or white adolescents used Panjabi against teachers, but everyone agreed that there was no one who could conduct a conversation. Other-ethnic competence was restricted to swear words, terms of deprecation, perhaps a few numbers, a very small selection of stock formulae and one or two nonsensical pseudo-Panjabi inventions that non-Panjabis might themselves have had a hand in coining. Indeed, pronunciation difficulties were often mentioned, and informants frequently referred to the fragments of Panjabi that they had now forgotten. But in consequence and compensation for the linguistic difficulties that Panjabi was said to present to Anglos and Afro-Caribbeans, there were many accounts of the entertaining language teaching that went on informally in cross-ethnic peer group interactions. Indeed, despite its limitations, knowledge of Panjabi could be an important social marker:

Extract I.8

Participants: Manwar [14 Pa M], Faizal [14 Pa M], Billy Hayman [14 An M], BR

Setting: 1987 interview. 'Jabber' is an originally pejorative term for Asian. Peter is Anglo. [Simplified transcription]

Manwar: we've nicknamed Billy . . . for a about a year in our school . . . half, half, half-jabber
  Faizal: he's half-jabber now – knows most of the words – and so's Peter , he knows quite a lot of words too
Manwar: yeh, these two are one of us

Extract I.9

Participants: Faizal, Kuldip [14 In M], BR
Setting: 1987 interview. [Simplified transcription]

    BR: so who would you say knows most
 Faizal: Peter
 Kuldip: yeh he knows, he's been in our sort of community
 Faizal: he's been our friend long time, he doesn't like going with white people, just hangs around with us
 Kuldip: and Billy Hayman, he knows a lot

These characteristics and evaluations referred to the most general forms of cross-ethnic Panjabi use. There was however, another very important context for the use of Panjabi which entailed a rather different interracial dynamic. This was bhangra, a form of dance music that originated in the Panjab and that integrated a range of popular musical influences in its transposition to the West, including elements of hip hop (cf. Banerji and Bauman 1990). By 1987, bhangra was a major youth cultural force in the neighbourhood, disseminated on cassette, local radio and at a variety of both local and national functions (weddings, concerts, discos). Among many Panjabis, the knowledge and abilities associated with bhangra were valued and cultivated, and excellence was an important source of prestige. White and black adolescents encountered bhangra in a number of settings at school, and it served as the standard musical background on ordinary nights at the local youth club. There was however, relatively little active interest in bhangra among most black and white youngsters, even among those whose Panjabi was read as an expression of particulary close interethnic friendship. Comparably, Indian and Pakistani informants expressed little enthusiasm when they noted the participation of white musicians in top bhangra bands. There were, though, some exceptions to this broadly ethnic division in aesthetic taste, and as before, these generally tended to be white girls, sometimes from the other side of town.

2.3 Comparison of crossing in Panjabi and Creole

Compared with out-group uses of Creole, Panjabi crossing seems to be distinctive in several respects. In interviews, approval tended to be the first response of Indian and Pakistani informants, whereas Afro-Caribbean support for Creole crossing was more equivocal. The use of Panjabi by white and black adolescents was emphatically linked to hanging around with Asians, and there seemed to be no major line drawn between general joking uses of Panjabi and the way it was employed by very close friends. In contrast, other-ethnic uses of Creole appeared to develop outside extensive involvement with Afro-Caribbeans, and Hewitt reports that in fact 'whites who were well-established in their black friendship groups and fluent in Creole will claim never to use Creole 'jokingly'. It seems that to claim otherwise would admit to the merely borderline status from which they are at pains to dissociate themselves' (1986: 171). Asked to compare Creole and Panjabi, informants agreed that while the former was tough and cool, the latter was ordinary, funny or just like English. Indeed, although the individuals identified as knowing Panjabi were quite evenly male and female, Afro-Caribbean and Anglo, general statements about typical users suggested that white boys were the most common Panjabi crossers.[4]

But despite these differences, there were also major similarities. Hewitt's account of a folk distinction between joking and serious other-ethnic Creole applied in Ashmead, and it was extended as a basic structure in local perceptions of black and white Panjabi. There was recognition of derisive crossing in both languages; nonsense, abuse and pedagogic disrespect figured in their joking modes; and white girls were often most seriously involved in ethnically marked expressive culture, whether this was bhangra or hip hop.

Further similarities between Creole and Panjabi emerged when informants talked about the ethnic and class groups that were *least* likely to be involved in crossing. Ashmead adolescents echoed Hewitt's observation that Creole had connotations of lower class life (1986: 108) when they used it to emphasise opposition to poshness:

Extract I.10

Participants: Ian [15 An M], Richard [15 An M], BR
Setting: 1987. Interview. Ian is describing the expectation that his American cousins had about the way that he would use English. [Simplified transcription]

Ian: they think we speak really upper class English in England . . . they they see on the . . . they say that Englishmen has got such beautiful voices, and they express themselves so well . . . ((in an approximation to Creole:)) 'eh what you talkin' abaat, wha' you chattin' about, you raas klaat', and they don't like it! They thought I was going to be posher

More generally, the connotations of Creole contrasted sharply with the way in which informants described the white boys at their school that came from outside Ashmead. These non-local boys were classified as 'posh', 'snobs', even 'posh wimpies', and they were said to dress badly, to stick to themselves in one area of the school grounds during dinner-time, and to be capable of only the most laughably feeble gang-style activities. But Creole was not the only language that could be used to differentiate oneself from the posh wimpies. Panjabi also played a part:

Extract I.11

Participants: Peter [14/15 An M]. BR
Setting: 1987. Peter is listening to a recording of his own dinner-time interaction. Andrew, who he refers to, is of Afro-Caribbean descent. 'gorra' is a Panjabi word for 'white man' [Simplified and abbreviated transcription]

Peter: 'gorra' – white man . . . always call the people who didn't go to Southleigh gorras, yet I'm white myself
BR: the kids who didn't go to Southleigh you say
Peter: yeh cos we reckon they're a bit you know upper class (most of them)
BR: and what were they doing then, what were they doing, ((in the recording)), can you remember?
Peter: play it back . . . no they're drinking and chucking things about . . . what was it – apple cores! they chuck apples about, they're stupid idiots

((. . .))

BR: you also said, early in the dining hall, you said 'look at the gorras, the gorras are stupid, the gorra gang'

Peter: I might have said 'I'd get the gorra gang on you' – I always say that to Andrew

BR: what is the gorra gang?

Peter: it's just a load of white people . . . white boys, that ain't their name, I just call them it

BR: and these are the same kids who didn't go to Southleigh who were in the common room?

Peter: yeh

There was also a second social category that was generally seen as lying outside the social space in which Creole and Panjabi were considered legitimate interracial currency. This consisted of young people of Bangladeshi descent.

There were three Bangladeshi informants in my sample and it was clear that these three looked at Creole in much the same way as white and Panjabi teenagers: they liked it, they linked it with being hard or cool, they said they used it a bit, and they cited much the same stereotypical lexis. Beyond that, their ability to comprehend and improvise in Panjabi was much more extensive than that of black or white adolescents, and they showed a much fuller interest in bhangra and in Indian songs and films. But this was overwhelmingly ignored in the accounts of who used out-group Creole and Panjabi,[5] and instead, Bangladeshis figured in adolescent talk as the typification of unacceptable peer group characteristics. They were associated with unsociability, unfashionable dressing, linguistic incompetence and low educational performance, and the term 'Bengali' was repeatedly used in 'humourously' critical remarks about the conduct of associates.

The positioning of both non-local white boys and Bangladeshis outside the realms of likely or acceptable crossing in fact intimated a larger system of social stratification.[6] Broadly speaking, the typification of these two marginal groups provided contrasting points of negative reference that helped define the 'normal'. The 'otherness' of these two groups formed a number of polar contrasts. Posh Anglos resided in wealthier villages and districts outside Ashmead, while many Bangladeshis lived in much poorer accommodation in the central part of town where migrant groups had traditionally settled on arrival. Adolescents frequently associated posh kids with private schooling, while prior to its closure in 1986, the local ESL reception centre was often described as a Bangladeshi school. Even within Newton Upper, informants linked posh kids with the high curriculum sets, and Bangladeshis with the low ones. Beyond their exclusion from the arena of customary language crossing, posh kids' English was regarded as 'proper', while Bangladeshis were seen as speaking only an inadequate second language variety. In each case, 'ordinary kids' could position themselves between these polar stereotypes.

In fact, neither image was unproblematic or uncontested, but dispute around them took different forms. Informants generally felt guilty about the way in which Bangladeshis figured in peer group discourse. It was recognised that 'lots of people spread a lot of lies about them', and that people made remarks 'only because they ain't got anything else to say which is funny'. Though they themselves were actually involved, informants might say that 'it's just a few in the community, you know, muck-abouts, you always get them', or alternatively, they might mitigate their own participation: 'I do make fun of Bengalis, I must admit . . . I might make a bit of comments right, but I'll never say you're a tramp and all this'. In fact, the pejorative comments made about Bangladeshis were similar to what many recent arrivals have been subject to, and in 1951, letters in the local Stoneford press were saying the same kinds of thing about Italians. Particularly among Indian and Pakistani informants, there was recognition that some aspects of their migratory experience were shared. They had friends and relatives who had attended the language centre, and derogatory remarks could cut both ways: 'you laugh at it at the time, but when you think about it, I mean I wouldn't like that to happen to me . . . if anybody made fun of my language, . . . that would be worse than making fun of me.' But few claimed to be innocent: 'yes I think it is racism, but I just can't help it . . . I'm not as bad as some people'.

In contrast, there were no feelings of guilt expressed when 'posh people' were discussed. Poshness in the form of snobbery was widely disliked, but there was quite a lot of disagreement about what poshness actually entailed. In fact, when it was detached from an attitude of social superiority, posh in the sense of 'high class' was frequently admired along with the wealth, educational success and/or linguistic ability with which it often collocated:

my cousin come ((over from India)) . . . he's got a degree and everything, he speaks good English, but he didn't used to speak in English
with us though, 'cos they sort of speak perfect English, innit. We
sort of speak a bit slang, sort of innit – like we would say 'innit' and
all that. He was scared we might laugh at this perfect sort of English
. . . the good solid English that they teach 'em [In M 15]

Freddie – he could pull out all these complicated words and boggle
your mind – that man, he is the posh man, that man can boggle
anyone, oh man. He could blow anyone [AC M 15]

Sometimes, rather than objecting to poshness itself as a social
characteristic, criticism instead merely focused on the spuriousness
of the claims to it that particular people might be making:

she was talking to us in this high class ((voice)) – you know, she's
from _____ ((a Stoneford private school)) – she was talking to us in this high class, all of a sudden I heard her voice change
into different tones going down and down . . . until it got to this
Cockney . . . so it's just a put-on, most of them girls, they just put it
on [Martha AC F 15]

There was also a lot more disagreement about who was or was
not 'posh' than there had been with the term 'Bengali', where only
one boy was noted as an exception.

Overall, though 'posh' and 'Bengali' served together as categories of otherness delimiting the sphere of the socially
'normal/ordinary', the former represented a cluster of attributes
that many informants rated highly, while the latter stood for a
lower position from which all were keen to dissociate. This difference contributes to the explanation of two phenomena.

First, the ambiguities surrounding poshness suggest one reason
why relatively posh non-local white girls were able to gain access
to the most prestigious sites of black and Panjabi youth culture.
Inserted within the rivalry pervasive in interaction between adolescent males, poshness in white boys would be difficult to detach
from snobbery. In contrast to this – as a lot of the data below will
suggest – male–female interaction appeared to provide some
release from serious competition, and so here, less threatened by
struggles for superiority, there was maybe more scope for adolescents to participate in a dialogue between the posh and the local.

Secondly, the negative view of Bangladeshis was an important factor in the way that adolescents perceived and used the third language variety of central concern to this study – stylised Asian English. It is necessary to start the description of this by considering the groups that might provide models of Asian English.

2.4 Stylised Asian English (SAE)

Bangladeshis were one group that was generally seen as having only limited proficiency in English. So were a number of Indian and Pakistani adults.

This perception was certainly not invariable. A lot of South Asian adults were recognised as speaking perfectly ordinary English – parents, relatives, teachers, youth workers, local, national and international media figures. There were also local adults with roles in the education service and the community who informants respected without regard for the fact that they spoke English with marked Panjabi accents. And it was understood that there was no necessary relationship between Panjabi pronunciation on the one hand and on the other, limited proficiency and prestige in English.[7] Even so, many Indian and Pakistani informants indicated that competence in English was restricted among some of their older relatives and friends.[8]

Indian and Pakistani informants' accounts of this kind of limited proficiency were overwhelmingly solidary. For adults not brought up in Britain, the acquisition of English was often regarded as an achievement, and where deviation from local English norms was conspicuous, this could be a source of shared amusement ('sometimes my mum speaks English but I laugh cos she can't say it properly . . . she laughs herself'). There were accounts of young bilinguals translating and interpreting for their parents at home and in public settings, and there was a clear view of the links between linguistic proficiency and racism in cross-ethnic interaction:

> you should see the way they treat the Pakistanis or Asians ((at the airport)) – there's this woman standing there and she'll go 'Pakistanis, this way' ((spoken loudly and slowly)) and I think 'oh my God!' you know, I thought 'I do understand', I felt like going up to her and I go 'I can speak well you know, I can speak English perfectly and even better than you' . . . They're nice to Europeans

. . . You ask them a simple question and they make a big do out of it ((. . .)) old people cannot understand English as much as we can and . . . maybe older people don't understand the way that some people sort of really speak slowly to impress other white people around that go 'oh god, look at this one' – 'cos they think they're inferior to them . . . they can talk about equality, but when you go down the bloody shop, and there's the um post – and they and they're supposed to be giving a service to people ((. . .)) there's this woman at the counter and she sort of talks really slowly and she looks, you know rolls her eyes at some other white people, and then you know . . . that just shows right that people stereotype you immediately just because of the colour . . . [Yasmin, Pa F 15]

In fact there were clearly certain similarities in the way that adolescents regarded ESL among Panjabi adults and Bangladeshi peers. In both cases, proficiency in English linked up with issues of racism, social access and position, and with both groups, the use of English was intricately connected with awareness of migration and transition. Generally speaking, though, among Indian and Pakistani informants, shared kinship and ethnicity combined with generational differences, and awareness of adult language difficult-ies was tempered with personal loyalty, an understanding of recent family history, and a sense of continuity and broadly orderly change. In contrast, although attitudes to Bangladeshis themselves seemed fraught with feelings of guilt, similarities in age brought Anglo, Afro-Caribbean and Panjabi young people into contact with people with whom they shared few preexisting affiliations, and their perceptions of Bangladeshis were over-whelmingly negative. This difference contributed to the ambiguity surrounding restricted proficiency in English, and this increased in encounters with the mass media.

A brief glance at the British press and television reveals that although they are by no means the only form in which they have been represented, pejorative sociolinguistic images of South Asians have had a wide national currency. More particularly, many of these stereotypes have inherited ideas about 'babu' developed dur-ing British imperial rule in India (Dummett 1973: 279; Lawrence 1982: 73–4; Goffe 1985; Khan 1986; Matthews 1986). The *Oxford English Dictionary* reports the first use of 'babu' in English at the end of the eighteenth century and defines it as 'A native Hindoo gentleman; also (in Anglo-Indian use), a native clerk who writes English; sometimes applied disparagingly to a Hindoo or more particularly, a Bengali with a superficial English education'. Yule and Burnell ([1886] 1985: 44) have a further 1873 reference which characterises 'the babu' as 'pliable, plastic . . . receptive . . . [and] servile'. Adolescents recognised the potential significance of this racist imagery in shaping the way that Anglos (and others) perceived South Asians, but their reactions to these caricatures, and to the comedians that performed them, were varied and often ambivalent.

> you laugh at first but if you think about it, why should they take the piss out of the way we talk [Pa M 15]

> A [In F 15]: I hate that, especially when – they do it on the telly as well, don't they
> B [In F 15]: stereotypes
> A: I don't like it . . . it's sort of a shame

> some of the younger audience, white people, they think it's true' [In M 17]

> I think it's quite funny, I mean it's just part of life innit . . . not everybody can speak proper English can they' [In F 15]

> A [Pa M 15]: he's good, he's a laugh
> B [Pa M 15]: he's a big bastard he is, a racialist

> 'do you reckon he means it?' [In M 17]

The effect of all this was that in a number of often contradictory ways, the association between South Asians and limited English proficiency was an insistent part of the social knowledge that adolescents carried round with them, and this tied in with the stylised performance of Asian English that was common in local adolescent discourse.

Informants often said that young people put on an 'Asian' accent and projected a comic persona that was deferential, polite, uncomprehending and incompetent in English – 'jolly good', 'very good, very good', 'excuse me please' and 'I no understanding English' were the kinds of utterance they reported. This was most typically described as a subterfuge that Indian and Pakistani youngsters used to undermine white authority figures, and this sort of strategic exploitation of limited English has been quite widely reported elsewhere. But it could also be targeted at Bangladeshis, and there were accounts of its use between friends. In fact, the link between Panjabi accented English and the social imagery of 'babu' was certainly not invariant, and there were reports of it being either elaborated or displaced in drama lessons at school, when pupils sometimes played South Asian adults.

Evaluations of stylised Asian English were mixed. Some Panjabis were quite celebrated for their comic and/or daring performances, though by some informants, these were classed as 'full time dossers'. Using it 'to have a laugh' among friends was generally regarded as all right, and this could be extended to whites and Afro-Caribbeans. Their use of it however, was much more hazardous:

A: no no it's natural, man, it's natural
B: we can laugh at our own kind
A: when someone else, white, especially white . . . when a white person does it, we take it serious [In M informants]

A: Leander ((AC)) does it for a laugh in the class sometimes
B: I think she's a bit of a racialist if you ask me [In F informants]

It's more the Indians and these lot that put on the accent than us . . . we'd do it to people who we know who don't take offence . . . Like Asif and them. Asif wouldn't give two fucks, unless they've got a bad mood. If you did it with Ishfaq on a bad day . . . he's liable to go wild . . . say you're being a racialist and all that [An M informant]

In fact the use of stylised Asian English could sometimes express quite serious animosity:

Extract I.12

Participants: David, Paul and Cyril [all 15 AC M], BR
Setting: interview. Lenny Henry is a very popular black comedian [Simplified and abbreviated transcription]

David: 'jolly jolly good' ((laughter))
  BR: why laugh?
 Paul: cos that sounds so stupid when people do that,
    ((laughing:)) that is just really is taking the piss . . .

((serious:)) I mean if if I was an Indian, I wouldn't like that at all. I think that is really bad ((. . .))

BR: you never put on an Indian accent at all?

Paul: oh yeh, I've done that if they try and put on a black one. Simple as that.

BR: so you've done it back? . . . Can you give me an incident where you did that?

Cyril: well in my art lesson, there was this Indian guy, and he goes like this . . . what did he say David? he goes, he goes 'the four Lenny Henry's' and I go 'yes jolly jolly good' ((laughter)) he got really offended by that because it was funny

David: it was, I was rollin' on the –

Cyril: and after I said that he shut up straight away.

BR: who was that?

Cyril: some guy called Harbinder, he's my mate but he just came out with it 'the four Lenny Henry's' and I go 'jolly jolly good'

BR: but you say he is a mate?

Cyril: yeh, but even though they're mates, they still unconsciously, or sometimes on purpose, still come out with the stereotypes innit. Everybody does it

2.5 Comparison of SAE, Panjabi and Creole

Though there could clearly be quite a lot of variation from situation to situation, friendship appeared to play an important part in eliciting a favourable response to black and white uses of stylised Asian English. In this regard, it ressembled both Creole and Panjabi. However, as an intergroup (and indeed in-group) currency, Indian and Pakistani informants were generally rather less enthusiastic about stylised Asian English than they had been about Panjabi, and both in this respect and in terms of wider interethnic awareness of the dangers of crossing, SAE was closer to Creole. SAE and Creole were also similar in so far as in both cases, there was often a sense that crossing was least likely, least appropriate, or indeed most hazardous for Anglos. In contrast, in other-ethnic Panjabi, Anglos had often been mentioned as the group that were *most commonly* involved.

The common factor behind these responses to SAE and Creole might well lie in the extent to which adolescents could gain access to these languages *outside* local peer relations. Where neighbourhood social networks controlled the flow of linguistic knowledge, a crosser's disposition would be more or less known and there could be some guarantee of amicable intentions. In cases where a language variety was misused, effective means of redress would be on hand, and its inheritors could generally play a direct and active part in shaping the interracial meaning of a language. None of this could be assured if a variety was made available to a much larger audience through mass communication channels, as was indeed the case for both SAE and Creole. In this wider national context, they could accrete stigma or prestige in ways that lay far outside the sphere of local network influence. Whether or not adolescents embraced or abhorred their public meanings, these languages were now partially removed from the cross-ethnically privileging zone of neighbourhood familiarity, and so now in addition, majority–minority relations and white domination, derogation and expropriation could all become part of the socio-cognitive framework relevant to the evaluation of language crossing. There is some additional support for this explanation in the fact that it was precisely at the point where Panjabi acquired a more salient public profile that comments started to focus on the absence, inappropriateness, and incongruity of white participation. Through live performances, local radio and minority programmes on national TV, bhangra was starting to receive increasing amounts of public attention, and here comments about whites as a group were much more negative than before:

A: there were two white girls singing the chorus
B: yeh that was sick I reckon ((. . .)) that was shameful ((. . .)) it sounded all right, you could tell what they were saying, it sounded all right ( ), they should have Indian women there though innit [Informants: In and Pa 15 M]

he was an English guy . . . and everyone was just cracking up about him . . . he was a hippy ((laughs)) . . . his long hair, he was playing the guitar and um em he sang a song – first the Indian guy sang and then after a couple of songs he sang it ((. . .)) they were just taking the mickey out of the guy but he was good, really good ((. . .)) he cracked me up [In 14 F]

I don't think they let whites join, because ((. . .)) they probably think they're intruding and it doesn't concern them so why should they come ((. . .)) they jeer us, they mock us and then they want to join [Pa 15 F]

This linked into a second distinctive similarity in the interracial use of SAE and Creole. Both were linked to a set of well-defined attributes – one connoted linguistic incompetence and bumbling deference, and the other tough assertiveness, quick-wittedness, and opposition to authority. Behind these lurked variations on the victim/problem and clown/threat dyads endemic to the dominating discourses of British racism (Gilroy 1987; Dummett 1973: 212; Carlin 1975; Hebdige 1979: 2, 88; Walvin 1987; Verma 1985), in which Asians were stereotyped as compliant newcomers, ineptly orientated to bourgeois success, while Afro-Caribbeans were portrayed as troublemakers, ensconced in the working class and adept only in sports and entertainment (Cohen 1972: 29; Rampton 1983; Hewitt 1986: 216; Gilroy and Lawrence 1988: 143; Jones 1988: 217–18). In contrast, adolescents found it much more difficult to associate Panjabi with any set of well defined characteristics. For Panjabi, there was no equivalent to the phrase 'acting black' and on the one occasion when 'acting Indian' was used, it referred to stylised Asian English. This absence of a highly defined Panjabi stereotype was doubtless due to its interracial currency being much more exclusively tied to local neighbourhood activity.

Only analyses of interaction can give a full idea of the extent to which adolescents either endorsed or subverted these stereotypes when they were invoked. But in closing this initial description of the way that young people reported on cross-ethnic multilingualism, one clue to their orientation can be found in the time frame that they used to authorise language crossing. I have already described the way that out-group uses of both Panjabi and Creole were explained and justified as well-established local traditions, for many informants dating back to their pre-teens. Admittedly, the time-span in these legitimations was primarily biographical, but elsewhere, there was a sense of the role that language played in marking out the historical trajectory of social groups. There is an idea of forward movement in Asif's (albeit macho) intimation of the significance of Creole:

Extract I.13

Participants: Asif [15 Pa M], Sukhbir [15 In M], BR
Setting: 1987 interview. [Simplified transcription]

BR: do you think there's a lot of difference between the ways boys and girls talk

Asif: yes there is. . . . a lot
BR: yeh?
A: yeh
BR: like what
A: well, we you know think quick, we got . . . they you know . . . only some of the girls, some of the girls are . . . like the posh ones they know what to say innit . . . (but) some of them don't know the future language you see, we do . . . they only know the past, they're they history you see
BR: uhuh
A: yeh
BR: what's the future language then?
A: pardon
BR: what's the future language?
A: ah like all this 'raas klaat' and all this, man, nobody knows it you know
BR: right . . . future? how do you mean the future?
A: ah you know like er . . . we say all these 'kukabin' . . . them girls don't come out with no words you know, and they copy us
BR: and the past language?
A: they only know the past . . . like you know, just ordinary past language . . . English, they don't use no slang or anything . . . only some of them.

While these data only provide a glimpse of Creole conceived as 'the future language', there was abundant evidence that Asian English stood for a past that adolescents felt they were now leaving behind. This was seen as a language of transition, associated with adult migrants and new arrivals who were seen as having adapted only imperfectly to the vernaculars dominant in the new country. Many informants felt some loyalty towards varieties of Asian English ('I mean our parents speak like that ((. . .)) well he grew up here my dad, but my mum does, and you know it's sort of – just sort of becomes part of you'), but in striking contrast to both Creole and Panjabi, they were not associated with any prestigious youth creativity capable of attracting new adherents. Indeed, when stylised, secondary representations of Asian English were placed in time, it was generally proposed that these were declining in their influence (despite the fact that there were more instances in the 1987 recordings than there had been in 1984):

it's out of fashion now, they used to do it. ((It was)) in fashion in 1982. It was racism, more common then.' [15 year-old male of Bangladeshi descent]

it happened in the middle schools ((. . .)) I don't think it's popular in Upper Schools, no, cos you sort of grow up more and you just sort of forget it, don't ya [An M 15]

> A [Pa M 15]: did you watch the plays today? ((. . .)) it's out now 'yes yes' ((in SAE)), it's silly man . . . it's stupid all this 'very good very good', that's out now, it's not in, you know, when you talk ((. . .)) it didn't sound good ((in the plays)) ((. . .))
> BR: did people laugh a lot at that?
> A: no, they used to but not now, nobody laughed

2.6 Summary and overview: a local and historical setting for language crossing

To conclude, it is worth summarising the empirical description so far.

This chapter has looked at the understandings of language crossing that adolescents expressed in interviews, and considered the ways in which these were integrated with perceptions of class, race, gender and community. It started to build up an account of how national and local conditions could affect the social meaning of other-ethnic language use.

Among my informants, the interethnic mixing indexed by language crossing appeared to exist in a socio-cognitive space bounded by both race and class difference. Broadly speaking, crossing was not regarded as a legitimate or likely currency among either posh whites or Bangladeshis, who were seen respectively as superior and inferior groups lying above and below the ambit of 'ordinary' local adolescent practice (though of course, in actual fact, both groups might make use of out-group varieties, and Bangladeshi informants certainly employed all three). In part, this differentiation was undoubtedly informed by objective patterns of economic, residential and educational stratification in Stoneford, and it corresponded with the social network structures I outlined in Chapter 1.

However, an exception was made for white girls from outside

the neighbourhood, and this points to a dynamic element in local perceptions of the 'demographic' position of the people who participated in 'normal' peer group practice. The admission of non-local white girls to the most prestigious sites for Afro-Caribbean and Panjabi youth culture opened up a dialogue with the 'posh', without in any way abandoning the symbols of ethnicity that differentiated Newton and Ashmead adolescents from the rest of town. This tuned with evaluations of poshness that were often favourable when they uncoupled it from snobbery. An interest of social (and historical) movement upwards was also evidenced in the view that Asian English was a variety that adolescents were gradually leaving behind.

Neighbourhood co-residence was another factor that could mitigate the social divisions generated by the wider pattern of majority/minority relations in Britain. White boys often participated in mixed networks if they lived in Ashmead, and in the contexts of these friendships, they had access to the use of other-ethnic languages. However, if a language also operated conspicuously outside the confines of local peer relations, race stratification seemed to reassert itself as a issue, and white use appeared to become much more conditional.

Many of the quotations from informants have suggested that although it did not stand for a seamless racial harmony, as a general practice language crossing was capable of carrying solidary interethnic meanings. At least in its interview representation, the use of an out-group language could be cross-ethnically 'we-coded'. Set within larger coordinates of class and race, themselves cross-cut by community and gender, this chapter has tried to trace out local folk ideas about who 'we' was.

In addition, we have started to compare three varieties in the multilingual peer group repertoire in terms of their more specific symbolic meaning potential and their interethnic accessibility. There were several broad similarities in the way that adolescents described Creole, Panjabi and stylised Asian English: they could all figure in joking cross-ethnic interaction between friends, they could all be used competitively, all could be used against teachers and authority, and they were all ambiguous in so far as none was insured against racialist intentions. But patterns of divergence and overlap were more complex than that, and (albeit at a risk of oversimplification), they are summarised in Figure 2.1.

Figure 2.1: Interview discussion of crossing into Creole, Panjabi and SAE: Summary of major similarities and differences.

	Creole	Panjabi	SAE
Recognition given to serious youth cultural as well as joking uses	+	+	–
Fairly unqualified enthusiasm for out-group use	–	+	–
Close association with inheritors/experts[9] a basic requirement for access	–	+	–
Models widely available through mass media	+	–	+
Well-defined stereo-typic attributes	+	–	+
White (male) use especially dangerous, unlikely or incongruous	+	– (except in bhangra)	+

Within this, the images of Creole and Asian English made available through mass channels were also radically different. So much then for the chapter's descriptive contents – what of its wider relevance?

So far, my concern has been (a) with institutional organisation, (b) with social knowledge as this relates primarily to race but also to class and gender, and (c) with the relationship of both of these to crossing's symbolic meaning potential. In fact, in its discussion of the people, styles, contexts and evaluations typically associated with out-group language use, this chapter has followed a well-established path in the study of code-switching and bilingualism, where often a range of sociolinguistic data sources are analysed in order to produce an account of a language's symbolic association with particular socio-cultural domains or frames of meaning (cf. e.g. Blom and Gumperz 1972; Fishman 1972; Hill and Hill 1986: ch. IV; Heller 1988: 1–24). However, most studies address the relationship between bilinguals and the languages of their own inheritance, and attend much more closely that I do to language use in intra-ethnic spheres. Here, in contrast, the main focus is on the relationship between speakers and the languages of ethnic out-groups, and instead of looking at the ways in which intragroup practices enter, affect and adjust to intergroup experience, this study starts with a situation of intergroup contact and addresses the processes through which this might be reconstituted as a new, mixed, ingroup.

In stratified urban societies (and probably elsewhere), the language varieties associated with different social groups often become the site of diverse and conflicting symbolic meanings. At its simplest, speakers come to see their languages not only as a means for the direct expression of their intentions, but also as reified objects in the perception of outsiders (Bakhtin 1981: 367), so that their words 'are not simple acts of reference', but are seen as carrying an 'ideological burden' (Hill and Hill 1986: 392). In Bakhtin's terms, 'there are no neutral word and forms ... all words have the 'taste' of a profession, a genre, a tendency, a party, a particular work, a particular person, a generation, an age group, the day and hour. Each word tastes of the context and contexts in which it has lived its socially charged life' (Bakhtin [1935] 1981: 293). In fact, given the large-scale relationships between language and social organisation established in macro-sociolinguistic analyses, in mixed discourse 'there are not only (and not even so much) two individual consciousnesses, two voices, two accents, as there are two socio-linguistic consciousnesses, two epochs ... that come together and consciously fight it out on the territory of the utterance' (Bakhtin 1981: 360; also Hill and Hill 1986: 392).

Oriented primarily to the contradictory valuations set up in the context of ethnic stratification, the descriptions in this chapter have described some of the disparate and conflicting 'sociolinguistic horizons' that potentially converged on adolescent speech. If, like most other studies, my analysis of intergroup experience had started out in the close observation of one group's intra-ethnic discourse, it might have been difficult to avoid the impression that when groups came together this struggle between symbolic meanings could only create chaotic sociolinguistic diffusion, endemic conflict and communicative breakdown. Instead, however, there was quite a lot of consistency in what informants said about how people from different ethnic groups used one another's languages. This suggests that in fact in Ashmead, this 'heteroglossia' was itself partly conventionalised, with some agreement on procedures for handling the socio-ideological contestation that polyphony entailed. The task is now to describe some of those procedures, and to do so, interaction becomes a central object of attention.

Notes

1. My sample involved only 12 black informants (7M 5F), whereas Hewitt's black and white informant group totalled 70 (1986: 9).

2. In 1984, there were two Anglos among the 21 non-Afro-Caribbean adolescents singled out in reports, and in 1987, there was one white among 10 named individuals.

3. Each ethnic/sex category of Panjabi crosser – black males, black females, white females, white males – was illustrated in the reports of at least four or five informants (i.e. four or five people mentioned a crosser who was black and female, four or five people mentioned a white male crosser, etc.).

4. There was agreement between at least six informants (2 In M, 2 In F, 1 Pa M, 1 Ba M) that whites used Panjabi more than Afro-Caribbeans (in two interviews it was suggested that this was because 'black people have their own language'). Only one informant suggested that as a group, black peers (girls) used it most. Four pairs of interviewees (2 Pa F, 1 Pa M, 4 In F, 1 In M) attributed more Panjabi use to boys than girls, and three white informants (2F 1M) said the same thing specifically in relation to white users.

5. About 14 informants of Indian and Pakistani parentage reported black uses of Panjabi, and about 14 reported white uses. About 10 Afro-Caribbean and Anglo informants reported other black or white peers using Panjabi. Apart from Bangladeshi informants themselves, only two people noticed any convergence towards Panjabi on the part of Bangladeshi peers.

6. This exclusion was matched by the way that neither Bangladeshis nor non-Ashmead white boys participated in local white, black and Panjabi friendship networks to any significant degree (cf. Chapter 1.7 above).

7. For example:

    in India right, the people that I've seen that talk English . . . talk strict English, you know. Here, this is more of a slangish way . . . the English that people talk round here you know, they're not really talkin' proper English . . . if you go India right . . . they say it clear, in the proper words

8. In addition to many interview comments, evidence for this comes from a 1984 questionnaire given to 15 bilinguals of Indian and

Pakistani descent and five Anglo and Afro-Caribbean monolinguals. Among other things, they were asked to comment on their own English proficiency, and the English proficiency of people and groups around them. The results of this questionnaire are presented in Rampton 1987a, 1988.

9. 'Inheritors' of a language are people with family links to a particular variety. 'Experts' are people who use it well. This distinction is discussed at some length in Chapter 13.7.

Part II

*Interaction with adults:
contesting stratification*

3 Stylised Asian English (i): interactional ritual, symbol and politics

This part of the book focuses on adolescent code-switching that was either directly addressed to adults, or that occurred when adults were a significant presence. Chapter 1 asked whether language crossing could feature in the development of an active sense of urban community, in which different local groups came together and contested common forms of domination experienced in their everyday lives. After that, Chapter 2 reported adolescents saying that language crossing was an anti-teacher activity. It is the combination of these two possibilities that generates the central question addressed throughout Part II: how far and in what ways was adolescent crossing a strategy of resistance to adults in authority, helping to develop a sense of local group identity?

The next three chapters will look at the evidence on stylised Asian English, Panjabi and Creole in turn. The present chapter begins with a short outline of the linguistic features used to identify a stretch of speech as Stylised Asian English (SAE). After that, interview reports of SAE code-switching with teachers are considered, and these suggest quite a close connection with ideas about youth cultural resistance. However, when actual incidents are examined, it becomes clear that informant reports over-simplify the social relations involved in adolescent–adult SAE. At this point, the analysis of symbolic ritual in interaction becomes relevant. Ritual is a slippery concept, and so a special effort is made to define the way in which I shall want to use the term. In the process I also develop a view of the connection between micro and macro levels of social organisation, and the chapter concludes with a discussion of the links between interpersonal discourse and larger political processes.

3.1 Linguistic features marking speech as SAE

There was a range of grammatical, prosodic and segmental features that differentiated stylised uses of Asian English from the local vernacular variety of English. Sometimes it was signalled through deviant verb forms and by the omission of auxiliaries, copulas and articles. Where they did occur, verbal auxiliaries were rarely contracted. Prosodically, this code was generally characterised by the stressing of every syllable, with no apparent nucleus. Intra-sentential pitch changes sometimes seemed abrupt, often involving a greater range than was normal in vernacular English. In terms of its consonantal features, retroflexion was extremely common, and voiced and voiceless plosives were either heavily aspirated, or unaspirated completely. Whereas the local vernacular involved a good deal of T glottalisation and H dropping, these were rare in stylised Asian English. /w/ could be changed to [v] or [b] and there were also instances of epenthesis. With vowels, nasalisation was common and long vowels were often shortened. Dipthongs were usually changed to monopthongs, so that for example the vowel in 'go' was variously realised as [ɔ], [ɒ] or [o], and 'day' was realised with [e] or [ɛ]. A short central open vowel, roughly equivalent to RP /ʌ/ in 'cup', was very common as a replacement for vernacular English /ə/, /æ/, /ɒ/ and /aː/. There was often an absence of schwa reduction. The switch from vernacular to Asian English was often marked out by a change in loudness, pitch, voice quality and/or speed of delivery. Though there was variation in the density with which these features co-occurred, the emic status of this code was attested (a) by the fact that informants had no difficulty in identifying it when listening to recordings, (b) by the examples that they produced in interviews, and (c) by the systematic patterning of its use in spontaneous interaction.

3.2 Interview reports

It was commonly reported that when a class was faced with a new teacher, or a temporary supply teacher, Panjabi pupils might respond to being addressed by pretending that they didn't know much English:

Extract II.1

Session with Ian [An M 15] and Richard [An M 15] in which findings from the 1984 research were being discussed
[simplified transciption]

> Ian: if a copper comes up to you right, and you ain't done anything ((. . .)) or just say you got a supply teacher in, Ben, and she asks you a question and Asif or someone will say **'excuse me me no understanding'**
>
> Richard: yeh
>
> Ian: and and ((laughs)) you know it w- she she knows very well that you can understand her but it get her ff- ((quietly:)) do you mind if I swear – it gets her pissed off
>
> Richard: ((laughs))

Extract II.2

Interview discussion with Kuldip [In M 14] and Faizal [Pa M 14] of 1984 findings. Later on, Harbans was described as 'our clown', 'our clown of the year ((group))'. [Simplified abbreviated transcription]

> Kuldip: ((smile voice)) that's what Harbans ((In M 14)) does
>
> Faizal: yeh
>
> Kuldip: with teachers he does that ((light laughter))
>
> BR: he does it with the teachers?
>
> Kuldip: ( ) he goes **'what you talking about'**
>   [wɒt ju tɔkɪn əbɑːt]
>   ((. . .))
>
> Faizal: Harbans, he does it all the time
>
> BR: how do the teachers react?
>
> Faizal: they just say 'just sit down' and he goes
>   **'I no understand'** and they just go away then
>   [aɪ no ʌndəstɑːɳd]
>
> Kuldip: cos he does it normally with um stand-in teachers when they just,
>
> Faizal: come in you know
>
> Kuldip: for
>
> Faizal: supply teachers, ( ) messes them around
>
> Kuldip: cos he does it normally with stand-in teachers when they just
>
> Faizal: come in
>
> Kuldip: yeh for
>
> Faizal: supply teachers

```
Kuldip:  yeh
    BR:  aah
Faizal:  he messes messes (them) around
    BR:  right ⌈ but not
Kuldip:       ⌊um there's this white boy, Tony Marsh, he sits
         right next to him and he copies, ((smile voice)) he copies
         Harbans
Faizal:  he tries to mix in with us lot
Kuldip:  yeh
Faizal:  he tries to do it too
Kuldip:  and we sort of teach him some words ((in Panjabi)) and
         he sort of ((laughs quietly:)) says them ((the interview
         continues with Kuldip and Faizal explaining what Tony
         learns))
```

Four points can be drawn from these reports. First, SAE seemed to involve a rejection of the teacher's attempt to elicit the show of active commitment to some task or topic of his or her deciding, and as such it could be interpreted by those in the know as a suggestion that the teacher was being intrusive. Secondly, this rejection was superficially mitigated by the remedial politeness encoded in the disguise: terms of formal address (Miss) and an excuse in terms of personal inability (Goffman 1971: 111; Heritage 1984: 270). Thirdly, in addition to exploring the boundaries of teacher control, this fabrication might contain an element of political testing. There was a general consensus that at least on the surface, there was not much racism in the locality, but that it was in the areas beyond that you'd be much more likely to meet it: 'if you lived outside it would be racialist' [Pa M 15], 'our school is not prejudiced' [An M 15], 'Southleigh teachers aren't racist – been with Asian people for years' [In M 17]. In contrast, 'you find (it with) some teachers who come from villages outside' [In M 17]. The persona projected in these reported events reflected white stereotypes about Asians being polite but incompetent in English. If this was part of a new teacher's conceptualisation of their pupils, then they could be drawn into ineffectuality. And finally, Anglos (and doubtless also Afro-Caribbeans) could appreciate aspects of this strategem (even though the active character of Tony Marsh's participation was unusual and threatened to instantly expose the ploy).

From these accounts, it looks as though SAE constituted a form of resistance, and this is the interpretation that Parmar puts on comparable reports in an influential publication from the Birmingham Centre for Contemporary Cultural Studies (1982: 264–5; see also Chapter 5.8). Indeed, as Extracts II.1 and II.2 indicate, this interpretation made sense to informants themselves when it was discussed with them (see also Rampton 1992: 34–46). Even so, interview data often have distinct limitations. Analysis of situated interaction indicates that in fact there was a good deal of idealisation in these reports. In actual practice, the political significance of such acts could be much harder to adduce.

3.3 Incidents observed

In my data, SAE was quite often used where adults were a relevant presence, either as addressees or as butts within earshot. Although the quality of their recording varied and some were noted in my diary rather than taped, there were about 40 instances. These involved teachers, caretakers, dinner ladies, youth workers, and myself (either as a youth worker or a researcher). In one group of informants it was suggested that SAE was mainly used by 'full-time dossers', and there was some evidence that with adults, SAE was more commonly used by adolescents who had animated, fairly uneasy relationships with people in positions of authority at school or in the youth club. Indeed, in the extracts that follow, one group of boys figures disproportionately. But despite that, reports suggested that SAE to adults was quite common, and in my data, it was used by more than 20 males (of whom three were of Caribbean descent and two Anglo) and two females (both Panjabi).

This was one incident:

Extract II.3

Asif (Pa M 15, wearing radio-microphone) and his friend Alan (An M 15) are in detention for writing on desks during lessons. They are being temporarily supervised by Mr Chambers, standing in for Miss Jameson who is trying to see the Headteacher about something else. Around lines 31 or 32 their friends Salim and Kazim (both Pa M) arrive at the door at roughly the same time as Miss Jameson.

```
 1  Asif:  there's loads of writing on this table (2.0) I just wrote
 2         two words words on there and then she put me in
 3         detention [ɪ] (.)
 4  Alan:  ENNIT (1.0) guess what I put
 5  Mr C:  What were they (          )
 6  Alan:  I put M R
 7  Asif:  ((laughs)) I wrote mister right
 8  Mr C:  (        ) (.)
 9  Asif:  that's it (1.0)
10  Alan:  ennit that's it (     )
11  Mr C:  what (        ) was there?
12  Asif:  what?
13  Mr C:  what (       )
14  Asif:  yeh I know Alan wrote them
15  Alan:  don't be silly
16  Asif:  ((louder)) eh don't be silly now
17         ((half laughing:)) look you're in
18         detent⌈ion so tell the truth
19  Alan:        ⌊you can't blame it on me now
20  Asif:  ((loud)) tell the truth Alan (2.0)
21  Asif:  she goes I don't trust you (.) she goes ⌈well I–
22  Mr C:                                          ⌊(neither
23         do I Asif) (.)
24  Asif:  what?
25  Mr C:  I don't tr⌈ust (you   )
26  Asif:            ⌊I don't trust YOU(.)
27         ((half laughing)) I tell you straight right (7.0)
28         ((?Mr C? whistles for 4.0 secs))
29  Asif:  nobody trusts a cowboy (1.5)
30  Mr C:  (what?)
31  Asif:  ((laughing quietly)) (        ) (.)
((Kazim and Salim arrive at the door about now))
32  Mr C:  (         )
33  Alan:           ⌈(          )
34  Asif:  ((f)) Kaz ⌊[ethe ɾo   ethe ɾo]
                ((Panj: stay here stay here))
35  Mr C:  (  see you messing   around)
36  Alan:            ⌈(      )
37  Asif:  ((chants)) ⌊['te'ri _____ 'a:,di:,di:]
           ((ff))      ((Panj: your + (obscenity) + nonsense))
38  Ms J:  'after'you
39  Asif:  'after'you::ˋ
           [ʌftə juʊu]
40  Salim: ((at a higher pitch)) 'after'you::ˋ
                             [ʌftər juʊu]
```

```
41 Mr C: (              ) (1.0)
42            ((door bangs shut))
43  Ms J: ((f)) have we got another cloth?
44 Salim: ((f)) alright  (        )
45                  ((a lot of loud laughter))
46  Asif: ((f)) Kazim you want to help us?
47Kazim: pardon
48 Mr C: you want another cloth do you
49  Asif: ((f)) yeh yeh say yeh         [ɑː ɑː ɑː ɑː]
                                        ((Panj: yes yes yes yes
50 Ms J:                           (              )
51 Salim: yeh I might  (       )
52 Mr C:               (       )
53  Asif: yeh
54Kazim: I'll help 'em
55 Salim: yeh we'll help 'em
56  Ms J:           no you won't (.) out
57Kazim: ((l)) come on 'en
58 Salim: ((l)) come on
59  Ms J: OUT (2.0)
60Kazim: ((l)) we're not joking
61  Asif: ((laughs))
62  Ms J: disobedient yes
63Kazim: I know but I (don't)
64 Mr C: ((l)) come on Salim
65Kazim: ((f)) so what you doing here anyway
66  Ms J: ((f)) thank you  very much
67 Salim:              ((f)) you you try to chat her up
68        ennit (        )
69  Ms J: thank you very much
70        ((Salim and Asif (start to) leave about now))
71  Asif: can I go now
72  Ms J: no, and I want  these desks
73  Asif:               WHAT YOU ON ABOUT UUH
74 Alan:  Miss
75  Asif: two words I wrote (.) You sa- is this half hour job
```

Quite a lot was happening in this episode and I shall return to discuss it when the focus shifts to the use of Panjabi with white monolingual adults in Chapter 4. But in the meantime, the use of SAE in lines 39 and 40 certainly appears to endorse certain aspects of the report data. Stylised Asian English occurred at a moment when boundaries were at issue: Miss James was negotiating with the two new arrivals about access through a door that had special significance as a threshold to the classroom where the detention was being held. It also encoded a stereotyped politeness that could not be taken at face value, since a separation between the words uttered and the speaker's usual selves was indicated by a sharp change from normal pitch, tune and accent (in addition, Asif appears to be have been situated inside the classroom and was thus in no position to make a genuine offer). The episode also shows clearly that SAE could be inserted within the micropolitics of pupil–teacher interaction: skirmishing over the assertion of authority became overt in lines 56–64, and plainly a system of wider institutional sanctions was at stake throughout (detention as punishment for misconduct). On these grounds, SAE does indeed appear to serve as a double-edged instrument of resistance in institutionally asymmetrical cross-ethnic negotiation.

A closer look, though, indicates that the bald term 'resistance' does not adequately capture the spirit of this encounter. Contrary to the prototypical situation sketched out in interview reports, the teachers involved here were well known to these youngsters: elsewhere, Mr Chambers was favourably mentioned for his minor adventures into multiracial adolescent Panjabi (see Chapter 4 note 3), and when they were later left alone, there was quite a lot of relatively amicable conversation between Miss Jameson and Alan and Asif. Perhaps more significantly, the switch to stylised Asian English occurred within a sequence of *reciprocal* kidding that was actually initiated by Miss Jameson. In lines 38–40, it was her falsely polite 'after you' – equivalent to saying 'please, do come and join us in detention' – that constituted the first move away from straight, untransformed talk. Once this initial shift from normal politeness had been introduced, it was easier for Asif and Salim to increase the non-literal framing of the exchange through the addition of false accents (Goffman 1974: 159). Where one might usually expect a gradually attenuating sequence 'after you – thanks (– my pleasure)', the interlude now promised to develop into an immobilising spin of reciprocal deference (Goffman 1971: 143–4). The recording is unclear as to who entered the classroom first, but a non-literal frame was maintained subsequent to the use of SAE, with both teachers participating until their bluff was called and Miss Jameson tried to bring things down to earth in lines 56 and 59.

Taken as a whole, this episode undoubtedly did involve conflict, with the boys probing away at the limits of authority. But given the actions of Miss Jameson and Mr Chambers, the extract might be more easily be characterised as 'sport' (or as 'verbal duelling') than political resistance.[1] Indeed, in inviting Salim and Kazim into detention, it was the teachers who transgressed basic features of detention as an event where attendance is involuntary and made by prior arrangement. Asif's use of Panjabi still awaits analysis, but certainly in terms of the overall outcomes, there was not much evidence of students breaking out from institutional norms. Kazim and Salim left the scene, Alan and Asif carried on with detention, and generally, this episode might well represent the kind of interactive juggling between play and seriousness that has been well documented as a popular and enlivening feature of the teacher's professional experience (cf. e.g. Pollard 1985: 205–17).

The effect of this discussion must be to qualify any temptation to exaggerate the force of stylised Asian English as a language of resistance. However, there were episodes where SAE was used in more plainly oppositional exchanges. In the reports and extract cited so far, the use of SAE imported an element of apparent politeness into the (partly playful) sparring between pupils and teachers (**'excuse me Miss'**, **'I no understand English'**, **'after you'**). On occasion though, these surface elements were omitted. This can be seen in the two subsequent extracts.

Extract II.4

Salim, Asif and Kazim have devised an illicit but profit-making procedure ('sneaking') which involves obtaining more dinner than they are entitled to and selling some of it off at discount prices to their friends. Salim, Asif and Kazim have just sat down in the dining hall with their friends and prospective clients Cyril [AC M 15], Richard [An M 15], Jagdish [In M 15] and some others. Another, Conrad [AC M 15], is nearby, as yet unseated. Although standing at some distance, the suspicions of one of the white dinner ladies have been aroused (and after this episode, she comes up to Salim to make enquiries).

```
1     Asif:  lady's getting a bit suspicious man
2  Kazim:  mm
3        :  (   what's wrong with  ) (8.0)
4  Kazim:  (      )
```

```
 5        : (    )
 6        : (    )
 7        : (    ) (4.0)
 8  Kazim: nice ennit
 9        : (         [  football)
10   Asif:          └mm      (5.0)
11 Jagdish:  ‚I am'wat'ching‚you: ((others laugh))
           [aɪ əm wʌtʃɪŋ    ju:]
12    Salim:  ‚I am 'vat 'ching ‚you::
           [aɪ əm vʌtʃɪŋ     ju:]
13 Jagdish: ((light laugh))
14 Jagdish: Conrad (comes and leans ) there man
15        : (        )
16    Salim: CONRAD (.) CONRAD (.)
17 Conrad: what?
18    Salim: ((quietly)): come on (1.0)
```

The switch in SAE appears to be a response to the dinner lady's
gaze (see also Extract II.5), and it contains no elements of deference. In common with previous uses of SAE, however, this
utterance can be interpreted as registering boundaries. One of
these is the conversational enclosure consisting of the young
people seated at the table, which the adult has crossed into with
her scrutiny. Interlinked with this and giving the enclosure special
meaning, is the boundary between legitimate and illicit pupil conduct which these transactions with food are transgressing. It seems
to be both that are indexed in Extract II.5, recorded later on the
same day:

Extract II.5

Due to the watchfulness of the dinner ladies, Salim and Kazim have
had to abandon their plans for further 'sneaking'. The two are now
walking together away from the dining room. 'Kit Kats' are a type
of chocolate bar.

```
1 Salim: ( the common room) (1.0) put our bags upstairs (5.0)
2 Salim: ((makes a short high pitched noise))
3 Kazim: still not full up (.)
4 Salim: ((slowly)) "still "not 'fuc'king ‚bloody    ┌„full
         [stˈiː‚ ŋã:t fʌ̃:kˈĩŋ   blɜ̃:di:       │fʊl]
5 Kazim:                                        └I know
6        I'm starving innit
```

```
 7  Salim:    ((smile voice)) I was going to go there again ma:n
 8            do another sneaker, but (2.0) then
 9  Kazim:    should've went the first time (      ) (1.0)
10            then the bitch looked
11  Salim:    yeh I was going ⌈there
12  Kazim:                    ⌊I know you went like this (     )
13            the bitch looked and (you jus'  )
14  Salim:    I went like this when the bitch looks (.) I went like
15            this (1.5) ah fuck it (.) I go fuck it (2.0)
              ((l.))                  ((l.))
              [f:ʌ:kˀɪːtʰ]       [f:ʌ:kˀɪːʈʰ]
16            ((in American accent)) shark it man (.) ((seeing a
17            passing teacher)) GO ON MISS WITH THE KIT KATS
```

In line 4, Salim repeated most of Kazim's preceding turn, but upgraded it with swear words and an SAE accent. Without adding any propositional information, this seems to revivify the conflict over 'sneaking', and the subsequent exchange returned to address it explicitly. In line 15, this SAE voicing was relocated directly within the earlier confrontation, and the oppositional potential of SAE was here made plain and unmitigated (it maybe also provided a gloss on an illocutionary force that was more concealed in the SAE utterance that Salim actually used in Extract II.4). Salim was sometimes nicknamed 'Gabbar' by his close friends, after a locally notorious villain in the film 'Sholay' (Sippy 1975). These boys sometimes did 'Gabbar' impressions and it is quite likely that this character provided the model for Salim's voice quality and slow delivery in line 15.

Even so, oppositional potential of this kind was never openly declared in any of the institutionally asymmetrical interethnic exchanges that I recorded or observed (and even in Extract II.5, it was expressed *sotto voce* outside authority's earshot). In addition, it is important to try to distinguish the contingent features linked to particular occasions from more stable characteristics associated with the use of SAE. In due course, I shall argue that the discussion of conflict, resistance and social movements in Chapter 1.2 was indeed highly pertinent for an understanding of stylised Asian English, but to avoid confusion of the essential and the incidental, it is helpful to look at the use of SAE in interactions that were much more obviously cooperative. Here are two, recorded in my fieldnotes:

Extract II.6

As I was going down the stairs into the gym at the youth club, a small Asian boy (about 12 years old) was walking down in front of me. Jim Cook, the school caretaker, was at the bottom by the doors. He held them open for us and as the boy went through, he turned to Jim as he passed and said in a very strong Panjabi accent (not subsequently maintained in ordinary talk): '**how are you doing Mr Cook**'. As I passed through after him, without any hint of annoyance Jim said something like 'might as well keep the doors open all the time', which he did. [fieldnotes]

Extract II.7

I was standing behind the snack bar. Ishfaq (Pa M 15) came into the club soon after it opened and in our first exchange of the evening, he came up to me at the counter and said in a strong Panjabi accent: '**Ben Rampton can I help you.**' Though it was me doing the serving, I sustained the joke and asked for 20? Mojos (chews). Then in his ordinary voice he placed an order for 10 Refreshers – is this a party I asked, etc. [fieldnotes]

In these two extracts, SAE is used in opening encounters. In both, a young Panjabi bilingual walks towards a white adult and the use of SAE marks the beginning of a period of heightened contact between them, even if it is only very brief. Explicit greetings of the 'hello, how are you' kind were very rare in the face-to-face SAE encounters between adolescents and adults that I recorded, but the kind of encounter instanced in Extract II.7 was more frequent. In this particular incident, Ishfaq's role reversal – could *he* help *me* – was unusual (though cf. Extract II.4), but more generally, there were eight (possibly nine) instances when combining with a request, the transition to a period of heightened access was marked with stylised Asian English.

To understand what is happening here, it is useful to consider the usual structure of opening encounters. The opening of encounters – and even minor comings-together over a counter (Goffman 1971: 78) – can be most simply analysed into two stages: (a) cognitive recognition, in which each participant places the other within some framework of personal and/or social information about them; and (b) social recognition, which overtly welcomes the approach, shows that further communication is permissible, and acknowledges their specific personal and/or social identities and their membership of a shared relationship (see Goffman 1971: ch. 7 and Schiffrin 1977 for a more differentiated account). Functionally, the 'phatic' work done in openings

> allows [interactants] the opportunity to explore, in a tentative way, the social identity and momentary state of mind of the other participant, in order to be able to define and construct an appropriate role for themselves in the rest of the interaction . . . it would appear to have an important propitiatory function in defusing . . . potential hostility . . . [and] it allows the participants to cooperate in getting the interaction comfortably under way, using emotionally uncontroversial communicative material, and demonstrating by signals of cordiality and tentative social solidarity their mutual acceptance of the possibility of an interaction taking place (Laver 1975: 218–19, 220, 221; see also e.g Firth 1972; Laver 1981; Ferguson 1981: 23–4; Kendon 1990: ch. 6)

In none of the episodes in which adolescents approach with an SAE request was the need for phatic work very intense (for example **'we want lifting'** (a lift), **'you could take me in your car?'**, **'Ben can I come'**). The motives for the encounters were transactional/business-oriented (cf. Goffman 1971: 71), the participants already knew each other quite well, the adults addressed occupied institutional roles that made approaches and requests appropriate, and often there had already been an extended period of co-presence (and maybe an earlier exchange of greetings) (cf. Laver 1975: 218). Nevertheless, an understanding of the structure of opening encounters clarifies what appears to have been happening in these exchanges. The use of SAE can be seen as a social recognition that registered an identity contrary to the kind of cognitive recognition that the recipient might be expected to make in the circumstances. It foregrounded a *social* category membership ('Asian who doesn't speak vernacular English') at a moment when the adult would normally be setting him/herself up for interaction with an individual known to him/her in a primarily *personal/biographical* capacity. And in doing so, it promised to *destabilise* the transition to comfortable interaction and the working consensus that phatic activity normally facilitates.

Not that this led to conflict or communicative breakdown. As has already been suggested, in a great many institutional settings people perform their institutional roles none too seriously, displaying personality and humanness in a stream of minor acts that declare a distance from their official capacities (Goffman 1974: 297–8). If these deviations are considered to fall outside the limits of conduct deemed acceptable by the institutional authorities, they can become the site of serious conflict. But alternatively, if they can be accommodated within the institution, they provide the grounds for the growth of more rounded, three-dimensional relationships. The identity switches evidenced both in these approach sequences and in the pupil–teacher interaction can be seen as a small contribution to this unofficial sideshow, inviting the recipient to display their competence and understanding of the frame play in progress. Although the tipping of the balance would be affected by a range of additional contextual factors, in principle the recipient might either flounder, unable to decide on the frame or footing being offered (Goffman 1974: 423), or they might take it in their stride, showing deftness and a willingness to play. One youth worker told me that when Salim spoke to her in SAE, she thought it put her at a distance and made her feel embarrassed (and I too generally felt uncomfortable when addressed in SAE). But another, being told 'I go toilet' by a Panjabi boy walking back into the club after closing time, responded in SAE with 'oh you bloody loony you'.

But this discussion of (minor) disturbance to smooth interactional transitions is just the first of three analytic stages that we need to move through in order to grasp the relationship between SAE code-switching and a wider arena of social conflict. As a second step, it is useful to ask what it was in all of these interactions that prompted adolescents to code switch at all, and what was involved in the fact that they chose to do so in stylised Asian English.

3.4 Ritual, symbol and politics in interaction

In terms of its interactional occasioning, switches to SAE frequently occurred when Asian youngsters were negotiating participation in an interactional enclosure in which a white adult would have some control or influence over them. This influence might involve the distribution of goods or services, or it could occur at the threshold of activities such as detention or basketball.

Reputedly, youngsters used it in response to teacher elicitations and on a couple of occasions it was also used when I asked for more concentrated attention during interviews. Outside the negotiation of engagements immediately on hand, SAE was also used when knowledge was at stake that could affect the course of encounters at a later date. It was used when adults were felt to be gaining unratified access to information about pupil activities that they might subsequently use against them (Extract II.4), and it was occasionally used in closings, where it is quite common to 'sum . . . up the consequence of the encounter for the relationship, and bolster . . . the relationship for the anticipated period of no contact' (Goffman 1971: 79):

> BR: ((at the end of an interview)): okay, good, that's very
> good, I'm glad to have got a bit of that
> Kazim: **so am I glad too**
> [sɔ əm aɪ glɜd t̺ʰu]

In fact, understanding SAE's interactional location assists the analysis of its symbolic significance. To make the connection, it is necessary to draw the idea of ritual into the account. Though not all of these characteristics are relevant at this stage in the analysis, ritual was defined prototypically in Chapter 1.4 as (a) formulaic conduct, (b) displaying an orientation to issues of respect for social order and emerging from some sense of the (actual or potential) problematicity of social relations, (c) giving a more prominent place to symbols than to propositions, (d) eliciting a marked emotional response and creating an increased sense of collectivity between at least some of the participants, and (e) being itself subject to comment and sanctions.

Opening exchanges are often described as *low-key* rituals. For example, Laver suggests that they can be seen as 'rites of passage . . . easing and signaling the transitions to and from conversational interactions' (1975: 234; see also Firth 1972); characteristic (b) is clear in the earlier quotation on phatic communion; and in the routine enquiries about health that feature in much greeting conduct, it is easy to note (a) (and in so far as recipients do not normally treat 'how are you?' as a serious inquiry about their state of health, at least part of (c)). Goffman describes these as 'access rituals', but also argues that interpersonal ritual is much more extensive than this, generally becoming prominent whenever there are threats or uncertainties around social life's innumerable norms and boundaries. 'When individuals come into one another's immediate presence, territories of the self bring to the scene a vast filigree of trip wires which individuals are uniquely equipped to trip over' (1971: 106), and when this happens, ritual work is in order, as it is when someone looks like deviating from the lines of conduct expected of them (1967). The great range and often very minor scale of the actual and potential offences that occasion ritual activity can be seen in Brown and Levinson's account of face-threatening acts and politeness (e.g. 1987 [1978]: 65–7).

It is important to recognise, though, that interpretations of an offence do not limit themselves to the particular act or event in question, but instead, read a wider significance into the transgression. Goffman describes the way that people respond to transgression in the following way:

> Social norms [or rules] are almost always couched in general terms, as if applying to a particular event because the event is one instance of a class to which the rule applies. Any deviation . . . on any one occasion when the rule is supposed to apply can give the impression that the actor may be delinquent with respect to the whole class of events. And any compliance can carry assurance regarding the actor's handling of all other events that come under the rule . . . This tendency of individuals to read acts as symptoms gives an important expressive or indicative quality even to acts [that are significant in their own right], carrying as they do evidence of the actor's relation to a rule and, by extension, his relation to the system of rules of which the one in question is a part. And, of course, such information often is taken as relevant for an appraisal of the actor's moral character. (Goffman 1971: 97)

Complementarily, interpersonal ritual itself is not primarily concerned with compensating for the specific discomfort or injury suffered on a particular occasion (1971: 118). Instead it is 'a conventionalised communication by which the individual . . . expresses his [moral] character' (1967: 54) and indicates a more general relationship to 'rules, which his actions appear to have broken, and to persons whose territories should have been protected by these rules' (1971: 116).

Goffman's concern with interactional boundaries, with norms

of propriety, with the wider moral implications of action, and with participants' active orientation to actual or potential offence, are all crucial to my analysis. But there is one sense in which his use of the term 'ritual' extends beyond the way in which I would generally like to use it in relation to language crossing. In Goffman's approach (e.g. 1981: 21), sensitivity to the ritual significance of conduct is regarded as a pervasive feature of all socially situated speech and action, and it covers utterances in which explicit propositional meanings play a central role just as much as those in which symbolic connotations are primary. This has been a very productive assumption, as the work of Brown and Levinson (1987) testifies. But Brown and Levinson are sensible to talk of 'face work' and 'politeness' rather than 'ritual', since in much sociological and anthropological literature, symbolism is taken as a central feature in ritual, often counterposed to the modes of expression dominant in ordinary conversation.

The relationship between symbolism and factually oriented referential meaning is complex, and there is disagreement about the extent to which these involve different modes of cognitive processing.[2] Even so, whether it is a matter of degree or kind, a broad view of the difference between symbolic and ordinary communication is provided by Sperber 1975. Of ordinary communication he writes:

> Our knowledge of the world is formed by organising statements according to ... relationships [of implication and contradiction], by accepting a statement only with its implications – at least the most evident ones – and similarly, by avoiding contradictions. Experience shows that ... knowledge [of the world] is not immune to incoherences and contradictions, but all practical life is based on a continuous effort to avoid and correct them. (1975: 94)

When we process an ordinary utterance in everyday communication, we analyse its propositions and integrate this with relevant pieces of world knowledge that we have brought to bear. In contrast, symbolic statements present a problem for routine propositional interpretation: they are often paradoxical and fairly immune to empirical contradiction. It is much harder to reconcile them with the bits of encyclopaedic knowledge that we first invoke, and this sets off the more extended process of memory search which Sperber (1975) calls 'evocation'. A broadly comparable sense of the difference between practical and symbolic modes of communication informs many accounts of ritual:

> Rituals . . . convey meaning by means of symbols, defined by one anthropologist as the 'minimal units of ritual' (Turner). If rituals are to be seen as a means of communication, they use very peculiar means . . . Rituals use symbols to refer and connote only in the vaguest of ways. Rituals employ relatively fixed sequences of language, and, above all, singing which hinders analytic communication (Bloch 1985: 699)

'Ritual' in the present analysis will obviously need to refer to a much more general set of activities than the religious rites that Bloch has in mind, but by the same token, it will also be necessary to keep symbolism firmly in view. As a concept, symbolism allows one to make connection with the role that ritual plays in wider societal concerns – concerns that Goffman plays down, but that are foregrounded in anthropological accounts as well as in the Gilroy argument outlined in Chapter 1.2.

Let us return to the data on SAE. In the way that it was occasioned by movement across interactional enclosure boundaries, codeswitches into SAE can be closely related to Goffman's account of access ritual. They also conformed to Goffman's notion in so far as they situated particular incidents within the framework of a more general social or moral relation (the gist of Goffman's account is that normally, the ritual activity occasioned by an act of transition means that in addition to their personal/biographical identities, participants would recognise each other as being generally considerate, decent members of society).

Here, however, I have suggested that switches to SAE were designed to disrupt smooth transition and certainly, they partially obscured the speaker's personal identity. Beyond that, they appeared to evoke the wider relation of Anglo-Asian domination as a relevant interpretive framework. This should certainly not be seen as the sum total of SAE's connotational resonances (see, for example, Extract II.5, where these are plainly much more complex). But this interpretation draws support from interview discussions (Chapter 2.4), and it fits with these particular situations of use much more closely than those described in Chapter 6 (cf. Turner 1969: 53 on the multivocality of symbols decreasing when they are studied in context). This being the case, it is possible to make more specific proposals about the way in which SAE might ruffle the transitions that occasioned it. SAE seemed to make relevant social knowledge about problematic intergroup relations, and to generate the potential significance of a 'worst case' scenario in which one of the participants might be seen as a white racist believing in babu stereotypes, or the other as an incompetent Asian (or both). And all this could be done while preserving politeness in the stylised surface features of the utterance.

To complete this account of the political character of interactional switching into SAE, the final step in the analysis entails further cross-reference to accounts of ritual as a macro-social, institutional practice. There are in fact a number of precedents for a shift between macro and micro examinations of ritual: Goffman's ideas were heavily influenced by Durkheim's study of religion ([1912] 1975), and this influence is also significant in Brown and Levinson (cf. e.g. Goffman 1971: 62–4; Brown and Levinson 1987: 43–44; see also Alexander 1988: 190–1; Collins 1988a, 1988b). Durkheim's work on religion has also been important for recent sociological analyses of institutional ritual, though running counter to his account, scholars have been at pains to emphasise first that ritual action need not be accompanied by an intense charge of collective emotional effervescence (Alexander 1988: 190; Collins 1988a: 110–11); secondly, that it is essential not to expect value conformity or a consensual outcome from the ritual process (Lukes 1975: 296ff; Alexander 1988); and thirdly, that no ritual is so rigid that there is no room for at least some improvisation (Turner 1974: 82; also Parkin 1984).

Lukes' account is especially relevant to the present investigation. Lukes defines ritual as 'rule governed activity of a symbolic character which draws the attention of its participants to objects of thought and feeling [objects, relationships, situations, ideas, etc.] that they hold to be of special significance' (1975: 291). But he insists that this needs to be understood in the context of a stratified, conflictual and pluralistic society where there are 'socially patterned differences of interpretation among those who participate or observe' (1975: 301). The political analysis of rituals should go

> beyond the conventional study of politics which . . . concentrates
> on who gets what, when and how, on 'how people get the things

they want through government', and focus instead on mechanisms through which politics 'influences what they want, what they fear, what they regard as possible and even who they are' . . . It [should] explore the symbolic strategies used by different groups, under specifiable structural conditions, to defend or to attain power *vis-à-vis* other groups . . . It [should] also examine the ways in which ritual symbolism can provide a source of creativity and improvisation, a counter-cultural and anti-structural force, engendering new social, cultural and political forms . . . In this way, political rituals can be analysed as part of what has been called the 'mobilisation of bias' . . . – that 'set of predominant values, beliefs, rituals . . . and constitutional procedures ('rules of the game') that operate systematically and consistently to the benefit of certain persons and groups at the expense of others' . . . And parallel analyses could be made of rituals that are not 'predominant' or hegemonic – whether these are subordinate and oppositional but posing no challenge to the existing social and political order, or else radically oppositional and representing a real challenge to the existing order (1975: 302, 305)

Code-switching into SAE can be seen as a 'mobilisation of bias' at the level of interpersonal ritual. Taking its earlier description as a destabilising action sited at the boundaries of institutionally vested enclosures, we can say that it presents a challenge to the dominant social order in one of its most micro-interactional forms. But as Lukes and others emphasise, the outcome and interpretation of ritual action is open to variation and negotiation, and because of this, we need not lose sight of the fact that these uses of SAE often seemed amicable. It has already been said (a) that in principle, the recipients of SAE might either flounder or flourish, and that (b) it conjured social knowledge of a wider pattern of intergroup stratification. Putting these two points together, we can suggest that if the subsequent interaction went badly, the problematicity of Anglo-Asian relations would be confirmed, with the interactants located on what could be construed as politically opposed sides. Whereas if it went well, then interaction could generate some reassurance that although it could not be ignored, knowledge of ethnic stratification was not dangerous or threatening for the relationship of these particular participants. In turn, the reception given to SAE might contribute to a sense of the legitimacy or otherwise of institutional relations and ultimately (along with other factors) affect the user's willingness to participate in them.

How does all this tie in with more general political processes? To answer this question, it is helpful to return to our earlier discussion of urban social movements.

3.5 Interaction and social movements

As I have already indicated, a social movement can be seen as a loose collection of people drawn together outside the sphere of official political institutions by their active and enduring opposition to some very general socio-cultural pattern that oppresses them (Touraine 1985; Giddens 1989: 624–9). In the context of dispute about race and nation, Gilroy suggests that this provides a productive way of characterising the oppositional sensibilities developing in multiracial British inner cities. Since a social movement's fundamental concerns can cover 'personal identity, the time and the space in everday life, the motivation and the cultural patterns of individual action' (Melucci 1985: 796; Gilroy 1987), there are good reasons for using face-to-face interaction as an arena for their empirical investigation, and the validity of an interpersonal perspective is endorsed when Melucci suggests that the term 'social movement' should be supplemented or replaced with the phrase 'movement networks' (Chapter 1.2).

As the quotations from Lukes make clear, however, non-conformity and opposition can take a number of different forms, and some of these can be irrelevant to the kinds of resistance which sociologists identify with social movements. People may, for example, transgress dominant social codes in the course of a mass panic, but since this involves little more than a plurality of atomised individuals, it lacks the dimension of solidarity that characterises a social movement. To distinguish it from several other kinds of oppositional activity, Melucci describes specifically *social movement* conflict in the following terms: (a) A social movement involves struggle between two (individual or group) actors, competing for resources or influence, and both sides in the struggle bring specific solidarities with them. (b) Instead of negotiating within an agreed framework (as typified in employer-trades union negotiations), the participants in a social movement break out from the working consensus that has been governing the argument hitherto. (c) Because they are defined as breaking the rules set for a dispute, social movements have a tendency to spread upwards through social structure from the sites where the conflict begins (see also Touraine 1981: 87). They might start within a specific institution, but by challenging the power governing the local system of norms and roles, the argument soon becomes more than a matter of institutional business and a larger field of social contestation becomes relevant. (d) In the process, the scope for negotiation diminishes, and the symbolic content of the dispute increases (Melucci 1981).

In the presence of adults, code-switching into SAE bore a number of similarities to this account of social movement conflict. Adolescents often switched into stylised Asian English with white adults in positions of institutional authority when the adults were on the point of increasing their control or influence ($\backsimeq$ a). The switch cast doubt over the frame governing subsequent interaction at the moment when it was introduced ($\backsimeq$ b). In switching, young people moved beyond the local occasion and seemed to make relevant a quite fundamental field of social contestation. Through symbolic action, race stratification was made available as a wider interpretive context for interaction, and both participants momentarily confronted the possibility of their being on opposite sides in the conflict about race ($\backsimeq$ c and d).

Admittedly, this appropriation of Melucci's definition of social movement conflict entails quite a radical shift of analytic levels. As in most sociological discussions of social movements, Melucci takes fairly large-scale features of social organisation for his primary empirical focus – institutions, political systems and class relations. Phenomena such as these are rather more macroscopic than the main terms that we have been dealing with, and in this light, it would not be surprising if when we tried to adopt an interactional perspective on Melucci's model of social movement conflict, we had to readjust certain analytic expectations.

At first sight, for example, it may be hard to accept that the minor doubts which SAE placed over the frame governing subsequent interaction could be equated with a social movement's breaking out from conventional rules for dispute, and with the decreasing scope for negotiation which this generates ((b) above). As forms of disruption, SAE code-switching certainly looks very muted in comparison with the mass mobilisations which Melucci generally has in mind. On the other hand, this may be no more than one would expect in interaction. Grammars may not have rules for managing what happens when rules are broken, but interaction does (Goffman 1981: 21). The working consensus in interaction is often very far from fixed or inflexible, and conversationalists are famously adept at restoring orderly business when negotiation runs in to difficulty. This is not to deny that ruptures can occur (cf. Roberts et al. 1992), but they may be much less spectacular in interaction than in more macroscopic social processes, and they may also be more threatened than achieved (cf. G Turner 1983: 58–9).

But in other respects the shift to interaction produces analytic dividends. The analysis of macro-social phenomena necessarily involves the aggregation of a wide range of different events and practices, and in this light, Melucci's insistence that there is no essential, single meaning or purpose in large-scale collective action is entirely fitting: 'there are a plurality of analytical meanings which eliminate the apparent unity of the empirical object and yield a different evaluation of its structural components as well as its political implications' (Melucci 1981: 173). A move towards interaction certainly does not eliminate ambiguity and analytic uncertainty: in the data we have analysed, we cannot say categorically what it was that SAE opposed (was it the particular adult, the institution that gave them their authority, the system of values that rated white above Asian, or some actual or potential combination of these?). Even so, ambiguity and analytic uncertainty are much less problematic. The analysis of situated utterance meaning covers many more intimately related contextual clues than one is likely to find in the analysis of macroscopic phenomena such as, for example, the green movement or youth subculture, and these aid and discipline the interpretation of what a particular action means. Furthermore, we have seen that indeterminacy in the symbolic meaning of SAE was an active feature of the interaction itself, interrupting ordinary processes of communicative comprehension, making the recipient's subsequent turn a little bit more problematic, but also affording both parties an opportunity to calibrate their relationship in their interpretations of the ambiguity (cf. Sperber 1975). Ambiguity evidently mattered for participants themselves.

This leads into a second point. Studying interactional practices requires attention to the responses that code-switching elicits. These occur in close proximity to the symbolic action, and they not only display the recipient's orientation within the field that has been evoked, but also retrospectively affect the switcher's own interpretation of the significance of the political relations momentarily made relevant. This process means that to a considerable degree, an action's meaning is *jointly* constructed. One effect of this close relationship between utterance and response is to produce the relatively muted character of the frame disruption that we noted above. But more importantly, it provides a view of one of the ways in which urban communities can develop the heterogeneous solidarities described by Melucci and Gilroy. SAE appeared to raise controversial issues of identity, polarising black–white and dominant–subordinate relations. But, as the code-switching data emphatically underlines, identity is, in Moerman's terms, 'situated, motile, shaded, purposive, consequential, negotiated' (1988: 90; also e.g. Erickson and Shultz 1982; Levinson 1983: 295), and recipients could take SAE in their step, processing it in the context of other safer and more obviously bonding identity relations, which would be activated before, afterwards or during. In fact in consequence, though some differences in the evocations generated by this symbol would be inevitable, the ritual practice could itself become accepted as part of a *common* tradition, and contrary to the assumptions of ethnic absolutism, this embraced white peers and it might even extend to teachers.

Close attention to interaction also makes it clear that the linguistic resources in the multiracial adolescent repertoire in fact carried *different* kinds of political momentum, and that in their relations to institutional hierarchies, some were more oriented to autonomy than opposition. This will become clear as the investigation now turns to Panjabi.

Notes

1. The following quotation from Edwards and Westgate 1987: 96–7 meshes closely with the current analysis:

   a great deal of classroom humour takes the form of repartee, whether between teacher and class or between teacher and individuals who seem almost to have been granted, or have claimed, a jester's licence . . . Repartee trades on common knowledge, not only of particular events in past encounters which are referred to obliquely, but also of conventions which mark off permissable humour from humour which has 'gone too far' . . . [There is a] subtle line which can often distinguish cohesive from divisive humour . . . [and the] 'ritualising' of insults [can] remove any offence as long as implicitly agreed limits are not overstepped. [This might occur when] a teacher is checking a pupil's work at his desk, but the interaction is clearly in public view. We suggest that to interpret it as evidence of the teacher's relationship with his class, it would be necessary to know how often such verbal duelling occurred, at what stages of lessons, and how far they constituted breaks from otherwise orderly, 'working' transactions . . . [In addition, it is essential to address] the immediate sequences in which the 'acts' . . . are located. In particular, it is argued that the function of an utterance is often unintelligible without reference to what came next.

2. Sperber (1975) emphasises the difference between ordinary and symbolic interpretation processes by suggesting that they are handled by different cognitive mechanisms. Sperber and Wilson (1986) reject this view. Instead of seeing ordinary and symbolic interpretation as different in kind, they suggest that they differ in the amount of processing they require, the strength and specificity of the implicatures they generate, and the extent to which it is either the speaker or the hearer who takes responsibility for utterance meaning.

4 Panjabi (i): interactional and institutional participation frameworks

This chapter studies the way in which adolescents of Pakistani, Indian and non-Asian descent used Panjabi in the presence of white monolingual adults (drawing on about 16 episodes as well as on informant reports). It begins by discussing Panjabi's use in broadly conflictual interactions, but then moves on to illustrate Panjabi crossing in settings that were more cooperative. Central importance is attached to the ways in which the use of Panjabi structured the interactional participation of adolescents and adults (Goffman 1981). The latter were generally excluded from Panjabi exchanges, but the significance of this exclusion was very variable. Indeed, this exclusion was itself neither total nor necessary. A comparison is made with the participation frameworks entailed in the use of stylised Asian English (SAE), and the different social relations surrounding the use of these two varieties are interpreted as instantiations of their wider socio-cultural relationships to mainstream English. The micro-relations surrounding Panjabi reflected larger (though by no means universal) debates about cultural pluralism, whereas SAE's interactional relations were structured in the politics of assimilation.

4.1 Panjabi in conflictual interaction with adults

To start this analysis of how Panjabi figured in adult–adolescent relations, it is useful to return to Extract II.3 in Chapter 3.3, and to begin by noting the ways in which Asif played along the boundaries of teacher control. When he instructed Alan to tell the truth and show respect for his punishment in lines 16, 17 and 20 – 'look you're in detention so tell the truth' – he'd set Alan up (line 14) and was fabricating acceptance of a teacher's perspective. This was registered in Mr Chambers' 'I don't trust (you)' in line 25. The emphatic 'I don't trust YOU' in Asif's next turn does in fact look like a bald rejection of any interactional consensus that the teacher might try to establish, *except* of course, that it followed word for word what Mr Chambers had said and so in one sense it again respected the teacher's right to set the terms (if challenged, it would be easy for him to say that he was only agreeing).

The first use of Panjabi in line 34 – '[ethe ro ethe ro]', 'stay here, stay here' – continued this pattern of half-masked subversion. Admittedly, Asif was here addressing people who were not legitimate participants in the detention, and he was encouraging an action that was quite likely to disrupt it. But by doing this in Panjabi, which Mr Chambers did not understand, he hid its subversiveness and again, if challenged, he could deny any infraction (with for example, 'I was telling them to go away'). This use of Panjabi also illustrates the covertly directive role that Asif continued to play in the extract. In this friendship cluster, Asif was something of a leader (as is indicated for example in Extract I.2 where Hazel referred to this clique as 'Asif and them'), and this becomes apparent when Salim and Kazim enter the engagement. In fact, in addition to the opposition between school and peer group values, Asif's conduct during this interaction also produces a tension between his own authority and the teachers', and up to a point, he uses Panjabi as a way of preventing these two sources of influence from coming into direct confrontation.[1] Panjabi's function in concealing his own directives can also be seen in the switch in the reiteration in line 49.

However, the Panjabi used in line 37 – [teri _____ a:di:di:] – was rather different. The Panjabi utterances in lines 34 and 49 were clearly directed towards particular recipients, they carried propositional meaning, and they were simple but well-formed sentences that only the bilinguals present could be expected to decode. In contrast, the Panjabi in line 37 was an imprecation that veered into the nonsensical (according to the local translators), it did not appear to elicit any response, and it drew on a stock of playground Panjabi words and phrases with which Alan was also familiar (see Chapter 7). Rather than being used in covert tactical direction, here Panjabi's dominant function was to proclaim Asif's

own affiliation to the values and practices of peer group recreation, and as a result, in the subsequent interaction, none of his
peers could be in any doubt about what was really going on when
he appeared to follow the teachers in inviting them to stay.

From this episode, one might gain the general impression that
Panjabi was indeed an instrument of covert opposition. But as
with the analysis of stylised Asian English, it is vital to distinguish
between what is contingent to a particular situation on the one
hand, and on the other, the more stable social relations generated
by the code. Unfortunately, fully bilingual uses such as those evidenced in lines 34 and 49 fall outside the brief of my analysis, and
they would themselves need to be analysed as merely one register
among a number, many of these differing in the implied interlocutor relations. But given a governing interest in the
development of multiracial solidarities, interethnically accessible
utterances like the one in line 37 are of central concern, and other
episodes indicate that resistance to white adults was *not* a necessary feature in cross-ethnic uses of Panjabi.

4.2 Panjabi crossing in non-conflictual adult–adolescent interaction

Two points are important in the following extract: firstly, the axis
of opposition expressed in interracial Panjabi, and secondly, its
relation to the main activity in which a white adult was in charge:

Extract II.8

Participants: Asif [Pa M 15] Kazim [Pa M 15], Alan [An M 15], BR
[An M 30+]
Setting: 1987 – some days after the interaction in Extract II.3.
Dinner-time, during a playback session in a classroom upstairs. At
the outset, Asif asks BR not to stop one of the tape recordings of
spontaneous interaction, which they are listening to through headphones. Around that time or soon after, Alan (who hadn't been
involved in the recording that's currently being played) looks out of
the window and sees Salim. Until recently Salim had been a very
close friend of Asif and Kazim, but they have just had a big bust up.
It was quite common for peers to joke about Salim's nose.

1 Asif: ((l.)) 's leave it
2 BR: no, yeh that's the end of the extract

```
 3 Kazim:  ⌈no there's more
 4      :  ⌊(no it isn't)
 5 Kazim:  they say more fings there
 6    BR:  uh
 7 Kazim:  they say more things
 8    BR:  yes I know but I've er I've I've =
 9           = only made extracts     ⌈you see (        )
10   Alan:  ((calling out of window))  ⌊NOSE
11 Kazim:  ((to BR)) oh no (they were sayin   sayin      )
12    BR:  what
13 Kazim:  they were saying alright ma:n al:ri:ght =
14 Kazim:             = man  ⌈alright
15   Alan:  ((out of the window))  ⌊vədda na:] (3.0)
                                  ⌊((ff))
                     ((L2 Panjabi:  big nose   ))
16    BR:  ((?playing the tape again?)) (what's what's)
17   Alan:  Salim's a loner
18   Asif:  ((to Alan)) go on say [vədda nak] (.) say [vədda nak]
19   Alan:  [vədda nakh]
20   Asif:  go on
21 Kazim:  he's gone
22   Alan:  he's gone (.) I've said it to him
23   Asif:  who was he with
24   Alan:  himself ((laughs))  ⌈(he's a) loner (1.0)
25    BR:                       ⌊ right            right okay (.)
26          ((referring to an utterance on the recording)) wha-
27          wha- wha- what's dick gusty
28   Asif:  who
29 Kazim:  Dick Dastardly (.) he just said it you know some
30          ⌈(     ) people
31    BR:  ⌊ Dick Dastardly
32   Alan:  and Muttley
33    BR:  okay
```

Several important issues raised by Alan's use of Panjabi abuse in lines 15 and 19 – for example, its relation to [teɾi _____ a:di: di:] in Extract II.3, its status as a form of ritual action, and Asif's role as tutor – will be much fully explored in Chapter 7's discussion of peer group interaction. At this point, it is sufficient to say that it expressed antagonism *between peers*, and that this was its most common interracial form. Pupil–teacher conflict had no immediate relevance, and what is more, this episode did not arise as a subversive distraction welcomed within a larger context of adult–

adolescent opposition (as was the case in Extract II.3). Although they contain a disagreement, lines 1 to 7 indicate that the side involvement featuring Panjabi occurred within a main frame in which Kazim and Asif were keen participants (the listening activity that I was controlling). And rather than disrupting its central flow, their distraction from it synchronised with a temporary break that I had myself initiated (line 2). Indeed Kazim's interest continued for two turns after Alan had first introduced the tangential business of Salim (lines 11, 13 and 14). I did make one unsuccessful attempt to restart the main business while the talk focused on Salim (line 16), but after a short sequence in which all three boys discussed him, their attention returned to where I wanted it, with some only very light prompting (the boundary markers in line 25).

In both of the Panjabi episodes that we have examined so far, there are in fact two issues of interaction structure: (i) the framework of participation directly invoked by Panjabi, and (ii) the relationship between this and other participation frameworks. In both of these extracts, Panjabi utterances excluded adults, and in both, engagement in peer–peer discourse constituted time out from the lines of adult–adolescent communication that were dominant. The difference between them was that in Extract II.3, peer–peer Panjabi provided a hidden space for undermining the dominant involvement, whereas in Extract II.8, it ran as more or less separate business. I shall shortly return to this difference, relating as it does to the character of (ii). But before that, it's worth dwelling a little on (i), since it provides a useful way of contrasting the social relations in the company of adults set up by the use of Panjabi on the one hand, and stylised Asian English on the other.

4.3 Adult–adolescent participation frameworks in Panjabi and SAE

In settings where adults were a dominant presence – in classrooms, at counters and in interviews – the data suggest that stylised Asian English was frequently addressed to the adult in control. SAE belonged in exchanges in which utterances were directed between pupil and teacher, youth club member and worker, researcher and interviewee. With Panjabi, the addressees were normally peers. There were obvious linguistic reasons for this difference: most white adults did not understand Panjabi, whereas most Panjabi peers did (and within the restricted range of the playground variety, so did some white and black adolescents). In contrast, SAE was semantically comprehensible to teachers and others. The cultural frameworks that each evoked also differed in their accessibility. SAE drew on quite a full (and potentially troubling) set of images in dominant Anglo culture that were widely available to adolescents and adults alike; in contrast, most adults had very little view either of the playground practices where Panjabi was often relevant for non-Panjabi peers, or of the intra-ethnic themes and solidarities raised in its use among bilingual inheritors. The difference between them can be summed up diagrammatically, with arrows indicating the direction of address:

SAE		Panjabi
P P		P $\longleftrightarrow$ P
$\downarrow$		
T		T

P = pupil/youth club member/adolescent
T = teacher/youth worker/adult

In fact, we can go further than this in the light of the preceding analyses: SAE was occasioned at the edges of interactional enclosures, generally suggesting to its adult recipients that in spite of their overall institutional control, adolescent participation might be less than full-hearted. Panjabi was involved in no such adult–adolescent boundary negotiation. Instead, it set up an interactional enclosure that simply excluded monolingual adults. In the relation with adults that they set up at the moments of their use, one variety was about opposition and the other about autonomy.

But so far, the account only describes the most immediate participation frameworks invoked by these two codes. In classrooms and the other settings we have referred to, adults have overall responsibility for what goes on, and this makes them important as bystanders when Panjabi was being used. Their relation to peer–peer discourse is depicted by a dotted line in the diagram below, and it now requires more discussion.

Panjabi

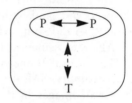

4.4 Bystanding as a contingent relationship

The relation between white adults and the enclosure instituted in
Panjabi was variable, and subject to a wide range of contingencies
such as for example, the tasks on hand, the adolescents' orientation to tasks and adult, and adult orientation to tasks and
adolescents. It could sometimes be used to subvert a teacher's
institutional authority, actively positioning him or her as a
bystander. This was evidenced in Extract II.3, and elsewhere it
was reported that, for example, Panjabi was used to 'pass the
answers around innit . . . if you're in class and somebody's stuck,
you know, it's a good code sort of thing . . . today in class I was
upset, and [the teacher] started saying you know get on with your
work and I started swearing at him in Indian' [informant: In F
15]. Black and white peers would not be able to understand all of
such usage, but they could often understand bits of swearing, as
well as a few Panjabi words which were quite widely used to refer
to adults around the school (for example, dinner ladies were quite
often known interethnically as '[buḍḍi]s' ('old women'), and one
bald-headed teacher was widely referred to as '[aṇḍa]' ('egg')).

Subversion, however, was by no means a defining feature of
Panjabi use with monolingual adults in authority. There was
sometimes a feeling that teachers' proscription of Panjabi was
unsurprising and acceptable given the requirements of classroom
control; there was one recording where a boy used Panjabi to support a youth worker and undermine his friend when he was
watching them play darts; and even in Extract II.3, Asif's swearing
in line 37 was mitigated by its deviant linguistic structure, which
could work to suspend consideration of whether the propositions
it expressed were true or false, maintaining it safely in the realms
of the comic (cf. Parkin 1980: 60,61 and Chapter 7.3).

Nor indeed was the exclusion of adults complete:

Extract II.9

Participants: Kuldip [In M 14 yrs], Peter [An M 14], BR
Setting: 1987. A play back session in the youth club. Kuldip and Peter have been listening voluntarily to recorded extracts on head-phones, but in line 1, Kuldip indicates that he no longer wishes to continue. (Perhaps it is worth adding that the dispute in this session was not typical).

```
 1 Kuldip:  oh be:N: (1.5) I can listen to this another day(.)you
 2          could sort of call me away │ from Maths
 3   Peter:                            │ shshsh
 4    BR:                              └no loo-listen I haven't- =
 5    BR:  =I really haven't got that much time (.)
 6   Peter: ┌(    )
 7 Kuldip:  └you ain't going away
 8    BR:   I am (.) I have to finish I have to f:inish the=
 9    BR:   =programme at in December so ┌(          )
10 Kuldip:                               └that's alright=
11 Kuldip:  = ┌I'll be at the youth club next week
12    BR:    └well I have- I have- I've I've got a really=
             ((acc))
13    BR:   = I've got a really crammed ┌time-=
14 Kuldip:                              └I'll be at-=
15    BR:   = you'll f- you'll have a reason not to do it then=
16 Kuldip:  = I PROMISE I'll do it then
17    BR:   no let's just finish this
18   Peter: Kuld just do it now::=
19    BR:   = just do it now get it over with
20 Kuldip:     [kɑḷi   ┌kətʃi ] shut up
             ((Panjabi: black │ pants ))
21   Peter:                   └[bandərə phʊddu]
             ((L2 Panjabi:      ?      fool ))
22 Kuldip:  ┌f:uck:ing
            │((l.))
23    BR:   └look we'd have finish- we'd've-we'd've finished=
                                       ((dec.))
24    BR:   =((slight laugh))now(.)┌if you 'd er just (cooperated)
25 Kuldip:                         └alright  CA:rry: on(.) major
                          ((l.))
27    BR:   ((playing the recording again)) (1.0) and so what was=
28    BR:   =he saying (.) he was saying ┌oggy oggy – oggy oggy
29 Kuldip:  ((repeating))                └that's two 10ps
             ((the session continues for a few more minutes))
```

Lines 1 to 26 were an insertion sequence set within a previously agreed activity that I was directing. It involved an escalating dispute about further participation, in which Kuldip mitigated his wish to withdraw by proposing alternatives (lines 1–2), elaborating them (lines 7 and 11), partially acceding to BR (line 10) and then finally promising to continue later (line 16). I countered these (lines 4–5, 8–9, 17), often with quite bald contradiction (lines 4, 8, 15, 17). In line 17, rejection of what Kuldip wanted reached its plainest expression: I told Kuldip to finish what we were doing, Peter upgraded by dropping my first person 'let's' and switching to a second person imperative (line 18), which I then repeated (reinstating the (meagre) incentive of satisfactory completion carried in the (more mitigated) directive before Peter's – line 19).

With the confrontation of wills reaching a climax, Kuldip addressed Peter (who had already interposed on my side – line 3 and perhaps 6), and swore at him in playground Panjabi, to which Peter responded in kind (lines 20 and 21). In doing so, Kuldip contained explicit expression of antagonism within his close relationship with Peter, thereby preserving the more deferential relations he maintained with me (ironic though these might sometimes be – line 25). But though I was momentarily excluded from the participation framework that Panjabi invoked, it was easy to audit what was going on, and to recognise that Kuldip was annoyed with a situation in which I too played an active part. Kuldip's subsequent 'f:uck:ing' was ambiguously sited at the border of the Kuldip–Peter enclosure: while it might be occasioned by their particular dispute, I could also understand it. It was probably because it was intelligible to me that Kuldip mitigated this imprecation by muttering it quietly (cf the discussion of Goffman's self-talk, response cries and imprecations (1981) in Chapter 7.5). His own effort to atone for leaving early ignored, he did have a grievance but in his relations with the bystanding adult, he kept this subdued.

The auditing by teacher bystanders could in fact provide some of the entertainment in pupil–pupil Panjabi use:

> this is a good one, this is one we always use . . . if there's a teacher who we hate right, like my tutor, and I'm talking to a friend . . . say me and Imran are talking right, then I'll be um you know talking to Imran in Urdu, and swearing at [my tutor] but looking at Imran

((laughs)) . . . wicked one! If he saw me looking, I'd get done you know what I mean [Pa M 15] (cf. Pollard 1985: 85)

More than this, the bystanding adult's response could feed into adult–adolescent relations:

Extract II.10

Participants: Ian [An M 15], Peter [An M 14 with radio-mike], Richard [An M 15], Ishmael [Pa M 14]
Setting: 1987. Youth club in the evening. Ian, Richard and Peter are watching badminton in the gym, discussing other matters. Ishmael comes in on line 4. Gwen is a youth worker, whose relationship with Ismael was generally quite poor.

```
 1    Rich:   try to tief that 10p and I'll tief you
 2   Peter:   ((half laugh))
 3   Imran:   ((playing badminton)) (       ⌈      )
 4  Ishmael:  ((to Peter, Ian and Richard)) ⌊guess what Gwen said(.)
 5            she asked for 50p innit I gave her i- she gave me
 6            innit (.) an' I- I go to Salim (.) I go Salim you
 7            [gəndi kətʃi ] (.) right- and Gwen goes to me YOU
              ((P: dirty pants))
 8            WERE SWEARING TO ME you were swearing to me
 9            and all this
10            (10.0)
11  Ishmael:  ((offering sweets)) (d'y wn (.) d'y wn) d'you wan'
12      Ian:  no (thanks)
13  Ishmael:  d'you wan' (5.0) ((scuffles))
14  Ishmael:  oh- (.) oh- (.) oh- (.) I'm under (        ) (.)
15    Peter:  ((quiet laugh))
16      Ian:  how d'you do Ish
17  Ishmael:  how's life
```

In lines 4 to 9, Ishmael told a story about the youth worker's inept misinterpretation of his interaction with Salim. In intervening in what had been a separate engagement and in construing this as an offence, the youth worker had herself acted improperly. It is worth also noting that Ishmael expected the monolinguals to be sympathetic to his complaint, and in making it, he *both* coopted them into the group of people who wouldn't make silly mistakes misunderstanding Panjabi abuse *and* used Panjabi accordingly.[2]

Sometimes, rather than intervening from outside, teachers were themselves situated in the addresser–addressee framework that was normally reserved for pupils only. When the class register was being read out

> I get angry . . . some teachers sort of make out it's- you can't say it . . . 'oh I can't read these names', as in a generalised thing that you know you can't take Asian names, and that really gets me . . . my name's not difficult to pronounce if you tried it properly, if you try, but they don't even try, they go 'oh my god, you can't pronounce these names', probably don't even consider them as names, you know what I mean . . . and they sort of make a joke out of it . . . [it's] supply teachers mainly [informant: Pa F 15]

But once again, it is vital to emphasise that negative interpretations of this kind were contingent. After all, not all whites stuck rigidly to English. There were appreciative reports of teachers entering the same kind of gaming monolingual-bilingual Panjabi interaction that were a staple form in its cross-ethnic playground use, with pupils 'calling [the teacher] 'a dog' and saying it's 'hello' or something like that ((laughs))' [Pa F 15].[3] Teachers themselves sometimes knew a little Panjabi ('the problem is, a lot of them understand now', 'yes 'cos most of the words are common now' [In F 15]) and occasionally, a white teacher actually knew quite a lot ('we had this English teacher', 'we were talking Indian and everything and knew some Indian, he started talking in Indian 'do this, do that', we were all amazed, it's like he shut everyone up, innit' [In M 15]). Beyond that, there were ethnic Panjabi bilinguals on the teaching staff ('we've got an Indian tutor, so we can't say nothing', 'yeh ((laughs))', 'and she'd understand everything', 'and she's tell the head innit ((laughs))' [In and Pa M 15]).

And there were also periods in lessons and in the timetable when classroom activity was less centred on instruction, and teachers were no doubt happy to allow all sorts of informal language activity ('at tutor period, we swop [rude] words [in different languages], all boys together and all the girls'). In loosely structured settings of this kind, it would be much harder to construe Panjabi as a disruption of central activity.

In the presence of adults then, Panjabi usually set up a direct line of address between peers (who might be black or white as well as Asian). It opened into Indian and Pakistani adult and youth culture, and as subsequent chapters will clarify, as an inter-ethnic variety it drew on a set of social relations and practices that had their base outside lessons. It was not itself immediately related to issues of respect and regard for the order of the classroom. Certainly, Panjabi could become the focus of disputes about what was proper classroom conduct, but whether or not this occurred was open to negotiation. In this, the response of bystanding teachers or youth workers was a central factor, and evidently, there was a good deal of variation. While the proscriptive actions of some could be regarded as racist, others could be coopted as ratified participants in Panjabi interchanges, and there were also adult bilinguals and serious second language users who could wrong-foot any attempted covert activity. Overall, Panjabi created a rich field of play, both within peer–peer relations, and between the peer group and supervising adults.

In contrast, SAE was more exclusively implicated in adult–adolescent relations, providing an opportunity for (minor) disruption beneath the guise of deference. Certainly, peers of different ethnic backgrounds could all play a role as collusive spectators or confederates. But though they apparently did on occasion, there was less scope for non-Asians to adopt the role of addresser.[4] As Chapter 6 will show, SAE was also used in the playground and sometimes, peer–peer uses might occur in class. But interethnically, these again appeared to be more problematic (cf. Extract I.12, Chapter 2.4).

This difference in the way that Panjabi and SAE were used in asymmetrical interethnic interactions corresponded with differences in the institutional position of these two languages.

4.5 The institutional embedding of interactional relations

The micro-relations existing around classroom Panjabi bore some ressemblance to wider negotiations within school organisation. As already mentioned, there were adults of Indian descent on the teaching staff, Panjabi and Urdu were available as options in the mainstream timetable, and quite a lot of extracurricular provision was made for bhangra. Indeed, although of course there would be a great many additional contingencies at play, it is not hard to imagine how local engagements with Panjabi at both interactional and institutional levels could influence each other. On the one hand, monolingual teachers would be encouraged to show respect for languages that were offered on the curriculum and were spoken by their colleagues, and pupils could see that the school was not opposed to their heritage languages. Conversely, amicable informal interactions around Panjabi might well have been important in getting monolingual teachers to lend a hand in organising bhangra discos or performances after school or in assemblies. Of course, this state of affairs was by no means entirely rosy. Pupils were critical of the school's attempt to provide for Urdu, and when they were disaffected with curriculum business, they could also mess around in classes where Panjabi or Urdu were actually being taught. But overall, these interactional and institutional processes were part of the complex negotiations in which ethnic inheritances were asserted and several local state institutions made efforts to accommodate them. The central concern here was with the development of differences that the principal local parties had agreed to value positively.

In contrast, stylised Asian English was lodged within a central preoccupation with the eradication of negative differences. This was again reflected in larger patterns of local school life (as well as being a dominant theme in the discourses of British racism).

At school, limited proficiency in English was primarily associated with pupils of Bangladeshi descent, belonging to the most recently arrived migrant group. Until recently, ESL provision had been provided in a separate language centre, and after its abolition, Bangladeshis were disproportionately placed in lower sets and singled out for extra help by peripatetic or school-based specialist teachers. Among the majority of Caribbean, Anglo, Indian and Pakistani pupils, Bangladeshis were held in low esteem, and there were a number of complaints about the preferential treatment they received from staff, who were presumably trying to compensate for the educational and indeed peer group disadvantage that Bangladeshis suffered (assuming that these complaints were well-founded – such complaints also have a well-recognised place in racist discourses).

Again, it is possible to see some very strong correspondences between these local institutional processes on the one hand, and on the other, the stylised Asian English exchanges reported and analysed above. Although it might exist in Ashmead side by side with the positive valuations of ethnic difference associated with

Panjabi, for many people outside the neighbourhood, nationally and in government, the eradication of negative difference – cultural assimilation – is the *only* issue in majority–minority relations. This could explain why reports of SAE often specified temporary teachers coming from outside, who, incidentally, could also be expected to regard all Asians as being the same, another aspect of the prejudice on which SAE could play.

Beyond this, there are at least three ways in which the position of local ESL pupils could connect with elements highlighted in interactional analyses of SAE. First, recognition of the institutional disadvantage experienced by non-fluent speakers of English could contribute to the connotations of problematicity and low status that I interpreted as a major element in SAE's symbolic evocation in Chapter 3. Secondly, there was a remarkable correspondence between on the one hand, the marginal position of a group of second language learners struggling to gain a decent foothold in school (and elsewhere), and on the other, the use of SAE at the boundaries of interactional engagements in which white adults held institutional sway. Transition was centrally at issue, both at the level of social groups and institutions, and at the level of interpersonal conduct. Finally, (at least in the interpretation offered in the last chapter), in the same way that the school hoped to minimise Bangladeshi disadvantage, in interaction the best adult response was to show that SAE was no threat to the working consensus. Neutralisation of difficulty was the optimum outcome, again at both levels. Overall, it is as if knowledge of the precarious institutional position of relatively recent immigrants acted as a cognitive template which sensitised adolescents to particular micro-political moments which they then marked out with SAE. Equally, the interactional organisation of switches in SAE kept recent arrival alive as an issue on the implicit political agenda of local adolescent social life.

Complex historical and interactional contingencies invalidate any effort to characterise participants' general experience of reality as a set of straightforward and compelling antagonisms, whether these are Anglo versus Asian, adult versus adolescent and/or teacher versus pupil. *However*, micro-interactional code-switching did momentarily dramatise some important political oppositions. More than that, switching into different languages conjured *different* aspects of the broader social contestation around majority–minority relations. In settings where plurality is acknowledged, diversity raises two central questions: (a) does the recognition of difference entail detrimental bias? or (b) does it instead involve a constructive individualisation (Cazden 1986: 447)? Stylisations of Asian English in the presence of adults engaged with (a). In contrast, Panjabi was much more oriented to (b). Panjabi generally asserted a frame of reference that was independent of the dominant interaction. Sometimes, it could involve struggle for influence against white teachers, but contrary to stylised Asian English, this was *not* inevitable. Indeed, monolingual adults could themselves volunteer or be coopted into the alternative realm that Panjabi instituted. At the micro level, code-switching into Panjabi was more creative than SAE, capable of generating new lines of adult conduct, and this coincided with its larger role in local institutional negotiations. Figure 4.1 summarises these differences between Panjabi and SAE.

There is one more point that needs to be made about code-switching and the development of local adolescents' political understanding about race.

Because the micro-social arrangements and processes emerging around Panjabi and SAE instantiated larger problematics in majority–minority relations, watching or taking part in these code-switching interactions could help to sensitise black and white pupils to the political concerns of Indian and Pakistani peers.[5] In this way, we can see how such interactions might play a pedagogic role for non-Panjabi adolescents, assisting 'the growth of [their] social understanding and of [their] capabilities for the maintenance of social relations' (Cook-Gumperz and Corsaro 1986: 4).

But in mentioning interaction and pedagogy, it is important to emphasise the way in which the processes examined here differ from orthodox accounts of classroom learning. Many studies look beyond the acquisition of linguistic structure to the ways in which school students are socialised into relatively enduring roles and

Figure 4.1   Summary of discussion of Panjabi and SAE: characteristics of their use in interaction with adults, and the relation of these characteristics to local institutional arrangements and more general political processes.

	MICRO-INTERACTIONAL CHARACTERISTICS	STYLISED ASIAN ENGLISH	PANJABI
I N T E R A C T I O N	Participation frameworks:		
	Relation to adult-directed activity:	Opposition. Destabilises consensus at boundaries of adult-dominated engagement.	Independence, though adult a significant bystander to pupil engagements. Pupil engagements may be covertly opposed, supportive or unrelated to adult-dominated activity.
	Scope for Anglo and Afro-Caribbean pupils to participate as addressers:	Limited.	Quite good.
	Principal fields of symbolic evocation:	Anglo-Asian race relations.	Intra- or pan-ethnic Indian and Pakistani adult and youth culture. Multiracial playground culture.
	Effect on adult–adolescent relations:	Adult disconcerted, or both parties reassured of the irrelevance of threatening symbolic connotations.	Varied: adult ignores, reproaches, encourages or joins in with peer–peer Panjabi.
	(Kinds of teacher most typically reported:)	(Temporary teachers from outside)	(Permanent staff)
	CORRESPONDENCE WITH:	↕	↕
	LOCAL INSTITUTIONAL ARRANGEMENTS	No Bengali classes, only ESL and lower set placement for Bangladeshis.	Panjabi and Urdu as curriculum subjects, bhangra as an extra-curricular activity.
		Problems of access and transition for social groups with limited proficiency in English.	Panjabi as a second language classes locally available for adults.
	and		
	MORE GENERAL POLITICAL PROCESSES	Negotiations around the eradication of negatively valued difference.	Negotiations around the development of positively valued difference.

attitudes, and more recent interactionist studies have shifted away from emphasis on the dominating influence of schools, subjects and teachers, towards an account that recognises the active role that pupils themselves play in shaping both the classroom environment and their own socialisation within it (e.g. Mehan 1980; Cook-Gumperz and Corsaro 1986). These analyses of interactive negotiation are generally oriented to the conduct of official school business, concentrating on the way that pupils provide teachers with subtle (and by no means always progressive) guidance about how to do their jobs (cf. McDermott and Gospodinoff 1981: 226,228; Pollard 1985: 160; Cazden 1986: 440). There is a frequent interest in how kids 'teach teachers how to teach them'.

In the analyses offered in this chapter and the one before, adults in positions of relative authority were an indispensable presence, and in that regard, there was much in common with classroom interaction studies. But here the primary pedagogic relationship wasn't between adults and adolescents, and the knowledge at issue wasn't defined by the school curriculum. Teachers (and other adults) had a crucial role, but not as principal pedagogic agents. Instead, they functioned much more as instructional objects, focal components to be observed in interactional experiments run by one set of adolescents to the potential edification of others. Of course, this oversimplifies and adults too could learn from these episodes. But in the kind of political education specified here, the main pedagogic relationship existed between peers, and the 'lesson content' derived not from the adult but from adolescent knowledge and experience.

Notes

1. Another strategy that Asif used to prevent overt confrontation between his authority and the teachers' was what Goodwin and Goodwin (1990) call 'piggybacking'. A 'piggyback' is an utterance that is inserted immediately after a turn that is obviously directed to someone else. It is slotted inside an adjacency pair, after the first pair part but before the second pair part expected in the initial turn. As a result, when it comes, the response could be either to the first pair part, or to the piggyback, or to both (Goodwin and Goodwin 1990: 101–7). This can be seen in the SAE sequence:

38 Ms J: after you
39 Asif: **after you::**
40   Sal: ((at a higher pitch)): **after you::**

As already indicated, Asif was inside the detention room so it can not have been him that Miss Jameson was addressing. But he inserted a response before either of the boys standing at the threshold, so that when Salim replied, he could be taking his cue from both Ms J and Asif (note also how once again Asif shielded what was in effect a disruptive action by modelling it word for word (if not sound for sound) on the teacher's). Asif also piggybacked in line 49:

48 Mr C: you want another cloth do you
49   Asif: ((f)) yeh yeh say yeh   [ɑː ɑː ɑː ɑː]
                                           ((Panj: yes yes yes yes
50 Ms J: (   )
51 Salim: yeh I might (   )

and as a result, Salim's response was again ambiguous in terms of being oriented to either Asif or the teachers. This manner of intervention itself provided Asif with some protection from the teachers, in so far as censure would require some extra work, requiring them either to put 'on hold' the official exchange with the person that they'd addressed, or to return to the intervention after its moment had passed (which might also then involve dealing with an alliance created across the piggyback and the official second pair part) (cf. Goodwin and Goodwin 1990: 107). At the same time, piggybacking also allowed Asif both to coopt the teacher's authority and to dominate it (even though in principle, a person who piggybacks risks being ignored). He accepted the attentiveness in Salim set up by the teachers' first pair parts, but then attempted to subvert the responses that these expected, instead steering them in the direction that he chose.

2. The fact that as the recipients of this tale, Ian, Peter and Richard expressed no appreciation of it is of no consequence here – Ishmael's story contained only the briefest preface, it was not tied topically to anything in their previous discussion (Levinson 1983: 324, 328; Nofsinger 1991: 155–62), and he also muffed it up – in line 5, who gave money to whom? When the episode was replayed to him, Peter clearly understood the gist of the Panjabi, and so Ishmael's code-switch had been fairly well-tuned to his interlocutors' proficiency. As two other Panjabi informants reported about Peter:

he don't know all the words [in Panjabi] . . . if you were talking to him right, you would say [it] in English, but if you were talking about some other person who was swearin' in Panjabi, then you'd tell him the swearin' words he said and he'd understand straight away cos he only understands the swearing words

Even so, Peter did not know the precise meaning of the Panjabi words in Extract II.10, and it was plain that this kind of interaction was sustained more by interpersonal familiarity, shared institutional status, and contextual inferencing than by partially sychronised lexico-grammars.

3. This was another report of a teacher participating in the joking uses typical of cross-ethnic Panjabi among peers:

Extract II.11

Participants: Mohan [In M 15]; Jagdish [In M 15], BR [An M 30+].
Setting: 1987 interview. [Simplified transcription]

Mohan: Mr Chambers, he don't really say much if we swear, he don't say nothing to us . . . sometimes he asks us what the words mean, he wants to learn sometimes

Jagdish: yeh he's learnt quite a few of them, like we used to say [kətʃi] and all this

Mohan: yeh and he asks what it means

Jagdish: and he found out what it was, you know 'shorts'

Mohan: and then Jagdish told me to say it, and I said it to him

Jagdish: yeh, yeh because because then I told Mo to say words right, because I knew that Mr Chambers knew and I said 'you say [it], you watch what he'll do'

Elsewhere another informant of Indian parentage (F) criticised a good friend for making oppositional use of Panjabi in class on what she regarded as the false assumption that Mr Chambers was 'just another dry teacher'.

4. This was one occasion when a white boy used SAE to a man of Indian descent, who spoke local vernacular English and who was generally liked and respected:

Extract II.12

At the youth club on Friday evening. Gerry (An M 16) came up to Joginder (In M 30+) who was serving behind the counter and asked for some crisps in a strong SAE accent. Then, when he was given his change, he started counting in Panjabi [ɪk dɔ] ((one two)). [fieldnotes]

Gerry's initial use of an SAE opening-and-request utterance occurred at the boundary of an engagement that involved both asymmetrical institutional roles and ethnic difference, and in that respect, it was fairly conventional, corresponding to its use by quite a few Asian adolescents. On this occasion, however, the actual distribution of ethnic difference would warrant Joginder's taking offence, and Gerry's utterance could be seen as racist. Perhaps it was a realisation of this that then prompted Gerry to switch into an unstigmatised code that instead evoked multiracial neighbourhood community. The shift to Panjabi translated the recognition of ethnicity carried by SAE into a frame in which there were more secure connotations of inter-group solidarity.

5.   See Extract IV.4 and the comments on it in Chapter 10.3.

5 Creole (i): links to the local vernacular

This chapter continues the discussion of participation frameworks and their institutional embedding, and the first three sections try to clarify Creole's similarities and differences from Panjabi and stylised Asian English (SAE). Crossing in Creole was more flexible than either of the other two – it occurred in both adolescent–adult and peer–peer exchanges. But at the same time, it was much less clearly demarcated as an official variety at school. In terms of both its greater cross-ethnic utility and its more indeterminate school status, Creole was more like ordinary vernacular English, and it is this relationship that is considered in sections 5.4, 5.5 and 5.6. Initially, two episodes are used to show the way that Creole's connotations could be closely integrated with a crosser's serious interests. After that, Hewitt's account of the Creole/vernacular interface is discussed, and related back to the Ashmead data. Finally, adult reaction to Creole forms in adolescent speech are considered, and these confirm certain symbolic ties between Creole and traditional non-standard local speech.

After a summary focusing specifically on other-ethnic Creole use, the chapter ends with an overview of Part II. It draws the argument together, it specifies the contribution of sociolinguistic analysis to sociological research on youth culture, and it clarifies the way in which language crossing can indeed be seen as a small but significant contribution to the development of the political sensibilities identified in Gilroy's discussion of urban neighbourhoods with an active sense of mixed community.

5.1 Interview reports

In interview, black, white and Asian informants were unanimous in the view that Creole did not fit with conformity to mainline classroom business. Reports suggested that Creole was used both when addressing teachers, and in talk among peers.

This was one account of Creole being used to teachers:

Extract II.13

Participants: Kiron [In F 15], Sohan [In F 15], BR
Setting: 1987. Interview. Miss Wall had been a temporary supply teacher. [Simple and abbreviated transcription].

BR: is there any Asian or white person you know who uses more kind of Jamaican language

Sohan: yeh, Dev (([In M 15])) does a lot, he does

Kiron: yeh

Sohan: in drama especially,

Kiron: and in er

Sohan: ⌈ and Sewa (([In M 15]))

Kiron: ⌊when he starts being cheeky to the teachers like in computers

Sohan: ⌈ and Imran (([Pa M 15]))

Kiron: ⌊he uses a lot of sort of things like that ((. . . .)) especially when we had that teacher, (Miss Wall) remember . . . a lot of that language then ((laughs))

BR: what, a supply teacher?

Kiron: yeh, and then he uses a lot of that sort of language then

Sohan: and kept walking out of the classroom. Dev, acting tough to her

BR: he uses it in drama as well?

Sohan: when he's acting, and when he's speaking to the teacher

Kiron: especially the teacher he doesn't like . . . supply teachers

BR: how do teachers take it?

Sohan: she don't know what to say, she jus

Kiron: she didn't know what to say ((laughs))

Sohan: she just shuts up ((laughs))

Kiron: ((laughing)): she just shut up and sits there while he goes on at her

BR: what do the black kids in the class think

Kiron: we don't have any black kids in our class

Sohan: they join in they do . . . , start going, 'yeh you're right', carry on something like that

As noted in Chapter 3, there was likely to be a good deal of ideal-isation in this kind of retelling. Even so, Sohan's final point is supported by Hewitt, who found that white Creole use was more acceptable to black adolescents in the context of pupil–teacher conflict (1986: 154–5). Sohan and Kiron's account also partly resembles what other informants said about SAE addressed to teachers – compare, for example their comments on the supply teacher being dumbfounded with Extracts II.1 and II.2 in Chapter 3.2. In addition, other people suggested that there was a certain amount of scope for amicable pupil–teacher negotiation around Creole use. One black informant reported Kazim's saying the non-sensical 'kukabin' to teachers (cf. Extract I.2, Chapter 2.1), and the un-dry cowboy Mr Chambers featured yet again in another youngster's description of adolescent–adult Creole use (cf. Extracts II.3, Chapter 3.3 and II.11, Chapter 4, note 3).

Between pupils, Creole could also be a substantial source of entertainment, and here reports suggested some close interplay between Creole and Panjabi (cf. Extract I.4, Chapter 2.1):

Extract II.14

Participants: Asha [In F 14], Saran [In F 14], BR
Setting: 1987 interview. [Simplified transcription]

> BR: in any of the languages that you know, who do you think
>   is the most kind of inventive kind of speaker
> Asha: I think I am cos ⌈ I use all the . . . I use
> Saran: ⌊ modest! ((laughs))
> Asha: because I come up with the good words for
> Saran: make up new words
> Asha: such as [kʊn kʊn] and 'blaps'
> Saran: ((laughs)) she makes us crack up . . . you know at the
>   wrong time she comes up with these words, in the middle
>   of a lesson or something ((laughs)), we all have to laugh

Though it is impossible to say whether or not they were opposi-tional, these innovations sound at least recognisably tangential to official classroom business, and 'blaps', here claimed as Asha's personal invention (as it was elsewhere by at least one other informant) was characterised as black language later on in the interview. But [kʊn kʊn] (a word which informants invariably said they didn't know the meaning of) had probably more ambiguous origins that this: it was widely used in the 1984 data, it was occasionally attributed to Creole, but it also converged on [kʊs kʊs], another semantically opaque term in interethnic use, this time attributed to Panjabi.

Evidence from interaction elaborates the way in which Creole could be contiguous with both Panjabi and SAE. It also confirms that while SAE involved adolescent–adult address, and while Panjabi centred on peer–peer participation frameworks, Creole crossing embraced both.

5.2 Evidence from interaction

In my corpus, there were about 10 episodes when adults were a significant presence and white or Asian adolescents used Creole (overall, this involved four Anglos and three Pakistanis, all male). Two episodes from one interview illustrate the similarities and differences between Creole, Panjabi and SAE.

Extract II.15

Participants: Asif [Pa M 15], Kazim [Pa M 15], Alan [An M 15], BR
Setting: 1987 – a little later in the playback session cited in Extract II.8. Asif and Alan have been talking playground Panjabi loudly into the microphone from close up, and BR is trying to reestablish their commitment to the listening task.

```
 1     BR:   right shall I- shall we shall we stop there
 2   Kazim:  no
 3    Alan:  no come ⌈on carry on
 4    Asif:        ⌊do another extract
 5     BR:   le- lets have (.) ⌈then you have to give me more=
 6    Alan:                    ⌊carry on
 7     BR:   =attention gents
 8    Asif:  ((l.)) yeh alright
 9    Alan:  ((l.)) alright
10    Asif:  ((l.)) yeh
11   Kazim:  ((in SAE)) I AM VERY SORRY BEN JAAD
                       [aɪ æm veri  sɒri   ben  dʒɑːd]
12    Asif:  ((in SAE)) ATTENTION  BENJAMIN
                       [əthenʃaːn     bendʒəmɪn]
13      :   ⌈((laughter))
14     BR:  ⌊right well you can- we cn-
```

15   Alan: ⌊benjaademin
16   BR: ⌜we can continue but we er must concentrate a bit
17   ⌊ more
18   Asif: ⌊yeh=
19   Alan: = alright ⌜then
20   Asif: ((in SAE)) ⌊concentrating very hard
                         [kɔ̃nsəstretɪn̥ veɾi ɑɾ]
21   BR: okay right
22   :((giggles dying down))
23 Kazim: ((in SAE)) ((l.)) what a stupid (?boy?)
                         [vʌd ə stupɪd]
24   BR: ((returning the microphone to what he considers to be
           a better position to catch all the speakers)) concentrate
           a little bit
25   Alan: alright then
26 Kazim: ((in Creole)) stop movin **dat ting aroun**
                         [dæt tɪŋ əɹɑʊn]
27   BR: WELL YOU stop moving it around and then I'll- won't
28   need to (.)
29 Kazim: ((in Creole)) stop moving **dat ting aroun**
                         [dæʔ tɪŋ əɹɑʊn]
30   BR: right okay ⌜right
31 Kazim: ((f))   ⌊ben jaad
32   Alan: ((laughs))
33   BR: what are you doing
34   Alan: ben jaa ⌜ad
35   BR: ⌊well leave (   ) alone
36 Kazim: IT'S HIM that ben jaad over there
37   BR: right
           ((BR continues effort to reinstitute the listening activity))

This episode as a whole involved the destabilisation of a frame in
which I had central control. In it, *SAE* was used in apology for the
disruption I was calling attention to (line 11), in acceptance of the
conditions I was laying down for the continuance of the listening
activity (lines 12 and 20), and maybe in endorsing my complaint
about their conduct (line 23). Obviously, these expressions of
renewed support for my wishes could not be taken at face value,
and this frame play may have taken its cue from my non-serious
'gents' in line 7. 'ben jaad' was a piece of corrupted *Panjabi* that on
one occasion Alan was credited with having invented. According to
the local adolescent translators, it fell ambiguously between [ben

jɑr], 'Ben, friend', and [pɛn tʃɔd], 'sister fucker', and it maybe illustrates the way that adults could sometimes be coopted into the cross-ethnic addresser–addressee relation that was common in multiracial playground Panjabi (Chapter 7).

In line 26, the pronunciation of the second part of Kazim's turn sounds Creole – see, for example, Wells 1982: 565–7 on the British English and Creole contrasts between [ð] and [d], [θ] and [t], and on final consonant cluster reduction. Transgression was again at issue here, but rather than being oriented (pseudo-) affiliatively to offences that I had imputed to the boys, as their uses of SAE had been, here Creole served as a plainly *disaffiliative* 'prime', constructing *my* movement of the microphone as an impropriety (Goffman 1971: 154–7). This led to a short 'run-in', in which I excused my action by laying the offence with Kazim, a move which he then ignored by simply repeating his directive. As action generally oriented to the repair of transgression, and in being addressed to an adult, Kazim's Creole was similar to SAE. But there was none of SAE's superficial deference, and rather than being accepted by the speaker, fault was here attributed to the recipient.

Adolescent–adult conflict, however, was not a necessary element in Creole crossing with adults. Here is the second episode:

Extract II.16

Participants: Asif [Pa M 15], Kazim [Pa M 15], Alan [An M 15], BR, Jim [An M 15]
Setting: 1987 – later in the same playback session cited in Extracts II.8 and II.15. Jim, a friend, has now entered the room, and this time it is Asif who abruptly moves out of the listening activity, looking out of the window and noticing a couple involved in (light) sexual contact.

```
1    Asif:  he's got his hand round her thing
2  Kazim:  yeh I know (1.0) she's a slag (.) go on carry on (3.0)
3    Jim:  there's Philip with her thing
4   Alan:  where is he
5  Kazim:  there he is
6    Jim:  (who tha-) ⌈ who's Philip with
7     BR:           ⌊ right
8    Jim:  what's that girl's name
9   Alan:  ((in Creole)) DIRTY SLAG
                        [dɜti    slag]
```

```
10  Kazim:  she's a sl ⌈ ag
11    BR:              ⌊ right
12  Kazim:  Brenda Hill's a (      )
13   Alan:  ((ff. mixed English and Panjabi)) [jə khʊttii] (.)
                                              ((trans: you bitch))
14  Kazim:  Brenda Hill's a [khʊt ⌈ tii]
15     :                    ⌊(        ⌈       )
16    BR:                            ⌊ right okay
17          ((listening activity continues)) (5.0)
18  Kazim:  ((citing from tape)) 'skank' (1.5)
            ((listening and commentary on the recording continues))
```

The lowering of [æ] to [a] marked Alan's 'slag' as Creole (cf. e.g. Wells 1982: ch. 7), and this occurred in a side involvement that bore a lot of resemblance to the one in Extract II.8. In addition, he used Panjabi alongside the Creole. However, the immediate participation framework centred on peer–peer relations which did not necessarily come into open conflict with the main adult–adolescent involvement. In fact in this context, it is worth noting that although I made a couple of unsuccessful efforts (lines 7 and 16), it was Kazim who did most of the work achieving a smooth reconciliation of these two frames, responding to his friends' unofficial initiatives while at the same time steering a course back to the main business. In line 2, Kazim was the first to acknowledge Asif's noticing. He made an affiliative assessment but then redirected attention to the main task. In line 5, it was again Kazim that responded to Alan's clarification request. In lines 10, 12, and 14, Kazim was the one to agree with Alan's assessments (accepting his anglicising aspiration of [k] in line 13), but he did not upgrade them with any additional comments that would generate further talk on the topic. And finally, in line 18, Kazim was the first to show that he was back in the adult–adolescent participation framework.

Summarising the account so far, it looks as though crossing in Creole was like SAE in its concern with transgression in adult–adolescent interaction. On the other hand, it was also like Panjabi in its involvement with concerns that were independent of the classroom – as already indicated in Chapter 2, Creole was extensively involved in both playground and expressive youth culture. In this regard, Creole appeared to be more flexible than either of the other two, and this can be represented in the primary participation frameworks invoked by each code:

SAE	Panjabi	Creole
P P	P $\longleftrightarrow$ P	P $\longleftrightarrow$ P
$\downarrow$		$\downarrow$
T	T	T

At the same time, however, Creole was less well 'shielded' than either Panjabi or SAE. Creole crossing was protected from adults neither by superficial deference on the pupil–teacher dimension, nor by linguistic unintelligibility on the peer–peer axis. On these grounds, it is probable that when it was used oppositionally, it would be more likely to receive censure than SAE. Equally, it would be more vulnerable to intrusion when it was used autonomously between peers. On both counts, communicating in Creole, it would be harder to maintain distance from adults intent on taking control.

5.3 The correspondence between interactional and institutional organisation

This difference between Creole on the one hand and Panjabi and SAE on the other can be related to Creole's local institutional position. At school, Panjabi, Urdu and Asian English (in the form of ESL) were treated as distinctive, educationally significant categories, and adults encountering them would know that their handling involved special instructional procedures. There were many more Asian than black pupils at the school, and it was these languages that were the focus for much of the debate about how to respond to cultural difference. In contrast, Creole figured much less prominently. It was not a distinctive category on the timetable, and it generally received a great deal less of the school's official attention. Institutionally, there was comparatively little to single Creole out from the central flow of dialogue between pupils and teachers, school and community.

So relative to Panjabi and SAE, Creole was more flexible in terms of the people it could address, but it was less well provided with protective insulation at the levels of both interaction and institutional organisation. In combination, these factors doubtless contributed to the fact that it was more closely incorporated into those elements of everyday discourse that were counterposed to the values associated with adult, white and/or class dominance.

5.4 Interactional evidence of Creole's incorporation with oppositional vernacular discourse

Evidence of Creole's integration with vernacular speech at oppositional moments can be seen in the next two episodes, where linguistic structure was managed more subtly, evoking Creole's disjunctive connotations in a less spectacular way than in the two extracts that we have just considered. In examining these episodes, it will become clear that more than in any other kind of crossing, language form suggested quite a close relationship between the speaker's everyday personality and their temporarily adopted symbolic 'voice'.

Extract II.17

Participants: Asif [Pa M 15], Alan [An M 15], Ms Jameson [An F 25+], and in the background, Mr Chambers [An M 25+]
Setting: 1987. Detention. A very short while after the episode cited in Extract II.3. Kazim and Salim have left the room and frame play has been abandoned. Ms Jameson is saying why she arrived late for Asif and Alan's detention, and now she wants to go and fetch her lunch.

```
80  Ms J:  I had to to and see the headmaster
81  Asif:  why
82  Ms J:  (          ) (.) none of your business
83  Alan:  a- about us (           )
84  Ms J:  no I'll be ⌈ back
           ((l.))     |
85  Asif:             ⌊hey how can you see the=
                       ((f.))
86         =headmaster when he was in dinner (.)
87  Ms J:  that's precisely why I didn't see him
           ((l.))
88  Asif:  what (.)
89  Ms J:  I'll be back in a second with my lunch ⌈(        )
90  Asif:                                          ⌊NO [ɪ]=
                                                    ((ff.))
91         =dat's sad man (.) (I'll b     ) =
           ((f.))
```

```
92          =I ⌈ had to miss my play right I've gotta go
93  Alan:      ⌊(                 with mine        )
94          (2.5) ((Ms J must now have left the room))
95  Asif:  ((Creole influenced)) 1 l:unch (.) you don't need no=
                                    ((f.))
                                 [l l: ʌntʃ]
                                       ⌣
96          = lunch ⌈ not'n grow anyway ((laughs))
                    │ [natʔn  gɹəʊ]
97  Alan:           ⌊((laughs))
98  Asif:  have you eat your lunch Alan
```

Lines 80–88 involved a verbal tussle in which Asif and Alan used
questions to undermine the positions that Ms Jameson staked out
in what she said. Asif's question in line 81 treated the account she
gave of her late arrival as inadequate; her rebuttal of the legitimacy of his inquiry was then undermined by Alan (lines 82–4);
and she was delayed in the departure she announced in line 84 by
a question that upgraded the query over her initial excuse into an
explicit challenge (lines 85–7). All this time, she was locked into
the interaction by the adjacency structures set up by the boys'
questions, but at line 89, she broke out of this pattern, ignored
Asif's repair initiation (line 88), again announced her departure
and evidently left without saying anything further. With the
cooperative exchange structure now disrupted and Ms Jameson
apparently disattending to him, Asif launched into explicit complaint, invoked his own sacrifice, and produced a similar
announcement of intended departure, which, in its emptiness of
any genuine capability, pinpointed the power inequality defined in
their respective institutional roles (lines 90–2). In challenging the
reason that Ms Jameson gave for leaving, and in elaborating this
with a critical implication about her size in lines 95 and 96, Asif
appeared to be engaged in what Goffman calls 'afterburn':

> a remonstrance conveyed collusively by virtue of the fact that its
> targets are in the process of leaving the field . . . when one indi-
> vidual finds that others are conducting themselves offensively in
> their current dealings with him . . . he can wait until they have
> closed out the interchange with him and turned from the encounter,
> and **then** he can express what he 'really' feels about them . . . he
> may turn to a member of his encounter . . . and flood into directed
> expression (1971: 152,153)

Creole influences were present in what Asif said in lines 90 to 98, but their identity and location is sometimes difficult to determine. The origins of a form are often open to dispute among linguists, and as Hewitt stresses, there can be a good deal of variation in the extent to which adolescents themselves consider a form to be ethnically marked (1986: 128–9). In line 90, Asif's annoyance-expressing click was more alveolar than dental, so it sounded much like vernacular Anglo (cf. Hewitt 1986: 134). Three items in line 91's 'dat's sad man' could be construed as Creole-influenced: on occasion, 'man' was identified as a black English term; Hewitt identifies this sense of 'sad' as Creole in origin (1986: 129); and the same could be true of the plosive realisation of TH. But all three were so widely used that such group marking could be lost, and indeed a case can be made for a different provenance for stopped TH (see below).

Once Ms Jameson had left, however, in lines 95, 96 and 98, Creole marking was less ambiguous. The vernacular English back open vowel [ɒ] in 'not' was shifted forwards towards [a], a well-recognised Caribbean variant (cf. e.g. Wells 1982: ch. 7; Sebba 1993), and the initial consonant in 'lunch' was stretched and heavily voiced in a manner reminiscent of Hewitt's description (1986: 134). In addition, although the subject requires much more research, the very extensive elision of 'gonna' in 'not'n' grow anyway' produced a rapidity of delivery which was elsewhere sometimes associated with Asians and whites trying to use black speech.

From this pattern, it looks as though afterburn provided one way of reconciling the need to maintain workable pupil–teacher relations with the critical and disjunctive stance evoked by Creole. As with Kazim in Extract II.15, Asif's protest maintained a thematic link to issues of transgression and attributed fault – indeed injustice – to an adult in authority. But there was also an important difference. Kazim's 'stop moving dat ting aroun' occurred in an ongoing session of energetic code-switching frame play. This didn't. The early period of play had been closed down (see Extract II.3), and rather than trying to start an argument up, these utterances came at the end of a run-in in which Asif had been defeated. Goffman's account of 'muttering' is pertinent here: 'In muttering we convey that although we are now going along with the line established by the speaker (and authority), our spirit has not been won over, and compliance is not to be counted on' (1981: 93). Especially in the 'afterburn' (to which 'muttering' bears functional ressemblance), the assertive connotations of Creole helped Asif to display his resilience and to repair an image momentarily damaged by Ms Jameson's abrupt departure. This overlap of symbolic evocation and personal concern suggests a strong degree of alignment between self and voice, 'principal' and 'figure' (Goffman 1974: ch. 13, 1981: ch. 3). It would be difficult to argue that Creole was unique in its capacity to support the expression of serious, unambiguous meanings – Alan's use of Panjabi to abuse Salim in Extract II.8 was located in what were now very hostile relations, and the intentions involved in the Panjabi exchange between Kuldip and Peter in Extract II.9 hardly seemed playful. Nevertheless, in this episode, the incorporation of an outgroup code was more extensively woven into the user's ordinary speech style than in any previous extract. In previous extracts, the concentration of crossing in single, sometimes formulaic phrases and sentences suggested performance, with crossers stepping quite quickly in and out of roles that seemed semi-theatrical.

The linguistic demarcation of habitual vernacular and borrowed out-group speech styles is even less clear-cut in the following episode, where Peter's use of 'afterburn' to complain about mistreatment was very similar to Asif's:

Extract II.18

Participants: Peter [An M 14 – wearing a radio microphone], Tony [An M 14], Iqbal [Pa M 14], Joginder [In M 30+], Ishmael [Pa M 14]
Setting: 1987. Peter and Tony are teamed up in a game of badminton, playing against Iqbal and Joginder, who is a voluntary youth worker. Ishmael is spectating. In line 4 Peter tries to stop the play, saying that the service was improper. But play continues and apparently, Peter and Tony lose the point.

1	Peter:	your serve Iqbal
2		((shot))
3		((shot))
4	Peter:	hit the rope

```
 5              ((shot))
 6   Peter:    ((f.)) hit the rope
 7   Iqbal:    oh my word ⌈(      )
 8   Ishmael:             ⌊come on now come on
                            ((f.))
 9   Peter:    it did
10   Iqbal:    (do you believe that) oi did you hear what he said
11      :      ⌈(        )
12   Peter:    ⌊JOGS IT HIT THE ROPE
                 ((ff.))
13   Ishmael:  IT DIDN'T
14   Peter:    IT COME DOWN WIGGLIN
15   Ishmael:  IT DIDN'T HIT THE ⌈ROPE
16   Iqbal:                      ⌊(          ) see ((laughs))
17   Peter:                      ⌊[1]
18              forget it man (1.0)
19              shuttlecock ⌈don't start wigglin=
                  ((l.))    ⌊
20                          ⌊((shot: play has restarted))
21   Peter:    = for no reason (.) ((moves to return a shot))
22 Joginder:   (            n all) (2.0) (aaah      )
23   Peter:    cheat sad man
24   Tony:     they're just startin' ( ⌈ ) cheatin (       )
25   Peter:    hit that rope anyone ⌊can see it
26      :                           ⌊(         you)
27   Tony:     CHEA:TIN:
```

In line 12, after his opponents had won what he considered to be
an invalid rally, Peter appealed loudly to Joginder who he might
expect to be impartial in his capacity as youth worker. But
Joginder kept quiet, and in view of the audible resumption of play
in line 20, he and Iqbal were presumably preparing themselves for
the next service around lines 15 and 16, thereby declaring the
matter closed and the point legitimately won. After an alveolar
click expressing disapprobation, Peter's 'forget it man' in line 18
probably referred to the service preparations then underway, and
gave an explicit indication that his 'compliance [was] not to be
counted on'. With his opponents' attention now redirected to the
game, lines 19 to 25 look like afterburn, in which Peter restated
the evidence for his original case to Tony, classified Iqbal and
Joginder's conduct as transgression, and received Tony's support,
who then forcefully readdressed their joint analysis to the others.

There are striking thematic similarities to the incident with Asif and Alan: transgression, rough justice dealt out by adults in authority, events assessed as 'sad'. But almost everything that Peter said was couched in his normal speech style, with the exception of 'shuttle-cock don't start wigglin' for no reason' (lines 19 and 21). There was nothing unusual about this phonologically, but it was grammatically distinctive in one of two possible ways. Due to the vernacular regularisation of third person singular Standard English 'doesn't', Peter's generic statement can be translated as either 'a shuttlecock doesn't start wiggling for no reason' or as 'shuttlecocks don't start . . .'. In the first interpretation, he omitted the indefinite article, and in the second, plural 's'. Both zero forms can be identified with Creole (cf. e.g. LePage and Tabouret-Keller 1985: 88; Edwards 1986: 141; Sebba 1993; Sutcliffe 1984: 234).

These data indicate a proximity between Creole-influenced linguistic forms and local vernacular speech which warrants more extended discussion. To do so, it is necessary to shift away from interaction analysis, and to turn instead to some general observations about language structure, as well as to a number of interview reports. Before that, however, it would be sensible to review some of Hewitt's comments on this issue.

5.5 Creole and the local multiracial vernacular

The interpenetration of Creole and local vernaculars is an important element in Hewitt's analysis, and it is worth attending closely to his conceptualisation of the relationship between them:

> As I argued elsewhere: 'There has developed in many inner city areas a form of "community English" or multiracial vernacular which, while containing Creole forms and idioms, is not regarded as charged with any symbolic meanings related to race and ethnicity and is in no way related to boundary maintaining practices. Rather, it is, if anything, a site within which ethnicity is deconstructed, dismantled and reassembled into a new, ethnically mixed, community English. The degree of Creole influence on the specific local vernacular is often higher in the case of young black speakers but the situation is highly fluid and open to much local variation. There is, therefore, a two-way movement evident in the language use of black London adolescents in which a de-ethnicised, racially mixed local language is creatively being established alongside a

strategic, contextually variable use of Creole . . . often employed as markers of race in the context of daily anti-racist struggle' . . . Black ethnicity is, on the one hand, not so much *lived out* as constructed and used as a resource amongst other resources in daily political engagements; a political instrument, not a constraining, taken-for-granted medium subsisting through all interactions. If there is an 'ethnicity' that *is* lived in this non-reflexive way it is more likely to reside in the emergent hybrid culture [and language] of black and white urban youth (Hewitt 1989b)

Here Hewitt makes a basic distinction between (a) unselfconscious and habitual vernacular speech, which incorporates Creole influences in ways that are generally unremarked, and (b) strategic code-switching which is symbolically related to ethnicity/race and which is used politically in boundary maintaining practices. The second of these is the primary concern in my research, while the forms and processes entailed in the first would generally fall within the interests of variationist sociolinguistics (e.g. Labov 1972a, Trudgill 1978, Bell 1984). The relationship between these two is highly complex. Hewitt very briefly suggests that 'The existence of creole forms that are, in specific contexts, *unmarked* for ethnicity [= (a)] . . . is necessarily preceded by the use and absorption of these same forms, ethnically marked to some degree [= (b)]' (1986: 148). Before a developmental connection of this kind could be accepted, however, there is a need for much fuller empirical investigation than either Hewitt or I provide. But whatever their relationship in processes of language change, Hewitt found that the shifting boundaries between these two contexts for Creole were very significant interactionally:

what is regarded by one group of black and white friends as unmarked with regard to ethnicity may, in another group in the same locality, be regarded as marked, and therefore possibly as the subject of special negotiations in interracial usage. If a white youngster wishes to use a certain word, therefore, he or she may have to make it appear 'natural' to their speech if they are to avoid the possibility of being challenged, or of being thought to be appropriating a language which they have no right to use. The existence of a vernacular which already contains a number of creole-derived features provides a useful alibi, a kind of smokescreen through which words may be smuggled into white speech (1986: 151)

My own research adds little to this discussion of the ways in which crossers could strategically exploit the ambiguous border zones between Creole and the local multiracial vernacular. However, Extract II.18 indicates just how subtle the line between them could be. Although it is hard to be sure that any sense of specifically interethnic wrong-doing was involved, Peter's zero forms protested about putative injustice and as such, they appeared to draw on Creole's association with opposition to arbitrary official authority – a link that was structurally much more obvious in Extract II.17. In that regard, Peter's usage can be construed as political and it conforms to Hewitt's second context for the use of Creole. But clearly, this was achieved with only the slightest of linguistic adaptations.

In fact, in strictly linguistic terms, the origin of Peter's omission of the indefinite article/plural marker is not necessarily even Creole. As Hewitt recognises (1986: 126), vernacular speech is receptive to a wide range of different influences, and in the locality I studied, a number of the variable features that one might ascribe to a Creole influence could also be derived from Panjabi, Indian English or second language learner interlanguage. Grammatically, one or more of these could also serve as linguistic sources for: the omission of 's' in the possessive, in the plural and in the third person singular present tense; zero realisation of the indefinite article; absent past tense and participle markers; and copula and auxiliary omission. The roots of the invariant question tag 'innit' could be traced to Indian English as well as to Creole, and phonologically so too could TH stopping, clear L, r-colouration, consonant cluster metathesis, as well as a relatively narrow range on the dipthongs in 'day', 'nose' and 'right' (narrow in comparison with Midlands and Southern English white working-class accents – see Wells 1982: 626 and Sutcliffe 1984: 232). Change in standard patterns of word stress, fewer schwas, stepping intonation and a drift towards syllable rather than stress timing could likewise have Panjabi as well as Creole origins.[1]

Hewitt is right to call this vernacular 'multiracial': a small quantitative study of phonological variation in the interview speech of these informants revealed that, for example, traditionally white L vocalisation occurred among black and Asian adolescents as well, that white adolescents occasionally used Panjabi-influenced retroflexes, and that among Indian, Anglo and

Caribbean youngsters, TH stopping correlated positively with having Pakistani friends (Rampton 1987a, 1989). As Hewitt notes elsewhere, it was usually possible to tell a person's background from their ordinary speech, since there tended to be a greater incidence of forms deriving from their particular ethnolinguistic inheritance. Even so, to a very considerable degree, they spoke 'a new **ethnically mixed** 'community English' created from the fragments' of a range of language varieties (1989a: 139).

Inspite of these 'objective' linguistic possibilities, however, informants generally credited black adolescents with the leading role in the multiracial vernacular, introducing elements that others subsequently adopted. In this way, for example, 'innit' was analysed as being originally black, and young people most often ascribed Creole roots to new words in the local English vernacular.

In judging the origin of these linguistic forms, to quite a degree young people may have relied on roughly the same kind of *pragmatic* analysis that I used in interpreting the origin of Peter's 'shuttlecock don't start wigglin'.[2] Here, folk analysis of the linguistic sources shaping the local multiracial vernacular probably drew on more general social and cultural stereotypes. It is likely that in assessing why 'innit', zero past tense and zero past participle marking should be attributed to Creole rather than Indian English, the local symbolic connotations of these two varieties were a central factor. Past tense and participle markers were most commonly omitted in verbs describing conflict and energetic, sometimes illicit action – for example, 'beat', 'catch', 'vex', 'whiplash', 'boost', 'thrash', 'slap', and 'fuck' (also more obviously Creole 'tief').[3] Some of these could be accompanied by other linguistically differentiating elements (cf. Hewitt 1986: 132–3 on the particle 'up'), but more centrally, they were compatible with Creole's resonances of street authority, not with SAE's connotations of polite deference. More generally, Creole's tough, cool associations probably meant that many adolescents would be happy to detect its influence on their speech. In contrast, the obvious linguistic distance between Panjabi and vernacular English probably inhibited the recognition of Panjabi influences in local English, and anyway, transfer from Panjabi was normally linked to stigmatised Asian English.

So whatever a professional linguist might say about the origin of linguistic forms, Creole was much more extensively linked with adolescent perceptions of their own vernacular speech than either

Panjabi or Asian English. Creole and the local vernacular were also more extensively tied to a sense of youth and class identity. This emerged in patterns of correction that were produced or reported in interviews.

5.6 Correction by adults

Asian and Anglo informants sometimes commented on the inappropriacy of adults using words from the interface between Creole and the multiracial vernacular – 'it's just not on, is it, [when my mum says "wicked", "hard"]'. And black informants themselves emphasised the differences between their own uses of Creole and the varieties spoken by adult relatives who had been brought up in the Caribbean (see also Hewitt 1986: 103; Sebba 1986: 155ff).

But the feeling that there was a specifically youth cultural variety of Creole-influenced speech came out most clearly in reports about the way that parents and teachers drew attention to certain aspects of the local adolescent vernacular. With Indian and Pakistani informants, Panjabi and Urdu were very commonly associated with politeness to older relatives, who, it was often said, were keen that the younger generation should make use of these South Asian languages. In contrast, it has been widely reported that black parents generally discourage Creole in their children's speech.[4] In Ashmead, several *Asian* and *Anglo* informants also reported adults taking exception to (actually or putatively) Creole features being used at home:

> they [adults] use very sort of dated English, and we just- we have our slang words, like . . . 'ennit Richard ennit' . . . or 'he got catch innit' and they say 'no, he got caught' . . . my mum for example: 'Eh mum, Chris got catch at school today' and she goes 'what sort of English is that?' . . . Probably they were brought up to it but it's easier for us to use our language . . . especially when I want to get my mum angry . . . I just say to her to get her annoyed sometimes, I say 'ah bootoo ((L2 Panjabi)), a rass you klaat' or 'cha na' (Ian [An M 15])

> [My dad] complained. He said, 'you're Indian, why can't you speak like one' and all this. I just said 'blerd'. (Manjit [In M 15])

> I'm always saying 'innit innit', and my mum and my sister take the mickey out of me cos they say it's not proper English (Sally [An F 15])

It was often attendance at a specifically multiracial school that distinguished informants like these from their adult relatives. In fact, this kind of correction was just as commonly attributed to teachers:

> Helen   [AC F 14]: sometimes when we're just having a good conversation, they just go 'that isn't- that isn't proper English' or something like that
>
> Adrian   [AC M 14]: yeh, we're having our own conversation – they just join and say that's not proper English . . . They just jump into the conversation and they just say 'that's not right'

Significantly, in a very similar vein, informants also reported adults correcting non-standard Anglo dialectisms:

> we say 'I aint' and they go 'I haven't', or 'I'm no[?] goin [?]u' and they say 'noT goinG To' (Ian [An M 15])

> Mr Hibbert corrects. If I say 'twenny', he goes 'twenty', don't he . . . well they're right, but they're fussy. He's a maths teacher but he gives us lectures on English for 15 minutes sometimes . . . people take the michael out of him (Pat [An F 15])

Informants evidently regarded *both* Creole *and* vernacular South Midlands forms as targets for the corrective efforts of adults committed to cleaning up the spontaneous speech of the young people in their charge. At the same time, while accepting that these forms weren't 'good' or 'proper', the stance of these informants was far from universally submissive. In fact, in highlighting a mix of Creole and vernacular Anglo features and in counterposing them to Standard English, it looks as though adult correction helped to invest these forms with a sense of multiracial working-class identity distinctive to local youth.

5.7 Summary

From the interaction, report and other data considered in this chapter, it seems as though Creole was more closely linked with the everyday speech of Ashmead adolescents than either Panjabi or SAE. To say that this was due to its dialectal proximity to English would reveal relatively little (and anyway, while obviously true in relation to Panjabi, this might be hard to argue in connection with SAE). Lesser structural difference might sometimes be a factor, but social influences on its perception and use by white and Asian youngsters were obviously important.

In situations where adults were a relevant presence, Creole was more flexible than either of these other codes, being available for both peer–peer and adult–adolescent talk. At the same time, its linguistic form provided it with less protection from adult intrusion than Panjabi, and its more overtly oppositional symbolic and pragmatic value made it more vulnerable to reprimand than SAE. There was also less to set it apart in terms of the organisation of the school curriculum. As a distinctive symbolic voice, Creole seemed capable of closer fusion with the expression of a crosser's genuine concerns in his or her daily dealings with teachers and parents. It was sometimes hard to separate utterances which drew on Creole to add weight to the speaker's ordinary voice from those in which Creole forms had become 'naturalised', carrying no obvious extra resonances.

These linguistic, interactional and institutional reasons for seeing Creole as more intimately connected with ordinary vernacular speech than either of the varieties studied in Chapters 3 and 4 were matched in interview discussion. In actual fact, everyday adolescent speech was receptive to a wide range of linguistic influences (and of course also included more than just the three languages analysed here). But informants generally prioritised Creole in their accounts of the local vernacular, and in doing so, they were no doubt affected by its quite extensive symbolic congruence with vitality and the kinds of concern that are quite frequently identified as typically youth cultural. Reports of the way that adults corrected adolescent speech also appeared to establish quite a strong association between Creole and traditional non-standard Anglo forms.

In all, a number of local social processes and arrangements helped to differentiate Creole from the practices and values associated with 'educated' Standard English, as well as aligning it more strongly than either Panjabi or Asian English with local vernacular speech.

5.8 Conclusion to Part II: Crossing, youth subculture, and the development of political sensibilities

To conclude this part of the book, I shall first summarise the central points that have emerged from this and the two preceding chapters. After that, it is worth comparing the approach taken here with some influential sociological work on youth culture and resistance – specifically, research in the tradition established by the Birmingham Centre for Contemporary Cultural Studies (CCCS).

This part of the book set out to explore the political aspects of multiracial adolescent code-switching in the presence of adults, and it has suggested that the interactional structures and processes clustering around SAE, Creole and Panjabi can indeed be seen as small but significant building blocks for the kind of collective interracial sensibility that Gilroy interprets in terms of the new urban social movements.

'Resistance' can be difficult to spot in everyday behaviour – most adolescents did not appear to want direct confrontation with their elders, and people are generally very good at repairing inter-actional difficulty. The argument has been, however, that acts of code-switching and language crossing foregrounded certain kinds of micro-social relationship, and that through processes of symbolic evocation they invited extrapolation to wider fields of political contestation.

To make these connections, analysis first focused on participation frameworks. Two were basic. The first involved an engagement between adults in superior institutional positions and adolescents in subordinate ones. The second involved interaction between adolescent peers. These then generated a third interactional relationship, in which institutionally powerful adults acted as bystanders to adolescent talk. When they were used, SAE and Panjabi generally entailed different participation frameworks: stylised Asian English normally occurred in adult–adolescent interaction, while Panjabi was used between peers with adults looking on. Creole could involve either.

Boundary negotiation was the second micro-interactional issue that regularly featured when any of these three varieties were used. The boundaries in question varied. Code switches into SAE were most often occasioned at moments when adolescents came under greater adult influence. Creole seemed to express concern at transgression of the norms of decent conduct. In this chapter, nothing was said of the ritual functions that Panjabi might serve between peers, but its use in arenas where the dominant activity was adult-directed did invite the people in charge to declare whether or not they regarded it as an *illegitimate* addition to the communicative flow.

In switching to symbolic voices that inevitably evoked connotational fields that stretched beyond the matter in hand, adolescents invited participants 'to read acts as symptoms' and to take a larger view. In this way, the particular participation frameworks and boundary negotiations involved in any one case of language crossing could be reinterpreted in terms of a wider set of political relations. Interactions between particular adults and adolescents could be reconstrued in terms of the domination of one social group by another. Adolescent–adolescent discourse could be taken to instantiate intra-group solidarity. And specific incidents involving subordination to adult influence, unfair treatment, or unwelcome interruption could be contextualised in a wider social order in which ethnic groups suffered disproportionate injustice, were accepted only in inferior positions or had to struggle for recognition of their independent traditions.

It seems fair to say, then, that interactional code-crossing provides a productive site for the analysis of informal political processes among youth in a multiracial urban setting. The connection with sociological discussion of social movements has already been pursued quite closely, especially in Chapter 3. But there is at least one other area of sociological research with obvious relevance to the present study, and it is worth briefly reviewing the kind of contribution that a fairly broadly based interpretive sociolinguistic analysis can make to this.

Work on youth 'subcultures' carried out in the tradition established by the Birmingham CCCS in fact forms a significant part of the background to my own research, and there is a very clear overlap in several central themes. Several commentators suggest that the most important CCCS contribution was to interpret the distinctive activities and 'focal concerns' of youth as a form of *ideological* contestation. Considerable weight was attached to the symbolic significance of style, dress, argot, ritual, activity and music, and it was through these that young people were seen as partially interrupting, adapting, resisting (but finally coming to terms with) the possibilities and meanings offered to them by the dominant society (P Cohen 1972; Hall and Jefferson 1976; Mungham and Pearson 1977; Willis 1977; Hebdige 1979; Connell 1983; Frith 1984; Brake 1985). Culture was examined as a political activity closely linked to the conflict of social interests, and an attempt was made to develop modes of analysis which could show

how the creativity of active human agents fitted in with the larger processes through which social stratification was reproduced (Willis 1977; Giroux 1983a, 1983b).

It has now been widely recognised, however, that during the 1970s (and sometimes later), work in this tradition often contained several fairly serious conceptual and methodological problems. In a number of respects, Gilroy's 1987 study represents a major development beyond these. But as I have already suggested, Gilroy provides relatively little systematic discussion of language use. In order to bring out the specific contribution of the kind of sociolinguistic discourse analysis involved in my own research, it is worth summarising some of the most important of the difficulties that CCCS research encountered.

1. Scholars in the CCCS paradigm attached considerable importance to ethnography as a way of studying youth's active reinterpretation of the specific local and historical conditions of domination in which it found itself, but the adequacy of their fieldwork and of their interpretive procedures has been questioned (Hargreaves 1982: 114; Connell 1983: 224). In practice, studies often fell short of the requirements for an adequate symbolic analysis, moving too rapidly away from the description of concrete instances and local interpretations into accounts of their wider sociological significance (S Cohen 1980: xvi; Turner 1974: 21). Indeed, inspite of its inclusion in the title of a seminal CCCS publication – *Resistance through Rituals* (Hall and Jefferson 1976) – very little sustained theoretical consideration was given to the concept of ritual.

2. These weaknesses in the empirical treatment of youth culture fed into at least two major conceptual problems: what kinds of activity actually qualified as resistance, and what were its targets? Ethnographies of schooling outside the CCCS tradition describe a number of different ways in which pupils express a lack of interest in classroom business – daydreaming is just one example (cf. Pollard 1979, 1985) – and if one interprets everything except willing and joyful compliance as a form of resistance, the concept's connection with ideas of collective social transformation gets lost (Hargreaves 1982: 113). Undifferentiating use of the term 'resistance' can also obscure moments in cultural expression when autonomy and alternative

identity have priority over active opposition, and therefore risks
the kind of reductionism which construes
minority experience exclusively in terms of antiracism (Hewitt
1986: 214; Gilroy 1987: 150,159)

3. At least in early CCCS work on subculture, these problems of
   interpretation were partially resolved in the view that class
   relations were always the fundamental issue, regardless of the
   apparent complexities of everyday life and of the
   interpretations that actors themselves might put on their
   conduct. As many later commentators both within and outside
   CCCS have noted, this led to the neglect of race and gender.

4. In order to explain the gap between ostensible conduct and the
   targets which they suggested it was directed against, scholars
   often described action as 'oblique', 'ambiguous' and 'displaced'
   in its meaning, engaged in struggles that were 'magical' and
   'imaginary' rather than explicit or well-focused. They also
   emphasised the contradictions within youth culture, frequently
   using the phrase 'accommodation and resistance'. But this
   idiom carried a number of risks: *self-conscious* resistances
   could be obscured, participants could be seen as inarticulates
   mired in a set of contradictions that blocked their vision, and
   indeed contradiction and ambiguity could be misattributed to
   informants when in fact the uncertainty lay in the analysis.

5. In CCCS work on subculture, a view of the many identities
   comprising a person's subjectivity was generally
   underdeveloped. As a result, members of subcultures and class
   groups were often treated as more homogeneous and more
   synchronised in their interests than one would now regard as
   empirically warranted. The boundaries around membership
   were seen as unrealistically clear-cut, and the opposition
   between youth and school was over-simplified (Connell 1983).

Clearly, then, there are a number of issues that have arisen in
debate about CCCS research that any study of the politics of
youth cultural practice now needs to reckon with, and my own
work tries to move past each of these difficulties by means of a
broadly based sociolinguistics. In the analysis presented so far, the
interpretation of ritual and symbol has involved a close reading of
particular interactional sequences, informant comments and
reports, and some detailed theoretical discussion of ritual and

symbolism themselves (cf. 1 above). In the process, it has become clear that 'resistance' is much too crude a term to capture the different political problematics made momentarily available in these code-switchings into Creole, Panjabi and SAE (cf. 2 above). The research here gives particular emphasis to race, but the difficulties of isolating this from class, neighbourhood and generation have become very apparent, particularly in the Chapter 5 (cf. 3 above). We have encountered 'ambiguity' in the symbolic meaning of for example SAE, and in many of the code-switches that have been examined, there was an obvious contradiction between the speaker's usual self-presentation and the particular persona that they momentarily projected. But rather than indicating the adolescent actor's confusion, contradiction and uncertainty at the level of interpersonal action seemed to be resources which the participants *skilfully* exploited (cf. 4 above).

Finally, the analysis has been underpinned by the assumption that individuals have many identities, and that differences in one of these can be attenuated by similarities in another (cf. 5 above). Code-switching has, for example, been studied as a practice that assists the political socialisation of friends, classmates and others *across* the boundaries of ethnic difference (e.g. Chapter 4.5). Overarching patterns of group stratification certainly cannot be denied, but they do not have to be oppressive in every local context, and through examination of actions and their responses, one can see how solidarities can develop between those who produce switches and those who merely receive them, in spite of the fact that they may be divided by major differences in institutional power. Unlike approaches which identify social or subcultural groups as the basic unit in their accounts of resistance (e.g. Willis 1977), the analysis of interactional practices does not prescribe who the proponents of these politics should be. Of course, not just anyone could use Panjabi, SAE or Creole, and in Part III, constraints on who could use which code will be discussed much more fully. Nevertheless, it is clear that given particular kinds of friendship and/or shared institutional position, whites could, for example, use Creole or Panjabi and evoke political relations that, in cultural or ethnic absolutist analyses, would only be available to the inheritors of those languages.

On a number of counts, interpretive sociolinguistic analysis of interactional practices avoids a crude determinism, and provides scope for understanding how urban communities can start to develop broadly shared political commitments in spite of their diverse constituency. How far this collective sensibility could develop, and what direction its political mobilisation could take, are not questions which this mode of analysis can answer. Important issues of that kind would require investigation of a far wider range of larger social processes, as well as a much fuller examination of local and national discourses about class, race and community. Even so, the analysis of interaction may play an important part in providing a view of the everyday understandings that lie at the roots of larger movements.

Notes

1. On Creole, see e.g. Sutcliffe 1982, Le Page and Tabouret-Keller 1985, Edwards 1986, Sebba 1986, 1993. On the English of people with Indian backgrounds, see e.g. Agnihotri 1979, Nihalani et al. 1979, Gumperz 1982a, Shackle 1987. On both, see Lander 1981, Wells 1982, Romaine 1983.

2. Up to a point, the folk attribution of a black origin to common vernacular terms could be based on attention to lexis. Some of the words and idioms that Hewitt lists as Creole features in white South London speech also had interethnic currency in Ashmead – for example, 'wicked', 'hard', 'bad' (all meaning 'excellent'), 'sad' (which Hewitt glosses as 'pathetic'), 'shame' ('[v] to shame or be shamed, and [n] state of disgrace') 'bahty' ('buttocks'), 'facety' ('cheeky'), 'tief' ('to steal, a thief'), 'cha' and tooth-sucking (both exclamations of annoyance), 'guy' (as a term of address), 'rass' (buttocks), 'soff' (weak, ineffective), 'wa appen' ('friendly greeting'). Whether or not they preserved the same forms and meaning that Hewitt ascribes to them is a question that would require much fuller and more systematic examination than I have been able to give them.

3. See Cheshire 1978 on similar verbs, which, in contrast to Ashmead, in Reading served as a site for the preservation of older dialectal forms rather than for the introduction of new ones.

4. Sutcliffe 1982: 152–3; Hewitt 1986: 105; Edwards 1986: 105–6; Dalphinis 1991: 49; though cf. Sebba 1993: ch.6.

Part III

*Crossing with peers:
negotiating solidarity*

6 *Stylised Asian English (ii): Rituals of differentiation and consensus*

Part III of this book focuses on the everyday recreational interaction between peers that comprised much the largest part of my database. In Part II, we looked at situations in which adults had (varying degrees of) official control over adolescents. These institutional power differences could themselves be taken to exemplify wider patterns of class and/or race inequality, and it was mainly through its negotiation with people in authority that code-crossing was considered as a micro-political phenomenon. In contrast, this part of the book is much more concerned with the role that crossing played in the organisation of interracial adolescent *solidarities*, and with the way in which in interaction, crossing foregrounded, obscured or redefined adolescent knowledge of wider ethnic stratification and division. Again, code-crossing's political character will be emphasised, but here, this will be conceived more in terms of (a) its orientation to ideologies of race, and then later on, (b) its implicit assumptions about social reality and the place that ethnicity occupied within it.

This chapter concentrates on the ways in which adolescents used stylised Asian English among themselves. They often used it to make critical comments about a peer's behaviour or appearance and here stylised Asian English (SAE) generally emphasised *differences* between the speaker and the target of their utterance. But it was also used in games, and there, in contrast, it was the participants' *shared* interests that utterances stressed. In both of these contexts, it was unlike SAE in adult–adolescent interaction, in that there was little evidence of its being the specialised practice of a few individuals. About 36 people used SAE in informal interaction outside games, 11 of whom were female. Of those, two were of Caribbean descent while among male users, five were Caribbean and three were Anglo. All of these non-Asian users had been closely associated with Panjabis for a long time.

After giving a description of different types of use, the chapter provides an overview of all the ways that SAE was used – with adults as well – and it clarifies SAE's status as a form of ritual action. In doing so, it ties interactional conduct back to the views that informants expressed in interviews and back to the position that Asian English occupies in British society. In ending, this chapter comments briefly on games as a special context for interaction, which then leads into the discussion of Panjabi crossing in Chapter 7.

6.1 SAE in criticism

With critical uses of SAE,[1] there was no systematic patterning in the data to suggest that the use of SAE by white and black youngsters was considered unacceptable per se, or that white and black adolescents carefully avoided its use in the company or presence of Panjabis. What mattered was the referent: for Indians and Pakistanis, for Afro-Caribbeans and for Anglos, licence and avoidance were closely connected with the social category memberships of the people that SAE utterances were intended to target as their butt. In fact, it is helpful to take critical SAE in two parts, one dealing with its use with adolescents with lower peer group status, and the other focusing on its use with friends and acquaintances.

6.2 Critical SAE to adolescents with lower peer group status

When either the speaker or the target was Asian, the use of SAE appeared to be least constrained when it was directed at people who were unknown to the user on a personal basis, but who could be identified in terms of a less prestigious social category. Typically, these uses arose in open settings in which a number of separate engagements were in progress and in which some kind of norm transgression was felt to necessitate the user's attention being temporarily diverted from his or her main concerns. In such gatherings, one can say that the multiracial peer group was experienced as a concrete collectivity, and within them, the noisy censure of conduct constituted one of the most public definitions of the social meaning of SAE, observable by anyone present.

Some of these utterances in stylised Asian English were directed at adolescents of Bangladeshi descent.

Extract III.1

Participants and setting: Ian [An M 15 wearing radio-microphone], Jagdish [In M 15], Richard [An M 15], Conrad [AC M 15]) and a lot of other pupils are queuing up in the corridor waiting to go in for dinner. A few moments earlier, Jagdish had said that there was a Bangladeshi pupil trying to push in, but for the time being attention has returned to soccer.

```
1      Ian:   ((to Jagdish)) you're gonna have to make Anil sub
              now
2 Richard:    you'll have to make Anil sub
3      Ian:   ⌈oi look (.) oi (.) oi Jagdish
4      :      |(        )
5      :      ⌊(        )
6      :      oi you (   )
7 Richard:    OI EH EH WHERE YOU GOING (.) GET BACK OI
8      :      (        )
9 Richard:    EH GET BACK (1.0) HEY WHAT A RAAS (.)
10     Ian:   EH (      ) EH MISS (.) WHERE THEY GOING (.)
11 Richard:   MISS THEY'VE PUSHED IN
12     Ian:   OI (.) LOOK Baker ((a 6th former)) THESE LOT
13            PUSHED IN (.) THEY JUST (      OUR DINNER)
14            THEY (BOUGHT    ) (.) GET BACK TO THE BACK
15 Richard:   GED OU'
16 Anon. A  [M]:        OUT:
                        [aʊth]
17 Richard:             GED OU'
18 Anon A:   ((slow)):  GE:T OU:T
                        [ge:t ʌʊ:th]
19  Anon B  [M]:((slow)) OUT BOY OUT
                        [ʌʊt bhɔI ʌʊt]
20 Anon A:   ((slow))   GE:T OU:T
                        [ge:t ʌʊ:th]
21 Richard:  (those others) pushed in (   )  ⌈
22 Anon B:                                   ⌊MOVE IT BO:Y
                                              [mʊv  It  bɔI]
```

```
23    Ian:  ⎡WELL WHAT'S THE MATTER WITH YOU BAKER
                (.)
24     :   ⎢(                              )
25     :   ⎣(                          )
26    Ian:  see if that was me innit (.) ([kɹɑɑf])
                                ((approximation to Creole))
27           ((more laughter and talk for 8.0))
28    Ian:  ((quietly)) fucking Bengalis
29 Richard: go:sh ma:n
30    Ian:  ((addressing microphone)) see Ben you- this- see-
31           this sch- there's something wro:ng with this school
32           man some ⎡thing wro:ng
33 Richard:         ⎣ennit  if that was us
```

Similar uses also occurred when older adolescents addressed younger ones:

Extract III.2

Participants and setting: Razia [Pa F 15 wearing radio-microphone] and two friends [Pa F] are walking around outside. They see a small Asian boy bringing a drink out of the canteen (this was explained retrospectively by the participants). Mr Cogan is the deputy head-teacher.

```
1  Raz:  you're not allowed outside with a drink
2   A:   ((high pitched)) OI COME INSIDE COME IN COME IN (HERE)
3   B:   ((high pitched)) (  ) 'MISTER ,CO ,GAN ,CATCH "YOU
                          [mɪstə   kəʊgən   kætʃ    ju]
4  Raz:  see look at 'at (.)
5 AorB:  what (.) (      )
6  Raz:  he just dropped it oh my go:d (26.0)
```

Extract III.3

Participants and setting: Mohan [In M 15 wearing radio-micro-phone], Jagdish [In M 15] and Sukhbir [In M 15] are in the bicycle sheds looking at bicycles at the start of the new academic year. Some new pupils run past them.

```
1 Sukhbir: ⎡STOP RUNNING AROUND YOU GAYS (.)
2 Sukhbir: ⎢((laughs))
3 Mohan:   ⎣EH (.) 'THIS 'IS ,NOT ,MIDDLE (SCHOOL) ,no ,more
            (1.0
            [aɪ    dɪs    ɪz ŋɒtʰ   mɪd̥              nəʊ mɔ:]
```

4   ‚this is a re‚spective (2.0
          [dɪs ɪz ə ɹəspektɪv]
5   : (school)
6 Mohan: school (.) yes (.) took the words out my mouth (4.5)

In each of these episodes, the speakers were claiming that an impropriety had been committed: that a queue had been entered improperly, that a drink was being taken into areas where it was forbidden, and that the norms of conduct appropriate to second-ary pupils during a breaktime gathering had been broken. To understand the use of SAE in these episodes, it is useful to return to certain key elements in Goffman's account of interaction ritual, and in particular, his view of remedial interchanges (1971: 95–187). As outlined earlier (Chapter 3.4), Goffman argues that two kinds of issue arise when infractions occur. One of these is 'substantive', relating to practical matters such as the offender making amends, and the offended showing that they are not going to accept the way they have been treated. The other is ritual (in Goffman's extended sense), which in contrast, is concerned with the way in which participants' display their more general respect and regard for social norms, personal preserves and the system of penalties and rewards that are intended to protect those norms and preserves (see Goffman 1971: 95–8, 100, 116). Here the con-cern is with 'indicating a relationship, not compensating a loss' (1971: 118). The structure of the exchanges in these three extracts locates SAE within this second dimension of the remedial process, and given the role that symbolism played, it can also be called 'ritual' in the narrower sense preferred in earlier discussion.

In each episode, the noticing of the infraction was announced by normal vernacular English 'primes' – attempts to get the (putat-ive) offender to provide a remedy, which they might do by desisting, apologising and/or giving an explanation (1971: 154ff, 109–14). In extract III.1, lines 7, 9, 14, 15 and 17 directed primes at the initial offender, and lines 10, 11, 12, 13 and 23 directed them towards a dinner lady and a sixth form prefect; they were aimed at the offenders in lines 1 (and perhaps 2) of Extract III.2 and line 1 of Extract III.3. Across these three episodes, the shift from local vernacular English to SAE was not accompanied by any obvious similarity in the surface illocutionary acts they performed:

in Extract III.2, SAE coincided with a warning about being appre-
hended (line 3); in Extract III.3 it ran with a reminder that old
rules of conduct no longer applied (line 3); and in Extract III.1 it
repeated the demands made earlier in vernacular English (lines 18,
19, 20, 22). Instead, the common feature can be identified in the
way in which SAE made a symbolic proclamation about the transgression's relation to a wider social order. In switching away from
their normal voices to stylised Asian English, the speakers aligned
the offence with a more general social type, so that the offending
act was cast as a symptom. Because SAE was stereotypically associated with limited linguistic and cultural competence, the switch
implicitly explained the transgression by imputing diminished control and responsibility to the offender. In doing so, it achieved the
same effect as a sanction – 'the significance of . . . rewards and
penalties is not meant to lie in their intrinsic worth but in what
they proclaim about the [actor's] moral status . . . and . . . [their]
compliance with or deviation from rules in general' (Goffman
1971: 95,98).

It is also noticeable that SAE came at or towards the end of a
sequence of primes and that it was not followed by intensifying
primes in vernacular English. In Extract III.1, SAE closed the
demands made directly to the person accused of pushing in. One
more prime was directed at the sixth former and then the clamour
died down, leaving an afterburn complaining about both offender
and official authority. In Extract III.2, SAE was immediately succeeded by an afterburn as the apparently unheeding transgressor
continued his drink. Admittedly, in line 4 of Extract III.3, there
was a second prime that had lost the Asian English markings of
the one preceding, but by this time, the new pupils had rushed off
out of earshot: far from upgrading, it petered out so that someone
else had to help to finish off the sentence. In general, it is as if at
least formally, this minor shift in pronunciation (or syntax with
Extract III.2's omission of auxiliary 'will') upgraded vernacular
English primes into an ultimatum, laying the prospect of outcast
status in front of the offender. At the same time, for the adolescents who claimed to be offended, the effect of SAE could be to
compensate symbolically for the disorder created by the putative
transgression. It would do so in the first instance by placing such
infractions in a larger scheme believed to predict and explain
them. And second, it could affirm social cohesion among the

'offended' by attesting to their common recognition of this higher level framework.

In fact, it is worth analysing the way in which this social cohesion was interactively constructed. In each episode, the primes before the switch to SAE referred to an event in the world, so that when it occurred, SAE connected an abstract scheme of stereotypes to (recently) visible activity on hand. In that sense, SAE was being stamped empirically with a link to questions of propriety, thereby doubtless facilitating its use on other occasions to imply infraction where none was obvious. But this link with the perception of conduct outside in the world should not lead us to underestimate the importance of interactive concerns internal to the group claiming that an offence was taking place. In Extract III.2, during a period in which the girls were walking with little to say to each other, the observation of infraction provided the pretext for talk and agreement. And in Extract III.1, the fact that Jagdish warned his friends in advance that someone was likely to push in, indicates that the ensuing primes were much more than mere reflexes to irresistably intrusive occurrences in the world outside. Perception and orientation to infracting events was selective – the order of queuing was by no means inviolable, and without any comparable fuss, black, white, Indian and Pakistani pupils often inserted themselves into places that weren't rightfully theirs.

It is also significant that offences were remedied in none of these episodes. This is consistent with the observation that disputes among children are often unresolved (e.g. Goodwin 1982: 87). Maynard explains this in terms of a basic function of conflict, which 'is to achieve a concrete, particular social organisation through the display of opposition and the constitution of accountable alignment structures' (1985b: 212). Outside the use of SAE in the episodes here, alignment among those claiming offence was displayed in the repetition and elaboration of other people's primes (Extract III.1: 7–15; Extract III.2: 1–2) and in collaborative afterburn and turn completion (Extract III.1: 28–33; Extract III.3: 4–6). Clearly, stylised Asian English occurred within sequences that expressed social affiliation among a subset of participants in the gathering, as well as their common orientation to external events on hand. But more specifically, in none of these episodes was it used in the first noticing of an infraction – in each, it built on prior speaker's primes, and was only brought in when a certain degree of common orientation seemed assured. So when SAE was used to connect the 'offence' with a wider sense of social order, it followed in a sequence of agreement, emerged with the force of a collective assessment, and led to no shows of dissent from the in-group. In this way, the ritual switch and the order it indexed acquired a general ratification.

Whatever their targets and intentions, there are several structural grounds for suggesting that the SAE in Extracts III.1, III.2 and III.3 was potentially offensive. Words were called out to 'offenders' without any of the minor shows of support that might give reassurance that the approach was made with good intent, and they were not based within relationships of personal acquaintance that might allow the recipients to come back at them.[2] Furthermore, located in gatherings, there was an element of very public shaming in these noisy primes. Certainly, with this particular combination of organisational characteristics, SAE was almost only ever used when targeting younger pupils and pupils of Bangladeshi descent.[3] With friends, acquaintances and age-mates with Caribbean, Panjabi and Anglo backgrounds, infraction-focusing uses took more mitigated forms, though these were not uniform and themselves showed sensitivity to ethnicity and gender.

6.3 Critical SAE between friends and acquaintances

As will emerge much more fully in due course, male-female interaction in this peer network generally involved a certain amount of special licence in the use of languages associated with ethnicity. This certainly seemed to be the case with SAE. In my data, there were no instances of black or white boys or girls themselves targeting SAE at an Indian and Pakistani agemate of the same sex. But there were two examples of black boys (not whites) addressing SAE to Panjabi girls, and this was one of them.

Extract III.4

1987. Cyril [AC M 15 wearing radio-microphone] is outside. Surjit [In F 15] approaches with a few friends [F]. In line 5 another boy (Anon M) arrives. Surjit is rumoured to have a boyfriend in his twenties.

1   Surjit: ((from some distance)) hello Cyril:
2   Cyril: hello are you alright Surjit (.)

```
 3  ?Surjit:  innit (1.5)
 4   Cyril:   remember the boyfriend (3.0)
5Anon M:  Surjit (          ⌐        )
 6  Anon F:                 └good mornin'
 7   Cyril:   ((loud)) ˌtwenty ˌone ˌyears ˌo::ˈld (1.0)
                      [twenti wʌn jiəz   o::ˈld]
 8  Anon F:  show him show him
9Anon M:  alright Cyril right
10    Cyril:   ((to Anon M)) dont mess ABOUT dont mess
```

In fact, this bore some ressemblance to cross-sex SAE between Panjabis:

Extract III.5

1987. It is non-uniform day, when pupils are allowed to come to school in their own clothes as long as they make a donation to charity. Mohan [In M 15 wearing radio-microphone], Jagdish [In M 15], Conrad [AC M 15] and Anita [In F 15] are talking outside. Mohan is trying to get Anita to speak into the radio-microphone: he has already asked her to 'make a comment' three times, but for the time being she is showing more interest in what Jagdish is saying about some people she knows.

```
1 Mohan:  would you like to make a comment
2   Anita: ⌐no
3 Jagdish: └Hari was dancing with 'im the other day (.) fuckin'
4          guy was pissed man
5   Anita: who?
6 Jagdish: Hari (1.0)
            (  )well pissed ⌐man
7 Mohan:   ((quite loud))  └ˈwhy ˈyou ˈvearing ˈdose ˌclothes
                            [vaɪ ju vɛɹɪn  dəʊz klɜ:z]
8   Anita: ((emphatically)) because it's non-uniform day
```

In both cases, SAE was used in jokey provocation. In each, it singled out unusual attributes that in other circumstances, one might expect to be a source of pride to their possessers – a mature boyfriend and casual clothes (skirt and yellow top). But evidently, the use of SAE made them seem like social improprieties. In extract III.5, Mohan's use of SAE appeared to give 'why are you wearing those clothes' the force of an interrogative challenge, so that Anita finally gave him the attention he had been seeking, in order to defend herself (since she knew that Mohan knew the reason as well as she did, her retort was justificatory, not explanatory). In Extract III.4, Cyril's initial, vernacular English reference to 'the boyfriend' elicited no response, but when he delivered the crucial details in Asian English, he set in motion some playful physical retaliation, with Anon M acting on Surjit's behalf.

Between age-mates of the *same* sex, there were about 10 clear cases of SAE being used to imply or refer to an interlocutor's infraction of normal propriety, and these were almost all male. The participation of Panjabis appeared to make some difference to the way that it was used in these same sex interactions.

There were six occasions when SAE was used between non-Panjabi boys (two between whites, two between blacks, and two between a white and a black). These marked or implied a variety of improprieties: eating too much and being fat, bumping into a girl in the dinner queue, talking out of turn, refusing to accept rejection from a soccer team, together with one summons to an engagement in which the addressee was due to receive jokey retribution for an earlier offence, and one summons away from an encounter in which the addressee was over-staying. The challenges and accusations encoded in these SAE utterances were often quite bald: for example, **'understand English, don't you understand English'**, **'fat bastard cunt like ___'**, **'shut your mouth'**, **'what you do man'**. But these didn't elicit any retaliation. On one occasion, SAE expressed quite serious irritation, but on three it was followed by laughter (and on another it was clearly playful).

There was no evidence as to whether or not Panjabis also found such uses of SAE entertaining, though most of them occurred well within their earshot. But on the occasions when Panjabis were involved as protagonists, the criticisms encoded in SAE-accented propositions were generally more mitigated: **'are you not there'**, and **'no problem'** between Panjabi boys, **'21 years old'** and **'yeh you got money, you got plenty money'** from black boys to Panjabi girls, and **'this nice'** and **'Eeny will play'** from Panjabi boys to whites. And on a couple of occasions, there was some dramatic retaliation. This was illustrated in extract III.4, and is evident in the following:

Extract III.6

Setting: 1987. Early on during an evening at the youth club, a basket ball game is being arranged. Ian [An M 15 wearing radio-microphone], Salim [Pa M 15], Kazim [Pa M 15], Sally [An F 15], Aziz [Pa M 16], and Raymond [AC M 15] are standing near the counter, talking to a youth worker, Gwen [An F 30+]. 'Eeny' is Ian's nickname. Gwen has just asked Salim if he wants to play.

1 Salim: **ˈNO ˋI AM ˌNOT ˌPLAY ˌBASˌKET BALL ˌOˈKAY** (.)
[no aɪ əm nɑʈ pɭe bɑskɪʈ bɔɭ okɛ]
2 Kazim and others: ((loud laughter for 4.0))
3 Salim: **ˈI ˈAM ˌNOT ˌLIKING ˌTHAT ˌONE ˌˌGAME**
[aɪ əm nɒʈ ɭaɪkɪn ɖeʈ wʌɳ ɡɛəm]
4 : ((laughter for 4.0))
5 Gwen: Eeny, you gonna play?
6 Ian: what (.) yeh (.) I am
7 Sally: Gwen
8 : ( )
9 : ((laughter continuing))
10 Salim: ((laughing)) **ˈEeny ˈwill ˈplay ˈthis** (2.0)
[( ) wɪɭ pɭe ðɪs]
11 Ian: FUCK OFF SAL (1.0) Sal the fucking ((rhyming mild
12 abuse term)) (.) you're gonna use your nose (1.0) I
13 know Sal's going to use his nose to play basketball
14 Salim: **ˌyou ˈare** (ˈ) (1.5)
[ju ɑɽ]
15 Ian: ((quieter, smile voice)) you alright Kaz
16 Kazim: what's goin' on man
17 Ian: nothing man
18 Kazim: come 'ere come close come close keep warm
19 Ian: wha- wha- wha-
20 what eh- they wer- alright how you do Kaz (.) like
21 your hairstyle man (.) we're- we're (gonna) have our
22 test tomorrow
23 Kazim: what on

Salim's initial utterances in lines 1 and 3 were addressed to the youth worker, casting her inquiry as an intrusion in a way that brought the oppositional force of adult-directed SAE quite close to the surface.[4] Gwen made no response to this, but when Salim then used SAE in line 10 to refer to an acceptance that Ian had already given, Ian replied with some jocular abuse (focusing on a physical characteristic that was very well established as an acceptable target – see Extract II.8, Chapter 4.2). Salim's utterance involved no factual misrepresentation of Ian's interest, but having just constructed an adult-adolescent boundary, its effect was to put Ian on the other side. The subsequent interchange between Ian and Kazim (lines 15–23) appears to involve a little bit of work rehabilitating Ian's relationship with Salim's close friendship circle, and as such points to some social tension contained within the abuse exchange. At the same time, there is little in it to suggest that Ian's response to Salim's stylised Asian English was way out of line, or that he was badly mistaken in his interpretation of its critical force.

In contrast to all of the incidents above, in which it marked other people's improprieties, stylised Asian English was also used by speakers to indicate infractions of their own.[5] In this context, SAE was much less a source of interpersonal controversy, though even here, if there was a possibility that blame could spread beyond the speaker, it might be challenged:

Extract III.7

Participants and setting: 1987. Razia [Pa F 15 wearing a radio-mike], Yasmin [Pa F 15] are with one or two friends outside during lunchtime. There are to be no lessons that afternoon (the tutor period normally comes at the end of the school day), but unlike their friends, Razia and Yasmin normally attend an extra-curricular typing class after 4 o'clock. Discussion has turned to this afternoon's activity.

```
1 Anon:  (you) have to come all the way back (1.0) innit
2 Razia:  what have we got next
3      :  tutor
4 Yazim:  ,we 'got 'ty,ping
         [wi  gɒt taɪpɪŋ]
5 Razia:  well 'I'm gonna come 'back 'A:NY`WAY: (1.0)
6      :  mm (1.0)
7 Razia:  I've got a typing (10.0)
```

Yasmin's switch to SAE in line 4 can be seen as a small piece of remedial work, making amends for the fact that her and Razia's line of activity is going to differ from the others'. The move to SAE accentuation seems to both recognise non-conformity *and* to display awareness of a larger set of typifications within which this can be placed. In this way, she can be seen to restore her reputation within the group by showing her regard for (a) the consensus that she thinks is emerging within the conversation, and for (b) the images and values current among the wider adolescent community. Razia's subsequent turn provides support for the view that Yasmin's utterance involves more than neutral provision of the information requested in line 2. If that had been Razia's interpretation, one might have expected 'oh yes' or 'ah that's right'. Instead, Razia's initial 'well' displays non-alignment with the prior turn (cf. Levinson 1983: 307, 334; Heritage 1984: 268, 272), as does her move from inclusive 'we' to differentiating 'I'. Her emphatic 'anyway' then indicates an element of defiant contrariness to the others' expectations (Leech and Svartvik 1975: 99), and in doing so, seems simultaneously to deny that returning is infraction and to distance her from Yasmin's implicit apology.

It is worth now turning to the radically different way in which SAE was used in organised games.

6.4 SAE in structured games

There were about as many instances of SAE in formally structured games as there were in informal peer–peer interaction. These occurred while playing cards, pool, bar football, table tennis, badminton, soccer, tennis and cricket, indoors and outdoors during breaktime at school and in the evenings at the youth club. This also involved about the same number of users, one of whom was black and four of whom were white. Since boys participated in organised games much more frequently, there were only a couple of instances of females using SAE in this context. Here, the person I observed using the code most often was an Anglo (Richard, whose eight uses in this context doubled what I saw anyone else do).

In games, SAE very frequently encoded terms of positive evaluation, most typically in forms like '**very good shot**', '**very good**', '**good shot**', '**shot**', '**shotting**' and also more rarely, with words like '**good hitting**'. This could be delivered in a variety of ways and could follow both good and poor performance: it could be said enthusiastically, ironically, nonsensically or indifferently (with little interest in the game in progress). SAE was also used in commentaries on cricket, soccer or tennis games, improvised by players themselves or by bystanding friends (Aziz [Pa M 13]: '**and Kapil Dev is batting now and Aziz is the wicket keeper for Pakistan . . . oh yes what a ball . . . what a save by the wicket-keeper**'). The role of spectator could merge with that of umpire and scorekeeper (Mohan [In M 15]: **'Jagdish to serve . . . ball please, new balls please . . . yes thirty all'**; Aziz: **'off off, ball this way'**), and players themselves could use SAE to keep the tally, to declare a change in the state of play and to remind others of the appropriate next action:

Extract III.8

Participants and setting: 1987. At the youth club in the evening, Chris [An M 14] is playing badminton doubles with Peter [An M 14, wearing radio-microphone] against Imran [Pa M 15] and Richard [An M 15].

```
1    Chris:  ((to Peter)) what you doin
2    Peter:  PLAYING BADMINTON (.)
3    Chris:  could have fooled me
4       ? :  (                    )
5 Richard:  go on you ser⌈ve
6    Imran:            ⌊(          )
7    Peter:  'ONE ‚NIL
             [vʌŋ  ŋɪl]
8    Imran:  love- love one
```

Extract III.9

Kazim [Pa M 15 wearing radio-microphone], Salim [Pa M 15 wearing r-m], Ranjit [In M 15], Darren [AC M 15], Gurinder [In M 15] and some others are playing blackjack (more commonly known as 'switch').

```
1    Kazim:  put the king down (.)change your cards⌈around
2        :                                         ⌊er there's=
3            =a phone ringin' (2.0)
4    Salim:  'DIA‚MOND
             [ɖhʌmʌ̃ɳɖʰ]
5 Gurinder:  ‚dia‚mond ‚d'you want ‚dia'mond (2.5)
             [ɖæmæ̃ɖə ʤũ  wʌ̃n  ðʌ̃mɔ̃n]
6 Gurinder:  eh (.) I thought I put that⌈down
7        ? :                            ⌊(('cunning' laughter))
8    Ranjit:  [ o he mərɡɛjɑ]
             ((Panj: I'm dead ))
9    Salim:  LAST CARDS
10       ? :  ((rhythmic beating on the table))
11       ? :  let me look let me⌈look
12    Salim:                    ⌊NO GET FUCKED
```

```
13   Ranjit:  go on (.) Kazim (1.0) (that's) [hi::re::]=
                                           ((Panj: diamonds))
14            = ⎡ what you do that for? come on (⎡        )
15   Kazim:  ⎣ go on Sal
16   Salim:                                   ⎣ my go (.) thank
17            you (got a pen)
18   Kazim:  oh you bastard
19      ? :  oh my- ⎡ o::h why the fuck did I do that
20   Salim:         ⎣ oh god
21         :  ((laughs for 4.0))
22   ? : ((counting out cards quietly to self)) (four six eight
23            ten twelve) (2.0)
24 Gurinder:  ˈfi ˈfer ˌteen ˌyou ˌpick ˈup=
              [pĩ pə̃ di:ŋ  jũ   pĩk  ɒ̃p]
25            =           [oe _____ kʊttiɑ̃] (2.0)
                          ((Panj: oh you + (obscenity) + bitch))
26   Ranjit:  go on Kazim
```

In both these extracts, it is clear that games involved dispute, criticism, personal abuse and expressions of surprise and dismay (cf. Ervin-Tripp 1986). It is also plain that some of this was conducted in languages other than vernacular English – in Extract III.9, for example, the use of Panjabi in lines 8, 13, and 25. In Gurinder's Asian English 'fifteen you pick up' (line 24) there is an ineliminable element of criticism of Anon's failure to pick up the right number of cards. But this criticism is closely tied to concern with proper observation of the rules of the game, and it is significant that in ending his turn with personal abuse, he shifts away from SAE (here, into Panjabi). Salim's use of Asian English in line 4 is consistent with this concern for the order of play: a change of suit constitutes an important juncture in the game's organisation, introducing a new set of constraints and possibilities for subsequent turns. Furthermore, in the Asian English that immediately follows, Gurinder emphasises and accepts the new suit without protest or complaint.

There were occasions during games in which SAE was used to swear, taunt or threaten, but these were rare – there were only five out of over 50 observed or taped instances. Furthermore, in three of these cases, the targets were not accepted peer group members (one was addressed to me, another to some peers of Bangladeshi descent and a third was directed at an opposing team from outside the area). This suggested that in games between peers, SAE was relatively 'inhospitable' to the serious or playful expression of personal animosity, and this was matched by the rarity of its use in the pursuit of practical personal advantage. Thus there were only a few instances in which it was used to call for a pass or to discourage a rival from trying to gain access to the play (and again the recipients were Bangladeshi or adult). On a handful of further occasions, personal responsibility for some failure or offence was at issue, but in two, the blame was much more self that other-directed ('**I make fuck up**'; '**I ain't got one of**') and in a third, SAE was used to release the offender from any sense of obligation ('**don't worry I be okay**'). In the remaining, overwhelming majority of uses, Asian English encoded scores, praise, commentary, and guidance on the subsequent actions required by the rules.

From the occasions in which SAE was used to abuse or to try to gain personal advantage, it was clear that involvement in games did not dissolve all sensitivity to ethnic and institutional category memberships,[6] and non-Panjabis still appeared to avoid certain uses – there were no examples of SAE being used by an Anglo or Afro-Caribbean to prompt a Pakistani or Indian peer on the next move, and there were no extended white or black commentaries. However, the announcement of scores constituted a use of SAE that was clearly consequential for any Panjabis playing, and in '**good shot**', non-Panjabis found the only context in which it was legitimate to use SAE to single out an Asian friend.

It is worth stepping back a little in order to summarise these uses of SAE and to compare them with earlier descriptions of its use with adults. In doing so, we can develop the sense in which its use can be seen as a form of ritual action, and make its link with macro-social issues more explicit.

6.5 Summary: SAE to adults, to adolescents and in games

Chapter 3 suggested that in cross-ethnic institutionally asymmetrical interactions, stylised Asian English was used by people in insubordinate positions rather like some kind of probe. Switches to SAE frequently occurred when negotiating participation in an interactional enclosure in which the adult would have some contact, control or influence over the speaker, and symbolically, the code seemed to conjure social knowledge about intergroup relations in a way that promised to destabilise transition. In these contexts, SAE was usually congruent with the speaker's ethnic background and it seemed to enquire: 'if I'm this, how will you respond?'. It claimed an identity and opened up questions about subsequent action. In contrast, most often in informal interaction with peers, SAE worked in the opposite direction: it was first oriented to some attribute or action, and then raised questions about its implications for the identity of the bearer or perpetrator.

Between peers, SAE was more often oriented to the norms of propriety than to the boundaries of upcoming interactional engagement. In this context, it was used to mark or imply a variety of non-conformities, for example in musical taste, dress (Extract III.5), accent, physical shape, physical control, conversational manner, behaviour in public places (Extracts III.1, III.2, III.3), and conduct in male-female relations (e.g. Extract III.4) (to name only some). In focusing on transgressions, SAE here seemed to be involved in the negative definition of social order within the peer group, appearing to defend it from infraction and negligence. Legitimate membership of the peer group seemed more immediately at issue than interactional participation, and SAE had more the character of a judgement than a probe. SAE introduced little of the strategic ambiguity that has been ascribed to its use with white adults. Instead, it was usually the addressee that was aligned with the social typifications evoked by SAE, so that he or she was invited to contemplate relocation to the outer margins of peer group culture. Whereas with adults SAE was most typically used at the outset of a sequence of actions, the sequential position of SAE frequently gave it the force of considered assessment. The pattern illustrated in Extracts III.1, III.2 and III.3 was often repeated: stylised Asian English came at the end of one or more vernacular English turns in which the offence was first noted, so that when it arrived, SAE had the weight of a summary evaluation (see e.g. Extract III.4). When the turns in this sequence were spread across several speakers, then it had the added assurance of collective expression.

In games as in unstructured interactions, there was a lot of variation in the spirit in which SAE was delivered. But whereas informal uses most commonly conjured the *external* boundaries of peer group culture, in games Asian English was overwhelmingly involved in the enunciation of *activity-internal* boundaries, sequences and junctures. Though participants might have temporarily lost their bearings, SAE utterances merely highlighted norms that were assumed to be known and agreed by everyone. Beyond providing a helpful point of joint orientation, the code was also used to praise and affirm the effectiveness of other participants' performance, and rather than warning about infraction, its standard illocutionary force tended towards celebration of a game's norms and ideals. Where before SAE had been a voice of negative sanctioning in unstructured peer–peer interactions, here its sanctioning was positive. In this context, Asian English was styled as the language of magnanimous authority. SAE pronunciation appeared to place the speaker at some remove from the competitors' concentrated struggle for advantage, and in doing so, it emphasised rules and ideals which all players had contracted to, but which their enthusiasm about winning would always make vulnerable. These uses of SAE can be typified by Salim's interjection into a discussion about financial stakes in a game of pool: **'no, you no play for money, you play for love'**.

6.6 Rituals of disorder, differentiation and consensus

There are grounds for regarding SAE as a form of ritual action in all three of these contexts. In games, SAE occurred in forms that were clearly formulaic – **'very good'**, and **'good shot'** – and although elsewhere the semantic meaning of SAE utterances was much more diverse, speakers were engaged in purposeful symbolic evocation, making relevant realms of significance that extended beyond the propositional meaning carried in surface form. Although its interpretation needs to recognise situational differences in emphasis, distance from normal adolescent conduct, capability and/or commitments was a constant characteristic in the imagery that SAE conjured.[7]

SAE can also be seen as ritual action in view of its recurrent orientation to issues of social order. SAE utterances repeatedly stepped outside a commonsense attitude in which social order was taken for granted, and its symbolic connotations of detachment from expected modes of participation in the ordinary run of affairs actually played a central but varied role in this. It focused on social order in three different ways. With adults, speakers' dressed themselves in SAE's symbolic connotations, momentarily disturbing their addressees' expectations about the action to ensue. Here SAE can be seen as an anti-rite, a *destabilising* ritual counterposed to the categories and conduct that participants would normally assume to be operating. This contrasted with critical uses of SAE. In this second context, SAE was clearly oriented to *re-establishing* the norms of adolescent conduct, and in focusing on improprieties, its effect was to situate addressees in the marginal zones that SAE evoked. The function of critical SAE can be described as regulative but *differentiating*. In the third context – games – speakers used SAE to step aside from the competitors' factional interests and tried to channel their conduct towards the rules and ideals entailed in proper participation. In this way, SAE in games can be regarded as regulative and *consensual*.

These three functions – the anti-structural, the differentiating and the consensual – feature in a number of important discussions of ritual. It would be difficult to import any one of these wholesale: some deal fully with ritual symbolism but neglect the details of interaction (e.g. Durkheim [1912] 1975; Douglas 1966, 1968; Turner 1974; Bernstein 1975), while in others these emphases are reversed (Goffman 1967; Brown and Levinson [1978] 1987). In the present context, however, it is worth supplementing this chapter's primarily interactional focus with an interpretation of the crucial role played by larger social and historical factors in the constitution of SAE. These have been referred to with varying degrees of explicitness in the analysis so far, and it is worth drawing them together.

Chapter 2.4 suggested that in its ordinary form as a language spoken naturally by a number of Panjabi adults and Bangladeshi peers, the English of second language learners was intricately connected with migration and social transition. It was also closely involved with questions about access and discrimination in British society, and there was a good deal of ambiguity and variation in adolescent attitudes to language learner English. Though not without some feelings of remorse, adolescents were largely antagonistic when they encountered it among their peers, while with adults at home, Asian English was viewed sympathetically, sometimes with a sense of political solidarity. So macro-social and historical circumstances (a) made Asian second language learner English a language of transition and gave it controversial political significance, and (b) led a large number of local adolescents to feel that this variety was both close to them but very different from their own vernacular.

Anthropologists have often interpreted collective rituals as attempts to resolve deep social anomalies and contradictions (e.g. Turner 1969; Sperber 1975), and according to Douglas, 'the more personal and intimate the source of ritual symbolism, the more telling its message. The more the symbol is drawn from the common fund of human experience, the more wide and certain its reception' (1966: 114). Even though much of the preceding analysis has concentrated on the ways in which SAE mapped into small-scale interactional concerns, there are good grounds for regarding the data as broadly congruent with these macroscopic accounts. In the use of SAE by fluent English-speaking adolescents of Asian descent, the unstable but insistent evaluative charge attached to Asian second language learner English was organised and distributed into three broadly distinct arenas, so that in one it became positive, in another it became negative, and in a third, ambiguity became a strategic resource in the management of asymmetrical institutional relations. In contrast to the uncertain and contradictory views about 'Asian' English as a natural language that informants expressed in interviews, as a ritual symbol there was a high level of assurance and consistency in its use by adolescents.

The intimacy of this code's association with migration and race politics was also reflected in systematic patterns of mitigation and avoidance in its use by black and white adolescents. These indicated that while Asians figured foremost in the 'sociolinguistic horizons' conjured by SAE, they did not stand alone there. Monolingual speakers of English were sensitive to the possibility that if they used SAE, they too could be implicated, in dominant positions of dubious legitimacy. Or at least, so it seemed with monolingual friends in the adult–adolescent and unstructured peer–peer interactions. In games, there seemed to be a difference – after all, it was a white boy that used SAE '**good shot**' most often.

6.7 Games

The special context provided by games needs further consideration. Indeed, the alteration in SAE that occurred within games extended beyond the loosening of constraints upon white crossing. Logically, SAE could have been as easily used to blame and criticise inside games as out, and yet in the way it was actually employed, it is difficult to see that the code's more general connotations of non-competence had any immediate relevance. Similarly, whereas its use can be seen as either contesting racism in adult–adolescent interaction, or as actually doing it when addressed at Bangladeshis, it is difficult to fit race conflict anywhere into the interpretation of SAE in games. Perhaps we ought not be too surprised in view of Hewitt's description of games as a 'charmed circle' in which whites were more able to make use of Creole (1986: 178). But since formal games played an important role in both Creole and Panjabi crossing among peers, it is worth briefly saying a little more about some of their distinctive features.

Games and play can be seen as set apart from routine everyday activity (cf. e.g. Huitzinga 1955), and as involving a simplification of social reality. Play is 'predicated upon a reduction in available types of roles and relationships . . . and . . . actors [can] 'forget' their social selves' (Handelman 1977: 185);

> a game's rules dismiss as irrelevant most of the 'noise' which makes up social reality, the multiform stimuli which impinge on our consciousness. We have to abide by a limited set of norms. Then we are motivated to do well by the game's intrinsic structure, often to do better than others who subscribe to the same rules. Our minds and our will are thus disencumbered from irrelevances and sharply focussed in certain known directions. (Turner 1974: 56)

At the same time, play and games can also be seen as 'an interpretation of society' (Sutton-Smith 1982: 70). This is obvious in various forms of make-believe play, but it can also be seen in games that are not obviously imitative or exploratory. Tag games, for example, can be seen as dramatising fundamental issues to do with boundaries, danger, approach and avoidance (Sutton-Smith 1971: 57), and in Sutton-Smith's view,

> play is not a preparation for life. It is life itself. It is life's interpretation in action, a making of life a meaningful event often in a largely symbolic manner. Play with peers allows for a buffered orientation to experience within which it can be restructured to afford more flexible control and excitement with others. (1982: 75)

The issue of continuity between everyday reality and play is somewhat controversial (Goodwin 1985: 315), and there is also likely to be a great deal of empirical variation in exactly which elements of ordinary life are bracketed out, and which are 'restructured to afford more flexible control'. But the data on SAE do indeed suggest that while its symbolic connotations of distance from the central flow of adolescent activity remained intact, the 'buffering' in games allowed more interethnic crossing and held in check the code's more negative and conflictual symbolic resonances.

The relationship between play and everyday reality, and the manner and extent to which games provided a privileged context for cross-ethnic language use, will be addressed more fully in the next chapter, concentrating on white and black uses of Panjabi.

Notes

1. In addition to criticism and games, SAE was occasionally used in greetings. Males and females appeared to be about equally involved in using SAE in approach work, though it was sometimes hard to tell from the radio-microphone data. One (or perhaps two) of these incidents involved interlocutors with different linguistic backgrounds, but most occurred in interaction between Panjabis.

   Interracially, there was one occasion where an Anglo boy addressed an SAE 'hello' towards a Bangladeshi peer [M], and this got an unamused 'fuck off' in return. After the greeter's (Anglo) friend had replied in kind, there was no further engagement. Elsewhere though, there was no evidence that the use of SAE in greetings was read as any kind of slight. It was used playfully (coming up and asking **'do you want to buy a Poppy'** in the middle of July [memorial poppies are normally sold in November]); on one occasion it was used to say hello at the end of a very extended period in which the participants had already been accessibly co-present to each other (cf. Goffman 1971: 62–94); and it was also used in greetings made in passing. Arguably, SAE was appropriate to greetings that were oddly placed or that did not lead into full engagement because of its connotations of limited social competence and/or communicative inability (its politeness associations also fitted). But at least in passing greetings, it certainly didn't appear to be well-established as a conventional signal that the user wasn't available for a full encounter.

Extract III.10

Participants: Kiron [In F 15 wearing radio-microphone], Pritam [In F 15], Anon [In F], others

Setting: Kiron and Pritam are walking down the corridor, when a friend/acquaintance approaches [In F].

((Speakers that K and P are walking past:))

      : I'm gonna kill him
      : you are (   )
      : Dev (give me the yoyo)
      : (I promise I'll give it to ya)
      : (   )
        (4.0)

Kiron: **hello**
        ['he‚ ‚ɔ:]
Anon: ((from afar)) (have you found 'im) (.)
Kiron: what?
Anon: ((still from afar)) where you goin'
Kiron: UPSTAIRS ((quietly:)) up your ass (2.0)
        ((whispers:)) is she coming? (2.0)
Pritam: ((l.)) don't you like her?
Kiron: no
Pritam: don't ya? (.) no? (.) why not? ((smile voice:)) same
        reason as I don't ((laughs))
Kiron: ((laughs)) I think she's a bitch (.) that's to put it mildly (.)

In this incident, the recipient of the greeting tried to start more of a conversation than the greeter had in mind. Indeed, though no offence was taken from the form of Kiron's greeting, it is difficult to be confident that none was intended in the light of K and P's subsequent character evaluation.

2.   cf. Goffman 1971: ch. 3, 1963: ch. 7. In both these respects, and in the failure to accord them 'civil inattention', the recipients were being treated as what Goffman calls 'non-persons' (e.g. 1963: 84).

3.   There was some comparability with the way in which on one occasion, during a period in which a group of friends were looking for something to do, an Indian boy started to interact with some wasps in a way that generated considerable entertainment among his companions. He talked to them in stylised Asian English (**'bloody kill the lot of you'**) and addressed them as 'untouchables' ([tʃuɾe]).

4.   Although technically his utterance in line 3 constitutes a remedial account (Goffman 1971: 109–13), the loudness with which he gives this account is inconsistent with any display of the hesitation that frequently mitigates dispreferred declinations (Levinson 1983: 334), as is his proffered explanation in terms of will rather than ability (Heritage 1984: 271). Salim did not have a good relationship with the youth club staff and was later temporarily banned from attending.

5.   This was evident on five occasions – twice by Panjabi girls in co-
     ethnic, same-sex interactions, once by an Anglo/Afro-Caribbean girl
     in cross-ethnic same-sex conversation, and twice by a Bangladeshi
     adolescent working alone on a computer. This was one example:

Extract III.11

Mahmud [Ba M 15, wearing radio-microphone] is working on a
programme in the computer room during lunch-time, when the
text on his VDU starts to slide downwards. There is a teacher in
the background. On later listening to a recording of this,
Mahmud glossed the switch in lines 1 and 4 by saying that he was
trying to act kind of silly, using an second language learner
accent.

```
1 Mahmud:   (18.0) eh? (3.0) ,what ,is 'this? (2.0) eh? (2.0)
                   [wɒd iz ðis]
2           ((exclamatives said with rapidly rising pitch level:))
3           eh? (9.0) uh! (3.0) help! (3.0) huh? (2.0)
4           "what "is "this (7.0)
                   [wɒt iz ðis]
5           Miss what's 'appening (1.5). what's 'appening here?
6 Teacher:  (          ) (.) is this your (1.5)
7 Mahmud: that's my programme
```

This use of SAE falls within the Goffman's description of corrective
self-talk, in which 'we kibitz our own undertakings . . . speak to ourselves judgmentally about our own doings (offering words of
encouragement or blame in an editorial voice that seems to be that of
an overseer more than ourselves)' (1981: 79).

6.   Once during a large game of cricket at the youth club, Richard's [An
     M 15] use of SAE (and Panjabi) drew critical attention from an older
     Pakistani adolescent (so that Raymond [AC M 15] felt it appropriate
     to explain that he had 'a frog in his throat'). But the person con-
     cerned came from another school and only infrequently attended the
     youth club: there was no evidence of Richard's gaming SAE being
     censured by the Panjabis with whom he had regular contact.

7.   With the stylised, secondary representation of particular language
     varieties, it may sometimes seem appropriate to look for some fairly
     direct correspondence with the speakers who make ordinary,
     straight use of it (see, e.g., Basso 1979). One might hypothesise, for
     example, that in games the use of stylised Asian English reflected
     adolescent perceptions of ESL among Panjabi adults. But there are a
     number of difficulties with that kind of explanation of the origins of
     SAE's symbolic force. If in games, young people were trying to copy

familiar adults (or perhaps Indian and Pakistani sports players and commentators), one would expect the use of Asian English to be much less restricted in the ways in which it was actually used. In addition, what of Panjabi adults who spoke vernacular or Standard English (as did a great many of the South Asians most commonly appearing on the broadcast media), and why not use Panjabi, Hindi or Urdu in its place? Furthermore, in interracial arenas, the accented Indian English of adults was occasionally the subject of disrespectful comment, so it would be difficult to argue that SAE's game role as the voice of positive sanctioning reflected a universal solidarity with adult speakers of ESL. Retrospectively, participants might be able to gloss the stylised use of Asian English as a copy of some specific person (though in fact this seldom happened), but this can not account for the particular forms and moments in which it actually occurred.

7 Panjabi (ii): playground agonism, 'language learning', and the liminal

This chapter shares Chapter 6's concern with the different ways in which relatively stable speaker characteristics either facilitated or inhibited out-group language use. But in contrast to stylised Asian English (SAE), which from a structural point of view involved young people in only rather minor phonological and grammatical adaptations of vernacular speech, Panjabi was a very different language for black and white adolescents. As second language learners, they often had to rely on the structure of specific recreational activities to help them overcome formal linguistic distance, and this is an issue that figures prominently in the interactional analyses contained in this chapter.

After giving an indication of how much Panjabi was actually known by adolescents of Anglo and Afro-Caribbean descent, the chapter begins describing chasing games, jocular abuse and their special value for crossing into a different language. A picture of uninhibited playground culture emerges, which subsequent sections then start to qualify. Rather less entertaining abuse exchanges are described, and so are occasions when crossers played safe and just spoke Panjabi to themselves. Longitudinal evidence is drawn in to show the way in which crossing got milder as youngsters grew up, and agonistic Panjabi's relative infrequency among white and black *girls* is noted. After that, the chapter summarises the factors influencing the risk associated with Panjabi crossing, and sets its interactional descriptions next to more macro-social discussion of conflict rituals and joking relationships. It ends with a general proposal about the connection between language crossing and Victor Turner's notion of 'liminality' –

interactive spaces where the dominant norms of everyday life are temporarily jeopardised or suspended. This theoretical connection is then further considered in Chapter 8.

7.1 Panjabi in the multiracial playground repertoire

It would be very difficult to provide a definitive inventory of the Panjabi known by particular black and white adolescents, since this was a learner variety, there was a good deal of ephemeral invention and nonsensical improvisation, and other than asking black and white monolinguals for the meaning of the Panjabi that had occurred in their recordings, no language tests were carried out. Nevertheless, accepting that few individuals might know all or even most of them, a collective core of about 20–30 Panjabi words and phrases can be identified in the productive repertoire of non-Panjabis in this peer group. Another 10 or so could be located in some kind of zone of proximal development.[1]

Over the period 1984–7, this linguistic stock remained fairly static. It comprised a selective if rather predictable cocktail of nouns referring to parts of the body, bodily functions, animals, ethnic groups and kin; first and second person singular possessive pronouns; adjectives describing personal physical attributes; locative and possessive postpositions; a few numerals; and verbs of physical violence or ingestion. These could be combined in short phrases or sentences seldom exceeding four words, or alternatively a single word could be used in utterances in English. There was a good deal of dependence on one or two phrasal formulae, [u] was used quite often as a general noun suffix, and a 'Panjabi effect' was sometimes achieved by rounding utterances off with [ha] or [e:]. There were about three or four grammatical constructions which a few individuals might have productive knowledge of: noun + gender inflection, which might be extended to nominalised adjective + gender inflection ([kʊtta– kʊtti] 'dog – bitch'; [kaɭa – kaɭi] 'black man or boy – black woman or girl'); possessive pronoun + noun ([meri ____ – teri ____]); more rarely, adjective (unmarked for gender, number or case) + noun ([vəɖɖa nak]); and perhaps noun + vocative suffix ([-a]). Terms of abuse were also produced through Panjabi-English compounding ('[lʊllə]-head', '[lʊllə]-nose', '[phʊddi]-pussy' and so forth).

These forms of Panjabi showed a good deal of discontinuity

with bilingual adult uses of the language. For bilinguals, this kind of Panjabi needed no special cultivation or expertise. Deviant and temporary forms emerged in its use by bilinguals, white innovations could be accepted into multiracial peer group usage (cf. e.g. Extract II.15 and the discussion of it in Chapter 5.2), and there were words in circulation which nobody could explain the meaning of ([kʊs kʊs]). As one bilingual informant put it when asked what [sɑlɑ] meant: 'I don't know . . . it's just a word, it's rude . . . I don't to go up to my parents and say what does [sɑlɑ] mean . . . (get) a clip round the ear!'

7.2 Playground Panjabi in games

The data from 1984 demonstrates that for white and black crossers, the linguistic resources drawn from Panjabi stretched back to pre- or early adolescence. Many of the referents lexicalised in Panjabi fitted easily with themes and concerns traditional in schoolchildren's lore (Opie and Opie 1959), and the language added to what was already a substantial stock of possibilities in English (indeed Creole also contributed to this – see also Hewitt 1986: 129–30). Panjabi's place within playground culture was further evidenced in the kinds of activity in which it occurred. Here is one example:

Extract III.12

Participants: Terry [12 An M; wearing radio-microphone], Imran [12 Pa M]
Setting: 1984. Breaktime outside. Terry and Imran are participating in a game of off-ground tig (in which being off ground gives the chasee immunity). Terry starts off as 'It', and is giving chase to Imran.

```
1 Terry:  ((laughs)) [fʊddu::] it ain't off ground (3.0)
          ((L2 Panjabi: idiot ))
2         ((halting, laughing and breathless)) that ain't off
3         ground
4 Imran:  ((from afar)) (yes) (1.0) that is ⌈(I'm off ground)
5 Terry:                                    ⌊YEH YOU WASN'T
6         THERE when I tugged yer
7 Imran:  Yes I was Terry (.) (I'm off ground)
8 Terry:  you have to take it
```

```
 9 Imran:  I'm off ground (1.0)
10 Terry:  you have to take the beetle
11 Imran:  (I'm not takin it)
12 Terry:  TAKE IT
13 Imran:  (not) takin it (1.0)
14 Terry:  you're it then=
15 Imran:  =you're it (1.0)
16 Terry:  [ bʌʃtɑː  ] (2.0)
           ((l.))
           (('Italian':bastard))
17 Imran:  [pʊtã (1.0) ɹɑːs ](2.0)
           (('Italian'   Creole))
18 Imran:  ((shouting and running off)) ['pʊtã `nã `tere `made ˌʈəʈʈe]
                               (('Italian' and Panjabi in an
                               Italian accent:your mum's balls))
19 Terry:  ((gives chase)) (10.0) YE::H GOT YA:: (.)
20 Imran:  ((from a little way off)) no (2.0)
21 Terry:  ((chanting)) ['baː`re ˌmaˌre e `gənˌda]
                        ff
           ((L2P:   ?    ?   is dirty))
22 Imran:  ((no response))
((the game continues: Terry stays as 'it' for the time being))
```

Terry later reported that [bʌʃtɑː] in line 16 meant 'bastard' in Italian; Imran's response took this up, and the second part (line 18) was emphatically identified by the translators as being Panjabi pronounced as Italian ('definitely . . . even I mess about at home, saying Panjabi in an Italian accent'). A little later, Terry responded to this with Panjabi, chanted with a taunting tune traditional among schoolchildren (line 21). In part, these Panjabi (and 'Italian') utterances were serving as goads, attempts to taunt the person who is 'It' into giving chase (Opie and Opie 1959: 63). Such uses were also evidenced among black, white and Panjabi children, and the conventionality of this function may be particularly important in this incident, where Terry was unable to get anyone to accept that he had successfully tagged them. The roles of chaser and chased were in dispute, and it looks as though in line 21 Terry was using a Panjabi taunt to try to affirm that he was now a potential chasee.

Out-group uses of Panjabi varied in the extent to which they achieved the effects they sought. But this extract usefully illustrates several other common features of multiracial playground Panjabi. In terms of linguistic structure, its use by Indian and

Pakistani bilinguals could be highly non-standard, as well as being propositionally or semantically nonsensical (line 18). Furthermore, for white and black monolinguals, Panjabi utterances were not necessarily set within any firm or enduring understanding of denotational word meaning. When this incident was replayed to Terry in 1987 (where he retained a reputation for knowing more Panjabi than most), he recognised episodes of this kind but either mistranslated what he had said or said he didn't know. Up to a point, the partiality of monolingual knowledge of Panjabi and latitude in bilingual use could be mutually reinforcing, and the episode itself illustrates something of playground Panjabi's receptiveness to improvisation. As the exchange moved from English and Italian, to Italian and Panjabi (with Creole), to English and Panjabi, both boys took part of their cue from the other's utterance but deployed alternative admixtures, as if to cap the other's.

In 1984, chasing games were a common context for interracial Panjabi, and there are a number of ways in which they helped to circumvent the obstacles that one might expect both limited linguistic proficiency and ethnic difference to produce.

In the first instance, it is especially easy to see how the players could 'forget their social selves' in games of tag. Specifically as 'It', the chaser takes on a non-human identity, and as a result, the relationship between chaser and chasees officially ceases to be interpersonal (in the rules of the game at least). In this way, the game itself permits the players to abandon ordinary politeness. Secondly, like a lot of other games, tag provides a pattern for the development of action which is largely language independent. In ordinary conversation, participants normally attend to the propositional meaning of an utterance and intricate conditioning exists between one turn and the next. Plainly, in the central stages of a game like tag, there are only the weakest traces of this. An addressee need only attend to the broad illocutionary force of an initiating turn, and it is the game rather than the utterance which provides a simple but adequate choice of nexts (chase or ignore – or make noises back). Thirdly, at least in principle, winners and losers are decided on the basis of non-verbal attributes such as speed and agility, and so the disadvantages associated with incompetent linguistic performance are further decreased. Fourthly, there is no great shame if your endeavours in another language are ignored. The game's central excitement lies in the chase itself, but with only one 'It' and any number of people wanting to be chased, everyone must have some experience of goading without getting a response. Lastly, the game provides opportunities for abuse that are clearly *unrelated* to any real deviation or infraction (mums, for example, don't have balls).

7.3 Jocular abuse

Many of the characteristics of tag that facilitated black and white ventures into Panjabi also operated in ball, card and table games. Panjabi abuse could up the stakes, and again, whether or not one was linguistically proficient in the language, winning in the terms set by the game could provide a satisfactory form of retaliation. Panjabi abuse was used in provocative invitations to compete, and it also occurred in playful challenges apparently designed to initiate some spontaneous playground chasing. Even so, not all other-ethnic Panjabi was tied to physical activity and neither was it always confined to games. In the following extract, it was used in entirely verbal competition:

Extract III.13

Participants: Raymond [13 An/AC M; wearing radio-microphone], Ian [12 An M], Hanif [12 Bangladeshi M], others
Setting: 1984. Coming out of lessons into the playground at break. Ian and Ray are best friends. Stevie Wonder is the singer whose song 'I just called to say I love you' was very famous. Ray has a bad foot – cf. line 17.

```
 1   Ray:  IA::N::
 2  Hanif: (          )
 3    Ian: ((from afar)) RAY THE COO:L RAY THE COO:L
 4  Hanif: yeh Stevie Wonder YAAA ((laughs loudly))
 5   Ray:       ⌈ it's worser than that
 6    Ian: ((singing)) ⌊I just called to say
 7  Hanif: ha (let's) sing (him) a song
 8    Ian: I hate you
 9  Hanif: ((loud laughs))
10   Anon: ((coming up)) (   ) are you running for the school (.)
11   Ray:  huh ⌐
12   Anon: are ⌈ you running for the school=
13   Ray:      ⌊no
```

```
14  Anon:  =⌈I am
15  Ian:    ⌊he couldnt run for th-he couldnt ⌈run for the school
16  Ray:                                      ⌊SHUT UP =
17  Ray:  =I couldn-I don wan- ⌈I can't run anyway
18  Hanif:                      ⌊right we're wasting our ⌈time=
19  Ian:                                                ⌊I did=
20  Hanif:  =⌈come on      (we're) wasting our time=
21  Ian:     ⌊you come last (    )
22  Hanif:    =⌈[mʌmʌmʌ:]
23  Anon:      ⌊I came second
24  Ian:  ((singing)) I just called to say ⌈I got     a big=
25  Ray:                                    ⌊I hate youl
26  Ian:  =[lʊɬɑ :]
             ((L2P: willy))
27  Hanif and others: ((loud laughter))
28  Ray:  ((continuing Ian's song)) so's Ian Hinks (1.5)
29        ((Ray laughs)) no you haven't you got a tiny one (.)
30        you've only got (a big arse)
```

In this exchange, Ian engaged in jocular abuse against Ray and
did so most effectively in lines 24 and 26. There he used a Panjabi
word to change his initial corruption of Stevie Wonder's song (line
8), he upstaged Ray's effort to preempt him (line 25), he elicited
an enthusiastic response from third parties (line 27) and he left
Ray 'blowing' back in a way that Ray himself evidently judged to
be rather weak (lines 28 and 29).

In certain respects this and other comparable exchanges fit with
Labov's account of 'ritual insults' (1972b). Any attempt, however,
to apply Labov's analysis to these data immediately runs into a
major obstacle. According to Labov, an effective 'sound' takes
what the opponent has said and 'tops' it with an insult that is even
more extravagant in its bizarre obscenity. So if one speaker says
'your father got buck teeth', a winning reply might be 'your father
got teeth growing out of his behind!' (1972b: 332). Among the
African American adolescents described by Labov, success in jocular abuse crucially relied on skill in manipulating propositional
meaning. In my own fieldwork setting, however, as I have already
pointed out, black and white adolescents had only a tenuous grasp
on the meaning of Panjabi words and almost no competence in
Panjabi grammar. How was it then, that Panjabi could figure in
playful insult exchanges?

One method was to just use single Panjabi words that were denotationally understood, as Ian did Extract III.13. Song parody is itself traditionally celebrated among schoolchildren (Opie and Opie 1959: ch. 6) and bilinguals themselves inserted comic Panjabi lines into popular tunes:

Andrew [11 AC M]: ((singing)) By the rivers of
Mohan [12 In M]: ((continuing)) Babylon
                  where Andrew [sɑrɑ pəd mɑrɪɑ hɛ]
                 ((Panjabi: is doing a dirty fart)).

But play with the formal structures of language extended beyond this, and Panjabi grammar and semantics sometimes played a much more subsidiary role in white and black kids' insult sequences. Instead rhythm, pitch movement, segmental realisation and semantically opaque particles could serve as the critical materials:

Extract III.14

Participants: Imran [Pa M 12; wearing radio-microphone], Terry [An M 12], Richard [An M 15], Chris [Greek M 15]
Setting: 1984. Breaktime. The four boys are hiding in the toilets under the youth club. In lines 4, 6, 10 and 12, Imran is looking out at the person who is 'It'. A short abuse exchange is developing between Richard and Chris (the quality of the recording is poor at certain points).

```
 1    Chris: (        ) bastard
 2  Richard: (             )
 3    Terry: ((laughs))
 4    Imran: look there ⎡he goes (1.5)
 5    Chris: ((to Rich.)) ⎣(           )
 6    Imran: ⎡he's looking at us
 7  Richard: ⎣(              ?custard?)
 8    Chris: you're the son of a bloody ⎡(      )
 9                                       ⎢((f))
10    Imran:                            ⎣there he go
11  Richard: ((to Chris)) (   ?fry ya)
12    Imran: (   ) lookin at the youth club (1.5)
13  Richard: ((singing voice)) [ˌsere ˌ(maᵇə) ˌmaːɖə "gʊtʃə ˋhã::= ]
              ((L2 Panjabi:   ?    ? ⎡mother's knickers))
14    Imran: ((talking)) = [ˌterə ˌmãdə "kə⎢tʃiː: ]
              ((your mum's kn⎢ickers))
15  Richard: ((talking)) ⎣[ˌt( ) ˌmadə ˌgʊˋtʃiə ˋha]=
```

16 Richard: ≡ 'suckin a 'pussy [„ha]
17   Terry: ⌈ ((laughs))
18   Chris: │ shut up
19   Imran: ⌊((laughs))

Although Richard certainly knew what [teri mɑdi kətʃi] meant, this sequence was limited in terms of its propositional development. Entertaining and effective abuse was produced by other means.

In line 13, Richard started off in a singing voice, and he set up a basic metrical pattern consisting of two-syllable measures with a stress on the first syllable (cf. Leech 1969: ch. 7). In the first three measures of this pentameter line, his pitch stayed quite low, but on [gʊtʃə] at the start of the fourth it stepped quite abruptly upwards (perhaps in imitation of pitch movement in Panjabi (Gumperz 1982a)). [hɑ::] was held much longer than any of the other words in this turn/line, and it accompanied a slight fall. Imran responded immediately with a three-stress line, but he began in a speaking voice. He started at a fairly low pitch and repeated Richard's 'trochaic' rhythm in the first two measures. Like Richard, his pitch level on [kətʃi::] was also much higher than it was at the start of his turn, but he now stressed the second syllable and instead of adopting an extended [hɑ] together with a slight fall, he lengthened the [i] of [kətʃi] and kept it at a high level.

Just before he finished, Richard recommenced with a four-stress line, this time following Imran's use of a speaking rather than singing voice. Also following the model provided by Imran, he cut out the rather indistinct and unnecessary second measure of his first line (ʔ[mɑᵇə]ʔ) and gave more emphasis to the second syllable of [gʊtʃiə], replacing his previous [ə] with [iə]. But he did not extend this second syllable as Imran did. Instead he completed the line with a reassertion of his former [hɑ], this time introducing the first fall rise. Maintaining a fairly high pitch level, he now switched to English, produced another phrase from the playground repertoire, and introduced the only three-syllable measure in the exchange. But the penultimate measure reestablished the two-syllable structure with which he began; in the last, the pitch moved back towards the starting level and [hɑ] comes as a final refrain which reasserted the rhyme's identity within playground Panjabi.

The symmetry within this collaborative exchange was enhanced by Richard's return in line 16 to the trimeter structure introduced by Imran in line 14. In all, this seemed a winning performance: Richard's switch into Panjabi, Imran's support for this move, and the pleasure it evidently gave to the uncommitted audience left Chris unable to compete (lines 17–19).

In fact, Panjabi was suited to interethnic jocular abuse precisely because of its status as a *language learner variety* among white and black adolescents.

This might seem surprising in view of the value set on linguistic skill in jocular insult exchanges, but since most young people of Caribbean and Anglo descent were expected to be almost completely ignorant of the language, even a little knowledge could be lauded as exceptional ability. The actual criteria used to judge accomplished performance were very different from those operated by Labov's informants, but linguistic ability per se was still at a premium.

Ignorance of propositional meaning and a pressing dependence on the linguistic models just recently provided by bilinguals also meant that rudimentary utterances in Panjabi as a second language (P2L) were actually well fitted to turn structure in joking abuse sequences. Goodwin and Goodwin suggest that in 'sounding',

> The recipient of an initial ritual insult ... must use the scene described in the prior speaker's talk to produce a second description that turns the initial insult on its head and is even more outrageous. As noted by Goffman (1971: 179), 'the structure of these devices establishes a move that is designed to serve as a comparison base for another's effort, his object being to exceed the prior effort in elegance or wit' ... The point is not to negate or contradict prior talk but to show that second speaker can take a feature of first speaker's talk ... and transform it (1987: 223–4)

This coincides with Labov's account, who also states that

> since ritual insults are not intended as factual statements, they are not to be denied ... the fundamental opposition between ritual insults and personal insults emerges. The appropriate responses are quite different: a personal insult is answered by a denial, excuse, or mitigation, whereas a sound or ritual insult is answered by longer

sequences, since a sound and its response are essentially the same kind of thing, and a response calls for a further response ... The denials that are normal and automatic for personal insults are unthinkable with sounds. (1972b: 332, 335)

In the first instance, limitations in their productive capability meant that Anglo and Afro-Caribbean users of Panjabi often had no option but to repeat quite a few features of first speaker's talk – the imitation of proficient speakers has long been noted as a strategy in L1–L2 discourse (e.g. Hatch 1978: 409ff). But though this might bear some superficial ressemblance to the 'meaningless' classroom pattern practice that has been criticised in the theories of second language pedagogy, in the context of an insult exchange even fairly exact surface structure imitation involves a change of meaning – the referent shifts with the alteration of speaker ('you cheat' 'YOU cheat' – cf. Goodwin and Goodwin 1987: 212, 218). So in principle, provided they could hold what they heard in their short-term memory, even the least competent speaker could participate with some degree of success in Panjabi reciprocal abuse. At the same time, there was scope for more proficient crossers to substitute novel elements into the format that they had adopted from the insult addressed to them, and in this way their performance moved closer to the basic pattern in more elaborate joking exchanges, in which the aim is to exceed the prior speaker (see also, e.g. Broughton et al. 1978: 77–82 on 'substitution drills' in foreign language pedagogy).

Secondly, since white and black crossers often had only a shaky grasp of the propositional meaning of what was being said to them, it was hard for them to respond effectively with the denial, excuse or mitigation that would cast the insult exchange as personal. Their status as non-proficient second language learners, who often did not even properly understand what they themselves were saying, often suspended consideration of truth or falsity and preserved insults safely in the domain of play.

Admittedly, the limited proficiency of white and black adolescents did generally prevent jocular abuse from taking the rapid, sustained and escalating form described by Labov. But it brought with it entertaining interactional possibilities of its own.

Dependence on the linguistic models provided by expert speakers combined with limited semantic competence to provide ideal terrain for the development of self-incrimination routines (Opie and Opie 1959). Here mirthful Panjabis tried to trap monolinguals into swearing at themselves by pretending to teach them rude words and phrases that they could subsequently use on others ('say it to him [meri mãdi _____]' ((my mum's _____)); 'say [mɛ̃] Hazel [de dədde tʃʊgɛɑ]' ((I sucked Hazel's breasts)); 'say [mɛ̃ ʈəʈi khɑndɑ]' ((I eat shit)); 'no! that means 'my mum's cock'!'). Alternatively, they could be invited to respond to compromising questions ('[tu lɔrə di bʊn mɑregɑ]?' ((do you want to bum Laura)) 'no, I don't think so . . . that means 'are you gonna make her pregnant'!'). According to informant reports, one strategy available to the monolingual recipients of uncomprehended Panjabi abuse was to consult a bilingual ally. The relationship that this entailed was commonly described in pupil–teacher terms, and in fact abuse exchanges sometimes spread beyond the principal antagonists, as black or white participants turned to their own Panjabi specialists ('my friend, you know, he swears in Panjabi to English girls, and they go and ask an Indian boy they know, and he tells them and tells them other words and they come and say it to us' – cf. e.g. lines 18–20 of Extract II.8, Chapter 4.2). In this way, abuse exchanges could assume something of a team character. At the same time, as the web of participants expanded, so could the play's complexity, along with the scope for double-dealing: 'like Ishfaq tells . . . you know Alan Timms, if Alan Timms says 'teach me some dirty words', Ishfaq makes him say swear words to himself ((laughs)), so he's saying it to hims . . . he goes up to Asif and he says it and Asif starts laughing'.

In the picture that emerged from informant reports, non-Panjabis were not necessarily always in the worst position in cross-ethnic abuse:[2]

Extract III.15

Participants and setting: 1987 interview. Khalil [15 Ba M], Mahmud [15 Ba M], BR. [Simple transcription]

    BR: what they [Panjabi kids] wouldn't mind if you said
 Khalil: something to them, swear, cos they know I don't know
       what it means
    BR: you don't know what 'sala kutta' means
 Khalil: yeh I know what it means, but

> Mahmud: they might think you don't
> Khalil: they think that you don't know what it means, that
> you've just heard it from someone

Indeed, the dependency of white and black youngsters introduced a further twist, opening opportunities for passing culpability back to other sources:

Extract III.16

Participants and setting: 1987 interview. Anita [15 In F], Pearl [15 In F], BR. [Simple transcription]

> Anita: . . . you always get Ricardo [Italian M] or somebody com-
> ing up to you and saying um . . . like last time, he come up
> to me and he says 'Harbinder says _____'
> Pearl: what does that mean?
> Anita: ((laughs))
> BR: translate for her after
> Anita: I'll tell you later alright ((laughs))
> Pearl: ((laughs))
> Anita: well any
> BR: he came up to you and said that
> Anita: yeh anyway he said that, the reason why he said that was
> because he was trying to be um . . . I don't know what he
> was trying to be but he wanted to . . . say something to me
> that was out of the . . . out of the usual ennit, he wanted to
> be different, he wanted to say something to me that was . . .
> and he expected me to say something to say back to Harbie,
> and because he sort of interprets like that, carries messages,
> he learns the language quicker . . . 'cos I'll probably tell him
> to say something to Harbie, and he'll probably catch up
> (   ) innit
> Pearl: ((laughs))
> BR: so okay, Harbie, why didn't Harbie come and say it to you
> directly
> Anita: I don't think Harbie actually said it to me, I think right, he
> must have asked Harbie 'how do you say this word in
> Indian?', Harbie told him and he came and said it to me

More generally, responses to Panjabi crossing initiatives were often positive, and Indian and Pakistani adolescents themselves appeared to enjoy the licence generated by the participation of second language learners. There were a number of occasions when they repeated or elaborated the insults initiated by non-Panjabis, and often in doing so, they preserved the deviant but innoculating surface forms unintentionally produced by black and white peers (cf Parkin 1980:60).[3]

7.4 Not-so-jocular abuse

So far then, we have looked at Panjabi crossing in games and in jocular abuse and we have seen how each of these provided structures and possibilities that fitted well with the requirements of people who had only limited proficiency in the language. The responses of its inheritors have also been described as positive. This was not always the case, however, and a closer look makes it necessary to modify the impression of relatively unconstrained language sharing that we derived from interview discussions (Chapter 2.2). It is now worth considering a variety of ways in which licence to use Panjabi could be qualified:

Extract III.17

Participants: Conrad [15 AC M; wearing radio-microphone], Sat [15 In M], Pete [15 In M], Surjit [15 In M], others
Setting: 1987. A game of black jack during dinner time

```
 1    Pete:   go on (.) GO ON
 2  Conrad:   [wæ:æ:ʔ]- ⌐ wait a minute- lo- oo- =
 3   ?Sat:             ⌊you guys are fucking slow man
 4  Conrad:   = ⌐ who's go is it my go
 5    Pete:     ⌊it's his go right (.)
 6     ? :    it's his go you [phʊddu]
 7  Conrad:   ((smile voice)) it's my: go (.) [phʊddu]=
                                              ((P: idiot))
 8  Conrad:   =((quiet laugh for 1.0))
 9   Surjit:  FUCK OFF you African: (.) ⌐ jungle bunny
10                                      ⌊((laughter for 3.5 secs))
11    Pete:   aahaha that was a bad blows (1.0) that was too bad=
                ((l.))
12    Pete:   ((smile voice))=for too bad (.) go on 'en (.)HURRY UP
```

In a number of ways the exchange in lines 7–12 chimes with the account given so far, but it also contains elements in common with incidents where Panjabi abuse was more serious.

Prior to this incident, bilingual uses of [phʊddu] had passed unchallenged in the game (as does indeed Anon's in line 6), and the same was true of much more offensive English swearwords. So it seems unlikely that in line 9, Surjit was taking issue with swearing per se. Elsewhere, Conrad's use of Panjabi numerals went unremarked, and immediately preceding this episode, he had heavily retroflexed an Indian player's name in a way that another had playfully echoed. So nor did it seem to be a question of just any use of Panjabi. Instead, in picking on Conrad's [phʊddu] in particular – and neglecting Anon's before him – Surjit seemed to be orienting to *abusive* Panjabi *crossing*, which evidently constituted a special kind of provocation. In the laughter immediately following Surjit's riposte (line 10), Conrad could not be heard on the recording joining in. But the tone of the interaction remained light, the game continued as before, and Pete's 'that was bad blows, too bad for too bad' explicitly cast the exchange as an equal contest and aligned it with jocular abuse – in one of its senses, 'blowing' designated 'ritual' insult exchange. Admittedly, in other contexts 'African jungle bunny' might be construed as serious racist offence, but playfully derogatory references to ethnicity were common in this peer group (there were at least three Panjabi words referring to black people current in the peer group, and some youngsters of Afro-Caribbean descent found them humourous and occasionally used them themselves). On these grounds then, the exchange between Conrad and Surjit resembles the jocular abuse already described.

However, it differed in not being safely insulated from questions of factual reality. Labov's central condition – 'that everyone present plainly knows that [the abusive proposition] is not true' (1972b: 339, 332) – did not apply. Conrad's utterance was prompted by a real infraction – Surjit's attempt to take a turn at the wrong time. Similarly, Surjit didn't retaliate by building on some part of the structure offered in Conrad's turn (contrast Imran in line 17 and Terry in line 21 of Extract III.12; Ray in line 28 of Extract III.13; Imran in line 14 and Richard in line 15 of Extract III.14; also Labov 1972b: 327; Goodwin and Goodwin 1987: 224). Instead, he stuck to English, his 'fuck off' can be construed as a *denial* of truth claims in Conrad's insult, and the boundary between joking and serious abuse becomes blurred.

There were occasions of interracial Panjabi when abuse could constructed in clearly serious ways:

Extract III.18

Participants and setting: 1987. A football game outside during dinner time. Salim [15 Pa M, wearing radio-mike], Kazim [15 Pa M], Asif [15 Pa M, wearing radio mike], and others on one team, Alan [15 An M], Nigel [15 An M], Jonesie [15 An M] and others on the other. Lines 1–4 involve a brief dispute between Anon 1 and Anon 2, with Kazim encouraging one side in Panjabi. In lines 5 to 15, Kazim's Panjabi intervention itself becomes the subject of discussion. Telly Savalas is an actor who starred in the TV series *Kojak*.

```
 1 Anon 1:  kicking me
 2 Anon 2:  what?
 3 Anon 1:  (      )
 4 Kazim:   [thəlle ʈɑ lɛs] ([thəlle ʈɑ lɛs])
           ((f))
           ((P: get him down    get him down))
 5  Nigel:  TELLY DARLESS (.)
 6  Salim   ((laughing)): Telly Darless! (.)
 7  Jones:  who- who's Telly Darlass
 8   Asif:  his bum (.) he wants ⌈ to bum you
 9  Jones:                       ⌊THA-      NO:: Telly Savalas
10   Asif:  no:: he said he wants-
11  Jones:  KO:JACK
12  Kazim:  NOT KOJACK ((laughs))
13      :   (            )
14   Asif:  HE SAID YOUR BU:M ⌈ not Koj-
15  Kazim:                    ⌊((laughing)) (KOPAT)
16      :   (quick go right)
17   Salim  ((starts running))
           ((A few moments later. A disagreement between Kazim and
           Jonesie is clear in lines 28 and 29, and this probably also
           involves lines 25–26. Although it cannot be verified on the
           audio-recording, it makes sense to suppose that Jonesie looks
           or moves towards Salim in line 30. After that, it is Salim and
           Jonesie who are the central protagonists in dispute))
25  Kazim:  ⌊          )
26  Salim:  ⌈ ((short quiet laugh))
27      :   ⌊what about (      )
28  Kazim:  (can't be- can't be) off-side [phʊddi:]
                                   ((Panjabi: fanny))
29  Jones:  [phʊddi] yerself
30         (1.0) ((?Jonesie looks or moves towards Salim?))
31  Salim:  ((sharp exhalation of breath))
```

```
32 Kazim:          [ləppəɽ   thəlle ʈɑ lɛs] (.)
                   ((Panjabi: slap him  get him down))
33  Jones ((to Salim)): fuckin' laugh at me I'll fuckin batter
34         batter ya
35  Salim: SHADUP YA STUP-
36         ((scuffles ⌈ and heavy breathing for about 4 seconds))
37  Kazim:          ⌊[ləppəɽ   de de ] (.) ooh no::
                   ((P: slap him  give him one))
38     :   (      'urt      )
39  Jones: don't try me Sal I'll ⌈ fuckin'
40  Salim:                        ⌊shshshu:du::p okay:: (.)
41         ((smile voice)) okay boys (.)
42         EH FUCK YOU
43         ((scuffling noises and exhalations for 2.5))
44  Jones: gonna fuck off my neck before I break break your back
45  Salim: WOW:: (.) you really are
46     :   GO ON JO ⌈ NESIE    GONE ALL RED
47  Salim:           ⌊you wish!
48  Alan:  AND JONESIE IS SERIOUS HERE
```

In the first part of this extract, the interaction around Panjabi
was largely playful. In line 5, Nigel's construal of Kazim's preceding utterance was a source of amusement (e.g. Salim's response in
line 6) and Asif joined in with an attempt to exploit monolingual
ignorance by launching a 'comic' distortion of the meaning of
Kazim's Panjabi in line 4 (lines 8, 10, 14). Admittedly, in actually
trying to correct Kazim (or Nigel, or Salim), Jonesie maybe overstepped the interpretive freedom allowed to non-Panjabi speakers,
and it looks as though he did not even realise that Panjabi was
involved. But there was nothing in the subsequent correction that
this received to indicate any noticeable shift out of a playful key.

However, in the second part of the extract, Panjabi crossing
clearly entailed more seriously conflictual social relations. A real
infraction of the rules of play seems to be involved in Kazim's
'can't be offside [phʊddi:], and Jonesie's '[phʊddi] yerself'
involved only the most minimal recycling of Kazim's turn (of the
kind that Labov 1972b: 343 regards as the denial of a personal
insult rather than the return of a jocular one). But the clearest
indication that this was not a playful display of skillful Panjabi
retaliation lies in Jonesie's response to Salim's laughter, which in
being largely inaudible on the recording, was itself fairly
restrained. In the joking abuse that was evidenced in many of the

previous extracts, the audience played an important part – 'besides the initial two players, a third person role is necessary' (Labov 1972b: 344) – and in Extract III.17, Pete's active orientation to the abusive interchange between Surjit and Conrad itself helped to locate it in the realms of the playful. Here, however, Jonesie treated Salim's laughter as an illegitimate intrusion (line 33), and in doing so, he cast his interchange with Kazim as a private difference of opinion, not a public performance. In this context, any intervention from outside could be construed as 'ganging up', and in the fight that followed, he experienced the real force of 'telly darless' as a Panjabi utterance factionally excluding monolinguals. Finally, it is worth noting that this interaction was embedded in a more generally distrustful relationship between Jonesie and Asif's close friendship circle (Asif: 'Jonesie, he's a pisstaker' – Extract I.7).

These last two extracts indicate that Panjabi crossing was not inevitably tied to run-away jocularity, as well as showing that although it might be a significant facilitating factor in certain specifiable respects, participation in games did not provide black and white adolescents with a *carte blanche* for the use of the language.

7.5 Self-directed playground Panjabi

Further evidence for the sensitivity of Panjabi crossing lies in its frequent location within utterances that were not directed to other people, and here there is a good deal of relevance in Goffman's analysis of 'self-talk' (e.g. 'how did I do that?!'), 'response cries' ('ouch!' or 'wow!') and 'imprecations' ('shit!').

Goffman attributes at least four characteristics to utterances of this kind. First, they are oriented to deviations from normal conduct (1981: 82, 89). Secondly, they do not necessitate a response. On the surface at least, they appear to be natural and spontaneous emotional expressions, and they do not seem to be recipient-directed (1981: 97, 112, 114). Thirdly, despite appearances, they are actually very sensitive to the people around them (e.g. 'sugar!' instead of 'shit!'). They are often styled to be overheard in a gathering, they can provide bystanders a half-licence to start interacting verbally, and they are often adjusted to the audience's sensibilities (1981: 97–8). Fourthly, particularly with response cries and imprecations, they often draw on taboo and non-words

(1981: 114). This last characteristic clearly makes these kinds of utterance compatible with the Panjabi competence of youngsters of Anglo and Caribbean descent, and the interactional data also demonstrates the operation of the other three.

According to Goffman, imprecations often close unsuccessful sequences of action that have been the focus of heightened attention. In my data, in addition to preceding the chase and being audibly addressed at an opponent (like goads and challenges), derogatory Panjabi could also be used quietly to oneself when coming to rest after a chasee had escaped:

Extract III.19

Participants: Richard [An 12 M, wearing radio-microphone], others
Setting: 1984. Break-time outside. Playing tig, Richard is chasing.

```
1 Richard:  ((chasing)) (GET) YOU (     HEAD) (.) YAA (     )
                                ((ff.))
2           you fucking wanker (4.0)
            ((f.))
3           ((slowing down, coming to a halt)): you fucking [fɪndhu]
                                                           ((l.))
4           ((Richard remains on his own, silent for 58 seconds))
```

And similar linguistic materials could also be used be used in self-directed commentary on the state of play in pool (cf. Goffman 1981: 113 on the 'grandstanding' function of self-talk):

Extract III.20

Participants: Raymond [12 An/AC M; wearing radio-microphone], Yacub [9 Pa M], Al [17 M], Terry [12 An M], others in the background.
Setting: 1984. Youth club. Raymond is playing Yacub at pool, and Al is giving advice. (It isn't clear whether Anon's comment in line 11 refers to the game or to some other activity in the vicinity).

```
1 Yacub:  ((plays a shot))
2   Ray:  what a B::ASTARD (5.0) I'll have to give 'im two
3         shots │(now)
4     Al:       └no you don't (1.0) come off over here (4.0)
5   Ray:  ((plays shot)) (1.5) that's alright
                            ((l.))
6 Terry:  yeh RAYMON::
```

```
 7 Yacub:  (                    )
 8  Ray:  ((smile voice)) WI:SE SHOT (1.5)
 9  Ray:      [ khalʌ (.) ᵍɪᶻˢ (.) │ fʌkkã̄ : ha:ha]
            ((L2P: ?the black   is │ fucked?))
10 Yacub:                         └((plays shot))
11 Anon:  YOU'RE RUBBISH
12  Ray:  (5.0) uh got- I gotta get that black away (.) I got
13        to do a curl
```

If they wanted to (and if they could understand what he was on about), bystanders could respond to what Raymond said in line 9, but if they didn't, there would be no loss to Raymond's face as long as the utterance maintained its credentials as self-talk. In fact it was also possible to make tactical play of the ambiguity between self-directed response cries and other-addressed abuse (invoking the former to excuse the latter). There were instances in both 1984 and 1987 where a Panjabi response cry – [mərəgi], commonly used to express trepidation – was exploited provocatively by a non-Panjabi (cf. Goffman 1981: 103 on 'threat-startles'), and within all three kinds of self-directed talk, more plainly vulgar or aggressively intended Panjabi could be kept within the bounds of safety.

More generally, self-directed utterances in Panjabi can be also seen as a way of keeping alert and staying in tune with a pre-dominantly Panjabi bilingual social situation, in circumstances where either one's linguistic resources were limited, or where one was not entirely confident of the response one's efforts would elicit (or both). In that way, no one was forced to the unambiguous approval or rejection that a first pair part would set up: self-talk, response cries and imprecations permitted a non-confrontational fellow travelling.

7.6 Mellowing over time

Yet further evidence of constraints on Panjabi crossing emerged through longitudinal comparison. Not only did it appear to become less common with time – in 1984, there were 43 episodes in 45 hours of recording, whereas in 1987, there were only 25 in about 100. Crossing also became more circumspect.

In 1987 there were no instances of the full voiced, sustained and highly public strings of abuse that had been evidenced in 84. In

1987, three sets of informants were replayed loud out-group Panjabi abuse sequences, taken from 1984 episodes in which they had been participants. They laughed a lot; Panjabi bilinguals said they still taught swearwords, sometimes so that people swore at themselves. But all three groups felt that abuse practices were different now and two of them remarked that it was wild then, that it was not as bad as this now, that they had 'mellowed' and were more mature.

There was other evidence of mellowing. There were seven instances in 1984 where monolinguals directed derogatory Panjabi terms at bilingual peers, but none elicited a serious challenge and several received the endorsement of good humoured Panjabi reciprocation. The four clearly depreciative utterances directed at Panjabis in 1987 tended to be less obviously jocular (see Extracts III.17 and III.18) and there were no longer any instances of bilinguals accompanying monolinguals in loud Panjabi chanting (cp. Extract III.12). Instead, reports described covertly preparing friends to go and 'swear' elsewhere: collaboration now took more surreptitious forms (cf. line 18, Extract II.8, Chapter 4.2). The quantity and intensity of swearing had also generally diminished in 1987. Whereas in 1984, about four-fifths of the monolingual uses of Panjabi could be classed as derogatory, involving rude words or critical comments about someone's appearance, ability or habits, in 1987 this was only about two-fifths.

In place of derogatory terms, in 1987 there were Panjabi nicknames, the occasional number, and one or two words such as [pɪtʃe] (meaning 'back') and [tʃəlie] (meaning 'let's go'). These were used to call the attention of a Panjabi teammate (often for a pass), and the fact that they hardly ever occurred outside structured games further indicates the constraints on white and black crossing. As if to emphasise the risks, there was an interethnic debunking routine in circulation that reinserted superficially affiliative [tʃəlie] within a fooling framework:

     A: [tʃəlie]
       ((let's go))
     B: [kɪtthe]
       ((where?))
     A: ((pointing to private parts))
       [ethe]
       ((here!))

A number of factors could be involved in this shift over time away from more openly abusive forms of crossing. In 1987, friendships no longer necessarily stretched back to early childhood, and Panjabi was much more actively valued as a language of youth cultural prestige (see Part IV). But this longitudinal change could also be closely correlated with the fact that people no longer played elaborate chasing games (cf. Extract III.3). In 1984, chasing games provided legitimate opportunities for extravagant abuse that could spill over to other activities contemporary with them. Without that institutionalisation, noisy agonistic crossing could become more fragile.

7.7 Girls and playground Panjabi: cross- and same-sex interactions

Partly due to the gap in the 1984 sample, the account has so far focused on interracial Panjabi among males. It would be a mistake however, to assume that females of Caribbean and Anglo descent were never involved in agonistic Panjabi exchanges. Fourteen and 15 year-olds regarded tag games as childish, and in their place, a substantial amount of recreational time in 1987 was spent in general sociability, either moving around common areas at school with a few friends, standing in a queue, or sitting in one place, greeting and calling to whichever people of interest happened to come into view. This was the source of considerable entertainment, especially where it concerned male/female relations. Here, even simple greetings could be put to gameful use, publicly proclaiming for example, an affiliation to which the recipient might be expected to resist. For example:

> Sally ((deliberately simpering)): Hello Micky
> Micky: fuck you!

and

> Pat (f): Hello Jimmy!
> ((turning to her friends, imitating Jimmy)) 'fuck off'
> Jimmy ((imitating Pat)): 'Hello Jimmy!'
> Pat ((to her friends)): oh, I thought he'd swear at me!

The permutations on this playful cross-gender provocation were very numerous indeed, and in interviews, male–female interaction was the most widely cited context for cross-ethnic Panjabi.

This was most often described as 'swearing', and the ethnicities of the participants seemed to be varied – though at least one participant was always Panjabi, this could be either the boy or the girl, and their opponent could be white or black. Although boys were most commonly reported as starting the abuse, there was not complete agreement on this (cf. Extract I.6), and there were a number of accounts of girls retaliating in kind. Some episodes involving cross-ethnic Panjabi use between males and females were described in terms of a teaching relationship (often involving swearwords) and in these cases, Panjabi boys were almost invariably cited.

Such reports may well have exaggerated actual practice (and one informant denied that Indian girls were involved in agonistic cross-ethnic Panjabi). In the event, only a handful of episodes were recorded in the interactional data, but in the three where they can be ascertained, responses appeared to be positive (as indicated for example by laughter). In fact, the only episode from 1987 in which a non-Panjabi initiative received any kind of sustained reciprocation involved a black boy with a group of Panjabi girls. In this regard, the Panjabi data synchronised with the evidence on SAE, where male–female interaction had also appeared as a privileged zone for critical language crossing (e.g. Extracts III.4 and III.5).

In settings where peer group recreation is predominantly single-sex, contact between the sexes is often regarded as special, serving as the source for a great deal of talk and teasing (cf. e.g. Sluckin 1981: 69–70). Particularly in South Asian families, interaction between unrelated male and female adolescents was frequently a matter of concern, and in Ashmead, the unusual quality of cross-sex relations was also suggested in reports of white girls gaining access to the heartlands of black and Panjabi youth culture, thereby by-passing the class, race and residence constraints that generally applied to boys. I shall return to the significance of cross-sex interaction as a privileged arena in section 7.9, where its relation to other sites for crossing will also be addressed. Before that, however, it is necessary to comment briefly on cross-ethnic Panjabi in *single-sex* female interactions.

According to informant reports, 'swearing' uses of interethnic

Panjabi were not just restricted to interaction with boys: 14 informants (12F, 2M) reported cross-ethnic tutoring exclusively among females, and black and white girls also demonstrated some knowledge of Panjabi swearwords in interview. To collect interactional evidence on this, radio-microphones were given out to six youngsters (2 AC and 4 An) who seemed particularly likely to use the language – they had good Panjabi friends, they liked bhangra, they attended a predominantly Panjabi youth club, or they had attended Southleigh. This produced more than 15 hours of school-based data, and these contained some talk about bhangra that will be analysed in Part IV. There were however, almost no instances in which these girls used Panjabi in the 'swearing' mode that we are discussing here.

Although no systematic attempt has been made to survey gender difference in language use in this peer group, a brief and impressionistic view indicates that as in boys' usage, girls' talk involved swearwords, disputes, insult exchanges, song corruptions, rude rhymes, vulgar comments, funny voices and improvised compound words in English. So at least at first glance, the non-occurrence of Panjabi abuse among girls can not be attributed to radical linguistic gender differences. Instead, two factors can be suggested in explanation.

First, at school, these girls didn't hang around much with Panjabi girls. In the majority of episodes in which boys crossed over into Panjabi, youngsters of Indian and Pakistani descent were closely involved (and these were usually friends). Panjabi crossing in exclusively black and/or white company was rare. If the presence of Panjabi peers was an important cue for agonistic crossing among boys, then their absence from the company of black and white girls might explain why they never used it. Secondly, the girls on these recordings very rarely took part in competitive games (a point that will be elaborated in Chapter 10.7).

It is worth now trying to provide an overview of the account so far.

7.8 Overview: opportunities, risks and the enunciation of 'tensed unity'

Incontestably, Panjabi formed part of the peer group repertoire of white and black adolescents. But it is equally clear that they did

not assume unconditional freedom in their use of it. A number of
factors seemed to be at play influencing the appropriacy of its out-
group use. Without claiming to provide a tight theoretical
statement about which factors were most critical, a summary can
be made of the circumstances in which crossing was likely to be
most and least acceptable.

Panjabi crossing was sometimes affiliatively geared to gaining a
team-mate's attention, but it was also very commonly oriented to
transgression and impropriety. With the latter, the transgression
could be either fantastical or real, and the perpetrator could be the
addressee, the speaker, or third persons (for example teachers).
Panjabi utterances could be both self- and other-directed, verbal
skill could make other-directed abuse a source of particular entertainment, games were a major, though not essential, context, and
so were friendship and male–female interaction. These factors can
be arranged in a set of contrasts:

Safe crossing	*Dangerous crossing*
Self-directed utterances	Other-directed utterances
Affiliative	Critical
Imaginary transgression	Actual transgression
Transgression imputed to self or third person referent	Transgression imputed to addressee
Skillful verbal performance	Unskilled performance
Part of an organised game	Not part of an organised game
Addressee either a friend or a member of opposite sex (or both)	Addressee a non-friend of the same sex

There were no cases in my data in which white or black uses of
Panjabi involved all of the factors listed on the right, though it is
not difficult to imagine a context of street racism in which these
might all occur in exclusive combination. But at the opposite end
of the scale, there were some instances which combined most of
the 'safe' characteristics. On scoring an own goal during bar football, Terry exclaimed 'ah god! I kicked that in myself, [gʌɖɖu]
((=?marrow/fattie?))!') – here a quite exclusive Panjabi word was
used in a self-directed utterance oriented to the speaker's own
transgression during a game with friends. But self-talk of this kind
did not generate much interaction, and there was more excitement
to be had when crossing integrated at least some risky elements. In

jocular abuse, this involved imputing an offence to the addressee ('dangerous'), but ensuring that this was imaginary and doing it with friends/members of the opposite sex ('safe'). With the more awkward interactions that we have seen, a greater proportion of 'dangerous' features appear to have been present. In Extracts III.17, III.18 and II.9 (in Chapter 4.4), other-directed utterances critically imputed real transgression to a member of the same sex. In Extract II.9 (Kuldip and Peter), this occurred outside games, but crossing was maybe mitigated by a display of some proficiency and it was certainly set within close friendship (the former in fact deriving from the latter). In Extract III.17 (Conrad and Surjit), less verbal skill was demonstrated, but the exchange occurred in the context of a game between friends. In contrast, Salim and Kazim did not have a particularly friendly relationship with Jonesie, and consistent with this, Extract III.18 appeared to be the most problematic crossing interaction in my corpus.

With this summary and the fairly detailed interactional analysis on which it is based, observations commonly made at an institutional level can be related to micro-interactional mechanisms. This was a central concern in Part II, where close situational analysis was brought to bear on sociological discussions of the politics of youth culture. Here, connection can also be made with anthropological discussions of 'joking relationships' and 'conflict rituals'.

Writing about interethnic relations in Southern Africa, Mitchell suggests that

> one possible mechanism for the control of inter-tribal hostility lies in institutionalised joking relationship ... Radcliffe-Brown... writes: 'The theory is that ... joking relationships which constitute an alliance between clans or tribes ... are modes of organising a definite stable social system of social behaviour in which disjunctive and conjunctive components are maintained and combined' (1956: 35, 36)

According to Turner, 'if mutually irrepressible principles or protagonists belong together in a human being or a social group, they can also constitute strong unities, the more so if both principles or protagonists in the conflict are consciously recognised and accepted' (1969: 83). Lukes also recognises practices connected with the 'tensed unity' that Turner describes, but he stresses that synchronised action and attention should not be mistaken for more widely shared social interests and commitments:

> conflictual rituals appear ... to express and institutionalise ... underlying social conflicts whose continued existence, together with the social order which contains them, is accepted as given and unchangeable by participants and observers. These rituals may be said to contribute to social integration but not to value consensus. (Lukes 1975: 300–1)

There can be no doubt that as a language, Panjabi was closely associated with particular ethnic backgrounds, and that these existed in a wider context of race stratification and division. The presence of Panjabi peers was an important motivating factor, but crossing was constrained and confined within a limited set of actions, activities and relationships, most of them competitive or superficially conflictual. For young people of Caribbean and Anglo descent, the encounter with Panjabi was not a process of free-flowing fusion or relaxed assimilation, and in this respect, it indeed makes sense to talk of Panjabi crossing as the enunciation of a 'tensed (interethnic) unity', encoding both separation and conjunction. From the outside it marked the multiracial peer group as a distinct collectivity, while at the same time on the inside, it continually registered internally transecting limits and divisions. More than a truce but less than a merger, playground Panjabi provided youngsters with a way of negotiating position within delicate interethnic border zones. Lukes' warning about not assuming value consensus is also borne out, since white and black adolescents in fact differed in their commitment to the interracial community that playground Panjabi ambiguously constituted. A couple of the most widely cited crossers employed racist discourses elsewhere. But for others, Panjabi 'swearing' was a valued part of the local multiracial inheritance. It had figured in a range of the entertaining activities in which they had been participating with bilingual friends for a number of years, and in consequence, Panjabis described them as 'one of us' and 'in our sort of community' (Extracts I.8 and I.9, Chapter 2.2).

But in giving this kind of account, it is vital to keep in mind the interactional processes through which this interplay of division and solidarity emerged. If these are neglected, it is easy to assume (incorrectly) that the combination of social proximity and ethnic difference is on its own enough to generate intergroup joking practices. In turn, this may lead one to overestimate the spread and stability of these displays of cross-ethnic accommodation. Contrary to the characterisation of gaming and joking practices referred to by the more macro-social analysts cited above, crossing was emergent, not well-established or highly institutionalised. Interactional analysis shows that a great deal of the impetus behind these multiracial playground practices emerged from the tenuous coincidence of particular forms of adolescent recreation (chasing games and jocular insult exchange) with the strategic needs of participants with limited proficiency in Panjabi as a second language. Playground Panjabi would be more difficult for white and black kids who did not join in with these activities, and it might become obsolete if people 'grew out of' the activities that it depended on. Indeed, within and beyond these supporting activities, effective crossing relied on the biographically contingent social and interactional competence and sensitivity of particular individuals.

The preceding analyses of Panjabi also suggest a second more general point about language crossing, which embraces the data on SAE as well.

7.9 Language crossing and the liminal

An enormous amount of the data that we have analysed suggests that language crossing was located in moments when the ordered flow of social life was loosened and normal social relations could not be taken for granted. Independently of any language selection that is made, the boundary phases around interactional engagement are occasions of relative uncertainty (as suggested in Chapter 3.4's discussion of access rituals); impropriety and transgression breach normative expectations of conduct; and self-talk and response cries constitute time away from the full demands of respectful interpersonal conduct (Goffman 1981: 81, 85, 99). Parallel to these weak points in the 'interaction order', organised games involve an agreed relaxation of the rules and constraints of ordinary behaviour (Chapter 6.7), and finally, in settings where most recreational activity is single sex, and where many parents discourage unmonitored contact between adolescent girls and boys, cross-sex interaction is itself likely to seem special, unusually vested with both risk and promise (also Chapter 10.8).

All of these occasions can be related to 'liminality', a concept developed by Victor Turner in particular. Turner begins by discussing anthropological studies of initiation rites in tribal and agrarian societies. These rites have three phases: separation, in which initiands leave their childhood life behind; transition; and then incorporation, in which they are returned to new, relatively stable and well defined positions in society, now a stage further on in life's cycle (Turner 1974: 24; also e.g. Bloch 1985: 699). Turner concentrates on the middle phase, designated 'liminal':

> during the intervening phase of transition ... the ritual subjects pass through a period and area of ambiguity, a sort of social limbo which has few ... of the attributes of either the preceding or subsequent [ordinary] social statuses or cultural states ... In liminality, [everyday] social relations may be discontinued, former rights and obligations are suspended, the social order may seem to have been turned upside down. (1974: 24, 27)

It is not possible to argue directly from this account of traditional ritual to urban social relations in Ashmead. But the notion of liminality has been extended into a form that fits more easily with practices common in industrial society, and Turner calls these 'liminoid' ('-oid' meaning 'like', 'resembling', but not identical). In complex modern societies, the liminal and the liminoid certainly coexist (1974: 55), but Turner suggests the following differences (1974: 54):

1. Liminoid phenomena *may* be collective (as in agrarian societies), but they are more characteristically individual products. Rather than being related to the cyclical calendrical, biological and social structural rhythms (= liminal phenonomena), liminoid phenomena are continuously generated in the times and places set apart from work and assigned to leisure activities.
2. Rather than being found in the formal activities of churches, sects and clubs, and so on, liminoid phenomena are located in the leisure genres of art, sport and games. Instead of participation being a matter of obligation as with the liminal,

the liminoid is a matter of choice: one works at the liminal, but one plays with the liminoid.

3. Whereas liminality in traditional rituals is centrally integrated into the total social process, liminoid practices develop apart from central economic and political processes, along the margins, in the interfaces and interstices of central servicing institutions. They are plural, fragmentary and experimental in character.

4. Rather than involving symbols with common intellectual and emotional meaning for all members of the group (as with liminality), 'liminoid phenomena tend to be more idiosyncratic, quirky, to be generated by specific named individuals and in particular groups – 'schools', circles, coteries – they have to compete with one another for general recognition and are thought of at first as ludic offerings placed for sale on the 'free' market' (Turner 1974: 54).

5. Liminal practices tend to contribute to the smooth functioning of social systems, helping them to operate without too much friction. In contrast, liminoid practices are often creative, containing social critiques, exposing wrongs in mainstream structures and organisation. Sometimes in the liminoid, 'the seeds of cultural transformation, discontent with the ways things are culturally, and social criticism, always implicit in the traditionally liminal, have become situationally central' (p. 45).

The notions of liminality and the liminoid have particular value in making an explicit connection between phenomena at a number of different levels of social organisation. Similarities between 'grand' rites of passage and interpersonal conduct at the opening and closing of encounters have been pointed out by other scholars (Firth 1972; Laver 1975; cf. Chapter 3.4), but Turner provides a more extensive account. More specifically here, there is a great deal in common with the different kinds of language crossing that we have described so far: in all its forms, crossing occurred at interstitial and ambiguous moments, and it bore many of the characteristics attributed to liminality and liminoidity.

Turner's emphasis on choice and individuality in the liminoid fits, for example, with the way in which crossing was often embedded within a competitive orientation to personal advantage, particularly with Panjabi in jocular abuse and games. So too does the occurrence of Panjabi in self-directed utterances, which can be interpreted as affiliative desire combined with uncertainty about personal entitlement to an out-group language. All of these uses would be hard to accommodate with an account of the traditionally liminal, where solidarity and collective commitment are dominant.

Group interests were not always excluded however, and it would be a mistake to assume that (a) there is a clear dividing line between the liminal and the liminoid, and that (b) crossing can only be linked to the latter. Collective concerns were prominent when SAE was used in games, as well as when it was used to reprimand 'improper' conduct in informal peer–peer interaction. Turner attributes two different relationships with social structure to liminality and liminoidity, but again crossing into SAE covered both. With teachers, SAE can be quite easily synchronised with Turner's view that 'liminoid practices are often social critiques, exposing wrongs in mainstream structures and organisation'. But at the same time, informally with peers, SAE's function was often conservative, stepping into the breach created by putative transgression to restore the orderliness held appropriate to adolescent conduct. Indeed, the relationship between crossing, social order, liminality and liminoidity was even more intricate in games: here, SAE was used to emphasise key structural elements in the organisation of activities that can themselves be regarded as lying outside ordinary social reality.

Although crossing was often inserted into moments and settings where a breach of the taken-for-granted patterns of ordinary life had arisen independently of ethnic language use, it was also used productively to enhance or create such loosenings. In this way, white and black young people crossed into Panjabi in games and joking abuse in order to provoke remedial action, and this also happened with SAE (cf. e.g. Extracts III.4 and III.5). And although situational contingencies would determine whether or not it was considered illegitimate, the use of Panjabi in class itself set up an unofficial zone of alternative communicative possibilities.

Clearly, then, Turner's ideas provide a very useful way of drawing the crossing data together, particularly when the notion of liminality is extended to encompass the liminoid (from now on, unless I specifically want to emphasise the distinction, I shall simply use the terms 'liminal' and 'liminality', on the understanding that this covers liminoidity as well). In fact, these concepts help us to pinpoint one very important implication that runs through all the different forms that crossing took. By definition, liminal activity departs from the patterns of conduct and systems of classification that are dominant in a society. The fact that language crossing can be consistently linked to the liminal indicates that in the social structures which were dominant and which adolescents treated as *normal*, there was in fact a *relatively fixed* relationship between language and ethnic inheritance. This counters any temptation to see young people's language crossing as a successful collective effort to eliminate wider patterns of ethnic stratification and division, at least within the protected boundaries of peer group recreation. Admittedly, something like this seemed to happen in particular activities (e.g. SAE in games), but the neutralisation of inherited ethnic difference was not successfully achieved within local adolescent social life more generally. If this had happened, then out-group language use would be in no way marked off from taken-for-granted everyday behaviour.

Or so at least the situation seemed to be with crossing in Panjabi and SAE.

Notes

1. A 'zone of proximal development' might be identified as the words or phrases either attributed to black and white peers by Panjabi friends, or commonly used by Panjabis with white or black peers as ratified participants.
2. At the very least, they might make defensive use of paralinguistic and contextual clues, which could be helpfully combined with the knowledge of a few key Panjabi words (cf. Hill and Coombs 1982: 228):

Extract III.21

Participants and setting: 1987 interview. Ian [15 An M], Richard [15 An m], BR. [Simple transcription]

> BR: what happens if you're talking to somebody and another person comes up and starts talking Panjabi to them, what do you do?
> Ian [An 15 M]: sit there and listen or sometimes (   ) say 'are you finished yet?' or
> Richard [An 15 M]: 'what you talkin' about'

Ian: yeh, 'what you talkin'', wha' you chattin' about, hope
       you ain't saying anything about me . . . you said some-
       thing about me! I'm gonna to hit you'
BR: is there any way in which you can tell whether some-
       body's
Ian: yeh when some, some people sort of look, they go
       'motia' ((= fatty)) and they go 'mutoo' and I look round
       and I go 'I know what that means you stupid . . .
Richard: . . . flid'
Ian: they think I don't understand any of it so I trick them
       and I do, I understand most of what they're saying when
       they're saying 'phuddoo' and this to me . . . and 'mari
       bunjii' and all this
BR: saying what
Ian: oh no . . . 'murri bunji', I don't know what that means, I
       just made that up I think

Indeed some claimed to be able to exploit such resources and regain
the initiative with surprise:

Extract III.22

Participants and setting: 1987 interview. Helen [14 AC F], Adrian
[14 AC M], BR

BR: how much kind of Indian do you know?
Helen: quite a bit . . . well I don't know that much, but when the
       Indian kids are talking I can understand what they're say-
       ing, but I wouldn't be able to say it, sort of, just get
       tongue-twisted and everything, I won't be able to say it
       but I can just understand by the expression on their faces
       and the way they use their hands to talk, I just watch
       them, and I think, 'yeh I know what you're on about' and
       everything. Most of the time I go up to them and I tell
       them what they were just talking about and they go 'how
       do you know?', and I go 'ah, it's easy'

3. This can be seen for example in line 14 of extract II.16, and in a
    couple of goads directed at a third party ('It'):

Richard: [derɪ madə   gʊs gʊs]
               ((L2P: your mum's [nonsense word]))
Imran: [tere mãde phʊdde]
               ((non-standard Panjabi: your mum's   ?))

According to the local translators, the [e] suffixed to each of Imran's words made little sense: 'it sounds more of a joke, you could take [=accept] it like that'.

8 Creole (ii): Degrees of ritualisation in Ashmead and South London

On the basis of analysis of stylised Asian English (SAE) and Panjabi, it was suggested at the end of the last chapter that language crossing was intimately connected with occasions when the hold of routine assumptions about the conduct of social life became less certain. If this is the case, then the use of out-group languages has to be taken as an implicit recognition that ethnic difference was an important part of adolescent perceptions of ordinary social reality. If it was confined within liminal actions and events, crossing can not be taken as an indication that adolescents had found a way of permanently transcending the knowledge of race division associated with linguistic difference, or that they could move unproblematically in and out of the heritage languages of their friends.

Creole presents an important test for these proposals. Chapter 5 suggested that it was felt to be more closely integrated into the habitual patterns of local vernacular speech than either SAE or Panjabi. Does this signify that hitherto limited adolescent efforts to overcome ethnic difference had been successful, and that from the confluence of black, white and Asian youth, the possibility of a new plural identity had emerged – an identity drawing on several distinctive ethnic sources that an adolescent could nevertheless sustain as a normal part of everyday social relations?

My data on Creole crossing has been analysed much less intensively than crossing in SAE and Panjabi. A good deal of out-group Creole has been classified initially in terms of participants, speech forms and functions, topics and themes, activities and key, but these categorisations have not been continuously reexamined in the course of empirical analysis. Because of this, my description of Creole use among Pakistani, Anglo and Indian adolescents in Ashmead must be regarded as more provisional than the account of crossing in the other two codes. Fortunately, however, reference can be made to Hewitt's study (1986). In fact, in a different form, Hewitt also addresses the question outlined in the previous paragraph, and he answers in the affirmative.

Hewitt suggests that in the context of close black–white friendship, interpersonal uses of white Creole develop in ways that lose all group-referencing function, that involve undemonstrative alignment, and that can be considered 'as part of normal convergence of cooperating interlocutors' (1986: 187). At the same time, he regards these as distinct from common forms of multiracial vernacular speech (cf. Chapter 6.5). So rather than reflecting a single *mixed* identity emerging from the fusion of different traditions as in the local multiracial vernacular, these interpersonal uses appear to represent a new white *biculturalism*.

This characterisation is difficult to assess independently of Hewitt's analysis of several other kinds of white Creole, and so it is worth considering his scheme of classification a bit more generally. This is the focus of the next section, where I shall suggest that there are certain weaknesses in Hewitt's analytic framework. However there is still a great deal in his account that can be reformulated into a more comprehensive theoretical analysis of language crossing, and the subsequent section starts to outline it. After that, data on Ashmead Creole crossing are brought to bear, these are then summarised in a rudimentary model, and Part III concludes with an overview of the differences between crossing in Creole, Panjabi and SAE, a discussion of Bakhtin's heteroglossia ('polyphony'), and a glance towards wider sociolinguistic implications.

8.1 Hewitt's analysis

Hewitt distinguishes several ways in which whites used Creole, some overlapping with local folk notions of 'joking', while others were considered 'serious'. He describes the first of the two joking styles as a light 'cultural self-contextualisation', 'little more than a flirtation with the public surface of black culture' (1986: 136). He designates this a 'cultural' mode, and contrasts it with competitive uses, which are also joking but which instead involve a lot of abuse. In this second mode, cultural self-contextualisation combines with a concern for personal positioning in 'the rivalries of verbal and other forms of play' (p. 136).

There is however a problem with this dichotomy, because it is based on the assumption that it is possible for talk to occur without regard for the participants' personal interactional positioning: 'the cultural mode . . . becomes evident where no strategic purpose with regard to the immediate discursive relationship between the interactants is served' (p. 142). This view that cultural uses are in some sense gratuitous, occurring without a warrant in the dynamics of the immediate interaction, leads Hewitt to describe them as 'exhibitionistic' (p. 149, 156, 163). This certainly tunes with the view expressed by at least some local informants (p. 155), but there are good grounds for doubting the basic premise that people can talk without regard for interpersonal position. To illustrate the differences between these modes, Hewitt cites a chip shop interaction, in which a white boy who is momentarily disengaged from the interaction, says 'Tarra, man!' to himself rather 'in the nature of a reflective exclamation of annoyance' (p. 146). Hewitt describes this as 'purely cultural marking', whereas in fact as an instance of self-talk, it is *also* likely to be closely tuned to the interactional environment. If Chapter 7.5's account of self-directed utterances in Panjabi is accepted, exclamations of this kind show much more sensitivity to possible criticism than anything suggested in the term 'exhibitionistic', and they emerge from spontaneous calculations of the local costs and benefits of outgroup language use that one could certainly call 'strategic' (in the sense that Hewitt uses the word – cp. Gumperz 1982a; and see Heritage 1990/91 for broader uses). In fact the difficulty surrounding this conception of 'purely cultural'/'exhibitionist' marking goes beyond merely joking uses: it also undermines the distinction between (joking) 'cultural' and (serious) 'interpersonal' uses of white Creole, since the latter are partly differentiated from the former in *not* being exhibitionist.

There is also another way in which the divisions in Hewitt's account seem rather artificial. In the chip shop interaction, 'competitive' and 'cultural' modes actually share a common orientation to transgression. In addition to the self-talk described above, which expressed annoyance at his friend's failure to arrive as arranged, the white boy refused a repeated invitation to play 'Space Invaders' with Creole 'I want **some'in'** fe eat'. As demonstrated in Brown and Levinson's study of politeness and in conversation analytic work on preference organisation, participants have a heightened orientation to the potential offence that they could cause one another at moments of this kind (in another supposedly 'cultural' instance, Creole was used across an engagement enclosure to make an assertive request, another face-threatening act ('Eh, tell 'er **fe com!**')).

Analysed in this way, there is also less of a difference between these joking uses, and those uses which Hewitt classifies as interpersonal (and serious). He cites the following interaction:

1 A (black): Jes' see how it goes . . . If it ain't got the plugs on it, jes' buy the plugs for it then jes' tune it up my yard.
2 B (white): Alright.
3 A: 'Cos I got the amps. I could take the amps down your yard . . . or somethin' like that
4 B: **Wha' 'bout de speaker-dem?**
5 A: Well . . . that means we're gonna 'ave to tune it at my yard. 'Cos that's the reason my ol' man [***]. 'Cos if I blow it I could pay thir'y quid to get 'em fixed (1986: 188)

Hewitt says that this interaction 'lacks any competitive dimension, and the Creole utterance shows only the slightest trace of Creole pronunciation. It falls within a merely technical discussion over arrangements to do with sound equipment. The white boy employs a Creole plural marker, without any attendant theatricality' (p. 187). However, as in the chip shop interaction, the switch to Creole coincides with a potentially face-threatening act. In turn 3, A makes a suggestion about going to B's house that clearly requires B's assent. B appears to pause slightly before responding (hence A's post-completer '. . . or something like that'), and he then raises a complication, which A subsequently recognises as an obstacle to his proposal with 'well' and an account of the disadvantages of not taking the amps to B's house. Although this disagreement is very mild, it still contradicts Hewitt's characterisation of interpersonal Creole as convergent, integrative and unconnected to personal opposition. He gives other instances of interpersonal white uses of Creole: 'Similarly, a white boy indicating to his black friends that he was going for a smoke in the lavatories used the phrase 'Mi a-go blango' with no special stressing and with all the appearance of matter of fact conversation' (p. 188). Once again, this arises at a moment when the solidity of interactional relations is temporarily weakened: this appears to be part of an access ritual, with the speaker accounting for his departure from the engagement enclosure (cf. Goffman 1971: 79 and Chapter 3.4).

Before relating these instances back to the question of liminality, it is important to point to one final problem in this account of 'interpersonal' cross-ethnic Creole. Hewitt describes other forms of crossover Creole as having connotations of dauntless assertiveness and of street life, and as often occurring in discussion of music and sound systems. But he then says that in its interpersonal uses, Creole is not used as an 'explicit marker of cultural affiliation with an idealised 'black group'' (1986: 187). This is not at all clear in the examples which he gives: for example, a discussion of music provides the context for B's use of Creole, and 'mi a-go blango' (in the loos) relates to activity with strong connotations of the unofficial street life stereotypically associated with black youth. So also on these grounds, Hewitt's typology of uses seems problematic.

My purpose in questioning this account is twofold. In the first place, it is by no means clear that Hewitt provides evidence to show that some adolescents transcended knowledge of ethnic division, entering black domains so completely that during participation, all sense of their cultural distinctiveness was neutralised. Contrary to the gist of Hewitt's analysis, these data *do not* indicate the development of open bicultural relations among a small section of black and white youth. Secondly, the different modes that Hewitt describes have more in common than he suggests. This second point is particularly important, because it creates the opportunity to formulate a general account of crossing, which can nevertheless embrace the real differences that his data do in fact display.

8.2 Crossing with degrees of ritualisation

The notion of ritual would occupy a central place in this general account of crossing. Judging from the data that we have so far considered, switching into out-group ethnic varieties either created, or was inserted within, periods when participants had heightened awareness of alternatives to the norms of everyday conduct. It also symbolically evoked 'sociolinguistic horizons' that were marked out from the routine of ordinary life, and in combination, these two characteristics provide a good initial basis for seeing crossing generically as a form of ritual action. In Hewitt's account, there are also other characteristics that are commonly associated with ritual. Black informants said that using Creole made them feel 'more lively and more aware' (1986: 107) and Hewitt describes its use as often enlivening interaction between ethnic Anglos (cf. e.g. Turner 1974: 81 on the 'performative plenitude' of ritual). White Creole use was widely commented on and strongly sanctioned – 'the notoriety of white Creole use is far greater than the activity itself . . . the incidence of white Creole speech is consistently overreported' (1986: 161) – and much of the same can often be said of SAE and Panjabi crossing, as was indicated in Chapter 2 in particular.

If we refer back to the discussion of liminality in the previous chapter, we can start to see how acts and events can in fact differ in the extent to which they are ritualised. Liminal periods in the main flow of social life differ considerably in their magnitude. Some liminal periods involve a relatively major suspension of the norms of ordinary conduct, as appeared to happen for example, in games, cross-sex interaction and in conventional joking abuse exchanges. Others are much more fleeting, involving momentary awareness of only potential offence – Brown and Levinson's ([1978]1987) account of face-threatening acts (requests, suggestions, disagreements, etc.) concentrates on this kind of minor uncertainty about the prospects for solidary interaction. Indeed, the evidence suggests that the relationship between crossing and the disruption of orderly business can be even more indirect: Creole forms occurred in white speech that merely reported past events where conflict and disorder had occurred – Ashmead adolescents used Creole forms with verbs describing trouble and counter-official action ('catch', 'vex', etc. – see Chapter 5.5), and Hewitt encountered dense Creole usage in Anglo descriptions of incidents involving knife fights and the police (1986: 190–1).

Admittedly, it would not be possible to arrange actions and events on a single linear continuum of ritualisation. Even with a relatively minimal definition in terms of liminality, symbolism and/or formulaicness, one can imagine combinations that would be hard to compare on any such scale – which should one consider more ritualised, a lightly ritualised utterance in a strongly ritualised activity (for example Creole 'cha' briefly exclaimed at an imaginary delict during a game), or a heavily ritualised utterance produced at a weakly ritual moment (a spectacular Creole string occasioned by actual transgression in a dinner queue)? Nevertheless, gross gradations can be drawn between fully liminal events which generate a marked emotional response and an increased sense of collectivity (see Part IV), spontaneous symbolic actions where practical concerns and truth claims are absent, and then finally, subtle ritual acts which insert a trace of symbolic significance over propositional utterances oriented to the transaction of serious affairs (as in the exchange between A and B in the section above).

In fact, one can proceed from this to suggest that there may come a point where the symbolic and liminal character of linguistic action gets lost. Peter's Creole in Extract II.18 approached this point of transition (see the discussion in Chapter 5.4 and 5.5) and it is very possible that the presence or absence of ritualisation was a critical issue when in Hewitt's research, white adolescents tried to disguise Creole forms in the local multiracial vernacular. Unfortunately, this is a complex issue that I cannot give adequate empirical treatment to in the present discussion. But more generally, it can be suggested that although an explicit statement in these terms is ultimately blocked by his awkward compartmentalisation of white Creole uses, a view of different degrees of ritualisation is implicit in Hewitt's concern with varying degrees of 'theatricality'. Much of what he describes could be broadly placed at different points on a scale of this kind.

8.3 Evidence from Ashmead

In now turning to a consideration of other-ethnic uses of Creole in my data, one purpose is to explore the extent to which different degrees of crossing can be arranged on a rudimentary scale of ritualisation. Another is to develop the comparison with SAE and Panjabi. The ensuing analysis is incomplete in so far as it does not consider what might in fact be the most delicate traces of Creole influence. I shall not consider tag questions, or TH stopping, or indeed the extensive elision that frequently figured in adolescent speech and that was sometimes considered Creole in origin. Clearly such forms could well be critical for investigation of the way in which out-group speech patterns move over from 'liminoid' to ordinary vernacular language practices. But as explained at the start of this Chapter, my analysis of Creole data can be regarded as only preliminary, and a full treatment would require much more space and time than is currently available.

Despite these descriptive limitations, however, it was clear that Creole features generally figured much more frequently in adolescent speech than either SAE or Panjabi. Even so, there were about five informants who did not use any obviously Creole forms during the time that they were recorded with radio-microphones (three girls of South Asian descent, one Anglo girl, and one black boy who went around with Indian friends).

From its use by the others, it is possible to set up three rather different kinds of Creole crossing. These can be initially distinguished as (a) minimal, (b) extensive but jocular, (c) extensive and serious. I shall take each of these in turn.

Minimal crossers

Creole features were used only minimally by my white informants, none of whom belonged to predominantly black friendship clusters. Even though there were substantial periods in which they participated in friendly interaction with black peers, they almost only ever used Creole with Anglos and Asians who were good friends (see Jones 1988: 148). Network relations appeared significant here: Ian and Richard, who were on very close terms with Raymond [AC], used Creole forms in slightly more ways than the white girls I recorded. Among the girls, Sally, who was going out with Imran, used Creole forms more than Kelly and Pat [F].

In terms of linguistic form, a Creole and/or black British influence was generally evidenced in a small set of fixed terms and formulae, 'cha', 'raas', 'wa'appen',[1] '**you know what I mean**', which in terms of segmental phonology, were delivered in the speaker's normal accent. Exceptions to this occurred in the use of names and '**gewaan**' ('go on'), which appeared to be the local equivalent to '**go deh!/there**' in South London, described by Hewitt as 'an exclamation of encouragement' (1986: 129). Thus, leaving the dinner hall, Terry called out to Richard (sometimes called 'bender' because he was said to be 'round the bend'/crazy): [gə'waan 'ben`daa]. The shifts from normal vernacular [ɒ] and [ə] towards Cardinal [a] marked this as Creole, and more generally among extensive as well as minimal crossers, the lengthening and placement of pitch movement on the final syllable of names was very common way of introducing a Creole effect.

Among minimal crossers, Creole forms were used in catching the attention of people at some distance from the speaker (see immediately above), and they also occurred in episodes oriented to transgression and negative deviation. Sally used 'cha' on several occasions, reacting negatively to unusual or disruptive phenomena ('**cha man!** check these hairy legs'; Imran:'ah there's the ((end of break)) bell' Sally: '**cha man**').

In the negative evaluation they implied, most of these uses of Creole bore some ressemblance to patterns that were identified in both SAE and Panjabi crossing. But in distinct contrast – at least as far as unstructured interaction is concerned – Creole was also used to mark occurrences that deviated from the ordinary in being excellent or impressive. This was the primary force of 'gewaan' (though of course it could also be used ironically or to embarass), and the use of Creole with a positive evaluative loading can be illustrated more fully if we turn now to the second very distinctive group of crossers, those that used Creole in more elaborate but primarily joking ways.

More extensive but jocular crossers

Creole was often used in Asif, Kazim and Salim's friendship cluster. Like a great many others who used more Creole than Sally et al., these three boys used most of the forms that the minimal users employed, and this suggests that words and phrases like '**gewaan**', '**cha**' and so on, formed a common base, beyond which more elaborate endeavours could be developed.

Interacting with white and Asian boys outside games, the Creole of these three tended to stay close to this minimal base ('if you get **catch** in there, you get done'; 'yeh after, you know, you ran, you stayed near the wall, **w'appn?**'), though at the same time, it was clear that Creole could also be used in expressions of strong approval (so, for example, on getting well-placed seats in the youth club TV room: '**gaan** the wicked seats boys! (.) the best seats in the house'). In games however, some of Asif's crossing took more innovative forms. Phonological segments were unambiguously Creolised outside the more conventional slots, and stylised prosody was laid over less predictable sentences:

> Asif: ((playing soccer outside)) yeh Glover ((An)) (1.0) Glover (3.0) ((moving and breathing hard:)) ooo! eeh! yeeh! yeeh! ((?now standing?:)) RUN DEN (.)
> Anon: go on then
> Asif: **run DMC rhyme**
> ["ɹʌn "di 'em 'si 'ɹaɪ:m]

> Asif ((playing soccer indoors)): ((laughing:)) uuh yeh (**?kick?**) **the ball over** ((laughs))
> [ki   'ðə baal: 'o:vˈɜ:]

Anglo and Asian boys were quite frequently the recipients of Asif, Salim or Kazim's Creole-ish utterances, but in my recordings, they only addressed black boys twice. In both cases, this involved merely recoding the recipient's names phonologically. One of these occurrences involved calling for a pass in soccer. The other had racist connotations, drew the addressee's attention to an imaginary danger and wasn't well received (Kazim: '**Cyril! Cyril!** Watch it man, she might flatten you with her lips'. Cyril: 'oh yeh that's very funny').

In distinct contrast, quite a lot of Asif, Kazim and Salim's more elaborate Creole was directed towards girls of Caribbean descent, with whom joking exchanges were well established (some girls had been in the same classes as Asif, Salim and Kazim at middle school). Whereas Creole had often been used in affiliative remarks to males, here it was most frequently used to impute impropriety. As in games, cross-sex interaction provided a context for more creative improvisations. Unambiguously Creole pronunciation was applied beyond the most formulaic words, the use of nonsense words was reported, and sometimes playground Panjabi was brought into close conjunction. For example:

> ((Kazim and Asif pass Laura [AC] and her friends in the corridor during dinner time. Micky is Anglo))
> Kazim: eh heard the new news (.) Micky's goin' out with Laura
> Asif: **AAH GO'AAN LAURA**
> [gəaan   ]

```
    Laura:  ((laughs)) (              )
  Anon F:  (              )
     Asif  ((smile voice)): EUGH! CHECK THE GIRL'S face man
                           ((dec))                [gɪjalz]
  Anon F:  OI!
   Kazim:  check the [gɪjalz] face
```

((K and A are walking around the corridors, as is a group of black girls))

```
   Girl:  ASIF! (2.0)
  Kazim:  GO AAN ASIF  YOU 'AVE LOTS OF (        )
   Asif:  ((laughs)) (3.5)
          WHERE Y' GOING (.) GRACE JONES   GO ON DERE
          ['wɛ    jə gə`ɪŋ::   ˌɹɛɪs  ˌdʒaːnz  gə`ᵂaan `dɛɹ]
```

Extensive and serious crossers

As I have already indicated, I managed only limited fieldwork access to the third kind of Creole crossing – 'extensive and serious'. But there were occasions when adolescents with a reputation for Creole use were recorded in interaction with black informants wearing radio-microphones. This was the clearest example, and it involved Mashuk, the adolescent of Bangladeshi descent who ran a sound system and socialised with a lot of black youngsters outside school:

Extract III.23

Participants and setting: 1987 dinner-time. Andrew [14 AC M, wearing radiomike], Adrian [14 AC M], Mashuk [14 Ba M], AnonF [An F], AnonF2 [F], Colin [? M] are in the bikesheds outside, a relatively secluded area where people used to smoke. Andrew is eating crisps up until line 38. In line 52, a conversational topic has started up independently of Andrew, who joins it in line 64.

```
1  Anon F:  what lesson have we got last
2  Andrew:  ma ⌈ths
3  Adrian:     ⌊we got maths
4  Anon F:  oh cor
5  Andrew:  the assignment
6  Anon F:  I know but um- I haven't finished my- task one yet
```

```
 7  Andrew:  ain't you
 8  Anon F:  no
 9  Andrew:  I ain't fin(ished) my task four
10  Anon F:  I ain't (started on) task one and (    ) two (I
11           haven't finished) task three and I havent done task
12           four
13  Mashuk:  ain't you done none of the tasks
14  Anon F:  no ⌈ no we've got 'em but I ain't done 'em
15  Adrian:     ⌊I've done all of 'em  I've done all of 'em
16           ⌈I'm on task six
17  Mashuk:  ⌊have you got 'em in rough
18  Anon F:  yeh- no (.) I ain't done anything
19  Anon F2: I've done it in rough
20 ?Mashuk:  when does it have to be in by this-
21           ⌈this Monday init
22  Anon F2: ⌊Monday
23  Anon F:  ooh shit
24  Anon F2: not this Monday next Monday
25  Mashuk:  what I've done is um (.)
26  Anon F:  we gotta do extension work as well, we got an hour
27           extension work
28  Andrew:  yeh
29  Mashuk:  ⌈yeh so have we
30  Adrian:  ⌊((laughs)) (    )
31  Anon F:  no you haven't
32  Mashuk:  yes we 'ave
33  Anon F:  yeh but at least you get- you get given what to
34           write we we're not allowed to th- what (.) we're
35           not told anything
36  Mashuk:  nor are we
37  Anon F2: no everyone gets the same
38  Andrew:  ((wrapping up crisp packet)) yeh YEH EVERYONE
39           GETS  SAME YEH (.) yeh (.)⌐
40  Mashuk:  it don't matter how thick or ⌈(     ) you are you get=
41  Adrian:  ((rapidly))                  ⌊ANDREW
42  Mashuk:  =the same t-(.)AAH CHAA ⌈ME LIGHT IT UP MAN
                     ['ɑɑ ˘tʃɑɑ   |'mi 'laɪt ʔə? 'ʌp mæn]
43  Adrian:                          ⌊Colin's behind you
44  Andrew:  ((rapidly)) wh' Col where's Colin man I can't-
45           where's Colin man where's Colin where's Colin
46           ((smile voice:)) aah dere you are (.)
47           Colin give me a pull please
48  Colin:   no hold on
```

```
49 Andrew:   mm?
50   Colin:   ⌊just I just lit it up
51 Andrew:   ⌈so? I wan- I z wan a pull on it
52       :   ⌊(                    )
53 Mashuk:   ((imitating an offer to fight)) come on 'en
54           come on ⌈come on
55  Adrian:          ⌊((laughs))
56 Andrew:   ((?looking at the microphone?)) (say⌈something)
57 Mashuk:                                       ⌊AND THE GUY
58           WENT DOW::N MAN ⌈=
                [↑daʊ::n]
59  Adrian:                  ⌊sweet
60 Mashuk:   =AND THE GUY AND THE GUY GOT UP (FOR
                                     SOME) MORE::
                                       [↑mɔ,::]
61 Anon F:   ⌈why did he say) come on 'en
62      :    ⌈(                    )
63 Anon F:   ⌊Andrew?
64 Andrew:   ⌊(ss she- )
65  AnonF:   what an 'en Andrew booted 'im and then he came up
66 Andrew:   zz the guy (sort of) ((makes fight noises
67           and ?gestures?)) the guy flew:
68 Mashuk:   (now right) ⌈the guy went like this
69 Anon F:   ⌈          ⌊(            ) come on 'en come on then
70      :    ⌈((laughs))
71      :    ⌊((laug⌈hs))
72 Mashuk:        ⌊AND ANDREW WENT LIKE DIS (.)
             ⌊(?gestures))
73 Andrew:   ⌈tssss ((laughs))
74 Anon F:   ⌊(              )
75 Mashuk:   ((laughing)) AND 'ANDREW 'JUS `PU:,:SHIN ,THE
                          GUY ´MAN
                                  [dʒəs pʊ::ʃɪn      ðə
                              gaɪ:: mæn]
76           and (him plus ) the ((name of the posse))
77 Andrew:   ah⌈ dᶻudᶻudᶻudᶻudᶻu ((=?sounds of punches?))
78 Mashuk:   ⌊((laughing) (YEH            ⌈        )
79 Andrew:                               ⌊(     clearin the
80           table man) AND WHEN Simons hit that ((laughs))
81           thing innit
82 Mashuk:   'member(.) 'member when we were doing the roll-up
83 Andrew:   OH YEH
84 Mashuk:   everyone come in though ⌈it was
85 Andrew:                          ⌊they thought it was
```

```
86                    ganja ((laughs)) (.) ⌈an' it wz jis-
87 Mashuk:                                 ⌊(            ) everyone
88                    ⌈(fucking) thought it was spliff
89 Andrew:           ⌊innit                              oh my g-
90 Mashuk:           the ˌwoːˌmeːn 'they 'were 'ready to ˌcall the ↑poˋliːce
                     [wɪːmɪːn deɪ wə rɛdɪ tə kɔːl ə pəliiːs]
91 Andrew:           ennit ((the account continues))
```

Formally, from line 42 onwards, there were a number of Creole features in Mashuk's speech. Lexically and grammatically (cf. e.g. Sutcliffe 1982), there was his use of '**chaa**' and '**me**' for 'I' in line 42; his non-use of a verbal auxiliary in line 75 ('Andrew _ just pushing'); and '**spliff**' (marijuana cigarette) in line 88. Prosodically (cf. e.g. Wells 1982: 572–3), the high falls over stretched syllables in lines 58 ('down'), 60 ('more'), 75 ('pushing'), and 90 ('police') contributed to a Creole effect, as did his stressing of the second syllable of 'women' (line 90).

Mashuk's speech bore a number of similarities to the way in which Creole was used by both 'minimal' and 'extensive but joking' crossers. Like both, Mashuk used '**cha**' and emphasised syllables that were unstressed in ordinary vernacular English, and there was an orientation to transgression and non-normal phenomena both interactionally and thematically. It is not clear exactly what the arrangements about lighting cigarettes were, but clearly, Mashuk treated his not doing so as an offence in line 42, and in his narrative, the women's action was cast as grossly misplaced in line 90. Beyond that, Creole coincided with references to unofficial activity: smoking, prohibited at school (line 42 – cf. Hewitt's '**mi a-go blango**'); spliffs, illegal; and fighting. In fact from line 42 onwards, Mashuk's utterances contrasted sharply with those preceding, where school work had been the topic and where there were no Creole features in his speech. With the shift towards the Creole-linked topic, the key of the interaction became much more energetic, with more loud talking, laughter, improvised noises (66–7, 77), and probably also gesturing (67, 72). In one way or another, symbolic connotations of lively vernacular adolescent life provide a common link between Mashuk's uses of Creole, Asif et al.'s, Sally et al.'s and those described by Hewitt. These connotations were counterposed to the norms of polite mainstream society, and broadly accommodated concerns with excitement, risk, trouble, unusual appearance, sport, and relations with the opposite sex.

Obviously, Mashuk's use of Creole differed from Sally et al.'s in being less formulaic, and in this respect, it was a little like some of Asif, Salim and Kazim's. But there were also major differences between his and theirs. In sharp contrast to Asif, Salim and Kazim, Mashuk did not use Creole vowels or consonants – his use of Creole lexis, grammar and prosody did not carry through into segmental phonology (Hewitt notes roughly the same in relation to 'interpersonal' users, 1986: 188). At the same time, his switch into a (still) distinctly Creole style of speech was not just short-lived, as it had usually been with Asif et al., who dropped back to normal pronunciation after just one or two turns at the most. Auer's (albeit fairly idiosyncratic) distinction between 'transfer' and 'switching' is particularly useful here:

> [In transfer], language alternation from language X to language Y is followed by further talk in language X, either by the same or by other participants. [In switching], language alternation from language X to language Y is followed by further talk in language Y, by same or other participants. [With transfer], no renegotiation of the language of interaction is observed. The stretch of speech formulated in the other language has a built-in and predictable point of return into the first language. [With code-switching], the new language invites succeeding participants to also use this new language (1988: 200).

Admittedly, the varieties involved in these data (vernacular English and Creole) are much less distinct than those that Auer has in mind (Italian and German). Nevertheless, the Creole of Asif et al. can be classified as 'transfer', while at the very least, Mashuk was engaged in a sustained 'switch' in register. Furthermore, though no one else used markedly Creole items, he was unambiguously supported in this shift into a Creole-friendly frame by Andrew, a black youngster of the same sex, who joined him in telling central parts of the story in lines 85 and 86, and produced strongly affiliative 'innits' to a couple of turns with clear Creole features (lines 88–9, 90–91; cf. Auer 1988: 203). Mashuk's Creole was embedded in a well-defined and relatively stable engagement enclosure/conversation. In contrast, Asif et al.'s most elaborate ventures occurred in games, or in fairly brief passing encounters with members of the opposite sex.

It is now worth summarising the implications of this sketch of different kinds of out-group Creole use in Ashmead.

8.4 Interracial Creole: summary

In the first instance, all these data suggest that Creole crossing was associated with phenomena that differed from the routine norms of everyday life. Admittedly, this account has neglected the most subtle grammatical and phonological penetrations of Creole into local vernacular speech. Nevertheless, it is noticeable that even in uses that were similar to the ones that Hewitt describes as 'interpersonal', there were still quite clear symbolic resonances – knowledge of ethnolinguistic distinctiveness had not been transcended.

Secondly, Creole was used in ways that varied considerably in the degree to which it was ritualised. Many of the uses exemplified most clearly among Salim, Kazim and Asif occurred in games and cross-sex jocular abuse, activities that bear strong ressemblance to Turner's account of the liminoid as a space where activity is freed from the normative expectations of ordinary conduct. Often, the use of Creole segmental features in their pronunciation signalled a separation between a special persona and their ordinary 'selves', the latter reemerging very soon afterwards. In this respect, these crossings differed substantially from all of Mashuk's and from some that occurred among minimal users such as Sally. In the rather different uses of the two latter groups, speech with Creole influences at the levels of lexis, grammar and/or prosody coincided with the expression of perceptions, concerns or narratives which fitted with the interactional positions that the speakers continued to maintain in ordinary vernacular discourse. Mashuk and Sally's utterances can still be considered ritualised – they were oriented to breaches and they drew on Creole's distinctive symbolic resonance to create special emphasis. But here, there was a genuine alignment between self and voice, 'actor' and 'persona'.

These 'groups' of speakers did not differ from one another categorically. Though the data on Mashuk was too limited to say very much, there was certainly some overlap between Asif et al.'s and Sally et al.'s uses of Creole. In Extract II.17 in Chapter 5.4 for example, Creole was influential at the point when Asif articulated a strong sense of personal grievance, and in several of the examples in the paragraphs on minimal users, Creole was either offered or taken as (more or less) joking abuse. However, there were quite sharp differences in the overall quantity of Creole use and in the extent to which it occurred within well-established relationships with black peers.

The white adolescents who used Creole least generally avoided it in the presence of black youngsters, which fitted the view expressed in interviews that crossing was least acceptable among whites. In contrast, again as suggested in interviews, Salim, Kazim and Asif's Creole was set within a familiarity with black peers that was long-standing but not intimate. They did use Creole with its inheritors, but only if they were female. Finally, in line with Hewitt's emphasis on the importance of close friendship, Mashuk socialised extensively with black young people outside school, and his use certainly was not limited to black interlocutors of the opposite sex. In contrast to the others, Mashuk's use was actively supported by his participation in recreational activities shared with friends of Afro-Caribbean descent. These differences are arranged schematically in Figure 8.1.

Figure 8.1:   Chart summarising Creole crossing

Everyday assumptions about social order have a full hold on conduct	The hold of normal assumptions is partially weakened	The hold of normal assumptions is more extensively weakened	
A	E		Arenas primarily occupied by the inheritors of the variety concerned
A	x	F	Intergroup arenas
A	G		Arenas where the inheritors of the variety in question are either absent or have little influence

A = speech in the local multiracial vernacular
E = weakly ritualised Creole crossing as exemplified in Mashuk's speech
F = more strongly ritualised Creole crossing as exemplified in (some of) the speech of Asif et al.
G = weakly ritualised Creole crossing as exemplified in the speech of Sally et al.
x = see the accompanying discussion in the text

Before explaining the location of E, F and G in this figure and relating the chart to the data covered in this chapter, it is worth just restating its theoretical basis and clarifying its layout. The underlying idea is that in the everyday assumptions about social order operating in this speech community, Creole was viewed as the language of young people of exclusively Caribbean descent. Asian or Anglo adolescents could and did make quite obvious use of this variety, but this entailed some movement away from the norms that participants oriented to in everyday life. If you could persuade others to momentarily move away from these assumptions (as in jokes), or if events occurred that temporarily suspended them (games, transgressions, and so on), crossing could sometimes be safely achieved. But if a person crossed at times that were not liminal, they risked being seen as making a serious claim about really being black.

The factors that weakened the hold of normal assumptions about the language-ethnicity relationship were numerous (see Chapter 7.9). It does make sense to talk about variation in the strength of the grip that quotidian assumptions had on conduct, but because the influences loosening this hold were multiple, it would be very difficult to arrange anything but the clearest instances on a continuum of liminality. For this reason the horizontal axis on the chart is treated as a set of fairly clear-cut divisions, even though with more data and more theoretical elaboration, one might ultimately want to deal with more subtle gradations. The vertical axis is fairly self-explanatory, and I shall try to use this as a (very approximate) sliding scale. Here, inheritors are adolescents whose parents or grandparents come from the Caribbean.[2]

In now turning to the points situated within this matrix, it is first worth briefly noting that A represents the 'taken-for-granted medium subsisting through all interaction' – one of the ways that Hewitt describes the local multiracial vernacular (see Chapters 5.5 and 8.2 above). Here, Creole forms mingled in generally unnoticed ways alongside Panjabi and other influences (though cf. Chapter 5.6 on adult correction).

A second point concerns the positioning of E and G – the uses typified in Mashuk and Sally. Their roughly similar positioning on the horizontal axis captures the similarity that Hewitt notes between segmentally unmarked 'interpersonal' uses of Creole (like

E), and the forms employed by minimal users (cf. Hewitt 1986: 188ff). At the same time however, it also highlights the substantial difference between them. This becomes clearer if one considers the point marked 'x'.

'x' represents the patterns of *avoidance* found among both minimal and extensive-but-jocular users. Minimal users almost never used obvious Creole when black peers were present, and extensive-but-jocular users only used it in jocular cross-sex interaction with inheritors. This pattern stands to reason. Weakly ritualised uses of Creole would be riskier than strongly ritualised ones, since there is a greater chance that they would be interpreted by inheritors as *real* claims to a black identity. Schematically this is shown by 'x' being nearer than F to the left-hand extreme of the horizontal axis, which represents the circumstances constituting everyday reality. Crossing in this far left-hand zone would be non-ritualised and it would imply that Creole really was the speaker's normal everyday language, a suggestion that would contravene the language-ethnicity relationships regarded as part of the normal social order. In the data I have analysed, neither Mashuk nor Hewitt's 'interpersonal' crossers actually appeared to make as strong a claim as this, but clearly, they came closer than anyone else.

Minimal crossers also used weakly ritualised forms, but they were still very different because they only crossed when they were outside the company of black peers. So the gap between E and G, Mashuk and Sally et al., is very significant. In contrast, one might want to draw a line of progression between F and G, which would accommodate the similarities that actually emerged in the crossing of 'minimal' and 'extensive but joking' users (quite a lot of other adolescents not considered in this discussion might fit along this line as well). This would also make theoretical sense – after its use outside the presence of inheritors, the next safest site for clear-cut Creole crossing would be activity that was unambiguously bracketed off from normal reality.

8.5 Conclusion to Part III: the polyphonic dynamics of language and social identity

There are a number of common features in the crossing that has been examined in this part of the book. In all three varieties, language crossing was intimately connected to moments (and/or themes) where normal social order was loosened, and it either responded to these, or indeed produced or enhanced them. Unsurprisingly, adolescents also modulated the strength and salience of SAE, Creole and Panjabi crossing acts, and these differed in how far they incorporated out-group features, in whether or not they were directed towards other people, and in whether or not they marked 'real' or imaginary transgressions. Games and male–female interaction also made a difference, as did status asymmetry and indeed friendship, itself a space where the dominant order can be at least partially renegotiated (this is made particularly clear in Hewitt's discussion of 'fictive social relations', 1986: 164).

But aside from the broad generic similarities that have received most explicit attention in the last three chapters, there were obviously major dissimilarities in the symbolic associations of Creole, Panjabi and SAE. These led to some systematic differences in crossing, and in concluding Part III, it is worth drawing these together. These differences were not always categorical, and a really robust characterisation would need to base itself on a quantitative analysis that is not being provided here. In addition, proper recognition of variation in contextual factors (of the kind that I have outlined) might generate qualifications to any general statements that could simply loop this conclusion back into the start of Chapter 6! Even so, with these hedges in mind, certain broad tendencies seem to be discernible.

SAE was often used as a 'say-for' (Goffman 1974: 535), a voice not being claimed as part of the speaker's own identity but as one that was relevant to the identity of some transgressor. In contrast, the much greater linguistic integration of Creole with local vernacular speech often suggested close identification between speaker and voice. Like SAE, Creole could be used to criticise, but (outside jocular abuse), its specific effect was to lend power to the speaker's position rather than to attribute weakness to the target. Most crossers avoided SAE with Panjabis and Creole with Afro-Caribbeans, but with the first, this was to avoid being seen as insulting, while with the second, the speaker was much more likely to be vulnerable to charges of pretentiousness. With SAE, deviation was attributed to non-competence, whereas with Creole, it seemed to be more a matter of will.

The distinction between deference (expressing a person's appreciation and respect for the interlocutor and their relationship, Goffman 1967: 56) and demeanour (conveying a person's confidence in their own interactional competence and self-control, Goffman 1967: 77) is useful here. Where deviation from normal conduct was at issue, SAE evoked excessive deference and insufficient demeanour as the appropriate diagnosis, whereas Creole reversed this, implying abundant demeanour and limited deference. This was reflected in the way that each related to male–female relations. There was not much vulgarity in SAE utterances, and when relations with the opposite sex were in question, SAE implied hesitation or ineptitude (**'what you do man?'**; **'are you not there?'**). In contrast, a lot of sexual terms figured in Creole crossing, and when focused on male–female relations, it tended to conjure the prospects of successful sexual engagement (**'gewaan Bruce gewaan!** Bruce's got two girls!'; 'Micky's goin' out with Laura' – 'aah **go'aan** Laura') (cf. Jones 1988: 151).[3]

While crossing was generally *inhibited* by the presence of people who had inherited ties to *SAE* and *Creole*, the participation of Indian and Pakistani peers was actually *central* to playground *Panjabi* crossing. Set within predominantly playful antagonism, cross-over Panjabi made provocative claims to an identity that speakers *wanted* their interlocutors to contest. Admittedly, adolescents sometimes inserted single Panjabi words into vernacular utterances in a way that suggested they were 'semi-nativised' ('it's them two [gʌndəz] (('dirties'))', and in explaining why he was universally nicknamed 'Mutsy', one white informant said that it was an adaptation of the Panjabi word for 'fatty' ([moʈa]). But generally, second language learner social relations and interactional practices figured prominently in the way that Panjabi crossing occurred, as well as in reports. The process of moving into a new language, and the identity risks that this involves, were given central emphasis.

Acquiring another language variety was also a major issue with crossing in Creole and SAE, and there too, the acquisition of new ways of speaking was closely linked to movement outside the identities assumed in habitual vernacular speech. But the social positions involved in language learning were much more highly defined, and because of this, adolescents were more hesitant, less willing, to adopt them than they were with playground Panjabi.

With Panjabi, bilinguals abandoned their sure-footing in mainstream Panjabi culture, crossers refused positions of interactional subordination, and they converged on one another in a no-man's land where questions of ascendancy were (temporarily) settled in the current interaction.

In contrast, in SAE and in Creole crossing, there was less equality and less status indeterminacy in the way that language learning was construed. With SAE, second language learning was generally salient, stigmatised and detached from the central currents of vernacular adolescent life. Code-switching (outside games) threatened the recipient with regression, symbolically isolating them on a path of historical development abandoned by adolescents who had arrived at an endpoint that they now took for granted. In contrast, particularly in Hewitt's account, Creole represented a well-defined destination that motivated many young people, but which lay on an acquisitional route set around with social constraints that encouraged them to camouflage their learning, obscuring it in the refracted Creole forms that collective aspiration had drawn into the local multiracial vernacular. The politics of identity were involved in all three learning situations, but they differed in their degrees of orientation to 'sport', fear and desire.

In order to clarify the identity of these different 'language learning' problematics with more general processes of language mixing, to capture their differences without reifying them, to integrate them within a general view of syncretic peer group culture, and to make a wider connection with sociolinguistic research and theory, it is useful to draw in Bakhtin's notions of 'polyphony' and 'double-voicing' ([1929] 1984; [1935] 1981). According to Bakhtin, 'a variety of alien voices enter into the struggle for influence within an individual's consciousness (just as they struggle with one another in surrounding social reality)' ([1935] 1981: 348). Recognising that words, discourses and languages participate in this as well as 'voices' ([1935] 1981: 360), he pays particular attention to 'internally persuasive' varieties:

> Internally persuasive discourse . . . is, as it is affirmed through assimilation, tightly interwoven with 'one's own word'. In the everyday rounds of our consciousness, the internally persuasive word is half-ours and half-someone else's. Its creativity and productiveness consist precisely in the fact that such a word . . . organises

masses of our words from within, and does not remain in an isolated and static condition. It is not so much interpreted by us as it is
further, that is, freely, developed, applied to new material, new
conditions; it enters into interanimating relationships with new contexts. More than that, it enters into an intense interaction, a
struggle with other internally persuasive discourses. Our ideological
development is just such an intense struggle within us for hegemony
among various available verbal and ideological points of view,
approaches, directions and values . . .

The internally persuasive word is either a contemporary word,
born in a zone of contact with unresolved contemporaneity, or else
it is a word that has been reclaimed for contemporaneity; such a
word relates to its descendents as well as to its contemporaries as if
they were contemporaries; what is constitutive for it is a special
conception of listeners, readers, perceivers. Every discourse presupposes a special conception of the listener, of his apperceptive
background and the degree of his responsiveness; it presupposes a
specific distance. All this is very important for coming to grips with
the historical life of discourse ([1935] 1981: 345–346).

In the Ashmead data on crossing, Creole, Panjabi and SAE can
all be seen as internally persuasive 'alien voices', the first two being
comparable to the 'contemporary word, born in a zone of contact',
while the last is more like 'a word that has been reclaimed for contemporaneity'. All of them entered into the consciousness of local
adolescents and each was tied to a special sense of the potential
social relations surrounding its use. In addition, they can be seen as
struggling with one another for supremacy, and we can gain a
broad view of different forms of influence if we move to Bakhtin's
characterisation of 'double-voicing', which is the way in which different internally persuasive alien voices act upon the utterance
([1929] 1984: ch. 5; also Hill and Hill 1986: 390–1). With double-
voicing, speakers/writers use someone else's discourse (or language)
for their own purposes, 'inserting a new semantic intention into a
discourse which already has, and which retains, an intention of its
own. Such a discourse, in keeping with its task, must be perceived
as belonging to someone else. In one discourse, two semantic intentions appear, two voices' ([1929] 1984: 189).

In fact, there are several kinds of double-voicing (or 'double-
languaging', Bakhtin [1935] 1981: 360), and one of these is
described as 'uni-directional'. With 'uni-directional double-voicing', the user employs someone else's discourse 'in the direction of

its own particular aspirations' ([1929] 1984: 193). Speakers themselves go along with the momentum of the second voice, though it retains an element of otherness ('a slight shadow of objectification') which makes the appropriation 'conditional', introducing some reservation into the speaker's use of the second variety ([1929] 1984: 189–90). However the boundary between the speaker and the voice they are adopting can diminish, to the extent that there is a 'fusion of voices'. In such circumstances, discourse ceases to be double-voiced and instead becomes 'direct, unmediated discourse' (p. 199).

Obviously, there will be substantial variation in the particular languages and discourses that are most closely synchronised with the abiding interests of any given individual, and indeed their influence is certain to vary contextually. But of the three varieties considered here, Creole appeared to be most closely integrated into the mainstream of adolescent activity, and its use was the most 'uni-directional'. A great deal of the time, there certainly was some reservation in the way it was used by whites and Asians, and this was most noticeable in the way they avoided it in the presences of black peers. Even so, crossers often used Creole to lend emphasis to genuine evaluations (that were also often positive). In addition, its proximity to the local multiracial vernacular reflects the fact that, much more than either SAE or Panjabi, Creole was used close to the point where uni-directional double-voicing shifted over into direct unmediated discourse. In spite of a good deal of variation across speakers, situations and moments (exactly as Bakhtin suggests), some version of the Creole's 'sociolinguistic horizon', some interpretation of its symbolic value, was being adopted by many adolescents in the enunciation of their own social identities.

Bakhtin contrasts 'uni-directional' with 'vari-directional' double-voicing: 'Here . . . the author [or speaker] again speaks in someone else's discourse, but . . . introduces into that discourse a semantic intention directly opposed to the original one'. In vari-directional double-voicing, the two voices are much more clearly demarcated than in the uni-directional kind, and they are not only distant but also opposed ([1929] 1984: 193). In certain respects, adolescent uses of Asian English appeared to be vari-directional. With adults and in unstructured peer group interaction, the orientation to deference superficially encoded in the Asian English persona was counterposed to an actual stance of disrespect. Double-voicing was brief and quite clearly set off from ordinary vernacular speech (in Auer's terms, it involved 'transfer' rather than 'switching'). However, perhaps more clearly than either of the other two, Asian English was a site for the convergence and contestation of different evaluations (loyalty to co-ethnic adults struggling with a sensitivity to stigma generated within an enduring context of British race stratification). Context made a major difference to the outcome of this conflict, and in games, the double-voicing of SAE became uni-directional. There still was not any movement towards a fusion of different voices – indeed it was SAE's separation from vernacular speech that allowed speakers to step outside the hurly-burly of competitive play. Nevertheless, the voice's connotations often worked in synchrony with the speaker's primary intentions.

In Part V, I shall return to some of these notions, give fuller consideration to Bakhtin/Volosinov's ideas about discourse and ideology, and following Hill and Hill, explore their wider relationship to language crossing and sociolinguistics. But before then, some attention needs to be given to a third setting in which crossing commonly occurred – performance art.

Notes

1. In Ashmead, 'wa 'appen' was generally used as an ordinary question ('what's happened?') and so it had moved some way from its original use as a greeting (Hewitt 1986: 130, 143).

2. 'Inheritance', rights accorded by descent, can be contrasted with 'affiliation', in which allegiance to a language is not regarded as a consequence of birth. Both types of (socially negotiated) language loyalty need to be distinguished from actual proficiency or 'expertise' – see Chapter 13.6–13.7 below for fuller discussion of this particular decomposition of the 'native speaker' concept.

3. In comparison with both SAE and Creole, references to sexuality in Panjabi crossing tended to be much more scrambled and outlandish, mixing sexuality in with words referring to non-sexual bodily functions.

Part IV

Crossing and Performance Art

9 Creole and SAE (iii): Rituals of morality and truth, falsity and doubt

So far, we have considered crossing in the presence of adults, and crossing in informal recreation with peers. The interview reports in Chapter 2 suggested, however, that performance art – particularly music – generated an interactional environment which itself served as a distinctive third context for crossing. It is this possibility that we shall explore in the next two chapters.

I ought to say at the outset that my own first-hand understanding and involvement with the musics preferred by my informants has been limited, and this accounts for Part IV being much shorter than Parts II and III. I did not go to any events where black sound systems performed, and I made no tape-recordings during the bhangra discos I attended. Nor did interview questions dwell on music in the kind of detail that would be required to do proper justice to this aspect of youth culture. Overall in my corpus, there was a good deal less data on music and dance as a context for crossing than there was on other kinds of peer group activity. Nevertheless, the close analysis of a few verbal exchanges can sometimes be more revealing than the cursory analysis of many, and fortunately, there are a number of relevant accounts of performance art which can serve as secondary sources.[1]

The present chapter starts out with a brief outline of the place that sound systems occupy in black cultures. It then looks at some Ashmead evidence on white and Asian participation being facilitated both by gender difference and by North American influences. It moves on to consider the way in which sound system events generate alternative social orders, and it draws on a distinction between play and ritual to differentiate the crossing discussed in this chapter from most of the uses evidenced earlier. This then leads into some additions to the model that was introduced in the previous chapter (Chapter 8). The chapter concludes with a brief discussion of stylised Asian English in local dramatic perform- ances. Discussion moves on to consider bhangra in Chapter 10.

9.1 Sound systems and black music

Black music has had a profound influence on generation after generation of white youth in Britain. The particular forms that have had this effect have varied over time – in the post-war period, rhythm and blues had greatest impact in the 1950s, but at different periods subsequent to that, soul, disco, funk, hip hop and house from the USA and ska, rocksteady and reggae from Jamaica have all been influential:

> black music has consistently acted as a carrier of oppositional atti- tudes and sensibilities, and of new, liberating possibilities and pleasures to young whites. For, time and time again, white youth have found in black music a more realistic and resonant account of their experience than established idioms of cultural expression could offer. (Jones 1988: xxi)

These musical traditions have entered the mainstream of commer- cial popular music to differing degrees, and it is there that most white youth have encountered them. But commentators stress the extent to which they have been independently sustained in the institutions of the black community, and to understand the Ashmead data that follow, it is necessary to give a brief account of the role played by sound systems (cf. Hewitt 1986: 116ff).

Sound systems were brought over from Jamaica in the mid- 1950s, but by the late 1960s and early 1970s, they were established in all Britain's major black communities (Jones 1988: 39). A sound system is a very large mobile hi-fi, generating a sound that is particularly distinctive in its reproduction of bass frequencies. According to Gilroy,

> perhaps the most important effect of the sound systems on the con- temporary musical culture of black Britain [in which they remain a core institution] is revealed in the way that it is centred not on live performances by musicians and singers, though these are certainly

appreciated, but on records. Public performance of recorded music is primary in both reggae and soul variants of the culture. In both, records become raw material for spontaneous performance of cultural creation in which the DJ and MC or toaster who introduces each disc or sequence of discs, emerge as the principal agents in dialogic rituals of active and celebratory consumption. It is above all in these performances that black Britain has expressed the improvisation, spontaneity and intimacy which are key characteristics of all new world black musics . . . (1987: 164; also Hebdige 1987: 84ff; Jones 1988: 28ff)

In the primacy given to live talk-over, sound systems alter the social relations dominant in commercial pop, subordinating recorded products to the changing demands of the collective event in which they are being consumed. The distance between audience and performers is reduced, and

at parties and small clubs, not only would the sound-owners themselves toast, but known and competent members of the audience would also take over the microphone for a few records, the aim especially being to brighten up the party or contribute to the mood of the occasion – in the common phrase, to 'nice up the dance' (Hewitt 1986: 116; also Hebdige 1987: 88; Back 1988: 213; Jones 1988: 29)

Beyond this,

Soundsystems vary in size from the largest, which have commercial identities and work professionally, to the small ones which provide entertainment for a small house party. A soundsystem can be passed down through the family. Thus the ability to own a soundsystem is not confined to those who can afford massive, expensive systems . . . It is important to stress that most black Britons can own, or be involved with, a soundsystem. Many smaller sounds build their own equipment to minimise expenditure, so it is viable to be a producer as well as a listener (Back 1988: 213; also Hewitt 1986: 116)

The extent of white involvement with sound systems has fluctuated quite substantially since the late 1950s (cf. e.g. Jones 1988; Hebdige 1979, 1987; Gilroy 1987: 122ff). During the late 1970s and early 1980s, the association of reggae with Rastafari led to an emphasis on black cultural exclusivity, but in the mid to late

1980s, this relaxed with the growing influence of soul and hip hop. Both of these provided much more of a warrant for inter-ethnic mixing, without in any way diminishing the centrality of the sound system (Gilroy 1987: 190, 193–4, 210–1; Hewitt 1986: 100; Hebdige 1987: ch. 16; Jones 1988: 139, 218).

So sound systems were (and still are) a central feature in black music. They entailed a close relationship between performer and audience, and it was not particularly difficult for black adolescents to become involved with a sounds of their own. Furthermore, during the 1980s, the move away from reggae to soul and hip hop made it easier for whites and Asians to participate. This information helps us to understand the kind of context that black music and dance culture provided for language crossing in Ashmead.

9.2 Crossing and black music in Ashmead

Accessed through the mass media, black American music was generally very popular among adolescents in Ashmead, and when compared with bhangra, it was often referred to as 'English music'. The spread of North American culture is a subject well beyond the scope of this study, but adolescents often switched into US speech forms in contexts that both were and were not directly related to performance art.[2] From the fragments that informants chanted with one another or into the radio-microphone, it was quite clear that in 1987 Creole now existed side by side with North American varieties as languages appropriate to oral performance. For example:

> Adrian [AC]: pump up the volume
> ((Creole [pɒmp ʊp ðə vɒlʲjʊm]))
> pump up the volume ((Creole))
> pump up the volume ((Creole))
> check it out!
> ((North American accent: [tʃek ɪᵈ æ::ə]))

And while 'pump up the volume' was frequently encoded in Creole, another common catchphrase 'pick up the microphone, excite the crowd' was realised in American pronunciation.

The opportunities for participation in sound system culture created by American influences was intimated in the following extract, and I shall briefly return to this after discussion of how sex difference facilitated access, another issue foregrounded this interaction:

Extract IV.1

Participants: Darren [AC M 15, wearing radio-microphone], Sue [An F 15], others bystanding
Setting: 1987, dinner time. 5th year common room. Sue has said that she's part of a sound system 'posse' – a posse is a group of people who follow a particular sound wherever it is playing (Back 1988: 214). Darren is quite closely involved with several other sound systems, and he has expressed doubts about Sue's claims, at one point asking 'so you want a challenge against us lot?', and at another inviting her to show her skills by 'chatting' on his radio-microphone (an offer she declined).

```
 1  Darren:  you lot are rubbish man ru:bbish you migh- well as
 2           soon as I hear you play right, you- you might be
 3           good for girls, but
 4           ((switches into a funny voice:)) not good for boys
 5           (.) so fuck o:ff
 6  Sue:     you're a boy innit (2.0)
 7  Darren: ⌈yi-
 8  Sue:    ⌊so it shouldn't (be much different so never mind)
 9           (2.0)
10  Darren:  you're shit
             ((l.))
11  Sue:     you ain't heard us yet
12  Darren:  I'd like to hear you
             ((l.))
13           when- when you lot playin' now
14  Sue:     (well   ) don't know yet we ain't decided (1.0) got
15           to get all our equipment together (3.0)
16  Darren:  they don't even know the ABC about it (.)
             ((l.))
17  Sue:     (we do know so just shut ⌈up)
             ((l.))                    │
18  Darren:                           ⌊I know more about- em-
19           sound ⌈system
20  Sue:          ⌊well who- who- (1.0)
21                what posse do you belong to
                  ((?US accent: [pʌsi]))
22  Darren:  we're the ((name)) posse
                  ((US accent:{pɑ̃:sĩ:]))
```

23   Sue: know that
24 Darren: along with the em _____ posse and _____ posse (.)
25   Sue: yeh but you're- you're- you're boys innit
26 Darren: yeah! so what's that got to do with it (.)
27   Sue: quite a lot (3.5)
28 Darren: ((singing)): we are the _____ **possee** yeh
                 ((North American accent: [pãsiĩĩĩ]

In this extract, Darren thought little of Sue's aspirations and said as much (lines 1, 10, 16). But he didn't express this through an unqualified dismissal of the possibility that her sounds might be worth listening to. In this extract, he twice expressed interest in hearing them (lines 2 and 12), and later on they shook hands on an agreement that he would pay £10 if, in the event, they impressed him. Up to a point, Darren appeared to accept actual proficiency, directly assessed through performance, as the best basis for evaluating Sue's claims, and this was in line with sound system convention more generally – according to Back 'there is a great amount of rivalry [between sound systems]. This is ultimately expressed in competitions or 'battles' between them' (1988: 208). However, *these* views were only partially meritocratic – expectations of competence were tempered by reference to sex difference.

In lines 3, 4 and 5, Darren expressed a patronising confidence in masculine superiority which Sue subsequently contested in lines 6 and 8, implying that if Darren was to be taken as a typical specimen, there could be little substance to such presumptions (a challenge which elicited no response). In line 25 however, after Darren had listed his affiliation to several local posses, Sue herself backtracked on this and toned down her claims to expertise by reasserting male–female non-comparability. Several commentators have suggested that although there are very significant exceptions, there has been a prevailing ethos of masculinism in sound system culture (Back 1988: 215; Hewitt 1986: 123–4; Hebdige 1987: ch. 13). In combination with the negotiations around gender evidenced in Extract IV.1, this helps to explain the wider observation that in Ashmead, it was white girls rather than white boys that gained access to the heartlands of black youth culture (Chapter 1.7; cf. also Jones 1988: 183). In the interaction above, both Sue and Darren expressed active interests in a prestigious youth cultural field, but the assertion of gender differences created an opportunity to locate themselves in different competitive arenas so that direct threats to the other's status claims could be avoided. And of course the relationship facilitated by this defusion of potential rivalry could also be enhanced by sexual attraction.

So relatively fixed social differences were actively cited in this interaction, but these related to gender, not ethnicity (later during the same dinner time, Darren engaged in mocking banter about sound system claims with another group of girls, only these were black rather than white). In fact, non-local/regional/ethnic cultural group membership was made salient during this exchange, but the form that this took synchronises with general observations about the shift to North American musical styles increasing interethnic access to central areas of black culture. In the word 'posse' in line 21, Sue switched from the back open rounded vowel /ɒ/ character-istic of local vernacular speech to an unrounded (and more central) variant – [ʌ]. In doing so, she performed some kind of cul-tural recontextualisation which Darren picked up in line 22 (and 28) and articulated as North American with an unrounded back open vowel ([ɑ]) (distinct from the front [a] that would be its Jamaican Creole realisation, cf. Wells 1982: 122, 576). Evidently, an American frame of reference constituted relatively neutral ground, open to both black and white.

So both sex difference and US influences were factors increasing the accessibility of sound system culture to non-Afro-Caribbeans at local level. But the case of Mashuk raises a rather more complex set of issues. As already indicated, Mashuk was male and Bangladeshi by descent. He was much more deeply involved in black culture than Sue, and he ran one of the sounds that Darren identified in lines 22 and 24 (indeed Adrian and Andrew, both AC descent, also claimed membership of the posse associated with Mashuk). Certainly, the American orientation still appeared to be important - invited to rap by Adrian, Mashuk's performance on the radio-microphone was North American accented. But a proper interpretation of the kind of crossing that Mashuk engaged in requires further reference to the character of sound-system events.

9.3 Sound systems, ritual and liminality

Gilroy describes the collective events at which sound systems per-form as follows:

The town halls and municipal buildings of the inner city in which dances are sometimes held are transformed by the power of these musics to disperse and suspend the temporal and spatial order of the dominant culture . . .

The oppositional implications of a culture which . . . rejects the legal subjectivity on which policing rests are compounded as these locations become the object of hostile surveillance by the police. However, more significant than the rejection of capitalism's legal system is the critique of the economy of time and space which is identified with the world of work and wages from which blacks are excluded and from which they, as a result, announce and celebrate their exclusion . . .

[Hip hop] forms and devices articulate particular conceptions of space and time . . . They combine with specific invocations of truth and causality . . . to facilitate the dispersal and carnivalisation of the dominant order. The past and the conceptions of truth which derive from meditating on it, not only provide an answer to the mystifications which are integral to racial subordination . . . They become central to the regulation of collective memory, perception and experience in the present, to the construction of community by symbolic and ritual means in dances, clubs, parties and discos . . . The extent of this alternative public sphere can be gauged from the stress which soul and reggae cultures lay on names. Performers and those who support them . . . take new names which are specific to their underground cultural networks . . . In rap and go-go . . . performances, naming is at the centre of elaborate rituals in which MCs and rappers establish their right to speak before doing so and connect collective identity to community territory. The impulse to cement a critique of the world by unnaming and renaming it also shapes the reggae underground profoundly. (Gilroy 1987: 210, 211, 215, 216; see also Jones 1988: 35, 44)

Two elements stand out particularly clearly in Gilroy's account of black music and dance events: their opposition to the values of a dominant society in which race stratification and oppression feature prominently, and their enunciation of an alternative history and social order ('The soundsystem and the microphone provide a platform from which Black [British] can re-write and document their own history', Back 1988: 216). Referring to these features, we can elaborate an account of the ritual characteristics of sound system events in a way that starts to suggest the distinctiveness of Mashuk's crossing.

In some respects, Gilroy's description resembles the conception of ritual that was used in Parts II and III of this book, where symbolic action and divergence from dominant social norms were foregrounded as constitutive elements. There are some quite strong echoes of Turner's notion of the liminal, where there are 'few of the attributes of either the preceding or subsequent . . . social statuses or cultural states', where everyday 'social relations may be discontinued, [where] former rights and obligations are suspended, [and where] the social order may seem to have been turned upside down' (Turner 1974: 24, 27). In sound system events for example, the 'pre-' and 'post-liminal' can be aligned with the conceptions of space, time, history and social relations dominant outside the dance hall.

But in Gilroy's account, there is also an element that was largely absent from the adolescent practices that we examined earlier. In sound system events, the elicitation of a marked emotional response and the generation of a strong sense of collectivity appears to be much more powerful than in any of the more fleeting, fragmentary and individualistic practices described above. To capture the difference, we can refer back to Turner's distinction between the liminal and the liminoid, and elaborate this in terms of Handelman's account of the difference between ritual and play (1977). Both ritual and play are liminal/liminoid, but *ritual*, says Handelman, is explicitly oriented to matters of morality and truth. Beyond that, with participants in ritual,

> the collectivity . . . also forms a 'community', or an important segment of a community which is articulated with a socio-political unit in the ordinary social order. It is such units which are limned as moral entities within the ritual frame, and are then returned to the mundane world as moral communities whose memberships continue to be affected by their experience. (Handelman 1977: 188–9)

This coincides with Gilroy's reading of sound system culture. In contrast, *play* carries messages of falsity and doubt to the participants, and rather than defining moral community, it 'accentuates the plasticity of ideation' (p. 190). 'Let us believe' in one becomes 'make believe' in the other, and

> if the symbolic types of the ritual domain should appear in the social world (viz prophets, incarnations and so forth), they are imbued with vigour to influence the arrangements of ordinary reality. But the symbolic types of the play domain, should they escape, are rendered

impotent: the sad clown, the happy-go-lucky joker, the pitiful fool, the irresponsible lunatic and so forth. (p. 189)

It would be a mistake to treat this dichotomy as absolutely categorical, since as we have already seen, ritual activities which seem to involve conflict and deception at one level can in fact contribute to a sense of community on a higher plane. Even so, Handelman's distinction helps to make sense of some of the differences between Mashuk's crossing and the crossing of, for example, Asif et al. I made no recordings of Mashuk's most spectacular performances, which doubtless occurred when he was in charge of the microphone at parties or dances. But even in the limited data reported in Chapters 2.1 and 8.3, it was clear that his membership of the moral community articulated in sound system events permeated through to his everyday experience. He emerged from these with considerable local prestige, and much greater licence to use Creole in ordinary talk than any other white or Asian. He co-participated with black friends in the elaborate alternative order developed within sound system culture, and they sustained his use of Creole in a way that made it possible for us to speak of 'switching' rather than 'transfer' (in Auer's sense – see Chapter 8.3). In contrast, other Asian and Anglo youngsters were involved with sounds either much more marginally (Sue et al.) or not at all (Sally, Asif et al.), and rather than connecting with participation in ritual events central to the black community itself, their crossing generally appeared to have emerged within much more open arenas of interethnic mixing. Admittedly, Asif, Kazim and Salim practised relatively spectacular Creole with black girls, but the play character of this activity was indicated by the way it earned them a reputation as jokers (see Extract I.2).

The suggestion is, then, that in the context of performance art, crossing involved some qualitative differences from crossing in ordinary interaction with teachers and peers. In due course we will consider whether there is any support for this in the data on SAE and Panjabi, but before that, it is worth completing the account of cross-over Creole by elaborating the figure that was first presented in the previous chapter (8.4).

9.4 Charting other-ethnic Creole

Figure 8.1 in the previous chapter represented the three different kinds of crossing that were observed in informal interaction between peers. Two entries now need to be added to this chart (see Figure 9.1) – D, typified in the crossing that I am assuming Mashuk made at sound-system events, and M, mass media representations of Creole.

Figure 9.1:   Chart of Creole crossing, revised to include its use in performance art

Everyday assumptions about social order have a full hold on conduct	The hold of normal assumptions is partially weakened	The hold of normal assumptions is more extensively weakened	
	E	D	Arenas primarily occupied by the inheritors of the variety concerned
		F	Intergroup arenas
	G	M	Arenas where the inheritors of the variety in question are either absent or have little influence

D = more strongly ritualised Creole and black English crossing assumed to occur when Mashuk took the microphone at sound system events
E = weakly ritualised Creole crossing as exemplified in Mashuk's speech
F = more strongly ritualised Creole crossing as exemplified in (some of) the speech of Asif et al.
G = weakly ritualised Creole crossing as exemplified in the speech of Sally et al.
M = uses of Creole and black English in the music propagated through mass media

Two points need to be made about the placement of D. In first instance, situating Mashuk's (presumed) microphone performances under the heading which refers to more extensive weakening of the normal everyday assumptions draws on Gilroy's description of the profoundly liminal character of sound system events. There were also likely to be a large number of other factors which mark these performances as highly ritualised (see Hewitt 1986: 116–19 on toasting). Secondly, the vertical axis can be used to accommodate the common observation that sound system culture shifted towards greater ethnic pluralism during the 1980s. When reggae was dominant, D would have been higher up on this vertical axis, and Mashuk's participation might have been more problematic.

M – the use of Creole in the mass media – involves crossing in terms of speech reception rather than speech production: broadcast or recorded performers were no doubt themselves normally Afro-Caribbean by descent. While this is clearly a different notion of crossing from any that have been used so far, it is important because it captures the way in which, alone in their bedrooms, white and Asian young people could actively engage with black language and culture outside the presence of black peers.[3]

Of course, familiarity with mass-marketed performances could obviously serve as a major reason for wanting to cross into the heartlands of black youth culture, and it could also provide quite a useful resource in trying to do so. Nevertheless, commentators suggest that a lot of complex negotiation was entailed in the shift from an engagement in exclusively Asian or white contexts to one in which most of the participants were black (cf. Jones 1988: Part II), and some of this was intimated in Extract IV.1.

Let us now turn to SAE.

9.5 SAE in drama

The dialectic between mass representations and local performance was undoubtedly an issue with stylised Asian English. Comedians on TV, for example, quite often used this variety and they elicited mixed reactions (cf. Chapter 2.4). At local level, there were also theatrical presentations in which adolescents made use of SAE. According to reports, these most often occurred in drama classes at school, and lessons of this kind involved a systematic cycle in which pupils planned and rehearsed in small groups, and then performed in front of the whole class, which subsequently made a critical assessment. In interview discussions, SAE performances of this kind also appeared to be the subject of conflicting evaluations:

> Asif [Pa M 15]: did you watch the plays today? . . . it's out now
> 'yes yes' ((in SAE)), it's silly man, it's stupid all this 'very
> good very goo', that's out now, it's not in you know . . . it
> didn't sound good
> BR: did people laugh at that?

Asif: no, they used to but ((now)) nobody laughed

Anita [In F 15]: Salim usually does typical Indian people who can't speak too well

BR: do you ever think that's kind of offensive?

Anita: not really, I mean our parents speak like that, I mean my parents don't because – well he grew up here my dad, but my mum does, and you it's sort of – just sort of becomes part of you

Although it was not clear whether or not this was part of a deliberate strategy, there are grounds for supposing that these local performances at least partially reclaimed this variety from the racist stereotyping common in its dissemination through mass channels:

Sohan [In F 15]: I hate that I think . . . I hate that, especially when . . . they do it on the telly as well, don't they

Kiron [In F 15]: stereotypes

Sohan: I don't like it . . . it's sort of a shame innit, not every Indian talks like that ((....))

BR: does it happen a lot do you think

Sohan: I've seen it on telly quite a lot, and . . . only when you're doing drama do people use it. Hardly anyone does an Indian play . . . but when we do an Indian play- I- I use that sort of funny sort of accent thing

BR: why is that, that isn't- if you hate it, why do you use it

Sohan: you gotta show how the older- . . . 'cos I was playing an older character and I had to show how the older people speak . . . Leela (([In F 15])) said that might do it, so we just tried it – it worked

BR: and you didn't think that was kind of doing a stereotype or kind of

Sohan: it's alright if we use it, 'cos we're Indian

This evidence suggests that in a number of ways, SAE in drama might be different from the uses described in Chapters 3 and 6. Dramatic performances could set out to address human and social issues that adolescents felt were important, and for both Sohan and Anita, SAE appeared to be a necessary component in the conscious effort to reflect local social life. Prepared through consultation in small groups and then performed and assessed in larger ones, these uses of SAE also had more of an obviously

collective character than the spontaneous, fleeting and more idiosyncratic uses outlined earlier, and even though actual
performance was improvised, not scripted, it appeared to be something that adolescents worked at (Turner 1974: 54, 55). In
discussion of *Creole*, Handelman's distinction between ritual and
play was useful in differentiating Mashuk's crossing from other
people's. It looks as though the same distinction also has a certain
amount of relevance for these different uses of SAE.

Even so, it was clear that SAE figured only *incidentally* in drama
– it was not an important constitutive element, in the way that
Creole counted with sound systems and Panjabi mattered in
bhangra. And even then, it was not used to represent youth. SAE
was not a key element either leading into or flowing out from rich
and prestigious arenas of emphatically youth cultural activity. It
was not vested with a pan-ethnic appeal that derived from any
intricate association with high status and specialised cultural
zones, and there was no question of defending autonomous SAE
heartlands against the encroachment of envious outsiders.

Admittedly, dramatic performance in SAE could be a source of
celebrity, but there was nothing to contradict this general assessment in the one recorded episode where outstanding theatrical
SAE was discussed.

Extract IV.2

Participants: Anita [In F 15], Clare [AC/An F 15], Salim [Pa M 15],
Richard [An M 15], others (including Sukhbir [In M 15], Ian [An
M 15])
Setting: 1987. Lunch-time dinner queue. Premi in lines 8 and 37
had a very good reputation as an actor. Anita later said that the
dramatic context for the appearance of the character in line 26 had
been a play about pirates, in which the Captain of the ship had
come up and asked for the name of the person Salim was playing.

```
 1   Anita:   Salim (.) are you going to be in the inter-house
 2            drama competition
 3 Richard:   ((to someone else?)) OH NO (.) (you and your    ) (.)
 4   Anita:   INTER-HOUSE DRAMA COMPETITION (1.0)
              ((dec))
 5 Richard:   ((to someone else?)) shut up
 6   ? [M]:   (oh sh            )
 7   Anita:   interhouse (.) Ira Dolby by Marisa Conway
```

```
 8   ? [F]:  YES Premi's⌈(              )
 9   Clare:           ⌊now they won't allow him
10   ? [F]:  (.) they will
11   Clare:  ⌈he's     too        dumb ((laughs))
12   Anita:  ⌊WHAT HOUSE ARE you in     NO HE'S QUITE
                                                GOOD
13   Clare:  {      he's not he's         ) (.)
14   Anita:  HE'S QUITE GOOD he makes ev- he allows himself
15           to be called a ———— in ⌈front of (any)body
              ((Panjabi rude word))   ⌊((laughs loudly))
16   Clare:
17   Anita:  (.) ((laughs quietly)) ennit (.) and and guess what
18           his name was in the last play (.) he's was
19           called [lʊlli] (.) ⌈that was his name ((laughs))
              ((Panjabi: willy))  ⌊
20   Clare:  ((laughing)):    ⌊NO:
21   Salim:  ((from a little distance)): what (          )
22   Clare:  ⌈((laughs loudly))
23   Anita:  ⌊((laughs⌈loudly))
24   Salim:        ⌊(              )
25   Anita:  he comes up (.) he goes (.) he goes (.)
26           ((in SAE)) „I „am „Captain [ˈlʊlˌli] ˈSIR
                          [aɪ əm kʌpʈɪn] ((willy)) [sɜː]
27           something like-⌈((laughs))
28   Clare:            ⌊((laughs))
29   Salim:  ((from some distance)) I GIVE YOU HARD TROUBLE
                          [aɪ gɪ    ju haː   tɽʌbl]
30   Anita:  yeh: are you gonna be in it (.) ARE YOU GONNA BE
31           IN IT (.)
32   ? [M]:  (      )
33   Anita:  YES ⌈YOU SHOULD
34   ? [M]:    ⌊(   try Premi) (.)
35   Clare:  ⌈he's too DUMB
36   Anita:  ⌊(              )
37   ? [F]:  you should get Premi to do it
```

Salim was clearly sought-after as an actor (see lines 30–33), and he evidently used SAE personae to publicly elaborate an alternative world. But in terms of Handelman's ritual-play distinction, he gained his reputation as a comedian, not as an influential proponent of prestigious activity in the manner of Mashuk. It was also clear that Salim's performances led back into the kinds of agonistic activity described in Part III – it drew on the lexis of playground Panjabi, and a few moments after this extract, it was inserted back into cross-sex jocular abuse. 'Captain Lulli' the character also had a rather tenuous hold on school drama classes. The convention was that only English would be used, and Anita reported that the (very highly respected) teacher who usually took the class had been away on that particular day ('that's why he was saying it'). Furthermore, the remark in line 9 was correct – Salim had in fact now been banned from these classes. By definition, all this makes his acting atypical of the way in which SAE usually figured in drama lessons.

If SAE had been at the centre of a prestigious strand of artistic activity among youth, one might have expected discussions of theatrical SAE to have occurred with the same frequency as adolescent talk about sounds and bhangra. They very clearly didn't. In school-based groups that were organised to encourage discussion and reflection, adolescents could attempt to reclaim Asian Englishes from the representations that they were given in dominant discourses. And indeed in games, we have seen that SAE was used to enunciate some sense of shared communal interests. But this was only ephemeral, and neither of these practices generated any authority or commitment outside the well-demarcated events in which they occurred. Overall, the lack of wider institutional support severely limited the value of Asian English as an emblem of belonging with which adolescents could seriously identify.

What was the situation with bhangra?

Notes

1. Particularly Hebdige (1979, 1987), Gilroy (1982, 1987), Hewitt (1986), Jones (1988), Back (1988), and Banerji and Baumann (1990).
2. Outside settings closely related to performance art, US accent and dialect forms were used in swearwords like 'ass' ([æ:əs]) and 'bastard' ([bæstəd]), and in assertive remarks made during games ('**I can kill anyone**'; '**y' goin' down boy**'). In these non-artistic forms, they mingled with, for example, cockney rhyming slang ('**Yo China!**' [hello China plate/mate]) and also with Creole forms:

     Cyril [AC]: kick some [æəs]!
     Anon: fucking ____! they get me **vex**
              ((Creole or indeed American Vernacular Black English))

3. The significance of the difference between commercial and sound
    system performances was also evidenced in my own data when in the
    course of making a wager with Sue about the competence of her own
    sounds, Darren said 'and if you're playing, don- don don't give me
    those pop (.) music right' (Sue: 'alright').

10 *Panjabi (iii): looking beyond the borders*

The last chapter drew on a distinction between rituals which stressed deception and doubt on the one hand, and on the other, rituals which were oriented to truth and moral community. Empirical analysis of this has however remained rather tentative, partly due to my heavy reliance on secondary sources in accounting for sound-system events, and partly because this distinction applied only weakly with adolescent stylised Asian English (SAE).

My data on the crossing that was related to bhangra are more extensive, and so bhangra provides a context for continuing discussion of the 'play' versus 'ritual' – or indeed 'liminoid' versus 'liminal' – distinction. The present chapter begins with a brief account of bhangra, its presence in Ashmead, and its interethnic spread.[1] After that, it turns to one subsection of the social network I investigated, and it uses this to address a number of empirical questions: why were white girls much more enthusiastic about bhangra than white boys? What obstacles were there to their enthusiasm? How did they get past them?

10.1 Bhangra in Britain

Originally, bhangra was (and is) a form of folk music and dance closely associated with the harvest festival of Vaisakhi, performed and enjoyed by Panjabis of Sikh, Hindu, Muslim, Jain and Christian orientations throughout the India-Pakistan borderlands (Banerji and Bauman 1990: 137). During the mid-1980s in Britain, it started to incorporate the sounds, social forms and production strategies of Western popular music, and Banerji and Bauman report that at least from the early 1980s, young Asians were organising day-time events ('daytimers') in which sound systems and DJ crews played reggae, soul and then jazz funk and hip hop to mainly male audiences in community centres and hired halls. But around 1984, these events started to make more space for bhangra, and from 1986 onwards, big venues were being used to accommodate bhangra audiences of up to 3000 (1990: 146). But inspite of its professionalisation, however, and its popularity in Panjabi communities in North America, East Africa and Australasia (Banerji and Bauman 1990: 137), bhangra had not entered into the mainstream of commercial musical taste at the time of my research. It received quite a lot of attention in the British mass media around 1987 (p. 143) but it did not generally penetrate through into high street retail outlets. Instead, 'distribution continues to rely on a few specialist shops in areas of dense South Asian settlement . . . At present, even the most successful Bhangra musicians rely on daytime jobs for material security' (Banerji and Bauman 1990: 143, 144).

However, one effect of bhangra's non-commercialisation has been its maintenance of close community roots:

> privately booked live performances remain the mainstay of Bhangra musicians' efforts and reputation for all but a handful of groups. They also remain an indispensible source of feedback . . . between musicians and their audiences. Panjabi weddings excel in . . . long and enthusiastic dancing of bhangra, be it in a more traditional or in the 1980s disco style . . . [On] such occasions, two and three generations can mix on the dance floor and share . . . enthusiasm in a music and dance that . . . evoke Panjabi culture. Such privately booked performances contribute much to the continued vibrancy of Bhangra . . . [Even] a Bhangra style that relies on sampling and drum machines more than on the beat of the [traditional] dholak or the improvisatory finesse of a singer [can] command respect also from the oldest generation of Panjabis in Britain as a genre in the language and tradition of the region. Not all people of the parental generation . . . are happy with school students absconding to daytimers; but Bhangra, even where it takes its inspiration from disco or house . . . has retained its legitimacy and credibility as the music of a distinctive cultural community. As such, it continues to contribute both to its . . . traditions and to its internal debates. (Banerji and Bauman 1990: 151–2)

Much of Banerji and Bauman's account fits with reports and observation in Ashmead.

10.2 Bhangra in Ashmead

By 1987, bhangra was a major youth cultural force in the neighbourhood, disseminated on cassette (often through peer networks), in Asian programmes on local radio, and at a variety of both local and national functions (parties, weddings, concerts, discos). A substantial number of South Asian bilinguals did not particularly like bhangra (and in my sample, young people of Indian descent were more enthusiastic than those of Pakistani extraction, cf. Baily 1990). But many others valued and cultivated the knowledge and abilities associated with bhangra, and a significant number organised themselves into sound systems, bands and dance groups, and arranged discos, concerts, dance competitions and challenges (sometimes through the local schools or youth services). These varied in their scale and effectiveness, but due to social connections and first-hand experience of successful national bands, activity of this kind was much less remote from the creative centres of the cultural movement than anything that could be achieved in relation to commercial English pop.

For many local Panjabi youngsters, bhangra involved both intergenerational continuity and youth specificity (cf. Clarke, et al. 1976). On the one hand, it was performed at community events which were attended by all ages, and informants also said they asked their parents to explain when bhangra brought forward unfamiliar traditions and meanings. On the other, it was plain that their own tastes in bhangra often differed from older people's and these were sometimes the source of disagreement. Bhangra entailed both the inheritance and the reinterpretation of valued tradition, and in the wider context of race relations, it also challenged dominant conceptions of ethnic stratification and cultural worth, asserting an inheritance that had hitherto often had low status in society at large.

Bhangra offered local adolescents opportunities for distinguishing themselves within the hierarchies of peer group prestige that were loosely equivalent to the opportunities offered by rap and hip hop. In the same way that some young people aspired or succeeded in displaying expertise in the context of (originally) black sound systems, others sought to do so through Indian music and dance groups (though of course in both cases, performers could encounter just as much disparagement as admiration from the middle-of-the-road majority). Occasionally, there appeared to be some rivalry between followers of these two broad musical orientations, but many adolescents were eclectic in their tastes: 'I listen to a lot of Indian music, but just because I listen to Indian music everyone thinks . . . you know, 'cos of the dances [I organised] and that . . . everyone thinks I don't listen to English but . . . 'cos my brother listens to a lot of Eng . . . soul, so I like a lot of soul as well' [In F 15].

There were though, clear differences between black music and bhangra in terms of their pan-ethnic appeal and momentum. There were more white and Asian fans of black music than black and white fans of bhangra, and bhangra was seen as drawing on black sounds rather than vice versa. In fact, it is now worth turning to a fuller account of bhangra's cross-ethnic appeal in Ashmead.

10.3 Bhangra's local interethnic spread

Bhangra was influential in a number of ways in the interracial arenas where my research was set. During their dinner breaks, bilinguals sang (parts of) songs, talked about them and listened to tapes. Regularly supplied with cassettes by members, bhangra served as the standard musical background on ordinary nights at the youth club. School assemblies provided a platform for the performance of dance and music, and bhangra discos were sometimes held on the school premises and at the youth club, in the afternoons or in the evenings.

This sometimes had a big influence on non-Asian adolescents.

Extract IV.3

Participants: Jagdish [In M 15], Mohan [In M 15], BR
Setting: 1987 interview. Chris Hughes was Anglo, male, and about 17–18 years old. [Simple and abbreviated transcription]

Jagdish: it's like at my brother's wedding right, have you heard of
a guy called Chris Hughes

BR: yeh

Jagdish: him right, he was at my brother's wedding
((. . .))
and there was a group up there, (   ) quite famous one
innit, Alaap, they were there and their main song is

	really 'pabye ni pabye' like, and there's a new cassette, there was a new cassette out right called . . . what was it
Mohan:	'Best Wishes
Jagdish:	'Best Wishes From Alaap' right, and that boy he used to listen to these songs, and he used to come and everything, and when he was around, when he was around us Indian boys and everything, he used to start singing these songs and everything, so (we used to) really get amazed and once he went on the stage he did, and the singer was there right and he started singing in front of that singer, that singer's song right
BR:	in front of, when Alaap was there
Jagdish:	the actual singer yeh, and they got surprised they did you know, (he was) singing all these Alaap songs, they got really amazed they did, singing all the different Alaap songs

Other informants also reported this young man's expertise, but despite the fact that there were also accounts of local black and white DJs using Panjabi when they played bhangra at mixed discos, in this extended network, Chris Hughes' appeared to be fairly exceptional. Adrian was also identified as someone with a more active interest in bhangra than most, but his involvement seemed to be both more limited and more typical:

Extract IV.4

Participants: Adrian [AC 14 M], Helen [AC F 14], BR
Setting: 1987 interview. Warren, mentioned by Helen, was a very popular black youngster with a wide reputation for stylistic innovation. [Simple and abbreviated transcription]

BR:	people sometimes say that Adrian, he knows quite a few ((bhangra songs))
Adrian:	yeh 'cos I sing a ⌈ lot of songs . . . songs
Helen:	⌊ Indian songs yeh, it's mostly the songs
BR:	right go on give us a song
Adrian:	((sings)) 'pabye ni pabye ni soonu pabye, pabye ni pabye ni soonu pabye, hoorra hoorra hai'
BR:	((laughs)) right go on and another
Adrian:	((sings)): 'disco divaani aaha, aaha, disco divaani aaha neha'
Helen:	((laughs))

BR: know more of that song do you?

Adrian: no I can't remember the rest

BR: and how – where did you learn these?

Adrian: Iqbal!

Helen: Iqbal – always Iqbal. Iqbal teaches us the songs and he does the drums to it and everything, we just sit there singing the songs (the same)

Adrian: him and him, Balraj and Jins

Helen: yeh same

Adrian: Iqbal does the singing, and Balraj and Jins do the beats ((drums on the table himself))

Helen: yeh, say in something like English or something, they sit there, they're singing, we all join in

BR: so when is it that they teach you for example?

Adrian: economics

Helen: yeh, in lessons

BR: in lessons?

Adrian: yeh they were singing 'pump up the volume' just now in Indian

Helen: ((laughs)) yeh
((. . .))

BR: so how many songs do you think you've been able to sing at one time or another

Adrian: four, about four or five

Helen: 'Bhangra Fever'

Adrian: and 'Bhangra Fever' man

BR: go on sing that

Adrian: I can't remember how that goes now

Helen: no, it's just got a few words in it, but most of it is sort of

Adrian: beat

Helen: the beat, just er the music, instrumental sort of

BR: right, okay . . . do you buy bhangra cassettes

Adrian: ((laughs)) no thank you

Helen: no, er Warren, Warren had some once of er Iqbal's brother . . . and he brought, he brought one round to my house one time and he was sitting there and he was playing it right, and I recorded it but I can't remember what happened to it . . . 'cos he was sitting there singing to it and this is me: 'how do you know that song?' and he goes um 'F____ ((Iqbal's brother)) taught me it' and everything . . . and I taped it and I've lost the tape now, it's at home somewhere

BR: and what do the teachers say for example if you're doing that?

> Helen: teachers just tell us to be quiet 'cos they don't under-
> stand what we're saying
>
> BR: right right
>
> Helen: it would be different if they understood but they didn't
> understand what we're saying and they go um 'this is an
> English school, can't you speak *English*' and everything,
> and they start (   )
>
> Adrian: yeh there was a teacher in er Southleigh called Mrs
> D___, and she was a French teacher, and we were mak-
> ing too much noise on one day right, and she told all of
> us . . . it was mainly all er Pakistanis and coloureds in
> there . . . and she was going 'why don't you all go back
> to your own country' . . . and we just took it, we took it
> serious, we took it serious and we gave her a lot of stick
> and all that

Four aspects of this account are worth commenting on. First,
bhangra evidently contributed to the interethnic classroom Panjabi
discussed in Chapter 4. Secondly, it looks as though non-Asian
adolescents generally only enjoyed bhangra in the company of
Panjabi peers. There appeared to be relatively little independent
interest in it ('do you buy bhangra cassettes' – 'no thank you'). The
story of Warren's tape was the only instance I heard of separate listening, and Warren did not appear to have set a lasting precedent
('Warren had some once . . . I've lost the tape now'). This dependence on Asian friends was also noted with playground Panjabi in
Chapter 7, but it contrasted sharply with the spread of black music
– with black music, young people often listened to (more commercial) variants on radio or cassette on their own alone, and some
practised rapping outside the company of black peers. Thirdly,
despite being cited as someone with an unusually active interest in
bhangra, Adrian's repertoire did not appear to be very extensive.
No doubt the interview setting partially deterred him from displaying his full competence, and more subtle and knowledgeable
prompting might have elicited much more. But his close friendship
group did not provide him with any very special access to bhangra,
and this view of a relatively limited repertoire is at least consistent
with its being motivated more by sociability than independent
enthusiasm. Lastly, like Adrian, there were other non-Asian adolescents who were said to have a greater than average knowledge of
bhangra, but in interviews, this also seemed to be rather shaky.[2]

Quite a lot of local black and white youngsters were familiar with one or two bhangra songs, but their knowledge did not stretch much further:

> BR: do Cyril or Conrad [AC] know any songs?
> Jagdish: yeh, 'pabye ni pabye', stuff like that ennit, the main
>   ones, you know, most that . . . if there's a new
>   song out or anything, people are always playing it

And sometimes, they were merely tolerant:

> Paul: I think it's horrible, can't stand it
> Cyril: I don't like it that much either really . . . I mean it
>   wouldn't kill me to listen to it, it wouldn't kill any of us
>   to listen to it, would it
> Paul: no, I mean where there was something here ((at the
>   youth club)), at the disco thing, we were dancing to it,
>   weren't we

In fact, interviews and observation at several youth club bhangra discos produced two findings about the social distribution of out-group interest in bhangra. White boys were the category least likely to show interest or to attend discos (Kuldip: 'I've noticed that but I don't know why'), while white girls were the non-Panjabi category *most* likely.

Among the adolescents I interviewed, the white female friendship cluster involving Sally, Kelly, Lorraine and Pat were much more consistently positive about bhangra than any other. For these four girls, Imran played an important role as a point of access, and this actually highlighted the male–female contrast. Imran also played a significant role providing white boys with opportunities to cross. In the 1984 data, he had been involved in the use of agonistic playground Panjabi with white and black boys – particularly with Ian, Richard and Terry [all white] – and he was still very good friends with them. But although they heard bhangra during their very regular attendance at the youth club, these boys showed no particular enthusiasm for it in interviews and they did not go to bhangra discos. Their Southleigh grounded familiarity with competitive Panjabi did not carry any further. So, on the one hand there appeared to be a fairly settled male tradition of cross-ethnic Panjabi, unreceptive to new forms of prestigious youth culture, and on the other, a more adventurous female interest in bhangra, emerging from a position of relative unfamiliarity among girls who had not been to Southleigh and who lived outside the locality.

This striking difference in the interest in bhangra displayed by white girls and white boys is one of the issues that the rest of this chapter tries to address. How was it that girls rather than boys became enthusiastic about bhangra, and what were the strategies they used to gain access? These questions will require explicit comparison between playground Panjabi crossing and Panjabi crossing in expressive youth culture, and this will in turn provide an opportunity to reconsider the play–ritual distinction that we highlighted at the start. For most of this analysis, I shall continue to focus on Sally, Imran and their friendship clusters, moving between particular interactions and a more general account of the way they managed male–female relations.

We can start with the interaction.

10.4 An interethnic conversation about bhangra

Here is the longest example of one of the rare tape-recorded occasions in my corpus when non-Asians paid explicit attention to bhangra:

Extract IV.5

Participants: Sally [An F 15, wearing radio-microphone], Gurmit [In F], Lorraine [An F], Anon A [An F], Anon P [Panjabi F]
Setting: 1987. Dinner-time, sitting outside. One of the girls has a cassette player and is listening to bhangra on headphones. These headphones are fairly inefficient and the music can be overheard by everyone. During the interaction, there seems to be some play about who the bhangra cassette actually belongs to – cf. lines 23–28 and line 69.

```
1     Sally:    don't drink it all Iggy (.)
2  Lorraine:    you fuck off right (1.5)
3     Sally:    fuck you Iggy don't ea- I mean it don't drink it all
4               (.) EH WHAT's on there at the moment (.)
5    Gurmit.:   it doesn't forward
6    Anon A:   ⌈ wanna listen (.)
7              ⌊ ((someone bangs the cassette player))
8    Anon A:   ⌈oh you have to be very delicate ⌈(with it
9     Sally:                                     ⌊I've done it I
```

```
10              done it alright (1.5) you just have to bang it
11  Anon P:  nothing on yet (.)
12    Sally: ⌈no (that's cos its     )
13  Gurmit: ⌊it looks like the way I'm banging I'll probably
14              break the whole machine
15    Sally: d'you want to play
16  Anon A:  do you want me to bang you
17           one ⌈(        ) ⌈
18  Gurmit:     ⌊no ⌈these ⌈are boring songs
19    Sally:         ⌊what's │ on it can I
20  Anon P:                  ⌊try the other side (.) put the
21        ⌈other side (        )
22  Gurmit: ⌊it's the other side
23    Sally: ((high pitch)) cor who's song's this can I listen
24      ? : ((odd laugh))
25  Gurmit: ((laughing lightly)) Lorraine's
26  Anon P: ((?light laugh?))
27    Sally: is it Lorraine's
28  Gurmit: ((laughing lightly)) yeh
29  Anon A: (              )
30    Sally: OH LORRAINE ⌈EH LORRAINE HAS IT GOT=
31      ? :              │(              )
32      ? :              ⌊you want the other side
33    Sally: =[kenu mɪnu] ON it
              (( f.))
              ((words from a Panjabi song meaning 'she said to
              me'))
34      ? : ((the cassette is changed over to the other side, and
              after this, music can be faintly heard on my recording
              up until line 74. But it was evidently still audible to
              several participants at line 88))
35  Anon A: it's got ((singing)) [hɔʊli hɔʊli]
36    Sally: ((sings)) [ɒ kennu mennu] I love-
37    Anon: HELLO
38  Gurmit: oh that
39    Sally: ((speaking)) my favourite song that is you know
40  Gurmit: it's from Heera (.) ((a very popular bhangra group))
              ((l.))
41    Sally: is it on here (1.0)
42  Gurmit: no not on here (1.0)
43    Sally: ((sings)) [uər tʃə ti he] ((speaking)) that's a
              ((ll.))                    ((l.))
```

```
44              good 'un as well (.) Imran likes that one (.)
                  ((l.))                  ((l.))
45              ((louder:)) what's on that side (2.5)
46              ((overhearing a song)) I LIKE THIS ONE
47   Anon A:   let me listen (1.0) what is it
48     Sally:  go on (2.0)
                  ((ll.))
49   Gurmit:  │I better have a check (.)
50   Anon A: └oh this is the one I like (.) Gurmit (.)
51              ((quietly, at a high pitch:)) (        )
52    Anon :   ((short half laugh)) (2.5)
53     Sally:  Imran's got this (2.0)
54       ? :   aah aah (5.0)
                  ((l.))
55       ? :   (shag bags) (6.0)
56 Lorraine:  OH this is the one we were takin' the marm- em the
57              mickey out of (    ) (.) sounds like marmelade (1.5)
58   Anon A: ((sings)) ⌈I love marmelade (2.0)
59       ? :          └((laughs))
60     Sally:  Imran's got an Indian tape and he won't⌈give me it
61   Anon A:                                          └I like
62              [hɔʊli hɔʊli] (.) (where          )
63   Gurmit:  that was the first one init
64     Sally:  ((sings quietly)) ⌈[olle olle]
65       ? :                     │ yeh (                )
66       ? :                     └yeh (              well you =
67       ? :   = gonna have to bring     ) (4.0)
68     Sally:  LORRAINE has it got 'I love you' on it (.)
69   Anon A: she don't know it ain't hers
70     Sally:  ((sings)) [o kennu mennu] I –
71              ((speaking:)) that's a good'un that's a good'un (.)
72       ? :   ((short quiet laugh)) (6.0)
73     Sally:  Imran's got this tape right and at the beginning
74              it's sort of Scottish music playing ((light laugh))
75   Gurmit:  (1.0) oh that's Heera (.)
76   Anon P: oh ⌈yeh
77     Sally:    └it's good that tape
78   Anon P: mm │ (    )
79     Sally:  I lo└ve that tape (.) he brings it round my
80              house and I listen to (3.0) [bɔr:dʊm ] (1.0)
81              that's how it goes it [ bⁱr:dəm ] (2.5) it sounds
82              English don' it (3.0)
83   Anon A: ( n          ) (.)
84     Sally:  it does dunnit a bit (.)
```

```
85        ? : (N  IT BREAKS    )
86     Sally: n all of a sudden it'll let go [bᵘrːrːrm] and it'll start
              ((f. acc.))
87   Gurmit: (nine minutes past) (
88     Sally: no this one's abit bo ⌈ ring
89    Anon A:                      ⌊ oh that's what I was thinking(.)
                                     ((acc.))
90            THE BEGINNING ONE is- (1.0)
91    Anon P: it's probably finished by (the          )
92    Anon A: take it over to the other side and put it to the
              ((acc.))
93            beginning (.) stop (.)
94     Sally: no they- (.) to get it to the beginning you (
95                 side) to get to the beginning of the other side
96    Anon A: No:: this side I want the beg ⌈ innin of   that's why=
              ((f.))                         ⌊            ((l.))
97     Sally:                                ⌊OOH:
98    Anon A: =I'm just saying turn it over=
99     Sally: =((laughs)) I SHOULD BRING MINE mine's got fast
100           forward and rewind on it
101   Anon A: well it would do winnit (1.0)
102    Sally: I'm a snob
```

((the conversation turns to cassette players, with Sally describing hers))

Close analysis of this interaction reveals (a) bhangra's role as a prestigious cultural form worth competing about, (b) the rather unwelcoming reception that its inheritors gave to white enthusiasts, together with (c) the kinds of obstacle that the latter had to overcome as a result.

10.5 Competitive incentives and obstacles to white participation

The most persistent antagonism in this episode involved the two white girls, Sally and Anon A. They shared an interest in listening to the bhangra music on this cassette, and both asked to listen properly through the headphones (lines 6, 19, 23, 47). But differences in opinion made themselves apparent throughout the interaction. Disagreement was obvious at the start and the finish of the extract (lines 8 and 10, and lines 92 to 102), but there were also a number of more subtle competitive moments.

In line 35, Anon A inserted herself as the respondent to Sally's question to Lorraine about the cassette's contents, ignored the yes-no format of Sally's question, and instead stated its inclusion of a song that she showed she knew (and liked – lines 61 and 62) by briefly singing:

30   Sally: OH LORRAINE EH LORRAINE HAS IT GOT
33   [kenu mɪnu] ON it
35 Anon A: it's got ((singing)) [həʊli həʊli].
36   Sally: ((sings)) [ɒ kennu mennu] I love-

Sally's subsequent turn did not treat Anon A's prior utterance as any kind of reply to her inquiry. She also reiterated her interest in [kenu mɪnu] (in a different form), and in doing so, rejected any bid that Anon A might be making to introduce her preference as a topic for discussion. But at the same time, her own brief switch into song gave some recognition to Anon A's previous action, and as a result, their failure to coordinate a coherent question–answer sequence looks more wilful than accidental.

In line 61, Anon A overlapped Sally's turn:

60   Sally: Imran's got an Indian tape and he won't ⎡give me it
61 Anon A: ⎣I like
62   [həʊli həʊli] (where   )

This was well past the first transition relevance place in Sally's turn (cf. Levinson 1983: 296–7). While the effect of her onset might be to treat what Sally was going to say about Imran as a highly predictable 'last item' (cf. Jefferson nd) – itself perhaps a strategic move, implying Sally's tedious lack of newsworthiness on this subject – she could not in fact know how Sally was going to complete her turn. This was a competitive, disaffiliative interruption, reintroducing the subject that Sally had ignored in lines 35 and 36 in a way that bore little relation to the prior turn.

In line 69, Anon A told Sally that the cassette did not belong to Lorraine, thereby revealing the trick that Gurmit had played (lines 25 and 28), her own position as a confederate of Gurmit's, and

Sally's position as the pig's ear. Sally gave no acknowledgement of this, once again singing [o kennu mennu] as she had when Anon A had previously replied to the question addressed to Lorraine. Even so, she did not persist with this inquiry (maybe now accepting the authority of the answer that Gurmit had given her earlier in line 42).

Some of these competitive exchanges might have occurred when any music being played, but on at least two occasions (lines 30–36 and 60–62), these girls competed in their expression of particular bhangra preferences. Evidently, an interest in bhangra was something that individuals thought they could draw on to show themselves to relative advantage.

What role did the Panjabi girls play in this? Gurmit generally stayed aloof when Sally and Anon A stated their tastes. Both white girls quite often offered assessments of particular songs, but the Panjabi girls generally neither endorsed these evaluations, nor indeed took issue with them. When speakers introduce an assessment into a conversation, there is an implicit invitation for recipients to respond with evaluations of their own: 'A recipient of an initial assessment turns his or her attention to that which was just assessed and proffers his or her own assessment of this referent' (Pomerantz 1984: 62). In general, second assessments that agree

> are performed with a minimization of gap between the prior turn's completion and the agreement turn's initiation; disagreement components are frequently delayed within a turn or over a series of turns . . . Absences of forthcoming agreements or disagreements by recipients, [absences realised with] gaps, requests for clarification and the like, are interpretable as instances of unstated, or as-yet-unstated, disagreements (Pomerantz 1984: 65)

Sally and Anon A's assessments often encountered the signs of unstated disagreement outlined by Pomerantz. In lines 43 and 44, Sally rated [uər tʃəti he] positively, elicited no response (marked by the micro-pause) and then elaborated this evaluation on her own:

```
43    Sally ((sings)): [uər tʃəti he] ((speaking)) that's a
                       ((ll.))                    ((l.))
44             good 'un as well (.) Imran likes that one (.)
```

Her assessment in line 71 was also followed by a gap, and then only a short laugh. One of her assessments did elicit an agreement marker in line 78:

```
76   Anon P:  oh⌈yeh
77     Sally:     ⌊it's good that tape
78   Anon P:  mm  ⌈(    )
79     Sally:     I lo⌊ve that tape (.) he brings it round my
```

But Anon P's 'mm' was ambiguous – while it might be a weakened 'yes' (cf. Maltz and Borker 1982: 202), it could also have been the preface to a disagreement (Pomerantz 1984: 72) – and by this stage of the conversation, after making four assessments that had not elicited any signs of affiliative agreement from her bilingual interlocutors (lines 39–40, 43–44, 46, 70–71), Sally didn't hang around to find out and instead supplied an upgraded second assessment herself. Since Anon A's assessment in line 50 was over-lapped, her interlocutors may not have been attending, but in lines 61–63 she also received a response that can be interpreted as an unstated disagreement, this time in the form of a clarification request (cf. Pomerantz above).

```
61   Anon A:                              I like
62          [həʊli həʊli] (where      )
63   Gurmit: that was the first one init
```

Disagreement however, does not adequately capture Gurmit's mode of participation in this extract. On one occasion, she res-ponded to one of Sally's assessments by providing some information about the songs in question, in a noticeably unenthusiastic lowered voice:

```
39     Sally: ((speaking)): my favourite song that is you know
40   Gurmit: it's from Heera (.)
              ((l.))
```

Here, she acted as a source of knowledge rather than as a fellow bhangra fan, and her self-positioning as an authority placed above the commitment of Sally and Anon A was made clearer in line 49:

```
46     Sally: ((overhearing a song)) I LIKE THIS ONE
47   Anon A: let me listen (1.0) what is it
```

48   Sally: go on (2.0)
             ((ll.))
49   Gurmit: I better have a check (.)

Without (deigning to make) any elaborate show of it, Gurmit indicated her superior knowledge on a couple of further occasions (lines 42 and 75), and in combination with her persistent refusal to engage in agreement, or indeed *explicit* disagreement, Gurmit's style of interaction continually suggested that her knowledge of bhangra placed her own tastes in a different league from Sally and Anon A's, making it impossible for her to engage in any meaningful discussion about likes and dislikes.

Gurmit and Sally were not good friends and spent little time together. But Gurmit's attitude towards these white girls' interest in bhangra did not appear to be untypical. Chapter 2.5 provided some interview evidence of a general lack of enthusiasm about white participation in bhangra, and here is Sally's closest Panjabi female friend, commenting during a playback session on the way she had agreed when another friend had said she 'hated explaining' bhangra:

hard yeh cos it's different, it's different way of them saying it and different way of English way of saying it and I find it hard . . . I dunno, I just cannot explain Indian music, it's as simple as that . . . I understand it myself but I wouldn't explain it 'cos if I said somebody, it sounds stupid . . . it don't make it sound as if it's really like that . . . a lot of people at school and everything, they always say 'what are they saying, what's happening, what's this, what's that' it's like when we do discos at school, very grand discos, or it's like when . . . somebody brings in a cassette to school and we play Indian music, then they say 'what's happening, what's this' or it's when we actually do something with Indian music, a dance or something and they like to know what's going on, I don't usually (say) but I just try and get out of it, I just don't like it, and they've all my other friends there and all . . . I think they can do it better than what I can

Bilinguals often valued bhangra too highly to accommodate in any major way to the competence of monolinguals, even if they were good friends. To understand how monolinguals actually overcame this reluctance, it is important now to clarify the difference between crossing in bhangra and crossing in playground recreation.

10.6 Playground and bhangra crossing compared

Generally speaking, in its commonest *playground* form, Panjabi crossing was part of a set of recreational activities which appeared to decline rather than increase in their influence as adolescents got older (Chapter 7.6), and black and white adolescents simply drew Panjabi into familiar break-time practices as an auxiliary element. Crossing was intricately connected with an awareness of group boundaries and ethnic difference, but the exploration of different cultural traditions was very limited. Playground Panjabi appeared to enunciate a 'tensed unity', in which speakers with different types and levels of expertise and inheritance were drawn into a social coalition that was variously fractious, comic and familiar.

Interactionally, competitive differentiation was inscribed into the most basic routines of playground Panjabi crossing, and it did not necessarily involve black or white youngsters in any plain acceptance of subordinate status. In fact, crossers had a special licence because of an assumption that as second language learners, what speakers said was generally only tenuously connected with what they actually meant. Crossers sometimes claimed that the knowledge displayed in their use of Panjabi derived from other people, but when they did so, the aim was to exculpate themselves from responsibility for the import of their message. Winning, losing and deception were essential elements in the interethnic relationship involved in Panjabi crossing, and to facilitate the play, bilinguals were quite happy to converge towards the rudimentary competence of their monolingual friends.

The general context provided by bhangra was very different from this. A complex and prestigious cultural movement was in the process of developing around bhangra, and black and white young people could really only hope to play a novice role in it. But if they were uninhibited by their relative incompetence, bhangra offered them much more scope for the exploration of cultural alternatives than playground Panjabi. Though for the most part social and linguistic difference held them standing at the threshold, non-Panjabi adolescents here looked beyond the commonest boundary rituals towards different cultural traditions with non-indigenous origins that could be part of their appeal, and it was consistent with this general orientation that when asked whether they would like to do Panjabi classes at school, it was precisely those who were most interested in bhangra who expressed the greatest interest. In this setting, crossing was generally oriented to integration into the heartlands of ethnic youth culture.

In interactional terms, crossing no longer proposed a gap between speaker and voice, and Panjabi was used in the expression of meanings with which the speakers would align themselves. As could happen with playground Panjabi, crossers might explain their knowledge of Panjabi by referring to their relationships with bilinguals who were not present. But whereas with playground jokes this was done to extricate themselves from blame, in bhangra it served to corroborate the speaker's interest (this is illustrated in Extract IV.5, where Sally's four references to Imran (lines 44, 53, 60, 73) can be seen as efforts to authenticate her interest and to summon some indirect support in the absence of affiliative second assessments from others (especially in line 44)). Another contrast lay in the responsiveness of bilingual peers. In games and jocular abuse, local Panjabi bilinguals were uninhibited about adapting the forms of their linguistic inheritance to the capabilities of monolingual friends. But they were not enthusiastic about accommodating monolingual peers inside bhangra's creative heartlands. Admittedly, mixing in the art form itself provided non-Asians with some foothold – in Extract IV.5, bhangra's incorporation of western cultural influences provided Sally with points of connection on which she could start to form and discuss her tastes ('I love you' line 68; the Scottish music in lines 73–4), and more generally, bhangra's adaptation to a disco format allowed white girls to start out by dancing in non-Panjabi styles. But evidently, bilinguals were not routinely welcoming at such access points.

The evidence on Panjabi does in fact lend support to Chapter 9's suggestion that crossing practices can be broadly distinguished in terms of those where activity was conventionally geared to deception, doubt and the 'plasticity of ideation', and those where there was a more explicit orientation to commitment, truth and moral community. Playground Panjabi exemplifies the former, Panjabi in bhangra illustrates the latter, and the pattern initially suggested for Creole appears to have more general applicability. I am in no position to try do develop a detailed comparison of the kinds of social, moral and aesthetic experience which bhangra and black musics offered to crossers, but both figured as vital influences contributing to a major qualitative difference in the forms that crossing took.

With an understanding of the broad differences between Panjabi crossing in these two contexts, we can now ask how it was that some young people achieved a degree of success in crossing towards bhangra. As before, Panjabi was very different linguistically from the varieties normally spoken by white and black youngsters. But now, in addition, it was also part of an ethnic tradition that was valued very highly by its inheritors.

10.7 Interactional practices facilitating access to bhangra

Extract IV.5 indicates that in the absence of encouragement from Panjabi interlocutors, white girls could support each other in their interest in bhangra, at least up to a point. Though there were a number of competitive moments, Sally and Anon A's interactional relationship consisted of more than efforts to self-differentiate.[3] Anon A supplied Sally with the only affiliative second assessments that she received (lines 88 and 89, and perhaps 46 and 50); Sally picked up and ratified Anon A's reference to 'holle holle' by singing brief snatch of this song to herself (lines 61,62 and 64); and it was clear that this extract was set within a wider pattern of shared involvement when Lorraine and Anon A joked about 'marmelade' in lines 56–8 ('taking the mickey' out of songs was not something they only did with Panjabi lyrics – songs in English were often playfully corrupted[4]).

Even so, this kind of mutual support was evidently rather fragile, and it does not explain how these girls gained access to bhangra in the first place – the cassette they were listening to *didn't* belong to Lorraine (line 69), and Imran never gave any to Sally (lines 60; Extract IV.5). A more adequate account starts to emerge when we consider the structure of the activity in which they were engaged.

The activity type that Sally and her friends were engaged in can be designated 'listening to music', and this presented an opportunity for crossing that was distinctive in a number of ways. Listening to music did not generally force monolinguals into a moment-to-moment, face-to-face dependence on bilinguals as a source of Panjabi. In agonistic playground Panjabi exchanges, black and white youngsters frequently copied the linguistic models recently provided by bilingual peers, and/or reproduced ones that they'd been taught before in interpersonal tuition. Those situations relied on the friendship of Asian bilinguals, and on their active, utterance by utterance willingness to share their language. In contrast, when music was being played aloud, bilinguals would have to be quite aggressive – we don't want you round here – to prevent others from listening and from picking up some Panjabi in the process.

Beyond that, activities like listening to music involve 'parallel rather than tightly interdigitated' action from participants (Goodwin 1988: 88). In games and jocular abuse, most actions were inextricably tied to those that participants produced immediately before and after, and Panjabi was specifically used to provoke a response or respond to a provocation – participants were highly attentive to each other, and indeed in these tight exchanges, winning and losing were normally at stake. In contrast, talk could be much more desultory in the context of music, with a looser interpersonal focus. Goffman's description of 'open states of talk' fits with this activity type: '[when] an open state of talk [develops], participants [have] the right but not the obligation to initiate a little flurry of talk, then relapse back into silence, all this with no apparent ritual marking, as though adding but another interchange to a chronic conversation in progress' (1981: 134–5). In open states of talk, there is less pressure to attend to what other people say and minimal or non-responses can seem less offensive. In the particular activity type in Extract IV.5, the primary participation framework sometimes consisted of the recorded musician and each girl attending separately – this certainly seemed to be the case in some of the longer pauses (lines 54, 55, 67), and more generally, their orientation to the music was clearly evidenced in the way they used exophorically deictic 'this' in lines 46, 50, 53, 56, and 88.

Listening to music also created a legitimate context for response cries and self-talk, in which participants produced utterances that could be taken as merely auditing the music's development. As argued in Chapter 7, this kind of sequentially non-implicative utterance allowed some Panjabi fellow-travelling among black and white kids, since unlike the first part of an adjacency pair, it didn't force any show of bilingual acceptance or rejection. Sally and Anon A's utterances in lines 50, 51 and 53 could be taken as music-focused response cries and self-talk. More generally, this kind of event softened any offence that might be caused when

Sally and Anon A's evaluations failed to meet with affiliative second assessments, since there were other activities going on (the songs) that also had a legitimate hold on the attention of their interlocutors. Sally's relatively hushed utterances in lines 43, 44 and 64 could be taken as an acceptance of these other claims on their involvement.

So as an activity type, listening to music provided good opportunities for crossing. It permitted access to stretches of Panjabi in the absence of active bilingual support (in contrast to agonistic playground crossing); it allowed adolescents to continue their involvement in a relatively independent manner (again, contrast Chapter 7); and it also constituted a favourable setting for the face-preserving, sequentially non-implicative expression of affiliation to Panjabi youth culture. To that, it is worth adding that in music, of course, a great deal of enjoyment can be gained without any understanding of what words mean. In fact, the scope for crossing provided by this type of event – an event that enabled participants to engage in 'parallel' rather than directly competitive, 'interdigitated' (tightly interwoven) actions – was evidenced more widely. At bhangra discos, dance conventions seldom required partners to coordinate their movements very closely, and this meant that Anglos could use western styles alongside the Panjabi dancing of Asian peers.

In addition to the details of interactional practice, discussion of bhangra crossing also needs to address adolescent social relations and identities more generally, and at this point, gender moves to the foreground as an issue.

10.8 Gender relations and movement towards bhangra

It is very noticeable that this chapter has concentrated on girls, whereas the chapter on playground Panjabi crossing focused mainly on boys. Indeed the contrast between 'parallel' and 'interdigitated' interaction – primarily female and male respectively – comes from an article on pre-adolescent sex differences in language use (Goodwin 1988). Adequate treatment of sex differences in language would require much fuller analysis than I provide, and the interaction we have been examining shows just how difficult generalisation about competition, cooperation and gender styles can be. The Goodwins, however, comment quite usefully on research in this area: 'if we are to describe accurately the organisation of male and female language, we shall have to go beyond global generalisations that contrast all men with all women in all situations and instead describe in detail the organisation of talk within specific activity systems' (Goodwin and Goodwin 1987: 241).

This accords well with the central gist of my own analysis, which shows how crossing varied in character according to the kind of event ('specific activity system') in which it was embedded. It also points to one of the factors linking gender to broad differences in types of crossing. In the adolescent peer group which I studied, it was quite clear that males and females differed in what they most often did during their free time at school (cf. also e.g. Lever 1976; Maltz and Borker 1982). While boys usually played games, girls spent much more time during dinner breaks listening to music.[5] So in the first instance, the relationship between gender and type of crossing derives in part from the different recreational activities that adolescent males and females engaged in.

But as well as their often independent leisure pursuits, it is also important to address the relationship *between* the sexes. The case of Sally and Imran suggests that romance and sexuality also played a significant role providing girls with access to bhangra. Sally and Imran's courtship was very serious: they marked the anniversaries of their first date, Imran spent Christmas with Sally's family (overcoming her brother's initial disapproval), and they thought a great deal about the best way of making their relationship acceptable to Imran's parents (from whom at this time they concealed it). They were very conscious of their relationship's potential for development and they mentioned marriage as a goal (though not common, there were quite a few Asian-Anglo married couples in Stoneford). Cultural accommodation was one strand in this commitment to growing interpersonal convergence and bhangra was an important part of it.

The relationship between Sally and Imran was also significant for their wider network of friends, and through it, a number of other white adolescents became more extensively involved with bhangra. Very few black or Asian girls attended the local youth club, but Sally introduced a number of her girlfriends. Though some dropped out or came only occasionally, others attended quite regularly and one or two started to go out with Panjabi boyfriends (the fact that they came from different neighbourhoods made this easier, since it increased the scope for liaison away from the surveillance of parents who might disapprove). As Sally and others indicated in interview, the youth club was strongly associated with Panjabi music, and whether or not they were interested in dating, friendship with Sally provided white girls from outside the area with opportunities to visit a location in the 'Asian part of town' where bhangra was played in an atmosphere that seemed more relaxed and 'authentic' than what they would find at school.

Crossing of this kind was doubtless facilitated by gender-related asymmetries of status. Both males and females could recognise the personal prestige that came from association with bhangra, but they might manage to avoid too much competition if they assumed that gender differences were normal, and that it was natural for the sexes to excel in different kinds of activity. Assumptions like these would legitimate major differences in actual knowledge, and encourage adolescents to compare themselves with members of the *same* sex if they wanted to approach bhangra competitively. Agreement that the comparisons most crucial to status assessment should be single-sex would mean that *cross*-sex interaction could be relatively relaxed, even though the two parties had very different amounts of the relevant cultural capital. The influence of this differentiation was suggested fairly clearly in Extract IV.1 in Chapter 9.2, and more generally, boys often assumed superiority and gave patronising support to girls in a range of youth club activities. Even so, though this might account for differences in the access to prestigious youth cultural sites that was granted to white males and females, on its own it does not really say enough, either about why girls would want to participate in the first place, or about their willingness to persist in what promised to remain a subordinate position for quite some time. The distinctive influence of actual or potential romance also needs to be recognised.

Though there are obvious cultural variations in the particular points and sequences involved, in romantic relationships people often think in terms of reaching quite clearly marked stages much more than they do in friendship (so that in a lot of contemporary Anglo conduct, the pattern often runs from first meeting to first date, first sexual contact, first family introductions, then cohabitation, maybe marriage, and so on). Admittedly, the development of friendship also involves stages that participants often reflect on (and maybe cross-ethnic friendship increases this, cf. Jones 1988: 131). But anticipation of reaching these 'milestones' is not so often built into the participants' current sense of their relationship. This being the case, standing at the threshold of an unfamiliar cultural activity like bhangra would probably seem less daunting for any adolescents gearing to the possibility of romance. Rather than being inhibiting, its unfamiliarity could be appealing, and a young person looking out for a romantic relationship might relish the prospect of the closer cultural involvement that this could bring.

Finally, it is worth connecting this account of romance back to the notion of liminality. In the first instance, liminality is relevant in its reference to periods and activities that are in one way or another located outside dominant social orders. Even though courtship involves a number of conventional expectations and practices, for adolescents who did not have long-standing dates (and most of my informants didn't), it was new territory, potentially quite distinct from the predominantly single-sex recreation that they had been engaged in hitherto. Admittedly, Sally and Imran's steady relationship was well-established, involving regular activities that also drew in other people (see above). Nevertheless, the fact that they concealed their courtship from Imran's parents suggests that it still was not fully integrated into the everyday social realities in which they lived, and that it retained something of an alternative, non-routine character. Beyond that, particularly in anthropological accounts of initiation rites, liminality is also sometimes associated with an active sense of transition and development. This links with the heightened orientation to progression and change that we have attributed to courtship, which in turn supported involvement in bhangra. In these connections, we can see yet another dimension of the intimate but many-sided relationship between liminality and language crossing.

10.9 Summary

Crossing in the context of performance art will be set next to other kinds of crossing in Part V, which also contains extensive discussion of wider implications. Before that, it is worth briefly summarising the main points that have been made in the last two chapters.

Important similarities and differences in the social distribution of SAE, Creole and Panjabi in their performance modes are summarised in Figure 10.1 (which takes the vertical axis from Figure 9.1).

Figure 10.1:　Performance events associated with different varieties and their distribution across ingroup, intergroup, and outgroup arenas

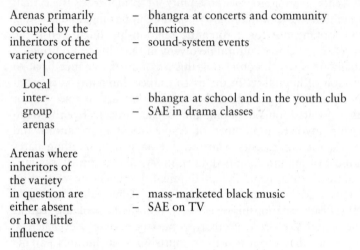

Arenas primarily occupied by the inheritors of the variety concerned	– bhangra at concerts and community functions – sound-system events
Local intergroup arenas	– bhangra at school and in the youth club – SAE in drama classes
Arenas where inheritors of the variety in question are either absent or have little influence	– mass-marketed black music – SAE on TV

In different ways, both bhangra and sound-system events involved a fairly close relationship between performers and audience. In contrast, SAE was not strongly identified with any creative centres of youth cultural activity, and relative to the others, this doubtless contributed to its symbolic status as a relic of the past. Like contemporary black musics, bhangra drew on a wide range of influences and this facilitated crossing. But it was not well-established in white youth culture, it was much less widely disseminated, and as a result, its interethnic appeal was more limited.

Consideration of sound-system culture produced a provisional distinction between crossing in which trickery and playfulness were foregrounded, and crossing that sought serious alignment with concerns and events important in black youth culture. If my data on this had been more adequate, it might have been possible to connect this with (a reworked version of) Hewitt's distinction between joking and serious Creole use among whites. However, my fieldwork covered Panjabi and bhangra rather more fully, and so this served instead as the context for a more empirical discussion of this dichotomy.

Figure 10.2: Summary of major empirical differences between Panjabi crossing in informal playground recreation and in bhangra.

	Panjabi crossing in the context of . . .	
	informal playground recreation	bhangra
The cultural arenas evoked by Panjabi	playground japes	performance art
The prestige of Panjabi for bilingual inheritors	low	high
Inheritor responses to the crosser's rudimentary efforts	convergent	non-supportive
Pretexts allowing crossers to partly disregard the proprietorial rights of bilinguals over Panjabi	games jocular abuse self-talk and response cries	listening to music self-talk and response cries
The relationship between turns at talk	'interdigitated'	'parallel'
The intentions conventionally motivating crossing acts	victory through deception	acceptance in the community of Panjabi inheritors
The crosser's status within the arena evoked by Panjabi	guilefully incompetent competitor	novice
Crosser's personal commitment to the meaning of their utterance	fairly limited	quite strong
Purpose in referring to a Panjabi source	to exculpate the crosser	to authorise the crosser
The reputation acquired through crossing	joker	style leader[6]
Sex of the crossers most evidenced in my data	male	female

Figure 10.2 provides a broad characterisation[7] of Panjabi cross-ing in informal playground interaction, and Panjabi crossing around bhangra. It outlines major differences in the cultural horizons which Panjabi conjured in each context, in the positions adopted by bilingual inheritors, the organisation of typical interactions, the social relationships claimed in crossing, and the kinds of wider status which it generated. The notion of liminality helps to illuminate all the crossing we have examined, but whereas the shift away from routine practice was commonly linked to deception and doubt in informal playground crossing, in performance art, movement away from familiar terrain was much more geared to commitment, truth and moral community. The distinction that first emerged from discussion of Creole appeared to have wider validity.

Admittedly, the interconnections between adolescent life and mixed urban art forms deserve much fuller treatment than I have given them, since influence is likely to flow in both directions and both share something of the same social and political problematics. Even so, this book provides a more comprehensive and more detailed description of different kinds of local vernacular syncretism than many others, and as such, it may serve as a useful reference point for deeper analyses of performance art in contemporary urban contexts.

Notes

1. It is worth noting that bhangra in the UK has received a good deal less scholarly and journalistic attention than sound-system culture, and that there are a several issues requiring consideration that the present discussion neglects. The notion of cross-over has figured very prominently in general discussions of bhangra, but the concern has been with its potential for entry into the mainstream of British popular music, not with the participation of black and white people in events which are closely rooted in the local Indian and Pakistani youth community. Bhangra's uptake among South Asian subgroups differentiated in terms of age, sex, religion and region of origin is another important issue which I cannot properly address (cf. Baily 1990; Banerji and Bauman 1990).

2. Sally had special access to bhangra through Imran, and she was also cited as knowing more than a lot of other white and black adolescents. But her knowledge didn't appear to be very robust:

Extract IV.6

Participants: Sally [An F 15], Kelly [An F 15], BR
Setting: 1987 interview. [Simple transcription]

BR: do you listen to black music at all
Sally: yeh, sometimes
BR: like like what
Kelly: even if I can't understand it I still enjoy it
Sally: sometimes I watch Soul Night and that on telly, they have quite a few soul programmes, I watch them they're good
BR: and what about Indian music?
Kelly: yeh I like that
Sally: I love Indian music
Kelly: yeh
Sally: yeh Imran's got some tapes, and he recorded two tapes for me, and he'll let me listen to them but he won't let me have them
BR: uhuh
Sally: that's why I like going up the youth club 'cos I like listening to the music ... I mean a few of the songs, I know some of the words ... that I can say them properly but ...
BR: you know what they mean, or you sing along with
Sally: no, don't know what they mean, just sort of sing along
BR: right, and you like
Kelly: yeh, I like them, I don't know what they mean but I still sing some of the words
BR: do you ever buy them yourselves
Kelly: no
Sally: no, Imran records, Imran records them for me but he never you know leaves the tape at my house, he takes it home
BR: that's stingy, you ought to work on him ((laughs))
Sally: yeh ((laughs))
BR: what groups do you like best?
Sally: what, do you mean
Kelly: Indian
BR: Indian, Indian groups
Kelly: I don't know any of their names
Sally: don't know any of their names

3. The second part of Sally's turn in line 60 – 'Imran's got an Indian tape and he won't give me it' – could be seen as an attempt to mitigate the advantage that her relationship with Imran gave her. And one could also construe Anon A's '[Lorraine] don't know it ain't hers' in

line 69 as at least partially conciliatory, since it now let Sally know that her leg had been pulled and stopped her making more of a fool of herself (cf. Goffman 1974: 87–9 on benign fabrications).

4. In fact, comic bhangra modifications were very common among bilinguals, though these could obviously be more elaborate and more pointed than anything these white listeners could achieve.

5. My data contained quite a few instances of female groups sitting around listening to commercial pop, and in ways similar to Extract IV.5, conversation turned to the cassette players, participants said they loved particular songs and Sally expressed her tastes with the phrases 'it's a good'un' and 'I love that' (cf. lines 43–4, 71, 79). Such events were much more rare in the recordings of boys.

6. This was very clear with Mashuk's crossing in the context of sound system culture. Sally's involvement with bhangra was much less sophisticated, but personal prestige beyond the sites where bhangra was played was still an issue, certainly among her small circle of white female friends. Up to a point, her four references to Imran and bhangra in Extract IV.5 can be read as efforts to authenticate her interest. But they can also be interpreted as quite strong status claims. Her relationship was important to members of her network and perhaps itself a source of prestige (cf. Eckert 1990: 93, 95; Goodwin 1985: 317); the fact of its existence could not be denied; and the importance of bhangra in her private transactions with Imran was not a matter that outsiders could dispute (cf. Goodwin and Goodwin 1987: 228). Her associates certainly did not have to be enthusiastic in according her prestige: her allusions to Imran in Extract IV.5 were generally ignored, and elsewhere, Kelly and Lorraine complained that 'she has to be better than us', a view with which Anon A and Sally herself evidently concurred (lines 101, 102). Even so, higher status was at stake, and this status was clearly very different from the reputation for joking generated in agonistic play-ground crossing.

7. The differences between Panjabi crossing in these two contexts were not absolute. For example, white girls sometimes joked about bhangra (cf. lines 56–9 of Extract IV.5), and Panjabi response cries and self-talk occurred in both settings. Goffman's notion of 'open states of talk' was applied to listening to music, but it is also relevant, for example, to a game of pool.

Part V

Conclusions

11 *Crossing and the sociolinguistics of language contact*

Drawing the strands of the empirical analysis together, Part V of the book tries to define language crossing's identity as a sociolinguistic practice (Chapter 11), to clarify its political character (Chapter 12), and to consider its implications for some dominant educational discourses on language (Chapter 13).

In the study of language contact, scholars have used a number of classifications to analyse the linguistic and pragmatic phenomena arising in bilingual interaction. The limited intrusion of linguistic items from another language is often discussed under the title 'borrowing' and 'interference' (cf. e.g. Romaine 1988). When speakers make more extensive use of two varieties and switch between them purposefully, scholars generally use the term 'code-switching' (cf. Blom and Gumperz 1972: 424–426; Gumperz 1982a: 60–61; Heller 1988: 5). In addition there are also cases where two varieties alternate rapidly in a stretch of speech without creating meaning through the code changes themselves (e.g. Poplack 1988: 217–19; Swiggart 1992). Here two codes combine into what seems to be a distinctive new variety and this is sometimes called 'code-mixing'. But there is in fact a great deal of disagreement about these categorisations. Terminology varies substantially (Romaine 1988: 114), and the distinctions are themselves the subject of dispute (cf. e.g. Hill and Hill 1986: ch. 7; Eastman 1992: 1; Gysels 1992).[1]

Engagement with the linguistic literature on borrowing and interference lies outside this book's primarily pragmatic and sociological brief. However, I have used the term 'code-switching' in a general way throughout, and at this point, it is important to explicate my understanding of the concept, to align it with particular accounts, and to suggest certain refinements. After that, and at somewhat greater length, I shall try to argue the case for my introduction of the new term 'code-crossing'.

11.1 Crossing as a form of code-switching

My own interpretation of code-switching follows Auer, who uses the term 'code-alternation': 'code-alternation (used here as a cover term . . .) covers all cases in which semiotic systems are put in a relationship of contiguous juxtaposition, such that the appropriate recipients of the resulting complex sign are in a position to interpret this juxtaposition as such' (Auer 1990: 71; see also Gumperz 1982a: 97). Code-alternation is one kind of 'contextualisation cue' (Gumperz 1982: ch. 6; Gumperz and Cook-Gumperz 1982; Auer 1990, 1991). Contextualisation cues are 'constellations of surface features of message form . . . by which speakers signal and listeners interpret what the activity is, how semantic content is to be understood and how each sentence relates to what precedes or follows' (Gumperz 1982a: 131). They provide information which enables participants to coordinate the interpretive frameworks that they use as a basis for inferring utterance meaning: in Auer's terms, they 'make relevant, maintain, revise, cancel . . . some aspect of context which, in turn, is responsible for the interpretation of an utterance in its particular locus of occurrence' (1991: 334; see also Goffman 1974: ch. 7 on the 'directional track'). The aspects of context manipulated in this way are numerous and diverse, encompassing for example activity types, mood, participant roles and identities, or the relationship between speaker and the propositional information being expressed. In this way for instance, a change of accent, speech rate or pitch level might indicate that a speaker does not seriously mean what they say, or it might signal an informal aside.

In fact, contextualisation cues can be kinesic and gestural (e.g. McDermott and Gospodinoff 1981; Kendon 1990), but obviously one form of verbal cue – code alternation – is of particular interest to Auer:

> Code alternation may work as a contextualisation cue simply because of the contrast it is able to establish between two contiguous

stretches of talk. It is a very convenient way of setting off what has been said in language A against what is going to be said in language B, and works, in this respect, like prosodic and gestural cues. This contrast can be used for conversational tasks independent of the social meaning of the languages involved, e.g. for setting off side remarks, marking new topics, switching between participant constellations, etc. But code alternation may also work as a contextualisation cue because (in addition) it plays with the social values and attitudes associated with the languages in question, such as they have been established in the course of an individual's history of interaction by the recurring coincidence of language choice and particular conversational activities (1990: 81)

All code alternation involves a change in some aspect of contextual framing, and in noticing the contrast between current and preceding codes, participants are prompted to do some extra inferential work as they try to establish what the new frame is, how it relates to the old one, or whatever. Auer's empirical work leads him to distinguish several kinds of code alternation, which he defines in terms of the types of account that participants are likely to come up with when switching prompts them to process issues such as 'why that now?' and 'what next?' (1988: 192). Two of these are particularly important. With 'discourse-related' alternation, participants make sense of a switch by interpreting it as marking out a different addressee, a new topic, a distinct narrative segment and so forth (see the instances cited above in relation to contextualisation cues). With 'participant-related' switches, recipients focus on the speaker's more stable attributes, and settle for an account which explains the code change in terms of his or her linguistic preference and/or proficiency.

Though Auer himself rejects it (1984: 90–91), this approach to code alternation can be married with Gumperz's early distinction between situational and *metaphorical* code-switching in a way that takes us to the heart of the issues addressed in this book.

In most of the cases that Auer describes, code alternation would appear to elicit only rather limited amounts of inferential work. Once they have resolved the initial interruption to the contextual frames prevailing hitherto, participants find little to contradict their basic assumptions about orderly conduct. With recipients reconciled to switches through the kinds of 'discourse-' and 'participant-related' interpretation that Auer proposes, the flow of unexceptional co-occurrence patterns can continue, albeit now in a slightly different path. In contrast, the code alternation that we have considered involves a more fundamental contravention of routine expectations – it entails a disjunction between speaker and code that can not be readily accommodated as a normal part of ordinary social reality.

It is at this point that Gumperz's situational versus metaphorical distinction becomes relevant. With situational code-switching, participants shift from one contextual frame over into another and then continue their interaction in a different gear, just as they normally do in Auer's account (Blom and Gumperz 1972: 424–6). In contrast, metaphorical code-switching involves a 'partial violation of co-occurrence expectations' and participants do not settle into the newly introduced contextual frame as an easy basis for further interaction (Gumperz 1982a: 98).[2] Like metaphor more generally, which a number of scholars characterise as a kind of 'double vision' (Wellek and Warren 1949), an 'interaction between co-present thoughts' and 'a transaction between contexts' (Richards 1936: 93,94; Black 1979; Tourangeau and Sternberg 1982), the new code ushers in a contextual frame that acts as a rather problematic *adjunct* to the current frame, not simply as a replacement for it. Because of this recipients attend simultaneously to *two* interpretive contexts when trying to infer the significance of the switch.

The basic disparity between speaker and voice that is fundamental to language crossing means that potentially, it has a good deal of symbolic resonance as a form of code-switching. In figurative language generally, the fairly extensive violation of normal co-occurrence expectations makes it much harder for recipients to end their search for meaning in the relatively neat solutions normally achieved with ordinary discourse (Sperber 1975; Levinson 1983: 109). Instead, recipients have to run through a much more extensive set of possible inferences in order to make sense of an utterance, and in Sperber's theory, it is this often unfinished process that generates the symbolic resonance around an utterance.

'Situational' code-switching – code alternation as a relatively routine contextualisation cue, in which speakers introduce a footing that is familiar and accessible to their addressees – is likely to have less symbolic salience than metaphorical code-switching. But clearly, this distinction is not at all absolute. As studies of dead and 'sleeping' metaphor make plain (e.g. Leech 1969; Lakoff and Johnson 1980), the distinction between the literal and the figurative, between the ordinary and the exceptional, is highly variable and often far from clear-cut. Taken as a form of metaphorical/figurative code alternation, the same was obviously true of crossing in Ashmead. While speaker and voice were quite easily differentiated with stylised Asian English, this was often much harder when Creole was used. Crossing in the latter looked much more towards their fusion into a new identity capable of holding an uncontested place in quotidian reality.

A range of factors affected the extent to which crossers were able to use Creole in acts of serious self-contextualisation. Whether or not white and Asian uses of Creole were seen as an authentic reflection of the person's identity depended on who the speakers and recipients were, what their relationship was, the degree of their involvement with black culture, the particular occasion, the specific contours of the character being claimed and so forth. But what was clear was that social reality, and the speaker's position within this, were the focus for some degree of interactional renegotiation. In some exchanges, Creole only occurred in actions that were offered and taken in a figurative spirit, while in others, the same acts might be taken for real. If code-switching research is to make some contribution to wider social analysis, it needs to give proper recognition to the *negotiably* figurative status that code alternation can have. Interpreted along the lines proposed above, Gumperz's early distinction between metaphorical and situational code-switching provides an important tool for analysis of the potentially creative explorations of social order in which speakers sometimes spontaneously engage.

In fact, our analysis of Ashmead data allows for some more subtle differentiations within the metaphorical/figurative category. To capture the different ways in which crossers aligned themselves with Creole, Panjabi and stylised Asian English (SAE), we have already had cause to make use of Bakhtin's notions of vari- and uni-directional double-voicing (Chapter 8.5). These ideas constitute an elaboration of key elements in Gumperz's original insight (see also Hill and Hill 1986: 387–401).[3] Figurative/metaphorical code alternation is the same thing as double-voicing/double-languaging, and the theoretical apparatus accompanying the latter provides a very useful way of thinking through the different empirical forms that 'metaphorical code-switching' can take.[4]

These then are the assumptions underlying my use of 'code-switching' as an umbrella concept, as well as one or two suggestions about how the terminology current in this field of study might be refined. But although they can be accommodated within this general framework, some of the most important implications of 'crossing' still need to be drawn out. As far as I am aware, the term 'crossing' – central to my own analysis – figures nowhere in the literature. For this reason, the case for its wider value needs to be argued. This will involve (i) highlighting the ways in which crossing *differs* from other kinds of code-switching; (ii) pointing to comparable studies and intimating the range of linguistic phenomena it draws together; and (iii) identifying its general implications for the sociolinguistic conceptualisation of code-switching, second language learning, and ethnicity.

11.2 Crossing as a distinct but neglected practice

According to Woolard, '[in] most . . . sociolinguistic analyses . . . [code-switching] is an in-group phenomenon restricted to those who share the same expectations and rules of interpretation for the use of the two languages. Code-switching is thus usually seen as a device used to affirm participants' claims to membership and the solidarity of the group in contrast to outsiders' (1988: 69–70). Certainly, many of the most influential studies have looked at the conduct of groups in which the use of two or more languages is a routine expectation, either because they have grown up with a multilingual inheritance, or moved into areas or institutions where the use of additional languages is an unremarked necessity (e.g. Blom and Gumperz 1972; Gal 1979; Duran 1981; Grosjean 1983; Auer 1988; Romaine 1988).

Crossing, in contrast, focuses on code alternation by people who are not accepted members of the group associated with the second language they employ. It is concerned with switching into languages that are not generally thought to belong to you. This kind of switching, in which there is a distinct sense of movement across social or ethnic boundaries, raises issues of social legitimacy that participants need to negotiate, and that analysts could usefully devote more attention to.

We have already seen that language crossing takes many shapes, and that these are influenced by socio-historical factors, by local social relationships and by specific interactional dynamics. Crossing into Asian English took very different forms from Creole crossing, and Panjabi crossing was also sometimes distinct. As an activity, crossing could either be an end in itself (e.g. in play-ground competition), or the first step in a longer journey (in romance or performance art); it could emphasise disdain or respect; it occurred when people were (more or less) on their own, when they were among co-ethnics, and also when they were with members of ethnic out-groups. The amount of support offered by the inheritors of the codes involved also varied considerably.

But inspite of all this variation, quite a clear pattern emerged from the data considered both in this study and in Hewitt's. The ethnolinguistic boundary transgression inherent in code-crossing responded to, or produced, liminal moments and activities, when the ordered flow of habitual social life was loosened and when normal social relations could not be taken for granted. Code crossing occurred at the boundaries of interactional enclosure, in the vicinity of delicts and transgressions, in self-talk and response cries, in games, cross-sex interaction and in the context of per-formance art. Adolescents used language to cross ethnic boundaries in moments when the constraints of everyday social order were relaxed.

In fact, we have tentatively proposed a 'scale of ritualisation': some acts of crossing co-occurred with a major suspension of the norms of ordinary conduct (games, performance art and joking abuse), while others arose with a fleeting awareness of a breach that was only potential (see Chapter 8.2). And although we have not tried to assimilate all our data to this model, the extent to which any crossing act was ritualised appeared to depend on a number of factors: the variety selected, the crosser's network rela-tions, ethnic and gender identities, his/her orientation to the socio-ideological horizons indexed by the code, his/her linguistic competence, the presence or absence of inheritors, and the size of the switch itself.

Certainly, on its own, ritualisation does not constitute an empir-ical characteristic that categorically distinguishes crossing from in-group code-switching. Ritualised language use is not confined to people who are using a language that is not considered to belong to them, and recognised bilinguals code-switch in artistic performance (e.g. Stølen 1992), in face-repair (e.g. Valdes 1981), in jokes, wordplay (e.g. McLure and MacLure 1988), and no doubt in most of the liminal moments described in this book (for example, games, cross-sex interaction, self-talk, and so on). Instead, the difference between out-group crossing and the in-group code-switching is likely to reside in the fact that in *in-group* practice, both languages can *also* be used in the unexceptional conduct of everyday life (at least up to a point). Crossing does not generally have this flexibility, and the code alternation it entails is much more likely to be 'flagged' (for example, 'marked by pauses, hesitation phenomena, repetition and metalinguistic commentary', Romaine 1988: 141). In in-group practice, it needn't be. Members may alternate between codes without even being consciously aware of it. One correlative of this is that non-liminal in-group code-switching is likely to require some productive and/or receptive competence in the semantico-referential dimension of both languages. Proficiency in this aspect of language may also feature in crossing, though as we have seen, this can be very minimal.

So the interactional character of in-group code-switching is likely to be more diverse than it is with crossing, at least in principle. But this does not necessarily make it a more fertile field of study. According to Auer,

> Three dimensions have to be taken into account [in both participant and analyst interpretations of code alternation]. The first dimension is that of the speaker's and of the recipient's individual competences and preferences. The second dimension is that of conversational structure. The third is that of the values and social meanings attached to the languages of the repertoire. In any particular instance of code-alternation, all three dimensions may play a role, or just one or two of them. (1990: 78)

Auer's first two dimensions refer to the distinction between 'participant-' and 'discourse-related' alternation outlined in Chapter 11.1. In in-group code-switching, an example of purely participant-related code-alternation would be bilingual adult–child conversations in which the child consistently used one language and the adult another. Exclusively 'discourse-related' alternation occurs when a change of code is simply used for setting off side remarks, marking new topics, repeated questions and requests, and so on (Auer 1988: 199). In both cases, there need be nothing in the social connotations carried by the language itself that make it appropriate to the particular topic being addressed.

In contrast to this account of in-group code-switching, crossing seems guaranteed to involve all three of Auer's dimensions. Crossing involves a disjunction between speaker and code that can not be readily accommodated as a normal part of ordinary social reality. This incongruity necessarily entails (a) that crossing is participant-related, and that (b) the language involved has a wider social meaning. The 'newsworthiness' of this anomalous combination then makes crossing a practice that (c) participants interactionally orient to in the intricate but extensive ways that we have documented – in other words, crossing's sociolinguistic incongruity is intimately connected with its discourse-relatedness.

The relevance of all three of these dimensions make crossing a particularly fertile site for the investigation of social processes. Apart from any presupposition that the analyst might have about the anomaly of white Creole, black Panjabi, or third generation Indian English, their location in liminal moments, activities and events provides independent confirmation of crossing's heterodox character. More important than this, the fact that it combines highly salient issues of ethnic identity with very distinct actions and occasions makes crossing an excellent empirical site for examining the ways in which social knowledge about ethnicity is actively processed in informal interaction within different social networks.

In this respect, *in-group* code-switching would appear to offer less analytic potential when it is only either participant- or discourse-related. On the basis of bilingual adult–child interactions in which each participant used a different language, one might suggest that the two codes broadly connoted different groups or generations, but there would be little in the texture of the discourse itself to suggest that each language had a set of symbolic associations that fitted it to only some social actions and not to others. Discourse of this kind reveals nothing about the way in which quite general social evaluations are displayed or generated through strategic interactional code selection. Equally, where code alternation is purely discourse-related and the proficiencies and preferences of participants are not at issue, interaction provides little purchase on the micro-political dynamics of linguistic entitlement and access, or on the interpersonal negotiation of linguistically marked social and cultural difference. If a language used in code alternation does not have any extrinsic social meaning, the study of interaction can have little to say about the ways in which dominant ideologies and ethnolinguistic stereotypes are processed in local contexts.

To sum up, we can say that although crossing subsumes a wide range of different practices, it is still likely to differ from in-group code-switching in being more exclusively ritualised. However, in being more restricted in this way, it is participant-related, discourse-related, and the language selected carries social meaning. Though the same can be true of in-group code-switching, it isn't necessarily, and so in this regard, crossing is likely to be a more consistently fruitful site for examination of the intersection of macro and micro social processes.

In spite of this, code-switching research has generally adopted an in-group perspective. Is this because crossing is actually rather rare? To controvert this possibility, it is now worth turning to a few studies in the code-switching literature which can be construed in the terms we have elaborated. After that, we can briefly glance at the wider span of sociolinguistic phenomena that the notion of crossing brings together.

11.3 Crossing's generality

Some of the code-switching practices described by Hill and Coombs (1982), Hill and Hill (1986), Heller (1988, 1992) and Woolard (1988, 1989) bear a striking resemblance to the liminal sociolinguistic practices observed in Ashmead (and South London). In all of these studies, ethnolinguistic boundaries were well defined, though to differing degrees.

Woolard's concern was with Catalan and Castilian in Barcelona (1989). There had been a considerable amount of structural convergence between these two languages, but (purposive) code-alternation within a single discourse – what Gumperz (1982a) calls 'conversational' code-switching – was rare (Woolard 1988: 55). Instead, the choice of which language to use was strongly influenced by the identity of the interlocutor. Catalan was only addressed to people whose primary linguistic allegiance was to Catalan, and in mixed company and in public arenas, Castilian was chosen. According to Woolard, code-switching was inhibited by 'generalised anxiety about ethnic boundaries' (1988: 56). More generally, ethnic identity and language choice were very salient macro-political issues (1988, 1989).

During the period of her fieldwork, however, a professional comedian achieved enormous popularity, and 'the most distinctive feature of his joke-telling was his "promiscuous" mixing of Catalan and Castilian' (1988: 57). Woolard summarises his appeal in the following way:

> Eugenio demonstrates a use of the two languages that is different from their use in the community, and one that breaks down two of the most tension-creating associations in the sociopolitical context of the time: the identification of language choice with ethnic boundaries (i.e. Catalan for native Catalans only), and the entrenched but besieged norm of selecting Castilian for public uses. It is not an absence of reference to group boundaries through language use, but the explicit *overriding* of them that is appealing. A bilingual Catalan and a monolingual Castilian can equally participate in the event and not lose any enjoyment of the humour . . . But the actual use of both languages . . . is an important denial of the boundary identifying force of the two languages (1988: 70 – original emphasis)

Eugenio's code-switching fits well with the account of crossing and liminality articulated here. His language use was set within a frame of performance art that marked it off from the ordinary, and as a joke-telling comedian, his transgressions could be seen as non-serious and not really real.[5]

In the domination of Nahuatl by Spanish, described by Hill and Hill (1986) and Hill and Coombs (1982), borrowing and interference were very common. But considerable effort was made to keep these languages apart, and code-mixing was very widely stigmatised. In the agrarian settings where Nahuatl was regarded as the main language of community life, Spanish was partly associated with the political power of a small elite who operated as brokers with outsiders (Hill and Coombs 1982: 227; Hill and Hill 1986: ch. 4). But for speakers outside this group, Spanish was the language of obscenity, of cursing, and of drunkenness. Hill and Coombs are explicit in aligning this kind of code-switching with 'the liminal stage of ritual, where social differentiation breaks down and new identities can be forged in the absence of structure' (Hill and Coombs 1982: 231).

In the Canadian situation described by Heller (1988, 1992), the dominance of English over French was gradually being reversed, and as a result of state legislation, French was becoming increasingly important as a language of upward social mobility. For some of the people that Heller describes – for example Franco-Ontarian women married to anglophone men in English dominant networks (1992: 134–5) – the boundary between these two languages was unproblematic, and code-switching that was both recognised and frequent could be used to signal 'a double affiliation'. But for others, language choice was politically more difficult. Heller describes the situation in a commercial company where proficiency in French had been introduced as a criterion for promotion, and where anglophone managers had either moved elsewhere, or had decided to stay and 'reorient themselves within a new framework' (1992: 129). Inspite of this change in power relations, it was still in the interests of both francophone managers and their anglophone colleagues to maintain a good working relationship, and to do so, they code-switched during interactions that were clearly geared to the conduct of serious business. In that regard, there was much less of the carnivalesque and/or oppositional in their movement across historically entrenched ethnolinguistic boundaries than there appears to have been in the situations described by Woolard and the Hills. Even so, Heller characterises the anglophone managers as switching into French for 'greeting routines and other fixed expressions', and in 'light-hearted joshing' (1992: 133–4), the kinds of usage that seem typical of the crossing that we analysed in Ashmead.

With a lot of the liminal code-switching in these different situations, crossers seemed to move towards a new identity, shifting across into codes that were prestigious and powerful, at least within one or two quite well-established sociolinguistic domains (cf. Hewitt 1986 and above on Creole; Woolard on Catalan; Hill and Coombs on Spanish; Heller on French). However, the use of stylised Asian English in Ashmead controverts any temptation to elicit a general rule on this, and in fact, in situations of advanced language shift, people may well make liminal use of the language that they are 'losing'. Hewitt suggests that the Creole use of a substantial number of black adolescents was actually fairly similar to that of their white peers (1986: 114,153), and in a study of massive shift from Gaelic to English in Nova Scotia, Mertz describes residual Gaelic being used in ways that bear a lot of ressemblance to the crossing we have examined – greetings and closings, pet-names, rebukes, response cries and self-talk (Mertz 1989: 113–14; see also Ferguson 1981:32).[6] Here, rather than being associated with processes that one might characterise as some kind of broad convergence, ritualised language use appears to reflect a recent history of sociolinguistic estrangement.[7]

Any attempt to use these findings to build up a comprehensive theory of language crossing would require much more than the limited sketches provided above. My own inductive generalisations about code crossing among youth in England relied on extensive and fairly intricate data analysis, and even in these brief outlines of other research, it is clear that the complexities of variation and change are likely to be just as substantial in other situations where people use languages not normally associated with their own, situationally negotiated, ethnolinguistic identities. However, to underscore crossing's importance as a sociolinguistic practice, it is worth glancing at some of the other phenomena which come within its orbit.

Sensitivity to the experience of anomaly that code-crossing entails can lead reactively to several practices with a very different character. One of these is 'passing', where, in order to avoid all the talk that draws attention to their use of an out-group code, people pretend that the out-group code is actually part of their own inheritance. Trosset (1986) describes the difficulties encountered by people learning Welsh as a second language. Speakers of Welsh as a first language were generally very pleased by any progress that learners made, largely because of its symbolic implications for the survival of Welsh. As a result,

> the aesthetic function is commonly dominant when Welsh speakers listen to Welsh learners. They focus primarily on the medium rather than the content of the learners' speech. Second language speakers are often frustrated to find how difficult it is for them to engage in normal conversation with native speakers – not because their own Welsh is inadequate, but because the attention of the native speakers seems irrevocably fixed on the linguistic skill being displayed by the learners. (1986: 179)

To escape from this, some learners 'attempt to 'become' native speakers – that is, they lie about their place and language of origin' (1986: 187–8). In South London, where rather than being celebrated, crossing into Creole was generally criticised by black adolescents, some white and Asian adolescents also tried to 'pass', saying 'I was born in Jamaica, my grandmother was half-caste and all things like that' (Hewitt 1986: 165,195; also Garfinkel 1967: 125,136–7).

'Refusal' lies at the opposite extreme to 'passing' as a way of avoiding the experience of anomaly that crossing entails. Where there is a common lingua franca, this may present no difficulties, but in other circumstances, this can have significant political dimensions. In consequence of 'permanently experienced frustration' in their negotiation with German-speaking bureaucracy, Hinnenkamp describes a disaffection among 'Gastarbeiter' that increases with their second language proficiency and that can culminate in refusal to use the 'host' society's means of communication (1980). Among Francophones in Canada, the experience of domination in anglophone domains can also result in conscious resistance to code-switching, a form of refusal which Heller ties in with larger processes of ethnic mobilisation (1992: 130–3).

Code-crossing's sociolinguistic significance extends beyond the negative impetus it gives to 'passing' and 'refusal'. It is obviously also the focus for a great deal of debate, play and meta-commentary. Drawing on the contact between standard and American Vernacular Black English, and between Spanish and Quechua and Nahuatl, Hill and Coombs (1982) summarise some of the ways in which in in-group settings, vernacular speakers exploit the dominant language 'as a source of symbolic material for the management of their oppressed status' (1982: 224). Prestige languages become the object of intensive play, remodelling and transvaluation, their meaning reshaped in ways that ultimately (though by no means harmoniously) consolidate group solidarity. Of course, the secondary representation of experiences with an out-group language does not only occur among people in subordinate social positions. The literature on 'Secondary Foreigner Talk' illustrates the ways in which, outside contexts of direct intergroup interaction, speakers of a dominant target language can caricature the efforts of second language learners (Ferguson 1975; Valdman 1981; Hinnenkamp 1984; *primary* FT is a term used to describe the simplified language that first language speakers sometimes produce when talking to foreigners considered not to know the language very well). Indeed, these stereotypes can themselves be inverted and turned back on members of the dominant groups in which they originate. This is illustrated in much of the data on stylised Asian English, which in its repositioning of white images of 'babu', might actually be designated an instance of *tertiary* 'foreigner talk'.

These instances are probably just a small fraction of language crossing's forms and ramifications. In second language learning classrooms, crossing obviously receives much more institutional support than anything we have considered so far, and the research literature on second language acquisition shows just how elaborate the metacommentary on crossing can become. Bourdieu's account of condescension (1991: 68–9) falls within crossing's ambit, and there is no principled reason why attention should not focus on the boundaries between registers and dialects *within* a language. But at this point, a question arises. If the notion of 'crossing' embraces so much, isn't it actually rather vacuous? In the final sections of this chapter, I shall try to spell out its strategic value for sociolinguistic theory.

11.4 Crossing's value as a sociolinguistic concept

Crossing matters as a concept because it promises to integrate the analysis of code-switching with the study of second language (L2) learning. In doing so, it opens up opportunities for the investigation of ethnic processes that both areas of research have tended to neglect.

Work on bilingual code-switching (CS) frequently conflicts with second language acquisition research (SLA) (e.g. Duran 1981: ix; Penfield and Ornstein-Galicia 1985: 16; Auer 1990: 76). The two research traditions differ fundamentally in their assumptions about non-standard language mixture. With code-switching research, language mixing is generally construed either as a new form of bilingual sociolect, or as skilful and appropriate strategy. With SLA, it is generally interpreted as error and a lack of competence.

As section 11.1 above made clear, my own study draws heavily on analytic assumptions and techniques used in code-switching research. But at the same time, it is quite clear that error and incompetence were very salient in crossing, for both participants and analysts. Code-switching into SAE illustrated the local social salience of second language learner status, and in Panjabi

incrimination traps in the playground, the crosser's linguistic proficiency was focal (Chapter 7.3). Ritual abuse formats provided
young people with a form of scaffolding that enabled them to
cross into Panjabi, and this scaffolding partly resembled the sup-
portive exchange structures identified in SLA research. With
Panjabi more generally, white and black youngsters made use of
linguistically undemanding activities in which the propositional
dimensions of language use were relatively unimportant – chasing
games, self-talk, listening to music.[8]

As a concept, crossing flags up the importance of language proficiency issues, and in using a primarily code-switching idiom to
do so, it helps to prop open the door between code-switching
research and SLA. Admittedly, though linguistic proficiency may
not occupy an exalted position within the study of code-switching,
it is widely acknowledged as one explanatory factor,[9] and Auer's
framework in fact accommodates it very well. Rather than lacking
any conceptual awareness of language proficiency issues, the main
problem with CS research has been its tendency to neglect these
issues empirically – a neglect encouraged by its overwhelming preoccupation with bilingual in-groups.

With theories of second language acquisition, this situation is
reversed. SLA research is firmly focused on the same empirical
subject matter that crossing addresses, but there is an urgent need
for new analytic idioms. SLA is centrally preoccupied with movement across language group boundaries, but in general, it is
ill-equipped to draw out the kinds of significance discussed in this
book. As a concept advocated for SLA, 'crossing' tries to promote
the kinds of analytic perspective that are actually fairly routine in
the study of code-switching. If such perspectives are adopted,
some of SLA's most basic premises may have to be rethought.

To develop this point, it is necessary to offer a characterisation
of SLA. After that, we can sketch out crossing's contribution to
some basic reconceptualisation. (More detailed discussion – and
fuller references – can be found in Rampton 1987b, 1991b, forthcoming.)

11.5 The contribution to SLA

Although there are a few notable exceptions (e.g. Trosset 1986,
Roberts and Simonot 1987, Aston 1993), L2 research is firmly

focused on the acquisition of linguistic structure, not on socialisation. Cook-Gumperz's observation on first language research holds true in SLA: 'The study of language acquisition, even from a discourse or interactional perspective, has still focused on the acquisition of linguistic forms, but not yet [on socialisation and] the maturation of the social person' (Cook-Gumperz 1986: 55). 'By socialisation we mean the growth of social understanding and the growth of capabilities for the maintenance of social relations' (Cook-Gumperz and Corsaro 1986: 4).

Interaction certainly figures on the agenda of SLA research, but attention is directed to the ways in which learners negotiate the 'comprehensible input' thought necessary for the development of their L2 grammars (e.g. Wong Fillmore 1979; Long 1983; Varonis and Gass 1985; Pica 1987; cf. Aston 1986 for a trenchant critique). Routines, formulaic utterances and politeness are also addressed, but again, it is generally their relationship to processes of interlanguage grammar construction that is prioritised (e.g. Krashen 1981: ch. 7; Scarcella and Higa 1981; Selinker and Douglas 1985; Varonis and Gass 1985). When SLA borrows models from within sociolinguistics, its central preoccupation remains the same. The Labovian approach to linguistic variation provides an opportunity to reconceptualise grammatical competence and to consider which speech styles that are most receptive to new forms (Schmidt 1977; Krashen 1981; Tarone 1983; Ellis 1985), and the social psychology of language provides concepts for discussion of the motivational factors which impede or accelerate L2 acquisition (Schumann 1978; Giles and Byrne 1982).

Of course there is nothing intrinsically wrong with a clearly defined research interest, and many studies select methods very well suited to their goals. But in general in SLA, there has perhaps been an over-elaboration of theory and methodology, resulting in an unproductively restricted view of the empirical phenomenon that, in its name, it declares as its interest. Experimental methods occupy the dominant position in research on second language learning, and even within more inductive studies, the collection of data tends to be extensively prestructured through the advance preparation of questionnaire and elicitation tasks. There is not much holistic investigation of the ways in which meanings are generated through the contingent interaction of different levels of language and socio-cognitive context, and outside the classroom, SLA seldom draws

on participant observation in the local communities that its informants come from. Direct observation of naturally occurring
behaviour across a range of settings is rare, and informants are
themselves generally only differentiated in terms of their age, their
national origin and the stage they have reached in their (linguistic)
education. Admittedly, SLA is committed to the view that L2 performance is a systematic reflection of learning and not just a mad
jumble, but otherwise there is no sustained sensitivity to the risks
of ethnocentricity. In short, in SLA, there is very little of the
methodological approach that underpins the study of code-switching. There is hardly any ethnography.

One of the main values of ethnography lies in the challenge it
presents to assumptions developed in the laboratory or library,
and its absence from SLA has permitted the acceptance of a
number of generalisations that are actually rather questionable.
This is made apparent by some of the Ashmead data, which produces a somewhat heterodox picture of what it is to be a second
language learner.

In the 'root image' underlying SLA research, it is assumed that
L2 learning generates situational anxiety, that progression along
the route towards target language proficiency is (or should be) the
learner's abiding preoccupation, and that learner status is fundamentally stigmatised. All of these characterisations may be true of
some, or indeed many, situations, but they are certainly not invariable (cf. Rampton 1991b). For white and black youngsters in
Ashmead playgrounds, using Panjabi as a second language was
often very good fun, and more generally it is important to point
out that there are pleasures as well as fears attached to the
learner's liminal position (Borsch 1986; Aston 1993). Indeed the
pleasures may be such that, to the extent that it carries a sense of
progression towards a destination, the term 'target language' is
meaningless. There was no evidence that playground crossers
actually wanted to learn Panjabi properly – being a learner was an
entertaining end-in-itself – and my guess is that this is actually
quite generally true of, for example, the large numbers of English
people who attend the same intermediate foreign language class,
all year every year, in preparation for their annual holidays. The
SLA assumption that there is a stigma attached to second language
learning is also open to question, and it probably derives from
SLA's overwhelming concern with the learning of *dominant*

languages (and English in particular). Studies of the learning of *minority* languages show that second language acquisition can actually lead to learners being accorded prestige by the people that belong to the language from birth (Trosset 1986 on Welsh; Woolard 1989: 76 on Catalan).

The very undifferentiated portrait of the second language learner that emerges in SLA no doubt partly results from its tendency to thematise the learner's internal psychological condition. Rather than looking at interaction as a socio-historically sensitive arena in which language learner identity is socially negotiated, SLA generally examines learner behaviour for evidence of the determining influence of psycholinguistic states and processes. One exception to this, however, can be found in research on 'L2 communication strategies', which studies the cognitive and interactional procedures that learners and their interlocutors employ when they experience difficulties due to the learner's flawed linguistic knowledge (Faerch and Kasper 1983; Kasper and Kellerman, forthcoming). Here, learner identity is regarded as a salient issue that participants in interaction actively orient to. Indeed, the notion of the L2 communication strategy as some kind of improvisational procedure is ideally suited to a lot of the Ashmead data on Panjabi, in which black and white youngsters worked hard to compensate for the massive gaps in their Panjabi lexicogrammars. But once again, the overall account that emerges from this strand of SLA research is limited by the general absence of a contribution from ethnography.

In L2 communication strategy research, it is normally assumed that it is the learners that are the source of the difficulty, that the language they speak is a deficient version of their interlocutor's, and that learner strategies fall into two general types ('archistrategies') – achievement strategies, in which the learner tries to solve the communicative problem by expanding his or her communicative resources, and avoidance strategies, in which the learner reduces his or her goal in order to avoid a problem (Corder 1981; Faerch and Kasper 1983: 52). Ethnographic evidence qualifies all of these ideas (cf. Rampton, forthcoming). Work on interethnic communication by Gumperz et al. (1979) demonstrates that the first language (L1) speaker's assumptions about the L2 user and their competence can be as much an obstacle to communication as L2 proficiency itself, and in response to this, language classes have been developed which are addressed to *both* groups (Roberts et al. 1992). Trosset reports communicative difficulties – resentment or embarrassment – that can arise when L2 learners use Welsh that is actually *more* standard than L1 speakers' (1986: 176–7). And both the 'tertiary' foreigner talk evidenced in adolescent SAE and the 'transvaluation' and 'remodelling' of dominant languages discussed by Hill and Coombs (1982) suggest that in addition to 'achievement' and 'avoidance', recognition ought to be given to something like 'resistance' as an archistrategy.

Encouraged both by the international spread of English language teaching (ELT) and by the dominant position occupied by theories of universal grammar within autonomous/'core' linguistics, SLA may be strongly tempted to generalise its findings across a very wide range of different sociolinguistic situations. Generalisation certainly is one of the first responsibilities of scholarship, but this is only valid if it proceeds with a proper admission of the limitations of its database. Ethnography traditionally plays an important role pointing limitations out, and its absence from SLA increases the risk. By trying to introduce the ethnographic and interactional perspectives characteristic of code-switching research, the term 'crossing' is designed to inhibit any inclination to generalise prematurely. At present, SLA could probably benefit from an enhanced sense of the empirical world's complex socio-cultural diversity.

Crossing, then, aims to combine the methodologies of code-switching research with SLA's empirical focus on other-language use and learning. In what ways does this combination 'open up opportunities for the investigation of ethnic processes that both areas have tended to neglect'?

11.6 Revising sociolinguistic conceptions of ethnicity

In its overwhelming attention to the learning of English and other dominant languages, SLA's primary concern is with the ways in which 'outsiders' assimilate to majority groups. Though it is recognised that this process can falter, that learners give up, there is little recognition of the complex boundary negotiations that this can entail. There is no attempt to provide any detailed account of the ways in which people cultivate alternative *minority* solidarities, and the micro-politics of interethnic interaction does not really figure on the agenda of SLA (though cf. Hinnenkamp 1987; Roberts and Simonot 1987). In this context, it is easy to see how studies both of crossing and of in-group code-switching could uncover ethnic processes that SLA has neglected hitherto.

But crossing's contribution to the understanding of race relations in code-switching research is less obvious, and so it needs to be argued at greater length.

The view of ethnicity that has dominated code-switching research, as well as several other areas of sociolinguistics, is well expressed in Gumperz and Cook-Gumperz's distinction between what they call the 'old and the new ethnicity':

> The term 'ethnicity' has traditionally been used to refer to relationships based on the linkage of similar people, whose social identity was formed by influences from outside the society in which they now live; but increasingly it has come to indicate relationships based on differences distinguishing one, new, indigenous group from another . . . We shall refer to these two concepts as the *old* and the *new* ethnicity respectively. The old ethnicity was supported both regionally and interpersonally through reinforced social networks which joined people through clusters of occupational, neighbourhood, familial, and political ties. People of the same ethnicity often lived near each other and supported each other within their work and their political groups. Marriage and families continued these network linkages. In the large urban centres of the industrial world, the consciousness of immigrant groups' separate historical past was reinforced in the present by physical-geographic, friendship, and occupational ties.
>
> The new ethnicity depends less upon geographic proximity and shared occupations and more upon the highlighting of key differences separating one group from another. Michael Hechter (1978), in developing a general theory of ethnicity that accounts for changes in the modern urban world, has referred to the dual basis of modern urban concepts of ethnicity as (1) *interactive* group formation, whereby one group is distinguished from another by its similarities and overlapping networks; and (2) *reactive* group formation, whereby an ethnic groups reasserts its historically established distinctions from other groups within a common national polity. The new ethnicity is more a product of the second process, because this ethnic identity is defined more as a need for political and social support in the pursuit of common interest than as regional similarity or sharedness of occupational ties. (Gumperz and Cook-Gumperz 1982: 5, emphasis in original)

Gumperz's work is centrally located at the intersection of these two senses of ethnicity. In the study of code-switching in urban settings, he analyses the way in which members of minority groups strategically juxtapose the styles and languages of their ethnic inheritance to the styles and languages of the dominant majority. They produce a wide range of rhetorical effects by reasserting cultural materials acquired in the interactive networks typical of the 'old ethnicity' in settings where in its new form, ethnicity is now much more a matter of reactive, contrastive identity (Gumperz and Cook-Gumperz 1982: 6). Gumperz's research on cross-cultural communication addresses the same problematic in a different form. In spite of liberal ideologies which officially declare the importance of judging a person on their merits, ethnicity remains an important feature in the organisation of contemporary life. By examining interethnic encounters in bureaucratic settings, Gumperz and others attribute the reactive processes of race polarisation to the *hidden* influence of the legacies of discursive practice inherited through the interactive networks characteristic of the 'old ethnicity'.

This distinction between 'old interactive' and 'new reactive' ethnicities in fact relates back to the massive shift from rural to urban that accompanied industrialisation in the modern world. The contrast between rural and urban, traditional and modern, has been a major shaping influence on sociology generally (Giddens 1987: 15–16), and its impact can be detected elsewhere in sociolinguistics. It is evident in Fishman's discussion of 'experiential' and 'referential' group membership, a distinction close to the 'old interactive' and 'new reactive' ethnicities (1972: 22–8). It is clear when Bernstein's analyses of class differences in language use (e.g. Bernstein 1971) draw on Durkheim's 'mechanical' and 'organic solidarity' ('mechanical solidarity' is typically agrarian, while 'organic solidarity' is typically urban). And it also explains why processes of mutual adjustment in modern institutions have been such a central sociolinguistic theme (cf. e.g. Hymes 1972b, Philips 1972, Heath 1983).[10]

There can be little doubt that contact between people with different backgrounds is sometimes problematic. But the trouble with the influential rural/urban, old/new ethnicity dichotomies is that they distract attention from the solutions which people improvise together in the arena of intergroup practice itself. Their temporal perspective only runs between the past and the present, and ethnicity only matters either as some kind of (concealed) historical burden, or as the (aggressive) reassertion of inheritance, or as both. The only options for the future, it would seem, are neutralised reconciliation or continuing polarisation along the same lines as before. In contrast to this, it is worth considering the extent to which multiracial interaction might generate a sense of the historic emergence of new allegiances, cross-cutting ethnic-genetic descent.

Though it is notoriously difficult to define, ethnicity generally involves some combination of: a sense of place and of common origin and destiny, shared culture and/or language, a measure of consensus on the evaluation of out-group 'others', active self-identification with the in-group, ascription to it by outsiders, and/or some idea of bio-kinship. But there is no reason why all of these features should be active simultaneously, and neither is there any reason to suppose that the lines defining ethnic 'us' and 'them' are set for perpetuity (cf. Fishman 1977; LePage and Tabouret-Keller 1985).

The language use that we have studied in this book was often strongly articulated with a sense of distinctive local network identity and neighbourhood. It was embedded within a set of interactional and cultural conventions that adolescents often reflected on with pleasure (and sometimes with stronger feelings of affiliation). Language practices were also linked in to ideas of common historical trajectory (albeit in different ways; see e.g. 2.5, 2.6, 8.5). In the main, however, these linguistic enunciations of group identity *traversed* the boundaries of biological descent.[11] Without trying to obscure or obliterate some very considerable background differences, crossing involved the active ongoing construction of a new inheritance from within multiracial interaction itself. If one wants to use the term ethnicity to describe these processes, Stuart Hall's conception of 'new ethnicities' provides a more accurate account than Gumperz and Cook-Gumperz'. According to Hall, the new ethnicities emerging in Britain's urban centres provide some hope for the construction of a politics 'which works with and through difference, which is able to build those forms of solidarity and identification which make common struggle and resistance possible but without suppressing the real heterogeneity of interests and identities, and which can effectively draw the political boundary lines without fixing those boundaries for eternity' (1988: 28).

There *are* sociolinguistic theories which can accommodate the formation of new social groupings as well as the dissolution or reassertion of old ones – LePage and Tabouret-Keller's theory of acts of identity is perhaps most notable in this regard (1985). But the rural/urban problematic tends to obscure these processes of emergence, and in their search for explanation of intergroup dynamics, it has continually urged sociolinguists back to the domestic in-group settings where notionally, historic practice is preserved and transmitted. Without any doubt, early socialisation and continuing involvement in kinship networks make a very significant contribution to the ways that people communicate, and research on in-group code-switching has revealed an enormous amount about the ways in which established social groupings negotiate their position in plural societies. But these approaches produce an account of ethnic processes which is undoubtedly incomplete, and they also risk a rather crude cultural determinism.[12] These are problems that as a sociolinguistic concept, 'crossing' can help to overcome.

Notes

1. The fact that academics cannot agree on the distinction between borrowing and code-switching might tempt one to dismiss the attempt to classify language contact phenomena as an exercise in scholastic pedantry. But this would be unfair – the distinctions that scholars try to make often correspond to differences in language use that are important for participants. In Hewitt's data on white users of Creole, for example, the distinction between borrowing and code-switching was of crucial importance: if a Creole form could pass as a 'natural' part of their local vernacular speech – as borrowing – it was less likely to be challenged than Creole usage which was seen as a purposeful switch (Hewitt 1986: 151, cited in Chapter 5.5).

2. In fact, there are some difficulties in the way in which the notion of metaphorical code-switching has been used in the literature. Perhaps most noticeably, the notion of disrupted co-occurrence expectations has often been confounded with empirical observations about the frequency and duration of metaphorical code-alternation, so that there has been a temptation to regard any brief, intra-sentential language switch as metaphorical (e.g. Fishman 1972: 42; Genishi 1981: 137; McLure 1981: 70; Gumperz 1982a: 60–62, 98; Breitborde 1983: 10). There is a certain logic in this: where code-switching introduces a frame that partially violates normal co-occurrence expectations, it

is often hard for participants to agree on a footing that they can sustain together for any length of time, and there may well be a tendency to return quite quickly to modes of conduct in which the categories guiding action synchronise with one another in routine ways. But as earlier discussion of liminoidity and liminality made very clear, there are many occasions when the co-occurrence expectations constituting our sense of everyday reality are collectively suspended for quite substantial periods, and during these times, the double-vision characteristic of metaphorical switching can be collaboratively sustained and elaborated by a *number* of participants. Indeed it may well be that certain groups of speakers participate in these kinds of 'metaphorical situation' more than others – adolescents being a case in point. To avoid this rather well-entrenched confusion, it is perhaps worth talking of 'figurative' rather than metaphorical codeswitching, which still conveys the sense that participants have that they not involved in business quite as usual, that things are not quite what they seem, and that there are reasons for going beyond a literal interpretation of the situation.

3. Hill and Hill use Bakhtin in a way that, up to a point, I follow in my own analyses. I would query, though, the extent to which they give adequate recognition to interaction processes. For example, they suggest that hesitations and dysfluencies around code-mixing reflect the fact that an utterance has become 'a translinguistic battlefield upon which two ways of speaking struggle for dominance' (1986: 392–3). Here, it sounds as though the speaker is simply a vessel, and no account is taken of the role played by interlocutors. In contrast, a more fully interactional account would need to consider the extent to which, for example, hesitations and dysfluency were influenced by preference organisation, and so rather than being at the mercy of conflicting voices, these patterns could reflect the speaker's fully controlled display of the dispreferred status of the code-selection coming next. Gardiner notes of Bakhtin more generally: 'although the early Bakhtin railed against such linguists as Saussure for ignoring the embeddedness of discourse in concrete social practices, his analyses often (though not always) remain at a curiously rarefied level, as if linguistic communication essentially consisted in the interaction between disembodied individual "consciousnesses" ' (1992: 177). This serves as quite a useful caveat to those using Bakhtin in the study of code-switching – it also underlines the value of trying to integrate Bakhtin's approach with Auer's conversation analytic framework.

4. In fact, Bakhtin's distinction between uni-directional and vari-directional double-voicing (see Chapter 8.5) provides another good reason for preferring the phrase '*figurative* code-switching' to the much

more common '*metaphorical*' code-switching. According to Leech (1969), when people process *metaphors*, they work on the assumption that the figurative meaning is somehow complementary, or similar, to the literal meaning. In contrast, the interpretation of *irony* works on the assumption that figurative and literal meaning are somehow in contrast/opposition. Shifting over to bilingual language use, the element of complementarity in metaphor aligns it with uni-directional double voicing, while the dimension of contrast in irony links into the vari-directional type. In sum, if one wanted to use the term metaphor in relation to code-switching, it might be best to regard it as a *subtype* of figurative code-switching, as in the following scheme:

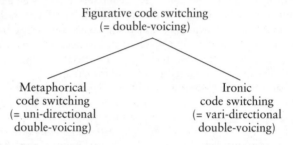

Figurative code switching
(= double-voicing)

Metaphorical
code switching
(= uni-directional
double-voicing)

Ironic
code switching
(= vari-directional
double-voicing)

5. In fact, in several important respects, Woolard's account of Catalan and Castilian resembles accounts of the relationship between Creole and local vernaculars among youth in England. In Hewitt's account, the extensive incorporation of Creole features into the South London vernacular was matched by a proscription of (purposive) conversational code-switching by whites (Hewitt 1986: ch. 4, 161–2; Woolard 1988: 55–6, 58–61). Comparably, where whites *were* accepted Creole users, the extent to which they really did code-switch was greatly exaggerated (Hewitt 1986: 161; Woolard 1988: 57). Finally, at least in the sociological literature, Eugenio's celebrity for combining Catalan and Castilian was paralleled by Smiley Culture's, a black British MC whose record 'Cockney Translation' mixed Cockney and Creole in a way that was accessible to both white and black listeners, and which Gilroy describes as composing 'a contradictory unity' that enunciates 'the basic framework for a potential black Britishness' (1987: 194–7; see also Hebdige 1987: 149–52; Jones 1988: 54–6; compare Woolard's comment 'Most importantly, in Eugenio's jokes, a fictional world is modelled where the two languages have found a peaceful coexistence' (1988: 71)).

6. Strong linguistic boundaries and the stigmatisation of both Gaelic and Gaelic-influenced English appear to have been the critical factors

pushing Gaelic into ritual zones at the margins of everyday reality (cf. also Hill and Hill 1986: 402 on the residual use of Nahuatl by Spanish dominant urban-dwelling Mexicanos).

7. There is in fact a considerable need for empirical studies which combine (a) analysis of language use among people losing a heritage language with (b) investigation of the ways in which ethnic outgroup members may themselves start to make use of that very same variety (cf. Gal 1989: 316). Most studies of language contact imply that it is the dominant language that provides the arena in which the language use of minorities overlaps with the linguistic practices of the majority. It is usually assumed that if, for example, native Britons share a language with immigrants to the UK, then that language is bound to be English. But in actual fact, majority and minority groups may also meet in liminal activities that are much more closely tied to the minority code (cf. Ferguson 1981: 32). And where this is the case, the ethno-political implications of language shift may be rather different from those most commonly ascribed to it (see the discussion in section 11.6 below).

8. In her study of advanced language shift in Nova Scotia, Mertz notices a similar pattern – Gaelic was increasingly concentrated in utterances that conveyed little 'semantico-referential information' (1989: 114). This was also crucial in Woolard's study of Eugenio's boundary crossing language use. To emphasise the difference, Woolard refers to a study of in-group code-switching in Yiddish: 'Kirshenblatt-Gimblett reports that speakers in the Ontario community are proud of their command of Yiddish and use it in structural slots that carry a high information load as a way of testing the competence of others who claim full membership in the community of Yiddish speakers' (1988: 69). In contrast, Eugenio only used Catalan in 'structural slots that do not carry a significant load of new information' (1988: 67). More specifically, the punchline of his jokes were almost invariably in Castilian: 'In Eugenio's performances, code-switching is used for boundary-levelling rather than boundary-maintaining purposes, and is popular for exactly that reason. The use of the two languages in a way that doesn't obscure critical information for any listeners eases rather than emphasises group boundaries, and allows the widest possible audience to participate' (1988: 70). In pursuit of the comparison initiated in note 5, it is worth adding that linguistic accessibility was also a key issue in Smiley Culture's celebrated record, which was, after all, called 'Cockney *Translation*'.

9. See e.g. McLure 1981: 74; Dorian 1982; Gumperz 1982a: 65; Auer 1984; Penfield and Ornstein-Galicia 1985: 16; Auer 1988: 196; Heller 1988: 78–79; McLure and McLure 1988: 45; Burt 1992.

10. Hymes' seminal notion of 'sociolinguistic interference' (1972b: 287–8) was also positioned at the meeting point between traditional practices and the demands of the modern state. It expressed concern that the discoursal habits and expectations that minority children acquired during their early socialisation might impede their performance at school in undetected ways, and this was supported by a number of important empirical studies reporting on the problems that arose when domestic in-group practices were transferred over into official intergroup domains that remained unresponsive and inflexible (cf. e.g. Philips 1972; Heath 1983).

11. Admittedly with SAE, Asian adolescents did introduce the language sometimes spoken by their parents into intergroup discourse. But contrary to the portrait of reactive ethnicity provided above, they did not necessarily align themselves with this in contradistinction to their white and black peers.

12. This is a point made by McDermott and Gospodinoff 1981. They argue that sociolinguistic studies of miscommunication have tended to overemphasise the determining influence of linguistic and socio-cultural convention. Sometimes, actors in cross-cultural interaction are seen as the prisoners of their communicative inheritances, it is forgotten that many people either enjoy or overcome differences in language or cultural style, and sufficient attention is not always given to the way in which participants can accentuate or play down cultural differences according to their immediate situational needs or purposes. In contrast, McDermott and Gospodinoff insist on a view that recognises ethnic difference, but which sees it as 'secondary to the political relations between members of different groups both in the classroom and in the larger community' (McDermott and Gospodinoff 1979: 212; see also Erickson and Shultz 1982; Cazden 1986: 446; Cook-Gumperz 1986; Roberts et al. 1992).

12 Crossing, discourse and ideology

Commenting on an important collection of sociolinguistic papers on code-switching, Susan Gal writes:

> we need a comparative analysis that interprets codeswitching practices not only as conversational tools that maintain or change ethnic group boundaries and personal relationships but also as symbolic creations concerned with the construction of 'self' and 'other' within a broader political economic and historical context. This suggests that the study of how codes are deployed in conversation is not only a sociolinguistic problem. Because codeswitching usually involves the use of a state-supported and powerfully legitimated language in opposition to a stigmatized minority language that has considerably less institutional support, it can also provide fresh evidence of what neo-Marxist culture theory (e.g. Williams 1973) identifies as 'consciousness': how speakers respond symbolically to relations of domination between groups within the state, and how they understand their historic position and identity within a capitalist world system structured around dependency and unequal development. (1988: 247)

Chapter 11 discussed code-crossing as a 'sociolinguistic problem', and it addressed the ways in which crossing serves to 'maintain or change ethnic group boundaries'. But there were only rather passing references to the way in which, through crossing, 'speakers respond symbolically to relations of domination between groups within the state'.

It is this political dimension that is the central concern of the present chapter. I shall try to characterise the kinds of ideological process that code-crossing encompassed. To do so, I will first sketch out some of the conceptual interrelations involved in Gal's attention to code-switching, consciousness and political domination. Once this has been laid out, three questions will be addressed: (i) How far did larger patterns of race division and hierarchy shape interactional language crossing? (ii) How far did language crossing contest, redefine or overcome these larger patterns? And (iii) what kind of political potential could it have? Because it embraces three minority varieties rather than just one, the setting for this analysis provides almost laboratory conditions for the *comparative* analysis that Gal proposes.

12.1 Discourse, consciousness and ideology: a map

To engage with the questions which Gal identifies, it is useful to begin with a discussion of Bakhtin/Volosinov, who qualifies as one of the most influential exponents of the culture theory that Gal refers to (cf. e.g. Williams 1977), and who has had a very considerable impact on the humanities and social sciences over the last 15 years. In what follows, I will lay out some of Bakhtin/Volosinov's views on the relationships between consciousness, interaction, ideology and domination. The purpose in doing so is not to give a detailed critique of Bakhtinian theory, but to provide an increasingly familiar and uncontroversial map of socio-cultural relationships and processes. This will then act as an explicit set of wider bearings within which it will be possible to recognise and place some of the fairly diverse issues addressed in the analysis of language crossing, my primary concern.

In considering the links between consciousness, interaction, and large-scale political processes, an initial bridge between consciousness and interaction exists in Volosinov's insistence on the essentially social and communicative character of mental life and inner experience.

> There is no such thing as [psychological] experience outside embodiment in signs ... expression organises experience ... [and] even in the original, vague form of glimmering thought and experience, [consciousness] has already constituted a social event on a small scale.

> From the very start experience is set toward fully actualized outward expression and, from the very start, tends in that direction. The expression of an experience may be realized or it may be held

back, inhibited. In the latter case, the experience is inhibited expression ... Realized expression, in its turn, exerts a powerful ...
influence on experience: it begins to tie inner life together, giving it
more definite and lasting expression. This ... influence by structured and stabilized expression on experience (i.e. inner expression)
has tremendous importance and must always be taken into account.
The claim can be made that it is a matter not so much of expression
accommodating itself to our inner world but rather our inner world
accommodating itself to the potentialities of our expression, its possible routes and directions. ([1929] 1973: 85, 90–1)

The way in which individuals orientate to actual and potential
communication in their immediate social milieux plays a fundamental role in organising their consciousness. Indeed, the
interpenetration of context with consciousness means that mind
'extends beyond the skin' (Wertsch 1991: 14):

Consciousness, while still inside a conscious person's head as inner-
word embryo of expression, is as yet too tiny a piece of existence,
and the scope of its activity is also as yet too small ... But consciousness as organized, material expression (in the ... material of
word, a sign, drawing, colours, musical sound, etc.), consciousness,
so conceived, is an objective fact and a tremendous social force.
(Volosinov [1929] 1973: 90)

To examine this development from inner action to material
force, Volosinov uses the term ideology to designate the different
sets of signs, representations and evaluations that constitute consciousness (Stewart 1981: 49–55; Todorov 1984: 18), and he
distinguishes two basic types – the 'behavioural' and the 'established'. 'Behavioural ideology' is located in the immediate social
situation: 'Behavioural ideology is that atmosphere of unsystemat-
ised and unfixed inner and outer speech which endows our every
instance of behaviour and action and our every 'conscious' state
with meaning' ([1929] 1973: 91). But despite their relatively
unstable and unformalised nature, behavioural ideologies are
closely intertwined with established ones. On the one hand
behavioural ideologies operate both as the immediate context for
the reception of established ideologies, and as their original
source. And on the other they draw from them part of their own
character:

The established ideological systems of social ethics, science, art, and religion are crystallisations of behavioural ideology, and these crystallisations, in turn, exert a powerful influence back upon behavioural ideology, normally setting its tone. At the same time, these already formalised ideological products constantly maintain the most vital organic contact with behavioural ideology and draw sustenance from it; otherwise, without that contact, they would be dead, just as any literary work or cognitive idea is dead without living, evaluative perception of it . . . Behavioural ideology draws the [ideological piece of] work into some particular social situation. The work combines with the whole content of the consciousness of those who perceive it and derives its apperceptive values only in the context of that consciousness. (p. 91)

To provide a schematic account of the way in which the meaning potentials in situated local interaction can become institutionalised as established ideologies,

We must distinguish several different strata in behavioural ideology . . . The world of an experience may be narrow and dim; its social orientation may be haphazard and ephemeral and characteristic only for some adventitious and loose coalition of a small number of persons . . . Such an experience will remain an isolated fact in the psychological life of the person exposed to it . . . Experiences of that kind, experiences born of a momentary and accidental state of affairs, have, of course, no chance of further social impact or efficacy. The lowest, most fluid, and quickly changing stratum of behavioural ideology consists of experiences of that kind. To this stratum, consequently, belong all those vague and undeveloped experiences, thoughts and idle, accidental words that flash across our minds . . . The upper strata of behavioural ideology, the ones directly linked with ideological systems, are more vital, more serious and bear a creative character. Compared to an established ideology, they are a great deal more mobile and sensitive: they convey changes in the socio-economic basis more quickly and more vividly. Here, precisely, is where those creative energies build up through whose agency partial or radical restructuring of ideological systems comes about. Newly emerging social forces find ideological expression and take shape first in these upper strata of behavioural ideology before they can succeed in dominating the arena of some organised, official ideology. (p. 92)

Before situating crossing within this general scheme, it is worth pointing out that with minor adjustments, these ideas tune quite extensively with contemporary discussion in a number of fields (cf. Gilroy 1987; Chapter 1.2; Gardiner 1992: ch. 3). The socio-cultural constitution of consciousness is by now a familiar idea (e.g. Vygotsky 1962; Wertsch 1991) and increasing emphasis is now given to the relationship between ideology and processes of signification (e.g. Thompson 1984; Fairclough 1989; Kroskrity et al. 1992). The connections that Volosinov makes between consciousness, ideology, signs and situated interaction entail a recognition that ideology plays an active role in the formation of human subjectivity and that it shapes and influences 'lived' social relations. In the emphasis given to behavioural ideologies, the idea that particular beliefs and values are simply imposed top-down by dominant groups is also clearly seen as inadequate (cf. Gardiner on the 'dominant ideology thesis'). Ideologies are plural and even the most established has to contend with the diffuse patterns of thought and meaning that animate local interaction. As Gardiner says 'ideology is not [now] conceived of as a highly systematic or axiomatic "belief-system", but as a disparate, contradictory and stratified complex of practices and symbols, which are pitched at different levels of coherence and social effectivity and which are subject to continual contestation and negotiation' (1992: 66).

Bakhtin/Volosinov's account of discourse, consciousness and ideology does have certain flaws,[1] but these do not seriously impair its value in helping us achieve an overview of language crossing as an ideological practice.

12.2 Discourse, consciousness and ideology: language crossing

To order and draw together all the evidence that we have covered, it is useful to address two basic questions:

1. How did established ideologies affect behavioural ones? How did the institutional and ideological positioning of a language and/or its inheritors affect the way in which social knowledge about race was displayed and negotiated in interaction?
2. In what ways was there a reverse influence? How (far) did discursive practices contest or reformulate more established representations and evaluations?

Two points need to be made in advance. First, there is no simple answer to these questions. As Bakhtin and many others would lead one to expect, the ideological understanding/social knowledge about race manifest in interaction was highly sensitive both to particular languages and to the immediate settings in which they were used. We have reviewed a wide range of different practices in this book, and their diversity must not be neglected or oversimplified. But secondly, in spite of its varied inflections, there was still, in the networks I studied, a certain common understanding of social reality and of the place in it occupied by race/ethnicity. Because of this, recognition of the variety in crossing need not drag us to a halt in a proliferation of hedges. The fact that adolescents were oriented to a shared sense of reality creates the prospect of some broad generalisation within this study.

12.3 The influence of established ideologies

How did a group or a language's positioning within established ideologies and institutions influence crossing as an interactional practice? In answering this question, it is first worth addressing some general remarks to Gal's concern with the ways in which 'a capitalist world system structured around dependency and unequal development' shaped and constrained the ideological terrain in which adolescents developed a sense of identity. After that, we can move to language crossing proper, drawing on more specific empirical descriptions.

The capitalist world system played a fundamental role shaping the history, structure and composition of Stoneford itself (see Chapter 1.7). It split, created, and/or reconstituted a range of different social groupings, placed them in different positions of power, and ultimately gave ethnicity and race much of their meaning. From the end of the nineteenth century, Stoneford changed from being a small market town and became a resort for Anglos returning from India, at the same time as Ashmead was emerging as a distinct working-class neighbourhood due to internal labour migration. After the Second World War, class stratification and the impact of imperial domination developed further, with migration from the Commonwealth and the development of local white suburbs. Race discrimination – itself intricately connected with imperial experience – in housing, employment, education and government meant that Afro-Caribbeans and Asians coming to Stoneford remained in positions of relative material disadvantage. Admittedly, there was some variation within this: families migrating from India appeared to have prospered more than other non-European groups, while disadvantage was greatest among those from Bangladesh, who had generally arrived most recently. But one result of these processes was that Ashmead was widely regarded as lower class and multi-ethnic – Stoneford's 'inner city' – and whatever their countries of ancestral origin, local adolescents were well aware of this identity.

It was not only a sense of neighbourhood that took shape within the processes associated with global and historical domination. They also affected the socio-ideological horizons associated with different language varieties. Among others, Gilroy describes the major impact that diaspora has had on black musics, and he identifies a critique of capitalism – its prioritisation of work, its oppressive state apparatuses, and its distortion of history – as a constant and crucial component in the sensibility expressed in lyrics, music and/or relations of consumption (1987: ch. 5). Elements of this doubtless had an influence on the way in which local adolescents saw both Creole and North American Vernacular Black English. Within Anglo culture, a great deal of the symbolic resonance of Asian English also has roots in a history of international domination (in colonial representations of babu). Among young people of Indian and Pakistani descent, family experience of migration meant that in conflict with this, accented English was also partially associated with transition in the recent past.[2]

Clearly, heritage languages were caught in a number of macro-ideological cross-currents. But of course ideologies are not like rarefied, disembodied voices, and are instead given material force in the practice of institutions. Certainly, language varieties derive a part of their social value from (a) the large scale socio-historical processes that operate across and through a *number* of social institutions (such as the ones outlined above). But to understand how established ideologies and institutional power relations influenced interactional language crossing, it is also necessary to consider (b) the *particular* (and sometimes distinct) sociolinguistic valuations operating *within* a given domain, as well as (c) the kinds of cross-ethnic social relations that the particular domain engenders. The interaction between these three socio-ideological levels is highly complex, as a review of code-crossing in three domains makes clear.

At *school*, Creole, Panjabi and Asian English all occupied a subordinate position to standard English in the educational ideologies materialised in the curriculum. But within that, Panjabi and Urdu were given (differing) degrees of prestige-generating recognition, Asian English was recognised in a way that contributed to its stigma, and Creole was largely ignored (Chapters 4.5, 5.3). For adolescents, the impact of these rankings was partly filtered through the particular role relationships that school produced. As pupils in classrooms, young people were placed together in positions of subordinacy, and up to a point, a common rejection of school values, symbolised in standard English, could lead either to tacit solidarity or to active convergence towards the language varieties valued beneath the 'posh' one. Even so, the larger frame of political relations remained important, either as a reference point or as an influence. In the first instance, adolescents themselves often foregrounded the intersection between local relationships and wider political problematics (a) when code-switching into stylised Asian English (SAE) indexed questions of disadvantage and access, and (b) when Panjabi switching raised questions of pluralism and autonomy (Chapters 4.5 and 5.8). Secondly, the wider social stigmatisation of Asian English set limits on adolescent solidarity, and there was hardly any sympathy for the Asian pupils who really did speak a second language variety of English.

In *expressive youth culture* – in drama, popular music, sound system culture and bhangra – the prevailing ideological valuations differed from those at school in several important ways. Creole had very high status, Panjabi was also valued, though not nearly as widely, and once again, Asian English tended to be the object of negative representation (Chapter 9.5). Opportunities for crossing also varied considerably, and were affected both by the ways in which the particular art form was disseminated, as well as by the interracial ideology that it articulated (Chapters 2.1 and 9.2). Generally speaking, both bhangra and sound-system culture involved competitive hierarchies in which adolescents of Asian and Afro-Caribbean descent did not readily cede advantage to outsiders. Here, rather than being allies in (classroom) adversity, aspirant Panjabi and Creole crossers were novices, engaged not in 'downward' but in 'upward' convergence towards what were now plainly prestigious varieties.

The third institutional arena considered in this study was *informal recreation*. This did not appear to be a zone in which comparative values had already been clearly ascribed to each language – here, 'behavioural ideologies' seemed to have a freer rein. Furthermore, in this domain, disrespect was a larger part of the prevailing social ethos than in either education or expressive art, and crossing occurred in actions that celebrated deception, doubt and individual advantage much more than truth, belief or moral community (Chapters 9.3, 10.6). Yet once again, crossing showed sensitivity to wider socio-ideological configurations in ways that differed for each code. A sense of ethnic 'otherness' occurred with crossing in all three varieties, but patterns of avoidance suggested that this sense of otherness took subtly different forms. If we ignore the special licence associated with sex difference, white and black youngsters generally didn't use SAE to target Indian or Pakistani friends: to do so could be interpreted as an unacceptable assertion of racial superiority (Chapters 2.4, 6.3). Whites and Asians also usually avoided Creole with Afro-Caribbean peers, either because this would be taken as pejorative stereotyping, and/or (more probably) because it could be read as a claim to the vernacular and artistic excellence stereotypically associated with black youth. In both cases, and in different ways, language crossing and its avoidance implied the relevance of race *hierarchisation* as an ideology. In contrast, playground Panjabi crossing generally *only occurred face to face* with Asian peers. Much more than elsewhere, language crossing here seemed to be guided by a view of ethnic difference that was relatively *uninhibited* by perceptions of wider ethnic stratification (Chapters 2.3, 8.5).

Summing up the discussion so far, we can say that the varying ways in which Panjabi, Creole and Asian English were positioned within different institutions had a major influence on language crossing actions. Taking the term to mean 'set limits and exert pressure on' rather than 'predict' or 'totally control' (Williams 1973), a number of different kinds and levels of established ideology certainly did 'determine' behavioural practice. But as has been repeatedly emphasised, the meaning of an action is finally shaped by a host of immediate interactional contingencies: who the participants are, what the activity is, where it occurs in the discourse, how it is received, its locutionary force and so forth. At this point, we should turn to the second question.

12.4 Local ideological creativity

How far did language crossing contest or reformulate established evaluations and representations? In what ways did behavioural ideologies affect established ones? In addressing this question, it is useful to start by considering crossing's general relation to the ethnic absolutism that underpins a number of powerful discourses in Britain. Through that, consideration will necessarily come to local ideological engagement with the values and images ascribed to particular groups and languages.

Ethnic absolutism is a term that Gilroy uses to characterise a cluster of assumptions that widely figure in a range of established discourses, articulating a number of different political viewpoints (1987: ch. 2; also Chapters 1.2 above and 13.3–13.4 below). Its two fundamental assumptions are (a) that a person's ethnicity is fixed, if not from their birth, then at least during their early home experience, and (b) that ethnicity is the most important aspect of a person's identity – other social category memberships are insignificant. In the discourses of the Right, this runs with a view that some ethnic cultures are superior to others; in those of the Left, it is expressed through the argument that minority cultures are different but equally valid. In addition to oversimplifying the nature of group membership, both discourses overlook culture's processual, interactive character and instead conceive of 'cultures' as a set of reified ethnic units.

If ethnic absolutism had been completely hegemonic in the network I studied, language crossing would have been unacceptable, a ceaseless source of local conflict. Of course, it might have occurred in the distancing, caricatural forms that one sometimes finds in the performances of commercial comedians, but this would have simply affirmed the emphatic and invariant otherness of ethnic out-groups. In contrast, in Ashmead, crossing arose out of solidarities and allegiances that were grounded in a range of *non-ethnic* identities – identities of neighbourhood, class, gender, age, sexual orientation, role, recreational interest and so on – and it was these that generated, among other things, the local multiracial vernacular. It was their base in these connections that allowed adolescents to explore the significance of ethnicity and race through language crossing. Indeed, crossing not only emerged from a plurality of identity relations: it also addressed a range of the meanings that ethnicity could have, and here it is worth turning to the different forms that crossing took.

As a form of local interactional engagement with the race stereotypes presented in dominant British ideologies, crossing practices varied in the extent to which they generally drew on these stereotypic images and valuations, and in the extent to which they accepted or rejected them.

Panjabi crossing was more independent of the ways in which ethnic minorities were generally represented than either Creole or SAE. In informal recreation, it took shape within the relatively subterranean traditions of playground culture (Chapters 7.1–7.3), and in the context of bhangra, crossing oriented to practices and images that had not yet been extensively processed and re-presented within commercial culture (Chapters 10.1–10.3). Though it has not been fully analysed, crossing in Creole tended to reproduce popular conceptions and to accept and embrace its stereotypic connotations of vernacular vitality, counterposed to the values of bourgeois respectability (Chapters 5 and 8.3; cf. also Hewitt 1986: 216–7; Back 1993: 229). With SAE, practical reinterpretation of established ideology took its most complex form. With white adults, crossing into Asian English evoked racist images of Asian deference in a manner that could subvert the action of any interlocutor that entertained them. Of course this could be done playfully, but at the moment when it was performed, crossing of this kind constituted an act of minor resistance to the smooth flow of adult-dominated interaction (Chapter 3.5). With younger children or with adolescents of Bangladeshi extraction, SAE also drew on popular stereotypes about Asian distance from vernacular culture, but this was unaccompanied by any radical inversion (Chapter 6.2). Here crossing simply endorsed and reproduced an image from racist ideology. In games, code-switching preserved Asian English's connotations of distance from mainstream adolescent culture, but here they were fused with celebration, largely extricated from any political problematic (Chapter 6.4).

The diversity of this patterning is very important for a general characterisation of the ideological significance of language cross-ing. Without it, it would be tempting to draw an unqualified parallel between code-crossing and Bakhtin's view of the speech at the marketplace and carnival:

> Abuses, curses, profanities, and improprieties are the unofficial ele-ments of speech. They were and are still conceived as a breach of the established norms of verbal address; they refuse to conform to conventions, to etiquette, civility, respectability. These elements of freedom, if present in sufficient numbers and with a precise inten-tion, exercise a strong influence on the entire contents of speech, transferring it to another sphere beyond the limits of conventional language. Such speech forms, liberated from the norms, hierarchies, and prohibitions of established idiom, become themselves a peculiar argot and create a special collectivity, a group of people initiated in familiar intercourse, who are frank and free in expressing themselves verbally. The marketplace crowd was such a collectivity, especially the festive, carnivalesque crowd at the fair. (Bakhtin 1968: 187–8)

Bakhtin's account of carnival and marketplace speech had other characteristics that resonate with aspects of the code crossing we have considered. In the terms of Gardiner's useful summary (1992: 44–58), carnival 'broke down the formalities of hierarchy and the inherited differences between different social classes, ages and castes' and involved 'carnivalistic mesalliances – the free and spontaneous combination of formerly self-enclosed and fixed cate-gories'; it 'underscore[d] the inevitability of change and transformation', and had 'a quality of "unfinished becoming" '; it emphasised the 'material bodily principle . . . incorporati[ng] images depicting the material functions of the human body (eating and drinking, defecation, copulation)'; and it drew together what 'are [Bakhtin's] primary values: incompleteness, becoming, ambi-guity, indefinability, non-canonicalism – indeed all that jolts us out of our normal expectations and epistemological complacency'. For contemporary sociolinguistic research on code-switching, some of the potential significance of this account is made clear by Hill and Hill:

> [in] Bakhtin's account . . . in the heteroglossic marketplace . . . common people can attack the monologic dominance of standard

language ... we do believe that mixing in language may carry a special resonance of resistance to official order ... For Bakhtin, heteroglossia in multilingual popular usage amplifies and opens up the possibilities for meaning and freedom. Here on the multilingual margins of society, official utterances will be removed from their sphere and clarified by exposure to parody and by confrontation with other ways of speaking. (Hill and Hill 1986: 398–9)

Certainly, as a general practice, language crossing was counter-posed to Standard English, it challenged normal expectations and it constituted a distinctive 'argot' that helped to create a 'special collectivity'. But it would be a mistake to push the relevance of Bakhtin's view too emphatically for at least three reasons.

First, if one wanted to insist on the similarity, it would be neces-sary to privilege certain types of crossing above others. There certainly was a great deal of the carnivalesque in multiracial play-ground Panjabi, but little of it transferred across to white engagements with bhangra. To neglect the difference between these two contexts would be to produce a partial and distorted account (cf. Bourdieu [1983] 1991: 98, 99). Secondly, Bakhtin in fact idealises the political character of carnival, regarding its laughter as invariably healthy and subversive, and neglecting its historic capacity to embrace racism and persecution (Gardiner 1992: 182). In the evidence we have considered, certain uses of SAE were highly illiberal, and more generally, to view language crossing as entirely 'liberated from norms, hierarchies, and pro-hibitions of established order' would be to considerably oversimplify the complexity of its engagement with dominant ideologies of race.

It would also be wrong to suggest that language crossing was entirely 'free and familiar', a process of run-away deconstruction indifferent to every significance that ethnicity might have (cf. also Gilroy 1987: 218–9). Broadly speaking, crossers were actually rather respectful towards the ethnic memberships traditionally associated with the language they were using, and this showed up in two patterns that ran throughout the data we have considered. (a) Certain types of speaker avoided language crossing in the pres-ence of certain kinds of interlocutor: members of ethnic outgroups did not usually take liberties with Creole and Asian English if there were inheritors on hand. And (b), crossing occurred in moments, activities and relationships in which the hold of ordinary assumptions about social reality was loosened in some way. In consequence, crossing did not ultimately claim that the speaker was 'really' black or Asian, or that their relationship with the minority group that they linguistically invoked entailed an open unrestricted biculturalism.

The fact that crossing occurred in liminal moments and events means, of course, that adolescents treated inherited ethnicity itself as a basic feature of social reality. Inherited ethnicity certainly was not regarded as either immutable or all-encompassing – this was not ethnic absolutism. But in the social ordering that people tacitly oriented to in the main flow of ordinary life, ethnic descent was evidently taken to be a significant category, clustering language, upbringing and other characteristics in a meaningful way. Indeed, this sense of the importance of ethnic descent synchronised with local social network patterns, and with Stoneford's distribution of material resources (Chapter 1.7).

In fact when they code-crossed, there was a tension in the way that adolescents treated the boundaries round an ethnic category – they both respected and transgressed them. In this light, it becomes possible to discern another very important aspect of language crossing's significance as a process of delicate political negotiation. In excess, both an acceptance *and* a disregard for these boundaries could slip into injustice, which can be defined as either (a) treating people the same when in relevant respects they are different, and/or as (b) treating them as different when, in relevant respects, they are similar (Halstead 1988: 154). For adolescents in a multilingual peer group, unrestricted use of an ethnic out-group language could constitute the first kind of injustice; on the other hand, if an individual resisted every temptation to experiment in an out-group code, they might also find that they had actually succumbed to the second. Crossing generally wove a path between these two forms of wrong-doing. Through it, adolescents actively explored the waterline where ethnic and interracial forms overlapped and intermingled with each other – here they challenged ethnic fixity and division (b). But at the same time, they normally only brought out their new acquisitions in places where it could be safely understood that they weren't making any claims to real, equal or enduring membership of an ethnic out-group. So in this way, they also avoided (a) – the insensitivity to difference instantiated elsewhere in race relations in 'colour blindness', eth-nocentrism and so forth. Crossing's capacity to manage this tension may have constituted its most important contribution to the emergence of a sense of multiracial youth community.

To summarise, we can say that at the level of interaction, code-crossing involved a rather complex set of engagements with established ideologies, images and valuations. It engaged with dominant stereotypes in a mixture of radical and reactionary ways, and sometimes it operated independently of these. In inter-ethnic discourse, it challenged ethnic absolutism, but it seldom dismissed ethnic descent as a significant social issue. One final question remains: how far up Volosinov's 'strata of behavioural ideology' did code-crossing move? As the articulation of a 'newly emerging social force', to what extent could it 'succeed in domin-ating the arena of some organised, official ideology'?

12.5 From behavioural to established ideology?

A response to this question needs to start with a denial. From the repeated emphasis given to liminality, it might be reasonable to ask whether code-crossing's synchronisation with the suspension of dominant norms meant that it was a fundamentally trivial prac-tice, confined within periods of unserious activity that necessarily prevented it from having any wider political impact. Eagleton raises this possibility in a critical comment on Bakhtin's utopian view of carnival: 'Carnival, after all, is a *licensed* affair in every sense, a permissible rupture of hegemony, a contained popular blow-off as disturbing and relatively ineffectual as a revolutionary work of art. As Shakespeare's Olivia remarks, there is no slander in an allowed fool . . . Can [this] intoxicating liberation be politic-ally directed?' (Eagleton 1981: 148, cited in Gardiner 1992: 231).

For a number of reasons, it would be wrong to use an argument like that to be dismissive about code-crossing's political potential. In the first instance, the fact that there were many different types of liminality in which crossing occurred was itself important – unlike carnival, these did not just occur at times formally prescribed in official timetables. Secondly, in spite of buffering out some quoti-dian expectations, many liminoid activities are a frequent and valued part of 'life itself' (Chapters 6.7 and 7.9). Some of the activ-ities that sustained crossing might have been ephemerally linked to childhood – chasing games are the obvious example (Chapters 7.2, 7.6) – but others, like listening to music (Chapter 10.7) could last a life-time. Thirdly, some liminal activities either articulated, or led towards, very fully elaborated alternative models of reality (cf. sound-system events, and crossing oriented to bhangra – Chapters 9.3, 10.8). And lastly, the dividing lines between 'real' and liminal situations, between ordinary and ritualised speech, and between dominant and alternative models of reality were themselves often very thin (Chapters 5.4, 8.2, 8.4, 9.3). So on all these counts, it is clear that liminal practices could enter into a productive engagement with social reality (which is why some version of Gumperz's metaphorical code-switching is so important) cf. Chapter 11.1).

But though it is quite easy to dispense with that particular objection to code-crossing's larger ideological potential, it is still necessary to admit that I cannot provide a full or systematic account of what this potential actually was. This study has taken interactional conduct as its central focus, and it has repeatedly stressed the way in which situational contingencies affect the impact and consequences created by any micro-political code-switch. If one intended to investigate the extent to which the sensibilities displayed and produced through code-crossing articulated with an organised ideology, it would be vital to pay fuller attention to the formulations offered for example, in music, drama, and in local debates about race. Certainly, I have made quite a lot of references to these, but my concern with these has been rather selective, treating them only when they were relevant to interactional code-crossing. I have not considered these kinds of larger cultural practice in their own terms, and a great deal more would need to be said about the different ways in which local adolescents participated in them.

That does not mean, however, that the present study is entirely irrelevant to questions about the broader ideological potential generated within local adolescent experience. The fact that we have attended to a set of rather fragmentary and small-scale actions is not in itself an automatic disqualification, since in the first instance, 'newly emerging social forces' do not actually have any single grand or essential ideological meaning. Melucci argues that 'A social movement is an object created by analysis ... [W]ithin historical phenomena of collective action, one should distinguish a plurality of analytical meanings which eliminate the apparent unity of the empirical object and yield a different evalua-tion of its structural components as well as of its political implications ... No phenomenon of collective action can be con-sidered in its entirety because it never speaks in a single language' (Melucci 1981: 173–4). In fact, rather than analysis being negative and undermining, Melucci believes that pointing to the many meanings embraced within a social movement can be politically constructive:

> This is not an easy task ... A strong resistance [to this] can be found ... in the movements themselves, given their immediate need to project a global and united image of themselves in order to secure mobilisation ... Collective mobilisation is fragile, since it often holds together around general and confused objectives a het-erogeneous 'base'. [But] I am convinced that reflection, even when it is theoretical, on the structural components of new movements plays an important role in the growth of collective action ... Knowledge, especially sociological knowledge, acquires a central importance for the collective phenomena before us. (1981: 178, 179, 192)

In fact, while conceding the absence of an adequate account of explicitly political mobilisation, a stronger claim can be made for the relevance of the present study. The investigation of face-to-face discourse has not just indicated a plurality of meanings around race and ethnicity: it has also suggested that these mean-ings are more than merely 'analytical'. The central idea in our interaction analyses has been that the participants themselves were oriented to the significances that we have drawn out. Through code-crossing in the spontaneous flow of everyday conduct, local adolescents themselves continuously exchanged the kinds of politi-cal meaning that we have been able to identify (cf. Chapters 3.5, 5.8). In consequence (and in line with Volosinov), we can in fact claim that code-crossing displayed complex interethnic under-standings that were in some sense *foundational* – code-crossing pointed to an intricate but distinctive web of sensibilities that would provide quite fertile soil for certain kinds of ideological development, and more stony ground for others.

The kinds of ideological elaboration that crossing could sustain were intimated in interview discussions,[3] and Chapter 2 described the ways in which crossing brought forth a range of local ideas about group similarities and differences, about interethnic accommodations that were permitted and proscribed, about idiosyncratic and shared historical trajectories, and about possibilities and limits to youth, class and neighbourhood co-membership.

These meta-sociolinguistic ideas did not themselves constitute the well-formed rhetorical package that Hill describes as a 'discursive system' – they were not enunciated in 'a set of characteristic formulas [that] develop a small set of major rhetorical themes' which speakers often chained together (1992: 264–5). They were drawn together around questions about language crossing, and they were too close to 'behavioural ideology' to allow the idealisation on which the discourses of established ideology rely. But these reflections on practice did not float like sitting ducks in a local ideological vacuum, prey to any political current that chanced past them from outside. In Ashmead as in other multiracial areas of Britain, there were locally generated discourses which articulated a strong sense of multiracial community. As Hewitt remarks,

> the local multiracial vernacular can be read from the outside as in some sense a sociolinguistic output of spontaneous multiculturalism [which] is essentially *unself-conscious*. However, where self-consciousness *does* seem apparent with regard to spontaneous multiculturalism is in the development of a coherent *discourse* of local community that is drawn on under certain conditions and has become very familiar to those researching in inner city areas . . . This discourse is . . . of considerable interest because in some respects, it has been generated from real social relations . . . and [it] constitutes an idealisation of the local imposed not from outside, like so many idealisations of the local, but from within. It is a discourse not only activated in response to the probes of ethnographers asking for accounts but may be drawn upon in many secondary accounts and evaluations of actual events. (Hewitt 1989b: 8–9; see also Jones 1988)

As Hewitt implies, this discourse obscures certain realities – politically regressive uses of SAE are one example. And so there is no guarantee of its perfect fit with every aspect of the practical interethnic sensibilities displayed and negotiated in code-crossing. Nevertheless, there was still a high level of congruence. Indeed, if Melucci is correct in believing that the effectiveness of a social movement depends on constant recognition of the heterogeneous meanings which it actually embraces, then analytic reflection on the complexities of interactional practice could ultimately make a useful contribution to these locally emergent discourses.

The time and distance between my writing this book and my involvement in Ashmead is now quite considerable, and though I did engage in a small amount of organised local discussion about my findings (Rampton 1992), this was far from being a proper project in empowering research, conducted on, for and with informants.[4] So there is relatively little to report on any live interaction between local Ashmead discourses and the analytic reflections on everyday practice contained in this book. It was quite clear, though, that in many respects, code-crossing shaped and took shape within behavioural ideologies of ethnicity and language which differed quite radically from the established ideologies governing policy in education, and it is this issue that I shall address in the final chapter.

Notes

1. As Gardiner notes (1992: 182–7), Bakhtin/Volosinov does not adequately address the issue of hegemony (Williams 1973: 8–10; Clarke et al. 1976: 38ff; McLellan 1986: 30).

2. Clearly, any sociolinguistic account that concentrated on *in-group* ethnicity would need to reckon much more fully with language, diaspora and international relations than I have.

3. Folk explanations of language crossing – adolescent attempts to produce *propositional* statements about crossing's symbolic significance – can themselves be seen as one step on the long road towards established ideology. As a communicative medium, propositional statements rely slightly less on local background understandings than does symbolisation, crossing's main expressive mode. The trans-situational intelligibility of propositional statements is likely to be greater, and they can engage more easily with the rationalist idioms to which British policy makers (at least used to) pay lip service. This is not to deny that propositional statements are themselves context dependent, or that they can sometimes have symbolic resonances which are much more important that their logical coherence (cf. e.g. Hill 1992). Nevertheless, propositional articulation is likely to be an important adjunct in any group's struggle to win recognition of its values and perspectives, and crossing itself appeared to prompt certain kinds of commentary.

4. For a full discussion of empowerment in language research, see

Cameron et al. 1993, and the peer commentary in *Language and Communication*, Vol. 13, Part 2 (1993). Heath 1983: Part II, Furnborough et al. 1983 are two good examples of sociolinguistic research projects that used empowering methodologies.

13 *Educational discourses on language*

The aim of this chapter is to explore code-crossing's implications for educational discourses in multilingual situations. The chapter falls into two main parts.

In the first, the data on crossing serves as the base for a discussion of some of the assumptions dominating English policy on language education. The issues addressed are (a) the teaching of English as a second language (TESL), (b) bilingual education, and (c) language awareness as a theme within the curriculum. The second part of the chapter addresses the notion of the 'native speaker'. In sociolinguistic circles there is a great deal of dissatisfaction with this concept, but it continues in international circulation because, so far, no alternative formulation seems to be available. Prompted by the Ashmead data, I try to suggest one.

13.1 Educational discourses on multilingualism in England

In general, the views of adolescents have been overlooked in discussions about language education, even though young people's well-being is often invoked as the central consideration. In educational debate, pupils generally figure as objects of concern rather than as potential partners in dialogue, in spite of the fact that as one Government report put it, 'many pupils in schools are bilingual and biliterate, and quite literally know more about language than their teachers, at least in some respects' (DES 1989: para. 6.11). My own research did not canvas young people systematically for their views on policy, and so it clearly did not provide any model of formal consultation. Even so, the attitudes associated with spontaneous adolescent conduct cast some interesting light on the assumptions underpinning official discourses.

13.2 SAE and TESL orthodoxies

In the UK, debate about teaching English as a second language has taken racism as a central issue. In general during the 1960s and early 1970s, pupils who were judged to have limited proficiency in English were either placed in specialist language centres, or were withdrawn from mainstream classes for specialist ESL instruction (cf. Reid 1988 for a summary of developments). In 1986, after an investigation of one local education authority, the Commission for Racial Equality formally decided that language centres constituted a form of racial discrimination. The Committee of Inquiry into the Education of Children from Ethnic Minority Groups – the Swann Report – also criticised separate forms of ESL provision, asserting that 'such provision merely serves to establish and confirm social and racial barriers between groups' (DES 1985: 392). In line with this, the late 1970s and 1980s saw an increasing consensus that it was best to provide for the English language needs of bilingual pupils *inside* mainstream classrooms.

The data on SAE makes it clear that limited proficiency in English was a salient issue for adolescents as well as for educationalists. To a considerable degree, it supports the link made between ESL and racism – indeed, when addressed to pupils of Bangladeshi descent who had come to Britain relatively recently, SAE code-switching often instantiated racism in one of its crudest forms. But in other respects, it intimated a perspective that could usefully help to broaden educational debate (for fuller discussion, cf. Rampton 1988).

Though they undoubtedly contributed to it, different types of language teaching provision can only account for part of the social stigmatisation of limited proficiency in English. More general processes of race stereotyping also need to be reckoned with. It is well recognised that there have been no reliable or widely accepted measures of proficiency in English as a second language available to schools, and that teacher assessment has occupied a central role in the identification of ESL difficulty (cf. Rampton 1983). In consequence, there have been many opportunities for the operation of covert biases in classroom language assessment, and at least up until the mid-1980s, much of the published discussion about ESL itself promulgated a particular stereotype of pupils of South Asian descent. British Asian pupils, it was often suggested, were typically industrious and keen to learn, but they were likely to be held back by hidden weakness in the English that they used. Fluency in their English was commonly considered to be 'superficial' and 'deceptive'.

Code-switching into SAE often pinpointed a racist image in the dominant culture that may well have had an unrecognised influence on this discourse about ESL. SAE often invoked the stereotype of 'babu', which casts Indians as 'pliable, plastic and receptive', with only a superficial command of English (Chapter 2.4). As such, SAE can be read as an oblique critique of the pedigree and integrity of contemporary educational judgements. In certain key respects, educational texts on TESL suggested an image of British Asian pupils that bore a disturbing ressemblance to the cruder stereotypes of popular racism.

By invoking a cultural image that stretches back to nineteenth Century imperialism and that indexes a relationship between Britain and India that has been longstanding, intimate and unequal in its distribution of power (e.g. Parekh 1978), SAE also provides the grounds for more philosophical engagement with educational discussion.

Where it has not been recaptured by right wing ideologues committed to the assimilation of linguistic minorities, debate about language education and majority–minority relations has generally been dominated by liberal pluralism. The tendency within liberal pluralism/multiculturalism is to speak of recently encountered difference rather than enduring domination, and the orientation is more to future prospects than to inherited legacies. Racism is commonly seen as 'hostility to diversity' (Levine 1990: 12), as 'negative perceptions of . . . strangeness' (DES 1985: 407), and this leads to the central recommendation that schools should be more hospitable.

There is a good deal to be said for the ideals in this approach, and it encompasses elements that really must figure in any decent pupil–teacher classroom interaction. But even so, it contains some serious analytic flaws. Although it makes space for polite discussion about language background diversity, it has been accompanied by a noticeable failure to address colonial and post-colonial language relationships in the countries where pupils have family ties. If one neglects historical and comparative sociolinguistic analysis, one loses a good deal of purchase on the ways in which British discourse about language, foreigners and education have been shaped within particular positions of power (cf. Said 1978; Howatt 1984: ch. 15). And more relevant to the present discussion, if they are only seen as relative newcomers unfamiliar with English ways, there is a risk of underestimating the sociolinguistic insights of minority pupils themselves.

Advocacy of the value of multiracial youth perspectives is not based on a spuriously romantic view of adolescent understanding. Of course, adolescent understanding is often inarticulate and it can be sometimes turned to bad effect. The central point, however, is that bilingual school students are not unformed innocents, waiting to be given shape and direction by the knowledge and wisdom of teachers and policy makers. Pupils and educationalists need to be seen as actors on the same historical stage, and neither party has privileged access to truth. Because their consciousness has been influenced by many of the same social and historical processes, there is likely to be a great deal of mutual intelligibility. At the same time, differences in position inevitably lead to the divergent perspectives that are commonly associated with antagonism, partiality *and* with insight.

We can summarise the discussion so far in terms of the distinction made in the last chapter between 'behavioural' and 'established ideologies' (Chapter 12.1). The TESL orthodoxies that I have sketched out can be considered as an established ideology, providing a nationally disseminated set of interpretations for particular kinds of language difference. Code-switching into SAE addresses the same type of difference, but as a form of spontaneous action delicately tuned to a range of situational contingencies, it needs to be construed as a form of practical consciousness/behavioural ideology. It appears that on the subject of ESL, there are important areas of potential dispute in the assumptions that educationalists and adolescents display at these two ideological levels. In this area of language education, the attitudes displayed in adolescent practice have generally been *ignored*. In another, one can make the case that they have actually been *misrepresented*.

13.3 Panjabi crossing and bilingual education

In England, government policy tolerates the use of minority languages as a transitional measure during the early years of schooling, and it also allows pupils to study community languages (such as Urdu, Italian, Panjabi or Polish) as examination subjects in their last few years at secondary school. But there is no encouragement for cultivation of bilingualism throughout a child's educational career, and there is no scope for bilingual education using minority community languages as media of instruction. The most influential document articulating this policy was the Swann Report, and its assessment was as follows:

> It is clear that both bilingual education and mother tongue maintenance can only be of relevance to mother tongue speakers of languages other than English, i.e. to pupils from certain ethnic minority groups. Where such provision has been made therefore it has inevitably meant that ethnic minority pupils have had to be separated from their peers for 'special' teaching. As we have stated throughout this report, we are opposed in principle to the withdrawal of ethnic minority pupils as an identifiable group and to the concept of 'separate' provision. We cannot accept that such provision can in any sense, as has been suggested, reduce social and cultural barriers between English speakers and ethnic minority pupils. On the contrary, we believe that any form of separate provision catering exclusively for ethnic minority pupils serves to establish and confirm social divisions between pupils. It also leaves the ethnic majority pupils' education impoverished and monolingual and the negative perceptions of the 'strangeness' of ethnic minority groups, which lie at the roots of racism, unaffected. Linguistic barriers between groups can, we believe, only be broken down effectively by a programme of language awareness for all pupils. (DES 1985: 406–7)

In this passage, there is a clear concern with the social impact of different types of language provision. In fact, the case against bilingual education is based on at least four assumptions:

1. there is a major risk of social fragmentation among youth;
2. minority languages are only of interest to ethnic minority pupils;
3. any kind of special language teaching is dangerous;
4. language awareness classes for everyone at school are the only effective anti-racist strategy.

Yet if one considers the empirical evidence outlined in this book, each one of these propositions starts to look questionable. We have seen that

1. there are many cross-ethnic friendships. Although there may not be seamless racial harmony, interethnic relations among youth can be much more robust than Swann assumes;
2. there can be a strong interest in minority languages among majority group peers. Indeed, far from seeming 'strange', for some black and white youngsters, Panjabi is part of their own youth community language repertoire;
3. adolescents do not necessarily require *all* members of their peer group to speak *all* its languages with *equal* proficiency. Linguistic specialisation may be well recognised: indeed, young people may enjoy the access to different cultural resources that the diverse linguistic backgrounds of their friends can provide;
4. there may be a good deal of language awareness *outside* the classroom, and some of it can be plainly antiracist in character.

Admittedly, the research described in this book was based in just one neighbourhood. But there is now good evidence that the kinds of social and linguistic dynamic described in Ashmead can be found elsewhere in Britain (cf. Hewitt 1986; Jones 1988). And even on its own, my data are sufficient to deny axiomatic status to Swann's claims about adolescent race relations. Intolerance among youth simply cannot be taken as some kind of invariant, self-evident fact, and so it provides no justification for a blanket decision not to permit bilingual education in England.

13.4 Language education, code-crossing and competing conceptions of ethnic identity

This conflict between the bilingual education policy enunciated in the Swann Report and the empirical sociolinguistic evidence on adolescent multilingualism needs to be seen in the context of wider dispute about British identity and 'national culture'. Ethnic absolutism – the view that ethnicity is the most important part of a person's social identity and that this is fixed during their early years of socialisation – has been discussed at several points in this book, and it is easy to see in the quotation from Swann. It is clear both in its assumption that 'bilingual education and mother tongue maintenance can only be of relevance to mother tongue speakers of languages other than English', as well as in the (extraordinary) idea that black and Asian pupils do not know English, which is what is implied in the dichotomisation 'English speakers and ethnic minority pupils'.

At the same time, it is worth noting that the Swann Report is generally regarded as liberal pluralist text, and that many of its other recommendations are quite clear in favouring multicultural education. Indeed in recent years, it has become a text that people look back to as the testament of better times. Since its publication, government education policy has moved rapidly away from ethnic pluralism, and with the development of a national curriculum, an exclusivist notion of Anglo ethnicity has become increasingly assertive. During the 1980s, the case against pluralism was stated in a number of pamphlets on language published by right-wing think tanks and pressure groups. In 1984, Honey attacked what he saw as the orthodoxies of sociolinguistic research by asserting 'the sad but true fact that in a plural society the handicaps of disadvantaged groups can be increased by promoting linguistic diversity, as they can be reduced by fostering greater linguistic uniformity' (1983). A few years later, this attack on liberal pluralism was carried over into English teaching in an influential text called *English Our English*, which concluded by proclaiming that 'in the future of its language there lies the future of a nation' (Marenbon 1987). Conservative education ministers have embraced these views, and in consequence, more and more emphasis has been given to (standard) English in language education policy documents.[1] The impact of this thinking was obvious for example in the preface to the chapter on 'Bilingual Children' in the Final Report of the Working Party on English in the National Curriculum – a document that in other respects was generally regarded as far too radical by the Conservative ideologues controlling education policy formation in the early 1990s:

Bilingual Children
Our terms of reference made it clear that we were to concern ourselves with the English curriculum for all pupils, whatever their mother tongue. In particular, they stressed that 'The framework (for English) should ensure, at the minimum, that all school-leavers are competent in the use of English – written and spoken – whether or not it is their first language'. The supplementary guidance also said: 'The group should also take account of the ethnic diversity of the school population and society at large, bearing in mind the

> cardinal point that English should be the first language and medium
> of instruction for all pupils in England.' (DES 1989: para. 10.1)

As a result, the Report could do little more than reiterate the
recommendations on bilingualism produced in the Swann Report.

In stark contrast to the notion of national identity being pro-
moted through recent developments in language education policy,
the evidence in this book points to the emergence of Hall's 'new
ethnicities':

> we are beginning to see constructions of . . . a new conception of
> ethnicity: a new cultural politics which engages rather than sup-
> presses *difference* and which depends, in part, on the cultural
> construction of new ethnic identities . . . What is involved is the
> splitting of the notion of ethnicity between, on the one hand the
> dominant notion which connects it to nation and 'race' and on the
> other hand what I think is the beginning of a positive conception of
> the ethnicity of the margins, of the periphery . . . this is not an
> ethnicity which is doomed to survive, as Englishness was, only by
> . . . displacing and forgetting other ethnicities. This is precisely the
> politics of ethnicity predicated on difference and diversity (1988:
> 29, emphasis in original)

The 'old' notion ethnicity is clearly articulated in the educational
documents we have considered so far, and it works with a 'notion
of the essential black subject' (p. 28). In contrast, the idea of the
new ethnicities is based on 'recognition of the extraordinary diversity of subjective positions, social experiences and cultural
identities which compose the category 'black'' (p. 289). The
empirical reality of the new ethnicities is extensively attested
throughout this book.

In many respects, Hall's discussion overlaps with Gilroy's (to
which it indeed refers). Hall's idea of new syncretic ethnicities
which embrace difference bears a lot of resemblance to Gilroy's
discussion of the interpretive sensibilities located in multiracial
inner city communities, and clearly, both can serve as useful
frameworks for understanding language crossing. Hall's formulation pinpoints ethnicity, and in doing so, it can be seen as a
strategic attempt to recover the term from the discourses of ethnic
absolutism. In some respects this makes it a sharper formulation
for public critique of, for example, the ethnic dimension in

national education policy. Gilroy's account is perhaps more extensively nested in sociological theory, and this makes it a little more unwieldy. On the other hand, the corollary of this is that it is richer in the suggestion of new analytic angles. We have already taken up Gilroy's interest in theory of the new social movements at several points in this book (Chapters 1.2, 3.5, 5.8, 12.5), and in fact, it has further relevance in the context of a discussion about the practical implications of code-crossing.

As has already been indicated at several points, research on new social movements rejects a sharp distinction between theory and application, analysis and intervention. In traditional models of inquiry, practical action comes after researchers have completed their description of a particular situation. In contrast, in research on the social movements, groups of activist participants analyse their own activity, and sociologists facilitate this process, introducing hypotheses and accounts that are discussed, accepted, rejected or modified by the groups in the course of their own social movement activism (cf. Frazer 1992: 179; Touraine 1981; Melucci 1981: 192ff). If we shift this model into the present context, we have to ask whether sociolinguistic analysis of code-crossing could be of any practical value to the young people who spontaneously engage in it. This question is by no means obtuse. It leads, in fact, into discussion of a third area of language education – 'language awareness' ('knowledge about language') as a systematic component in the school curriculum.

13.5 Language awareness as a curriculum subject

At the time of writing, the most recent government publications on language education (NCC 1992; DFE 1993) suggest that a pupil's conscious knowledge of language should cover little more than the shibboleths of prescriptive grammar. For the hard Right that has been directing education policy most recently, any kind of sociolinguistic understanding seems to be seen as a threat to its absolutist vision. However, outside this small (though very powerful) circle, there has been a steady growth in support among educational theorists and practitioners for the idea that schools should try to develop their pupils' conscious awareness of language.

Some of the main objectives of the advocates of language awareness are

-   to reveal to pupils the richness of linguistic variety represented in the class by speakers of different dialects or by speakers of a range of mother tongues and to show the relation of that variety to standard written and spoken English without arousing feelings of antagonism or inferiority.
-   to foster better relations between all ethnic groups by arousing pupils' awareness of the origins and characteristics of their own language and dialect and their place in the wider map of languages and dialects in the world beyond. (Donmall 1985: 7–8; see also, e.g. Hawkins 1984: 2; DES 1985: 407,419ff; DES 1988: 43; DES 1989: para. 10.12; James and Garrett 1991: 4)

Plainly, the relationship between ethnicity and conscious sociolinguistic knowledge is a concern central to mainstream debate about language awareness. Could language awareness sessions at school incorporate the kind of consciousness displayed in code-crossing?

Up to a point, curriculum attempts to incorporate the ideologies implicit in spontaneous adolescent interaction could be impeded by the rather blandly multiculturalist framing of many language awareness recommendations. The Cox Report (DES 1989) is fairly typical. Though it criticises 'emotive and prejudiced reactions' to language diversity, there is a failure to connect these with the history of group relations and with different positions in social structure (paras 6.13, 6.32). It advocates a stance of detached neutrality in the study of language, the only affective responses that it recognises are sensitivity and respect, and there is no reckoning with the possibility of just complaint. This in fact leads into another major problem. If schools expect their students to approach language difference in a non-prescriptive and respectful manner and then assess them accordingly (para. 6.32), they will find themselves delivering the self-contradictory edicts 'thou shalt not prescribe' and 'value judgements are bad'.[2] In this formulation, language awareness looks a little like ideological manipulation, and it is not difficult to imagine it coming into quite dramatic conflict with adolescent perspectives and experiences. (For more elaborate criticism of liberal pluralist approaches to race and language awareness, see Rampton 1991c, Bhatt and Martin-Jones 1992; for a critique of language awareness generally, Fairclough (ed.) 1992.)

There is, however, a much more fundamental difficulty which is seldom addressed in the literature on curriculum multiracial language awareness, either 'liberal' or 'critical', but which has been pinpointed in the cultural studies approach to antiracist teaching developed by Phil Cohen. Cohen (1987b) argues that two approaches have been dominant in teaching about racism. One advocates 'the learning of the real historical facts about colonialism, the application of reasoned arguments to understand the true cause of unemployment [which is supposed to lead] students to recognise that black and white people face many of the same problems' (p. 1). The other 'stresses the importance of direct experiential learning about 'other' (i.e. non-European) cultures to break down stereotypes and promote greater tolerance of diversity in society' (ibid.). There are problems with both.

The rationalist approach

> assumes that racism is primarily a doctrine or belief system which is falsely premised, and can be punctured by the application of a superior logic. But popular racism does not work in this way. Its appeal is precisely that it makes 'imaginative sense' of common predicaments; it is a practical, behavioural ideology, rooted in everyday cultural practices ... Moreover, rationalist pedagogies imply academic methods of instruction, which many working class students already resist. Social studies lessons on race relations spell instant boredom for this group. (ibid.)

The second, experiental approach fails to grasp the intricacy of the relationship between ideologies on the one hand, and practical experience on the other:

> it assumes that ... imaginary constructs or stereotypes can be separated from and dissolved by 'real experience' – the direct imprint of sense impressions on conscious attitudes. But ideologies work precisely by constructing experience in particular, largely unconscious ways. It is by organising certain structures of feeling and language that racism becomes 'common sense'. As a result visits to the local Sikh Gurdwara or a twin school in the West Indies may be enjoyable experiences for any number of reasons, but they may still provide grist to the mill of racist imagination, unless these underlying structures are also confronted 'en route' (p. 2)

Although the relationships between cognition, affect and experience feature on the agenda for language awareness teaching (James and Garrett 1991), proposals often only emphasise the 'access to alternative sources of experience or new means of intellectual understanding' that Cohen criticises. In spite of its designs on racial harmony, there are no accounts of how multilingual language awareness fares with the kind of recalcitrant teenager that Cohen alludes to, and so far in the school language awareness debate, the fact that perceptions of race and ethnicity constitute 'practical, behavioural ideology, rooted in everyday cultural practices' has not been considered in much depth.[3]

This is, however, exactly the level at which we have located the ethnic consciousness displayed in code-crossing. Code-crossing was intricately woven into 'lived cultures' and it can itself be seen as one of Cohen's 'new practices of representation which make it possible to sustain an imaginative sense of social identity and difference'. As such, code crossing had a social efficacy of its own which would need to be recognised prior to any well-meaning educational intervention. Admittedly, sometimes its use was plainly racist, but elsewhere it can be seen as a very delicate procedure for steering a course between the two kinds of racial injustice discussed in Chapter 12.4. Code-crossing processed ethnic difference and stratification against a highly complex set of situational contingencies – the stage and state of talk, the activity type, the institutional setting, the relationship between interlocutors, and so forth. Although there are no grounds for suggesting that these adolescents were exceptional in their interactional competence more generally, code-crossing entailed some very skilful negotiation around the meaning of race and ethnicity.

Both in analysis and in education, there is a danger of this being neglected or oversimplified. The risk arises when one tries to moves out of behavioural ideology, with all its contextual variability, towards more explicit and more general formulations. When one abstracts from the situational contingencies in which participants' sense-making procedures can be tracked and in which talk achieves coherence, one often encounters contradictions and inconsistencies. As long as the analysis remembers that it is no longer dealing directly with participant modes of understanding and action, there need be no problem. Unfortunately, however, slippage often occurs at this point and informants are themselves described as muddled. This is obviously unfair – if their discourses are decontextualised, most people look incoherent. Even so, this mistake happens quite often in sociological analysis, and in the sociology of youth, researchers have picked on confusion, contradiction and inconsistency as if they were the hallmark of adolescence (Frazer 1992: 100; Heritage 1984: 67–8; cf. Bourdieu 1977: 109–10).

School language awareness programmes themselves often try to get pupils to reflect on their own everyday conduct and understanding (cf. e.g. Tinkel 1984, 1991), and in this context, the risk of blaming actors for the contradictions created through abstraction is intensified. In principle, students should not be penalised or censored for the contradictions that they are encouraged to uncover in their own behaviour, but this may be hard to avoid in educational settings where moral norms are highly defined and/or there is emphasis on ranking performance. The perception of contradiction can also be very challenging for students themselves, particularly if these touch on personal and political relationships, as is likely in any effective discovery-oriented, student-centred approaches to multilingual language awareness. Student reactions may well be tense and emotional, and to work through these, there might be a need for more time and flexibility than the school time-table usually provides.

It would be a major mistake to rule out any possibility of schools engaging constructively with the 'new ethnicities' indexed through language crossing. Chapter 4 suggested that there could be indirect benefits from the implementation of quite simple measures, and with gifted teachers, flexible scheduling and a lot of sensitivity to local social dynamics, schools might be able to address this emergent interethnic consciousness directly, helping to develop towards more established status. It would be a delusion, however, to imagine that the processes and issues indexed in code-crossing could be adequately handled in any kind of tidily standardised package for the language awareness curriculum. Teachers and schools are an inextricable *part* of the social processes through which new ethnicities take shape. Their contribution is not easy to apprehend, it is even harder to control, and it is on (action-orientated) reflection on the school's own role that, above all, educational energies need to be expended. If standardised packages take the place of thoughtful and critical attempts to explore the school's own participation in ethnolinguistic processes, students may well be quick to detect the ersatz in language awareness modules on multilingualism, and respond to them accordingly.

So far in this chapter, we have focused on the way in which different social groups and institutions in one particular country have produced conflicting responses to processes and issues that they have experienced in common. The tension between absolutist and syncretic conceptions of ethnicity is likely to have wider resonances, and so too might our discussion of the varying relationships between behavioural and established ideologies. But in general, consideration of crossing's implications for education have been firmly set within the frame of social and political life in England.

But the sociolinguistic processes that we have identified with crossing also come into conflict with a notion of linguistic identity which has wide international currency, in folk, in educational and indeed in purely academic linguistics. This is the notion of the 'native speaker'. In crossing, the relationships between linguistic ability and language ownership are problematised – rights to the use of a language, the authority to grant them, and the actual capacity to speak it are all potentially open to dispute. In contrast, the concept of the 'native speaker' obscures and elides these issues, and so crossing clearly presents it with a challenge. In fact, there is nothing new in critical attention being directed both to the 'native speaker' and to the 'mother tongue': 'The whole mystique of the native speaker and the mother tongue should probably be quietly dropped from the linguist's set of professional myths about language' (Ferguson 1982: vii; cf. also, e.g. Paikeday 1985). Dissatisfaction with these terms is very pronounced, and they constitute a particularly crude form of the ethnic absolutism that we have criticised throughout the book. Even so, they have widespread currency, almost for want of anything better. With the Ashmead data as one empirical reference point, it is worth seeing whether we can develop a more differentiating set of terms with which to describe a person's linguistic identity.

In order to do so, it is important first to state exactly what the problems with the 'native speaker' are.

13.6 The trouble with the 'native speaker'

The idea of being the 'native speaker of a language' and 'having it as your mother-tongue' tends to imply at least five things:

1. A particular language is inherited, either through genetic endowment or through birth into the social group stereotypically associated with it.
2. Inheriting a language means being able to speak it well.
3. People either are or are not native/mother tongue speakers.
4. Being a native speaker involves the comprehensive grasp of a language.
5. Just as people are usually citizens of one country, people are native speakers of one mother tongue.

All of these assumptions are now widely contested. The capacity for language itself may be genetically endowed, but *particular* languages are acquired in social settings. People do not belong to only one social group, once and for all: people participate in many groups (the family, the peer group, and groups defined by class, region, age, ethnicity, gender, and so on), membership changes over time and so does language. Being born into a group does not mean that you automatically speak its language well – many 'native' speakers of English cannot tell stories or write reports, while many 'non-natives' can. Nobody's functional command is total: users of a language are more proficient in some areas than others. And most countries are multilingual: from an early age children normally encounter two or more languages. Sociolinguists have generally worked quite hard to deconstruct everyday folk conceptions of language, and to replace them with terms that are less laden with obstructive presuppositions. Instead of 'language' and 'dialect', they generally speak of 'varieties', and indeed for some, even this term is too laden with a priori assumptions (cf. Hudson 1980: ch. 2; also LePage 1980 and LePage and Tabouret-Keller 1985: ch. 5). But somehow, the 'native speaker' appears to have escaped this process of reformulation, and together with the 'mother-tongue' it remains in circulation, continuously insinuating its assumptions.

The political and educational effects produced by the native speaker's 'reign' (Mey 1981) are fairly obvious with English. Where it would be unacceptable to advertise language teaching jobs with 'only whites need apply', it is common to see 'only native speakers' (Seidlhofer et al. 1991: 23). The native speaker's supremacy keeps the UK and the USA at the centre of English language teaching internationally, and when attempts to establish the independent legitimacy of Englishes worldwide describe their object of their concern as 'nativized varieties', the English of ethnic Anglos is still there in the background as the central reference point.

The concept has also had a powerful influence on the educationally oriented study of bilingualism, institutionalising a fictional norm of perfect monolingual competence against which the abilities of bilinguals are measured. As Martin-Jones and Romaine note: 'Terms such as "semilingualism" are, in our view, misleading because they implicitly foster the belief that there is such a thing as an ideal, fully competent monolingual or bilingual speaker who has a full or complete version of a language' (1986: 32). The assumption that 'native speakers' have an excellent knowledge of one mother tongue generates the view that if you know two languages, you are likely to be less than 'fully competent' in at least one, if not both (e.g. Haugen [1973] 1979: 74)).

The idea that people really only have one native language, that really monolingualism is the fundamental linguistic condition, also underlies a widespread failure to recognise *new* and *mixed* linguistic identities. The measurement of bilingual proficiency and the investigation of bilingual language attitudes have generally both been very slow to acknowledge that the bilingual whole might be more than the sum of two monolingual parts. There has been an overwhelming tendency to treat languages in the bilingual repertoire as if they were separate entities, ignoring the ways in which they can combine to create new forms that are quite distinct from monolingual use in either language (Hamers and Blanc 1989: 15, 21; Auer 1988: 204; Baker 1988: 121–2; Romaine 1988: 256).

Finally the idea of the 'native speaker' connects with Chomskyan linguistics to privilege the view that it is a person's internal, psychological knowledge of language that matters most. Here language is seen as 'a supposed property of an individual, his 'native language' (or dialect). It is frequently supposed that we all have such a 'mother tongue' or 'native language' which represents some really fundamental properties of us as individuals who have grown up in a particular society' (LePage and Tabouret-Keller 1985: 188). This is a view that is often adopted in research on bilingualism. Auer makes this quite clear, and gives further details of the traditions in which this view holds sway:

Bilingualism (incl. multilingualism) is traditionally thought of as . . . a mental disposition which is accessible only indirectly by the usual techniques of psycholinguistic research. In the mentalistic framework of generative grammar, bilingual competence as a mental disposition is also accessible via the analysis of well-formed sentences involving two languages which may be treated as a window on the bilingual mind. Both the psycholinguist and the generative grammarian approach bilingualism as something which – like competence in general – is basically hidden underneath the skull; it can, and must be made visible by psycholinguistic methods, or the methods of generative grammatical research. Beginning with the discussion of compound vs coordinate bilingualism, and up to the present work on grammatical constraints on code-switching, there is an impressive amount of research which has been gathered from such a perspective. (1991: 319)

This is a perspective that also fits well with psychometric traditions in education, where indeed the relationship between bilingualism and IQ have been much discussed (cf. Baker 1988: Ch. 1). The problem with it is that it generally reduces social processes either to a source of data contamination (as in the Chomskyan notion of performance), or to some kind of socio-affective motivational filter on linguistic competence and its development (as in much of the research on second language acquisition). It provides no room for the view that a person's linguistic identity might be socially defined and interactionally negotiated (Auer 1991: 319–20), or that psycholinguistics and generative grammar might themselves be part of the cultural processes through which 'native speakers' and 'bilinguals' were socially constructed.

There are, then, quite a number of good reasons for feeling dissatisfied with the 'native speaker' as a way of formulating the relationship between speakers and their languages.

13.7 Expertise, affiliation and inheritance

If linguistic concepts are to be useful educationally, 'on the one hand, [they] should be compatible with current views of the nature of language and language acquisition; on the other [they] should be . . . simple, realistic, and practicable' (Brumfit 1984: 60–61). With this in mind, I would like to suggest that in the first instance, the 'native speaker' should be decomposed into the simple distinction between 'expertise' (skill, proficiency, ability to operate with a language), and 'allegiance' (identification with a language, with the values, meanings and identities that it stands for).

It is worth emphasising that 'expertise' and 'allegiance' refer to *linguistic identities* – to cultural interpretations of a person's relationship to a language. Though they undoubtedly relate back to the fundamental Western dichotomies of 'heart and mind', 'thought and feeling', they should not be confused with the functional dimensions of language use commonly distinguished in linguistics – the ideational versus the interpersonal, cognitive versus affective, transactional versus interactional. The sentence 'I love English' is an obvious demonstration that language allegiance can be expressed ideationally. It is also important to recognise that in practice, expertise and allegiance overlap in many different ways. People can be considered clumsy and inexpert in displaying their loyalties, they can use their expertise to demonstrate their allegiances, they can feign incompetence to express contempt (cf. e.g. Hill and Hill 1986: 122ff; Woolard 1989: 70–1; Heller 1992: 131). The 'native speaker' is indeed a potent folk concept, and competence in a language is often interpreted in terms of the speaker's regard for the identities typically associated with it.

But conflations like these do not undermine the utility of the distinction, which anyway is not being presented as a scientific framework designed for the unambiguous segmentation of empirical reality. The value of the terms 'expertise' and 'allegiance' lies (a) in the way they connect up with the distinction between proficiency and attitudes that is very common both in sociolinguistic research and in educational discussion of the curriculum, and (b) in the fact that in comparison with the 'native speaker', they are likely to have less morally and intellectually questionable consequences in education and the academy.

Expertise has the following advantages over nativeness as a metaphor for considering language proficiency:

1. Although they often do, experts don't have to feel close to what they know a lot about. Expertise is different from identification.
2. Expertise is learned, not fixed or innate.

3. Expertise is relative. One person's expert is another person's fool.
4. Expertise is partial. People can be expert in several fields, but they are never omniscient.
5. To achieve expertise, you go through processes of certification, in which you are judged by others whose standards of assessment can be reviewed and disputed. There is a healthy tradition of challenging experts.

In contrast to the 'native speaker', the notion of expertise emphasises 'what you know' rather than 'where you come from'. In an educational context, it also makes the learning goals more accountable. If native speaker competence is specified as the target, learners are left playing a game in which the goal-posts are being shifted by people they cannot often challenge. Talk about expertise requires a much closer specification of the types and levels of knowledge that students have to aim at.

In fact in multilingual settings, the notion of 'expertise' may also be more *practical* that the idea of 'nativeness'. Writing within the psycholinguistic tradition, Hamers and Blanc rather wearily aver that

> the impossibility of defining native-language competence ... makes the construction of valid and reliable measures of language competence extremely problematic ... [But w]hatever their shortcomings, tests of competence are useful, as they are the only means of assessing the bilingual's competence ... [Our] aim ... has been to draw the reader's attention to the difficulties inherent in the attempt to define and quantify languages in contact at all levels of analysis as well to the absence of adequate measures and the lack of refinement of existing ones. However, we have to use these measures, as they are the only ones available in the present state of the art. (1989: 16, 29–30)

The 'native speaker' idea fits in with an arduous and rather unrewarding quest for mental essences, pursued through esoteric tests that are always seeking greater powers to summarise and represent the very full range of abilities evidenced in language use (cf. Hamers and Blanc 1989: 14–25). Out of this endeavour, the psychological tradition of bilingual research – where the 'native speaker' resides as an awkward but unevicted lodger – has produced a number of highly abstract educational models of bilingual ability and development, represented by Baker as balloons, ladders and hydraulic think tanks (Baker 1988: ch. 7). Unfortunately, it is not at all obvious how these theories can be tied into language tasks in the curriculum. In contrast, the notion of 'expertise' is much more inclined to be satisfied with relatively hum-drum descriptions of performance in a set of quite familiar school activities. While there is no reason why its description should be rapid or easy, the idea of 'expertise' is perfectly compatible with the linguistic profiling of classroom achievement that is becoming an increasingly common part of the teacher's routine responsibility (cf. Barrs et al. 1989).

Of course, the terms 'native language' and 'mother tongue' also connote a person's affective ties to a particular language, and these are not covered under 'expertise'. So at this point, 'allegiance' becomes relevant. The data on crossing, however, suggests that it is important to make one further distinction within this. Two aspects of language loyalty need to be distinguished: *inheritance* and *affiliation*. In fact it is particularly important to use a specific term to stake out the claims of the second – language affiliation – in order to make sure that the shadowy authority of the 'native speaker' and the 'native/mother tongue' does not lead one to give pride of place to the first (inheritance).

Both affiliation *and* inheritance are socially negotiated. This is fairly self-evident with affiliation, which we commonly think of in terms of the social processes that it involves (requesting, applying, granting, agreeing, breaking off, and so on). But it is also true in the case of inheritance. Governments make laws about it, people try to decide what cultural and material items to include in their legacies, while others accept, claim, reject, and contest them. Certainly, there *is* genetic inheritance, but its effects never make themselves felt in any direct or absolute way – they are always interpreted in a social context and so to quite a considerable degree, they are only as important as social groups choose to make them. The crucial difference between these two concepts is that *affiliation* refers to a connection between people and groups that are considered to be separate or different, whereas *inheritance* is concerned with the continuity between people and groups who are felt to be closely linked. Inheritance occurs *within* social boundaries while affiliation takes place *across* them.

Because both inheritance and affiliation are matters of social negotiation and conflict, the relationship between them is always flexible, subtle and responsive to the wider context. It would be very hard to assert definitively that X is a language of inheritance and Y is a language of affiliation – indeed, in doing so, you would have to recognise that you were taking up a stance in social debate. People belong to many groups, feelings of group belonging change, and so does the definition of groups themselves. New but valued inheritances can emerge from powerful affiliations, while cherished inheritances can lose their value and be disowned. Wherever language inheritance is involved, there tends to be a sense of the permanent, ancient or historic, but it is important to underline the fact that affiliation can involve a stronger sense of attachment, just as the bond between lovers may be more powerful than the link between parents and children.

In combination with 'expertise', 'inheritance' and 'affiliation' constitute a simple but adequate vocabulary for discussing the intricate dynamics of the crossing that we have analysed in Ashmead. In crossing, some white and black kids were accepted by its inheritors as affiliates of Panjabi; young people of Indian and Pakistani descent disclaimed the inheritance of Asian English ascribed to them by white society; affiliates to Creole and Panjabi deferred to the expertise of inheritors, even though this might be minimal by the standards of their parents; and at a meta-level, the rituals of affiliation themselves developed into a new inheritance. Tied up with a sense of origin and of place, language ability and allegiance were continuously at issue, but the processes of their negotiation would, in contrast, be entirely obscured if we stayed with the 'native speaker'. With that, we would be tied to exactly the same kind of essentialism that we saw in the Swann Report.

The notions of expertise, inheritance and affiliation are likely to have quite wide educational applicability. They are relevant to *any* group, however you define it (by family, class, gender, race, region, profession, and so on). They can also be used to address the positions of individuals as well as groups, and this is convenient in education where there is generally a need to consider both. The emphasis on social processes and the cultural negotiation of a person's language identity is particularly important, and it allows linguists and educationalists to focus on the role that their own activity plays in helping to shape linguistic identities in the social world they share with their students and informants.

It would be folly to close one's eyes to the terms 'native speaker' and 'mother tongue'. LePage and Tabouret-Keller are perfectly clear about their political uses, but concede that these terms are 'very important to the personal identity of a great many people, and an important hypothetical base for many linguists and educationists. We must therefore accept [them] as part of our data on social institutions' (1985: 190). This is undoubtedly the case. But if the 'native speaker' is shifted over into the *data* of sociolinguistics, a gap appears in the vocabulary needed to analyse it. It is this gap that expertise, affiliation and inheritance are designed to fill. Expertise-affiliation-and-inheritance are a simple and workable set of terms that try to recognise rather than obscure the dynamic social and institutional processes through which sociolinguistic identities are defined.

Notes

1. To see this, one only has to compare DES (1989) *English for Ages 5 to 16* with DFE (1993) *English for Ages 5 to 16 (1993)*.
2. Admittedly, there would be no difference here from the stance adopted in much of twentieth century linguistics!
3. This is surprising in view of widespread sociolinguistic recognition that consciously expressed language attitudes differ considerably from the evaluations implicit in spontaneous linguistic actions and responses. It was this gap that led to the development of matched guise and listener reaction tests (Lambert 1967; Labov 1972a; also Gumperz 1982a: 62). In contrast to the debate about language awareness at school, it is worth noting that much more sophisticated forms of ethno-linguistic consciousness raising have been developed in the context of Industrial Language Training (cf. Roberts et al. 1992)

Appendix I
Descriptive Concepts

In this book, interactional activity is a central empirical concern, and in order to address the guiding questions listed in Chapter 1.3, four (interwoven) dimensions relevant to interaction will be given particular attention: (a) language use, (b) interaction structures and processes, (c) institutional organisation, and (d) participants' social knowledge about ethnic groups and their interrelationships. It is worth elaborating on each in turn.

(a) Language use

To a certain extent, discussion of language structure is necessary in order to distinguish the four language codes of particular interest to this study – Creole, Panjabi, Indian and local vernacular English. Language structure is also important because it is one factor affecting the manner and extent to which adolescents used each code. But generally, the analysis of language form is subsidiary to questions of use, and here more attention is given to pragmatic and contextual than to referential meaning.

The way in which particular stretches of language are analysed has not been programmatically determined in advance. But attention is often given to speech act functions and communicative intentions, usually assessed through sequential analysis and an account of the particular speech events in which they occur (Levinson 1983: section 5.7 and ch. 6). The symbolic connotations associated with particular language varieties is also of major interest, and there is a continual concern with similarities and differences in the connotational fields evoked by Creole, Panjabi and Indian English. Reference to a range of fairly large scale historical, social and political relationships is essential in the interpretation of language symbolism. But it is also vital to pay close attention to the particular conversational environments in which in which participants make use of this symbolism – symbolic interpretation is context-sensitive, drawing on the evidence presented in the talk on hand as well as on background understanding.

(b) Interaction structures and processes

The concern here is with the kinds of phenomena that Erving Goffman explored extensively, and which he located within what he called the 'interaction order' (1963a, 1967, 1971, 1974, 1981, 1983). The difference between on the one hand, the level of analysis that this entails and on the other, the levels more generally associated with the analysis of institutional organisation can be suggested by considering the difference between terms such as 'speaker and listener' and 'teacher and pupil'. 'Teacher' and 'pupil' are institutional roles/capacities that only certain people activate on rather particular occasions, whereas nearly everyone can be a 'speaker' and a 'listener' – these identities are activated on a vast range of different occasions of talk. Goffman's interaction order can be located at this much more general, cross-situational level, roughly in the same way that the syntax involves a relatively small number of basic patterns that occur in a huge number of different sentences.

In fact, the terms 'speaker' and 'listener' are much too crude for Goffman's analyses, and these are broken down into a set of more delicate distinctions. Speakership, for example, is subdivided into a number of 'production' roles: 'animator', which merely involves the articulation of words in sound (transmitting the message); 'author', which entails the selection/invention of words and meanings; and 'principal', which accepts responsibility for the import of the message (cf. Levinson 1988 for an elaboration). Often in ordinary conversation, a speaker occupies all three roles. But people can shift from being animator + author + principal to being mere animators, using a range of linguistic (and other) cues to mark the switch to a stretch of direct reported speech. Alternatively, in the role of newsreader, speakers operate primarily as animators (which broaches the way in which institutional and interaction analyses can interweave).

The apparatus that Goffman develops is much more elaborate than this, providing a comprehensive analysis of the ways in which participants arrange themselves, access one another and distribute their attention, both in verbal and non-verbal conduct. This can be explained as and when it becomes relevant in the chapters that follow. But it is important to qualify any idea suggested by the syntax analogy that Goffman is only concerned with structures. Every situation in which people are physically co-present involves a set of moral ground rules, and participants expect each other to display 'situational propriety', respect for the social occasion and participants in it, self-control and due deference to others. This respect (and the face-work it entails) is subject to very varied cultural expression, but in some form or other it is a fundamental concern in every gathering and interaction (see also Brown and Levinson [1978] 1987).

(c) Institutional organisation

Exactly how the 'interaction order' relates to institutional organisation is an open theoretical question that is not of central concern here (compare Goffman 1983 with, e.g. Collins 1981; Giddens 1988). The objective here is to outline the scope of the descriptive framework that I shall be using, and it is clear that the questions guiding this study require attention to concepts that are both more macroscopic and more culturally differentiating than those developed by Goffman.

To distinguish different interactional activities, Brown and Fraser's synthesis of a number of different frameworks is particularly helpful. They characterise 'situation' in terms of the principal elements 'setting', 'purpose' and 'participants', and they offer the following definition of 'activity types':

> There appear to be a considerable number of quite general types of activities which are identifiable virtually irrespective of their specific content matter; for example: buying, selling, chatting, lecturing, conducting a meeting, negotiating, playing a game. Such 'activity types' are culturally recognised units of interaction that are identifiable by constraints on (a) goals, (b) roles activated in the activity,

(c) interactional structure, and (to some extent) (d) participants and setting. In the activity of teaching, for example, the purposes (goals) of imparting information (and/or ways of thinking, attitudes, etc.) and the roles of teacher/student are activated. (Brown and Fraser 1979: 40; also Levinson 1979)

Interaction also needs to be situated in the larger structures that both constrain and are reproduced through specific activities, values, norms, roles, purposes and systems of stratification (cf. e.g. Hannerz 1980). One of these, the recreational domain, figures most prominently in the ensuing analysis, and it certainly entails a number of distinctive activities. But no domain can be studied in isolation: daily life moves across a number, transporting expectations and practices rooted in one domain across to another, and individuals are frequently subject to the heterogeneous and sometimes conflicting claims of several. In addition, domains need to be distinguished in terms of the strength and spread of their social influence, in terms of the power that they distribute to their members, and in terms of the unequal access that they afford to particular social groups and individuals. In this study, local recreation is closely bordered by school and home, and is extensively penetrated by popular communications media: potentially, these generate experience of a range of partially distinguishable discourses, practices, solidarities and other sources of influence and division.

An individual's participation and receptivity to the practices and meanings offered within any domain is mediated through interpersonal networks, in which interpretations of what's what are negotiated and relayed. Rather than assuming that people automatically internalise domain-specific values, social network analysis facilitates investigation of the processes through which within a domain, people develop and maintain diverse and often non-conformist orientations (Boissevain 1974: 4–5). To a substantial degree, network relationships are formed, enacted or indeed disrupted in interactional activity, and an account of interaction needs to recognise the histories of contact and familiarity that particular participants do and do not bring with them (e.g. Kapferer 1969). At the same time, because of differences in the overall range and character of every person's interactive contacts, social networks constitute an important mechanism through which individuals shape their feelings, knowledge and access to people, activities and domains with which they have only slight or non-existent first-hand personal experience.

(d) Participants' knowledge specifically as this relates to ethnic groups

This dimension is fairly self-explanatory. However, it is worth noting that positing this as a distinct analytic issue is simply a matter of thematic foregrounding. As discussion of knowledge and action in the main body of the text tries to make clear (Chapter 1.4), there is no implication that ethnicity is a socio-cognitive construct while other aspects of institutional organisation somehow have more material objectivity: they, too, are partly constituted in knowledge. Furthermore, like them, knowledge about ethnic groups affects and is affected by interactional conduct and experience. Indeed, here as elsewhere, knowledge about race and ethnicity is intimately interwoven with knowledge of other social groupings, domains, activity types, interaction structures and so forth, among other things producing the contextually contingent, multiple racisms and antiracisms that Gilroy and Hewitt describe.

Appendix II
Fieldwork procedures

I began the first year of fieldwork in 1984 in the neighbourhood where I had been working as a teacher and youth worker from 1978–80. From the outset I made it plain that I was interested in language and the way it fitted in with young people's social lives. My hybrid field role was made up of at least three components. In part, I was a (white male Anglo) ex-teacher, who had access to local schools and knew a lot of the teachers. This merged quite easily with a position as youth worker: I organised trips to sporting events, spent a lot of time on holiday play schemes and in the local youth club, and was addressed by my first name. Thirdly, I was a (PhD) student doing a project on language. My contacts with informants were largely limited to more organised areas of peer group recreation and to the more informal parts of the school day. This pattern was repeated in the second year of fieldwork that I carried out in the same neighbourhood in 1987, the only difference being that now I was a paid researcher.

There were some differences in the data collection procedures that I used during these two periods of fieldwork, but radio-microphone recording, interviewing, and participant observation featured centrally in both.

a) Radio-microphone recordings of recreational activity at the youth club and during free time at school serve as one of the main source of interactional data in this study. In 1984, radio-microphones were given out to 23 informants, producing about 45 hours of data; in 1987, 37 informants were involved, resulting in approximately 100 hours of data. These were annotated and indexed very soon after they had been made, and at a later date, sections of these were selected for detailed transcription. It is often hard to know how far the wearing of radio-microphones affects the naturalness of interaction, but they were normally given to informants on three or four consecutive days, so that their novelty would have time to wear off (cf. Hewitt 1986: 10). In addition in 1987, playback sessions (see (e) below) made it easier to decide whether or not particular episodes gave a reasonable indication of usual practice.

b) In 1987, interviews focused on two topics; language and adolescent social life. Most of these were carried out during school lunch breaks, lasting between 40 minutes and an hour, though a number were also conducted in a side room at the youth club. The issues that the language interview covered were: gender differences in the languages which informants knew well; generational differences; good and bad speakers (including inventiveness, correction, verbal art); bilingual code-switching; language learning at school; use of other kids' ethnic languages (learning, proficiency, use and users); and other kids' use of informants' own varieties. In the social interview, the topics I aimed to initiate were: habitual activities, alone, with family, with friends; friendships (past and present); relations with the opposite sex; the town and the neighbourhood; interethnic relations; gangs; styles; music. The data from these was then indexed and annotated on thematically organised protocols, and as with other elicitation procedures, some sections were later transcribed for closer interactional analysis. Interviewing in 1984 covered some of the same subjects, though language crossing was discussed much less consistently. In 1987, 35 informants participated in the language interview, and 39 in the one that addressed social issues. Serial interviewing in 1984 involved 23 informants (see also (g) below).

c) As a voluntary worker at the local youth club, I conducted participant observation on about 40 evenings during the 1984 fieldwork, and about 50 evenings during 1987. Observation focused primarily on language use, interpersonal and group relations and local forms of youth culture, and each visit to the club was written up in a field diary. Some less systematic observation was also possible outside the youth club, in the neighbourhood and at the local middle and secondary schools, and conversations with youth workers and teachers provided a useful additional perspective.

d) As my own proficiency is very limited, in 1987 two 17-year-old bilinguals from the locality translated and commented on all the examples of Panjabi recorded on radio-microphone during 1984 and 1987. This included Asian as well as black and white uses of Panjabi, and amounted to about 500 extracts.

The most relevant differences between fieldwork procedures in 1984 and 1987 were as follows:

e) Retrospective discussion with participants of extracts selected from the radio-microphone recordings. I did this during 1987 and it took the form of a 45–60 minute playback and discussion session. From several hours of recordings of each informant, between 12 and 20 extracts were selected, broadly focusing on code-switches, verbal play, references to distinctive aspects of peer group culture, and episodes that might afford insight into the interethnic and cross-sex relationships. These were then played back to a total of 33 informants (singly, in pairs or in threes), normally within three or four days of their being recorded by radio-microphone, although also, where I had recordings of particular informants from 1984, I occasionally played them extracts from these. This procedure was less systematic than the pragmatic elicitations described by Gumperz (1976: 284–9, 1982a: 136–40), and more directive than the relatively open ended playback sessions described in Erickson and Shultz (1982: 56–63), but it was still a productive strategy. It often helped clarify the details involved in recorded episodes – who the other participants were, what they were doing and so forth. It generated valuable commentary on peer group social life, focusing for example on sensitive issues which it might have been difficult to introduce 'cold'. It elicited quite a lot of adolescent metalanguage and resulted in the explication of word play which would have otherwise remained incomprehensible. And lastly, it contributed substantially to the understanding of language crossing, as for example when comments were made about its typicality, legitimacy and particular patterns of its social distribution.

f) Discussions of findings from the 1984 research. In 1987, I prepared a set of large diagrams summarising my PhD account of local sociolinguistic domains, code-switching, sociolinguistic stereotyping and educational theories of ESL. I then discussed this in small groups at the youth club with about 25 young people, 18 of whom had been informants during the earlier research. (This procedure is described in some detail in Cameron et al. (1992), together with a discussion of its implications for researcher–researched relations.)

g) Because it was partly planned with a quantitative analysis of the relationship between linguistic, social and psychological variables in mind, fieldwork in 1984 was much more elaborate in its elicitation of self-report data on patterns of bilingualism, local networks, domains, and social group identifications. It is not worth describing the details here however: the present account makes fairly peripheral use of these data, and relevant aspects of this methodology can be outlined as and when necessary (cf. Rampton 1987a: Part III, 1989, 1992).

Bibliography

Agnihotri R K 1979 *Processes of Assimilation: A Sociolinguistic Study of Sikh Children in Leeds*. PhD Thesis, University of York.

Alexander J (ed.) 1988 *Durkheimian Sociology: Cultural Studies*. Cambridge, Cambridge University Press.

Aston G 1986 Trouble-shooting in interaction: the more the merrier? *Applied Linguistics* 7(2):128–43.

Aston G 1993 Notes on the interlanguage of comity. In Kasper G. and Blum-Kulka S (eds) *Interlanguage Pragmatics*. New York, Oxford University Press, pp. 224–50.

Atkinson M and Heritage J 1984 *Structures of Social Action*. Cambridge, Cambridge University Press.

Auer J 1984 On the meaning of conversational code-switching. In Auer P and di Luzio A (eds) *Interpretive Sociolinguistics: Migrants, Children, Migrant Children* Tübingen, Gunter Narr Verlag, pp. 87–112.

Auer J 1988 A conversation analytic approach to codeswitching and transfer. In Heller M (ed.) *Codeswitching: Anthropological and Sociolinguistic Perspectives*. Berlin, Mouton de Gruyter, pp. 187–213.

Auer J 1990 A discussion paper on code-alternation *Papers for the Workshop on Concepts, Methodology and Data* ESF Network on Code-Switching and Language Contact. Strasbourg, European Science Foundation, pp. 69–91.

Auer J 1991 Bilingualism in/as social action: a sequential approach to code-switching, *Papers for the Symposium on Code-Switching in Bilingual Studies*. Strasbourg, European Science Foundation, pp. 319–52.

Back L 1988 'Coughing up fire': soundsystems, music and cultural politics in SE London, *Journal of Caribbean Studies* 6(2):203–18.

Back L 1992 Social context and racist name calling: an ethnographic perspective on racist talk within a South London adolescent community, *European Journal of Intercultural Studies* 1.(3):19–38.

Back L 1993 Race, identity and nation within an adolescent community in South London, *New Community* **19**.(2):217–33.

Baily 1990 Qawwali in Bradford: traditional music in a Muslim community. In Oliver (ed.), pp. 153–65.

Baker C 1988 *Key Issues in Bilingualism and Bilingual Education.* Clevedon, Multilingual Matters.

Bakhtin M 1968 *Rabelais and His World.* Cambridge, Mass , MIT.

Bakhtin M [1929] 1984 *Problems in Dostoevsky's Poetics.* Minneapolis, University of Minnesota Press.

Bakhtin M [1935] 1981 *The Dialogic Imagination.* Austin, Tex., Texas University Press.

Banerji S and Bauman G 1990 Bhangra 1984–8: fusion and professionalisation in a genre of South Asian dance music in Oliver (ed.), pp. 137–52.

Barrs M, Ellis S, Hester H and Thomas A 1989 *The Primary Language Record.* London, ILEA/Centre for Language in Primary Education.

Barth F 1969 Introduction. In Barth F (ed.) *Ethnic Groups and Boundaries.* London, Allen & Unwin, pp. 9–39.

Basso K 1979 *Portraits of 'the White Man': Linguistic Play and Cultural Symbols among the Western Apache.* Cambridge, Cambridge University Press.

Bell A 1984 Language style as audience design, *Language in Society* **13** (2):145–204.

Bernstein B 1960 Review of 'The Lore and Language of Schoolchildren' by Opie I and Opie P, *British Journal of Sociology* **XI** 178–81.

Bernstein B 1971 *Class, Codes and Control I: Theoretical Studies Towards a Sociology of Language.* London, Routledge & Kegan Paul.

Bernstein B 1975 Ritual in education. In *Class Codes and Control III: Towards a Theory of Educational Transmissions.* London, Routledge & Kegan Paul, pp. 54–66.

Bhatt A and Martin-Jones M 1992 Whose resource? Minority languages, bilingual learners and language awareness. In Fairclough (ed.), pp. 285–302.

Black M 1979 More about metaphor. In Ortony A (ed.) *Metaphor and Thought.* Cambridge, Cambridge University Press, pp. 19–34.

Bloch M 1975 Introduction. In Bloch M. (ed.) *Political Language and Oratory in Traditional Society.* New York, Academic Press, pp. 1–28.

Bloch M 1985 Religion and ritual. In Kuper A and Kuper J (eds) *The Social Science Encyclopaedia.* London, Routledge, pp. 698–701.

Blom J and Gumperz J 1972 Social meaning in linguistic structure: code-switching in Norway. In Gumperz J and Hymes D (eds) *Directions in Sociolinguistics.* Cambridge, Cambridge University Press, pp. 407–34.

Blumer H 1969 *Symbolic Interactionism: Perspective and Method.* Berkeley, Cal., University of California Press.

Boissevain J 1974 *Friends of Friends: Networks, Manipulators and Coalitions*. Oxford, Blackwell.

Borsch S 1986 Some ideas concerning the emotional dimension of foreign language teaching. In Kasper G (ed.) *Learning, Teaching and Communication in the Foreign Language Classroom*. Aarhus, Aarhus University Press, pp. 71–81.

Bourdieu P 1977 *Outline of a Theory of Practice*. Cambridge, Cambridge University Press.

Bourdieu P 1991 *Language and Symbolic Power*. Oxford, Polity Press.

Brake M 1985 *Comparative Youth Culture*. London, Routledge & Kegan Paul.

Breitborde L 1983 Levels of analysis in sociolinguistic explanation: bilingual code-switching, social relations and domain theory, *International Journal of the Sociology of Language* 39: 5–43.

Broughton G, Brumfit C, Flavell R, Hill P and Pincas A 1978 *Teaching English as a Foreign Language*. London, Routledge.

Brown D 1979 *Mother-tongue to English: The Young Child in the Multicultural School*. Cambridge, Cambridge University Press.

Brown P and Levinson S [1978] 1987 *Politeness*. Cambridge, Cambridge University Press.

Brown P and Fraser C 1979 Speech as a marker of situation. In Scherer K and Giles H (eds) *Social Markers in Speech*. Cambridge, Cambridge University Press.

Brumfit C 1984 *Communicative Methodology in Language Teaching*. Cambridge, Cambridge University Press.

Burt S 1992 Codeswitching: Black English and Standard English in the African–American Repertoire, *Journal of Multilingual and Multicultural Development* 13 (1 & 2):169–186.

Cameron D 1990 Demythologising sociolinguistics: why language does not reflect society. In Joseph J & Taylor T (eds) *Ideologies of Language*. London, Routledge, pp. 79–96.

Cameron D and Bourne J 1988 No common ground: Kingman, grammar and the nation. *Language and Education* 2 (3):147–60.

Cameron D, Frazer E, Harvey P, Rampton B, Richards K 1992 *Researching Language: Issues of Power and Method* London Routledge.

Cameron D, Frazer E, Harvey P, Rampton B and Richardson K 1993 Ethics, advocacy and empowerment: issues of method in researching languages. In peer commentary edition of *Language and Communication* 13 (2), pp. 81–94.

Carlin M 1975 Clowns for all races *New Society* 9 January, 75–6.

Cazden C 1986 Classroom discourse. In Merlin M and Wittrock C (eds) *Handbook of Research on Teaching* (Third edition). London, MacMillan, pp. 432–63.

Centre for Contemporary Cultural Studies (CCCS) 1982 *The Empire Strikes Back*. London, Hutchinson.

Centre for Multicultural Education (CME) 1992 *Sagaland: Youth Culture, Racism and Education*. London, University of London Institute of Education.

Cheshire J 1978 Present tense verbs in Reading English. In Trudgill (ed.), pp. 52–68.

Chick J 1985 The interactional accomplishment of discrimination in South Africa, *Language in Society* **14** (3):299–327.

Clarke J, Hall S, Jefferson T and Roberts B 1976 Subcultures, cultures and class: a theoretical overview. In Hall and Jefferson (eds), pp. 9–74.

Clarke M, Barr J and Dewhurst W 1985 *Early Education of Children with Communication Problems: Particularly Those from Ethnic Minorities*. Birmingham, Educational Review Offset Publication No. 3.

Coates E 1985 An examination of the nature of young children's discussions. In Clarke M M (ed.) *Helping Communication in Early Education*. Birmingham, Birmingham University Educational Review Occasional Publication II.

Cohen P 1972 Subcultural conflict and working class community. *Working Papers in Cultural Studies*. Birmingham, Birmingham Centre for Contemporary Cultural Studies, pp. 5–53.

Cohen P 1987a Perversions of inheritance: studies in the making of multiracist Britain. In Cohen P and Bains H (eds).

Cohen P 1987b *Racism and Popular Culture: A Cultural Studies Approach*, Working Paper No. 9. London, University of London Institute of Education Centre for Multicultural Education.

Cohen P and Bains H (eds) 1987 *Multiracist Britain*. Basingstoke, Macmillan.

Cohen S 1980 *Folk Devils and Moral Panics*. Oxford, Martin Robertson.

Collins R 1981 On the microfoundations of macrosociology *American Journal of Sociology* **86** (5):984–1015.

Collins R 1988a The Durkheimian tradition in conflict sociology. In Alexander (ed.), pp. 107–28.

Collins R 1988b Theoretical continuities in Goffman's work. In Drew and Wootton (eds), pp. 41–63.

Connell R 1983 *Which Way Is Up?* Sydney, George Allen & Unwin.

Cook-Gumperz J 1986 Caught in a web of words: some considerations on language socialisation and language acquisition. In Cook-Gumperz et al. (eds), pp. 37–64.

Cook-Gumperz J and Corsaro W 1986 Introduction. In Cook-Gumperz et al. (eds), pp. 1–11.

Cook-Gumperz J, Corsaro W and Streeck J (eds) 1986 *Children's Worlds and Children's Language*. Berlin, Mouton de Gruyter.

Corder S 1981 *Error Analysis and Interlanguage*. London, Oxford University Press.

Coulmas F (ed.) 1981a *Conversational Routine*. The Hague, Mouton.

Coulmas F (ed.) 1981b *A Festschrift for the Native Speaker* The Hague, Mouton.

Dalphinis M 1991 The Afro-English creole speech community. In Alladina S and Edwards V (eds) *Multilingualism in the British Isles: Vol. II*. London, Longman, pp. 42–56.

Davey 1983 *Learning to be Prejudiced*. London, Edward Arnold.

Department of Education and Science (DES) 1985 *Education for All: the Report of the Committee of Inquiry into the Education of Children from Ethnic Minority Groups* (Swann Report). London, HMSO.

Department of Education and Science (DES) 1988 *Report of the Committee of Inquiry into the Teaching of the English Language* (Kingman Report). London, HMSO.

Department of Education and Science (DES) 1989 *English for Ages 5 to 16*, (Cox Report). London, HMSO.

Department for Education (DFE) 1993 *English for Ages 5 to 16*. London, HMSO.

Dickinson L, Hobbs A, Kleinberg S M and Martin P J 1975 *The Immigrant School Learner: A Study of Pakistani Pupils in Glasgow*. Slough, NFER.

Donmall G 1985 (ed.) *Language Awareness*. London, NCLE/Centre for Information on Language Teaching & Research.

Dorian N 1982 Defining the speech community to include its working margins. In Romaine S (ed.) *Sociolinguistic Variation in Speech Communities*. London, Edward Arnold, pp. 25–33.

Dorian N (ed.) 1989 *Investigating Obsolescence*. Cambridge, Cambridge University Press.

Douglas M 1966 *Purity and Danger*. London, Routledge & Kegan Paul.

Douglas M 1968 The social control of cognition: some factors in joke production. *Man* (NS) 3:361–76.

Drew P and Wootton A (eds) 1988 *Erving Goffman: Exploring the Interaction Order*. Oxford, Polity Press.

Dummett A 1973 *A Portrait of English Racism*. Penguin (2nd edn 1984, London CARAF).

Duran R (ed.) 1981 *Latino Language and Communicative Behaviour*. Norwood New Jersey, Ablex.

Durkheim E 1912 [1975] *The Elementary Forms of Religious Life* (extracts taken from W Pickering *Durkheim on Religion*. London, Routledge & Kegan Paul).

Durojaiye S M 1971 Social context of immigrants learning English, *Educational Research* **13**: 79–84.

Eagleton T 1981 *Walter Benjamin: or Towards a Revolutionary Criticism*. London, Verso.

Eastman C 1992 Codeswitching as an urban language-contact phenomenon, *Journal of Multilingual and Multicultural Development* 13 (1 & 2) 1–18.

Eckert P 1990 Cooperative competition in adolescent 'girl talk', *Discourse Processes* 13:91–122.

Edwards A and Westgate D 1987 *Investigating Classroom Talk*. Lewes, Falmer Press.

Edwards V 1986 *Language in a Black Community*. Clevedon, Multilingual Matters.

Ellis R 1985 Sources of variability in interlanguage *Applied Linguistics* 6 (2):118–31.

Erickson F and Shultz J 1982 *The Counselor as Gatekeeper*. New York, Academic Press.

Ervin-Tripp S 1986 Activity structure as scaffolding for children's second language learning. In Cook-Gumperz et al. (eds), pp. 327–57.

Faerch K and Kasper G (eds) 1983 *Strategies in Interlanguage Communication*. London, Longman.

Fairclough N 1989 *Language and Power*. London, Longman.

Fairclough N (ed.) 1992 *Critical Language Awareness*. London, Longman.

Fasold R 1990 *The Sociolinguistics of Language*. Oxford, Blackwell.

Ferguson C 1975 Towards a characterisation of English foreigner talk, *Anthropological Linguistics* 17:1–14.

Ferguson C 1981 The structure and use of politeness formulas. In Coulmas F (ed.) *Conversational Routine*. The Hague, Mouton, pp. 21–35.

Ferguson C 1982 Foreword. In Kachru B (ed.) *The Other Tongue: English across Cultures*. Oxford, Pergamon, pp. vii–xi.

Firth R 1972 Verbal and bodily rituals of greeting and parting. In La Fontaine J S (ed.) *The Interpretation of Ritual*. London, Tavistock, pp. 1–38.

Fitzpatrick B 1987 *The Open Door*. Clevedon, Multilingual Matters.

Fishman J 1972 *The Sociology of Language*. Rowley, Newbury House.

Fishman J 1977 Language and ethnicity. In Giles H (ed.) *Language, Ethnicity and Intergroup Relations*. New York, Academic Press, pp. 15–58.

Frazer E 1992 Talking about gender, race and class. In Cameron et al. pp. 90–112.

Frith S 1984 *The Sociology of Youth*. Ormskirk, Causeway Books.

Furnborough P, Jupp T, Munns R and Roberts C 1982 Language disadvantage and discrimination: breaking the cycle of majority group perception, *Journal of Multilingual and Multicultural Development* 3 (3):247–66.

Gal S 1979 *Language Shift: Social Determinants of Linguistic Change in Bilingual Austria*. New York, Academic Press.

Gal S 1988 The political economy of code-choice. In Heller (ed.), pp. 245–64.

Gal S 1989 Lexical innovation and loss: the use and value of restricted Hungarian. In Dorian, N (ed.), pp. 313–31.

Ganguly S R 1980 The Ego Attitudes in the Second Language Learning of Asian Adolescent Bilinguals in England. PhD Thesis, Brunel University.

Gardiner M 1992 *The Dialogics of Critique: M M Bakhtin and the Theory of Ideology*. London, Routledge.

Garfinkel H 1967 *Studies in Ethnomethodology*. Oxford, Polity Press.

Genishi C 1981 Code-switching in Chicano six-year-olds. In Duran (ed.), pp. 133–52.

Giddens A 1987 *Social Theory and Modern Sociology*.Oxford, Polity Press.

Giddens A 1988 Goffman as a systematic social theorist. In Drew and Wootton (eds), pp. 250–79.

Giddens A 1989 *Sociology*. Oxford, Polity Press.

Giles H and Byrne J 1982 An intergroup approach to second language acquisition, *Journal of Multilingual and Multicultural Development* 3 (1):17–40.

Gilroy P 1982 Steppin' out of Babylon – race, class and autonomy. In CCCS, pp. 276–314.

Gilroy P 1987 *There Ain't No Black in the Union Jack*. London, Hutchinson.

Gilroy P and Lawrence E 1988 Two-tone Britain: white and black youth and the politics of anti-racism. In Cohen and Bains (eds), pp. 121–55.

Giroux H 1983a Theories of reproduction and resistance in the new sociology of education: a critical analysis, *Harvard Educational Review* 53 (3):257–93.

Giroux H 1983b Ideology and agency in the process of schooling, *Boston University Journal of Education* 165 (1):12–34.

Gluckman M 1962 Les Rites de Passage. In Gluckman M (ed.) *The Ritual of Social Relations*. Manchester, Manchester University Press.

Goffe A 1985 Black and brown in Brum, *The Guardian*, 19.9.85.

Goffman E 1963a *Behaviour in Public Places*. New York, Free Press.

Goffman E 1963b *Stigma*. Harmondsworth, Penguin.

Goffman E 1967 *Interaction Ritual*. Harmondsworth, Penguin.

Goffman E 1971 *Relations in Public*. London, Allen Lane.

Goffman E 1974 *Frame Analysis*. Harmondsworth, Penguin.

Goffman E 1981 *Forms of Talk*. Oxford, Blackwell.

Goffman E 1983 The interaction order, *American Sociological Review* 48: 1–17.

Goodwin M 1982 Processes of dispute management among urban black children, *American Ethnologist* 9: 76–96.

Goodwin M 1985 The serious side of jump rope: conversational practices and social organisation in the frame of play, *Journal of American Folklore* 98 (389): 315–30.

Goodwin M 1988 Cooperation and competition across girls' play activities. In Fisher S and Todd A (eds) *Gender and Discourse: the Power of Talk*. Norwood, New Jersey, Ablex, pp. 55–94.

Goodwin M and Goodwin C 1987 Children's arguing. In Philips S, Steele S and Tanz C (eds) *Language, Gender and Sex in Comparative Perspective*. Cambridge, Cambridge University Press, pp. 200–48.

Goodwin C and Goodwin M 1990 Interstitial argument. In Grimshaw A (ed.) *Conflict Talk*. Cambridge, Cambridge University Press, pp. 85–117.

Grosjean F 1983 *Life with Two Languages*. Cambridge, Mass., Harvard University Press.

Gumperz J 1976 Language, communication and public negotiation. In Sanday P G (ed.) *Anthropology and the Public Interest*. New York, Academic Press, pp. 273–92.

Gumperz J 1982a *Discourse Strategies*. Cambridge, Cambridge University Press.

Gumperz J (ed.) 1982b *Language and Social Identity*. Cambridge, Cambridge University Press.

Gumperz J and Cook-Gumperz J 1982 Introduction: Language and the communication of social identity. In Gumperz (ed.), pp. 1–21.

Gumperz J and Jupp T, Roberts C 1979 *Crosstalk: A Study of Cross-cultural Communication*. Southall, Middlesex, National Centre for Industrial Language Training.

Gysels M 1992 French in urban Lubumbashi Swahili: codeswitching, borrowing or both, *Journal of Multilingual and Multicultural Development* 31 (1): 19–40.

Hall S 1988 New ethnicities, *ICA Documents* 7: 27–31.

Hall S and Jefferson T (eds) 1976 *Resistance through Rituals*. London, Hutchinson.

Halliday M 1985 *An Introduction to Functional Grammar*. London, Edward Arnold.

Halstead M 1988 *Education, Justice and Cultural Diversity: an Examination of the Honeyford Affair 1984–85*. Lewes, Falmer Press.

Hamers J and Blanc M 1989 *Bilinguality and Bilingualism*. Cambridge, Cambridge University Press.

Hammersley M 1987 Ethnography and the cumulative development of theory, *British Educational Research Journal* 13 (3): 283–96.

Hammersley M 1992 *What's Wrong with Ethnography?* London, Routledge.

Handelman D 1977 Play and ritual: Complementary frames of meta-communication. In Chapman A and Foot H (eds) *It's a Funny Thing Humour.* Oxford, Pergamon, pp. 185–92.

Hannerz U 1980 *Exploring the City.* New York, Columbia University Press.

Hargreaves A 1982 Resistance and relative autonomy theories: problems of distortion and incoherence in recent Marxist analyses of education, *British Journal of Sociology of Education* 3 (2): 107–26.

Hatch E 1978 Discourse analysis and second language acquisition. In Hatch E (ed.) *Second Language Acquisition: a Book of Readings.* Rowley, Mass., Newbury House, pp. 401–35.

Haugen E [1973] 1979 The stigmata of bilingualism. In Pride J (ed.) *Sociolinguistic Aspects of Language Learning and Teaching.* Oxford, Oxford University Press, pp. 72–85.

Hawkins E 1984 *Awareness of Language: An Introduction.* Cambridge, Cambridge University Press.

Heath S 1983 *Ways with Words.* Cambridge, Cambridge University Press.

Hebdige D 1979 *Subculture: the Meaning of Style.* London, Methuen.

Hebdige D 1987 *Cut 'n' Mix: Culture, Identity and Caribbean Music.* London, Comedia.

Hechter M 1978 Considerations on Western European ethnoregionalism. Paper presented at conference on Ethnicity and Economic Development. Ann Arbor, University of Michigan, October.

Heller M 1982 Negotiations of language choice in Montreal. In Gumperz (ed.), pp. 108–18.

Heller M 1988 Introduction. In Heller (ed.), pp. 1–24.

Heller M (ed.) 1988 *Codeswitching: Anthropological and Sociolinguistic Perspectives.* The Hague, Mouton de Gruyter.

Heller M 1989 Speech economy and social selection in educational contexts: a Franco-Ontarian case study *Discourse Processes* 12:377–90.

Heller M 1992 The politics of code-switching and language choice, *Journal of Multilingual and Multicultural Development* 13 (1): 123–42.

Hester H and Wight J 1977 Language in the multiethnic classroom, *Forum* 20 (1): 9–17.

Heritage J 1984 *Garfinkel and Ethnomethodology.* Oxford, Blackwell.

Heritage J 1990/91 Intention, meaning and strategy: observations on constraints on interaction analysis *Research on Language and Social Interaction* 24: 311–32.

Hewitt R 1986 *White Talk, Black Talk.* Cambridge, Cambridge University Press.

Hewitt R 1989 Creole in the classroom: Political grammars and educational vocabularies. In Grillo R (ed.) *Social Anthropology and the Politics of Language* (Sociological Review Monograph 36). London, Routledge, pp. 126–44.

Hewitt R 1989b A sociolinguistic view of urban adolescent relations. Paper presented to a conference: Everyday Life, Cultural Production and Race. Institute of Cultural Sociology, University of Copenhagen 27028, April.

Hill J 1992 'Today there is no respect': Nostalgia, 'respect' and oppositional discourse in Mexicano (Nahuatl) language ideology, *Pragmatics* **2** (3): 263–80.

Hill J and Coombs D 1982 The vernacular remodelling of national and international languages, *Applied Linguistics* 3: 224–34.

Hill J and Hill K 1986 *Speaking Mexicano: the Dynamics of Syncretic Language in Central Mexico*. Tucson, University of Arizona Press.

Hinnenkamp V 1980 The refusal of second language learning in interethnic contexts. In Giles H, Robinson P and Smith P (eds) *Language: Social Psychological Perspectives*. Oxford, Pergamon, pp. 179–84.

Hinnenkamp V 1984 Eyewitnessing pidginisation? Structural and sociolinguistic aspects of German and Turkish Foreigner Talk, *York Papers in Linguistics*. York.

Hinnenkamp V 1987 Foreigner talk, code-switching and the concept of trouble. In Knapp K, Enninger W and Knapp-Potthof A (eds) *Analyzing Intercultural Communication*. Amsterdam, Mouton de Gruyter, pp. 137–80.

Honey J 1983 *The Language Trap: Race, Class and 'Standard English' in British Schools*. Kenton, Middx, National Council for Educational Standards. (extracts reprinted in Mercer N (ed.) 1988 *Language and Literacy from an Educational Perspective*, Vol. I. Milton Keynes, Open University Press, pp. 163–89.)

Howatt A 1984 *A History of English Language Teaching*. Oxford, Oxford University Press.

Hudson R A 1980 *Sociolinguistics*. Cambridge, Cambridge University Press.

Huitzinga J 1955 *Homo Ludens*. London, Paladin.

Husband C 1987 British racisms: the construction of racial ideologies. In Husband C (ed.), pp. 319–32.

Husband C (ed.) 1987 *'Race' in Britain: Continuity and Change*, 2nd edn. London, Hutchinson.

Hymes D 1972a Models of the interaction of language and social life. In Gumperz J and Hymes D (eds) *Directions in Sociolinguistics*. Oxford, Blackwell, pp. 353–37.

Hymes D 1972b On communicative competence. In Pride J and Holmes J (eds) *Sociolinguistics*. Harmondsworth, Penguin, pp. 269–93.

Hymes D 1980 *Language in Education: Ethnolinguistic Essays.* Washington, DC, Centre for Applied Linguistics.

James C and Garrett P 1991 The scope of language awareness. In James and Garrett (eds), pp. 3–20.

James C and Garrett P (eds) 1991 *Language Awareness in the Classroom.* London, Longman.

Jefferson G (nd) Notes on some Orderliness in Overlap Onset. MS, University of York.

Jones S 1988 *Black Culture White Youth.* Basingstoke, Macmillan.

Kapferer B 1969 Norms and the manipulation of relationships in a work context. In Mitchell J C (ed.) *Social Networks in Urban Situations.* Manchester, Manchester University Press, pp. 181–244.

Kasper G and Kellerman E (eds) (forthcoming) *Advances in Communication Strategy Research.* London, Longman.

Kendon A 1990 *Conducting Interaction.* Cambridge, Cambridge University Press.

Khan S 1986 Asian youth: Ill-educated sons of peasants? *Searchlight,* **132**: 22.

Kitwood T and Borrill C 1980 The significance of schooling for an ethnic minority, *Oxford Review of Education* 6 (3): 241–53.

Krashen S 1981 *Second Language Acquisition and Second Language Learning.* Oxford, Pergamon.

Kroskrity P, Schieffelin B and Woolard K (eds) 1992 Language Ideologies. Special Issue of *Pragmatics,* **2** (3), pp. 235–453.

Labov W 1972a *Sociolinguistic Patterns.* Oxford, Blackwell.

Labov W 1972b *Language in the Inner City.* Oxford, Blackwell.

Lakoff G and Johnson M 1980 *Metaphors We Live By.* Chicago, Chicago University Press.

Lambert W 1967 A social psychology of bilingualism *Journal of Social Issues* **23**:91–108. (Reprinted in Pride J and Holmes J (eds) 1972 *Sociolinguistics.* Harmondsworth, Penguin, pp. 336–49.)

Lander S 1981 Towards a reformulation of interlanguage in the light of work on pidginisation and ethnic minority English in Britain *Interlanguage Studies Bulletin* 6: 56–71.

Laver J 1975 Communicative functions of phatic communion. In Kendon A, Harris R and Key M R (eds) *Organisation of Behaviour in Face-to-Face Interaction.* The Hague, Mouton, pp. 215–38.

Laver J 1981 Linguistic routines and politeness in greeting and parting. In Coulmas F (ed.) *Conversational Routine.* The Hague, Mouton, pp. 289–304.

Lawrence E 1982 Just plain commonsense: the 'roots' of racism. In CCCS, pp. 47–94.

Leech G 1969 *A Linguistic Guide to English Poetry.* London, Longman.

Leech G and Svartvik J 1975 *A Communicative Grammar of English*. London, Longman.

LePage R 1980 Projection, focusing and diffusion, *York Papers in Linguistics* 9.

LePage R and Tabouret-Keller A 1985 *Acts of Identity*. Cambridge, Cambridge University Press.

Lever J 1976 Sex differences in the games children play, *Social Problems* 23: 478–83.

Levine J (ed.) 1990 *Bilingual Learners and Mainstream Classrooms*. Lewes, Falmer Press.

Levinson S 1979 Activity types and language, *Linguistics* 17: 365–99.

Levinson S 1983 *Pragmatics*. Cambridge, Cambridge University Press.

Levinson S 1988 Putting linguistics on a proper footing: explorations in Goffman's concepts of participation. In Drew and Wootton (eds), pp. 161–227.

Linguistic Minorities Project (LMP) 1983 *Linguistic Minorities in England*. London, Heinemann.

Linguistic Minorities Project (LMP) 1985 *The Other Languages of England*. London, Routledge & Kegan Paul.

Long M 1983 Native speaker/non-native speaker conversation and the negotiation of comprehensible input, *Applied Linguistics* 4 (2): 126–41.

Lucas E 1972 Language in the infants playground *Multiracial School* 1.(3): and 2 (1).

Lukes S 1975 Political ritual and social integration, *Sociology* 9: 289–308.

McDermott R and Gospodinoff K 1981 Social contexts for ethnic borders and school failure in H Trueba, G Guthrie and K Au (eds) *Culture and the Bilingual Classroom*. Rowley, Mass., Newbury House, pp. 212–230.

McLellan D 1986 *Ideology*. Milton Keynes, Open University Press.

McLure E 1981 Formal and functional aspects of the code-switched discourse of bilingual children. In Duran (ed.), pp. 69–94.

McLure E and McLure M 1988 Macro- and micro-sociolinguistics dimension of codeswitching in Vingard (Romania). In Heller (ed.), pp. 25–52.

Maltz D and Borker R 1982 A cultural approach to male–female communication. In Gumperz (ed.), pp. 195–216.

Marenbon J 1987 *English Our English*. London, Centre for Policy Studies. (Extracts reprinted in Crowley T (ed.) *Proper English?: Readings in Language, History and Cultural Identity*. London, Routledge, pp. 243–60.)

Martin-Jones M and Romaine S 1986 Semilingualism: a half-baked theory of communicative competence, *Applied Linguistics* 7 (1): 26–38.

Matthews B 1986 Bad news for race relations, *Times Educational Supplement* 24 January.

Maynard D 1985a How children start arguments, *Language in Society* **14** (1): 1–29.

Maynard D 1985b On the functions of social conflict among children, *American Sociological Review* **50**: 207–23.

Mehan 1980 The competent student *Anthropology and Education Quarterly* **11**: 131–52.

Melucci A 1980 The new social movements: a theoretical approach, *Social Science Information* **19**.(2): 199–226.

Melucci A 1981 Ten hypotheses for the analysis of new movements. In Pinto D (ed.) *Contemporary Italian Sociology*. Cambridge, Cambridge University Press, pp. 173–94.

Melucci A 1985 The symbolic challenge of contemporary movements, *Social Research* **52** (4): 789–816.

Melucci A 1988 Getting involved: identity and mobilisation in social movements in *International Social Movement Research* Vol. 1. 329–48.

Mercer N, Mercer L and Mears R 1979 Linguistic and cultural affiliation amongst young Asian people in Leicester. In Giles H and St Jacques B (eds) *Language and Ethnic Relations*. Pergamon, pp. 15–26.

Mertz E 1989 Sociolinguistic creativity: Cape Breton Gaelic's linguistic tip. In Dorian (ed.), pp. 103–16.

Mey J 1981 'Right or Wrong, My Native Speaker', Estant les Regestes du Noble Souverain de l'Empirie Linguistic avec un Renvoy au Mesme Roy. In Coulmas (ed.) (1981b), pp. 69–84.

Miller J 1983 *Many Voices*. London, Routledge & Kegan Paul.

Milner D 1983 *Children and Race: Ten Years On*. London, Ward Lock.

Milroy L 1980 *Language and Social Networks*. Oxford, Blackwell.

Mitchell J C 1956 The Kalela dance. In *Rhodes Livingston Papers 27*. Manchester, Manchester University Press, pp. 1–52.

Moerman M 1988 *Talking Culture: Ethnography and Conversation Analysis*. Philadelphia, Penn., Pennsylvannia University Press.

Mungham G and Pearson G (eds) 1976 *Working Class Youth Culture*. London, Routledge & Kegan Paul.

National Curriculum Council (NCC) 1992 *National Curriculum English: The Case for Revising the Order*. York, National Curriculum Council.

Nihalani P, Tongue R and Hosali P 1979 *Indian and British English*. Delhi, Oxford University Press.

Nofsinger R 1991 *Everyday Conversation*. Newbury Park, Sage.

Oliver P (ed.) 1990 *Black Music in Britain*. Milton Keynes, Open University Press.

Opie I and Opie P 1959 *The Lore and Language of Schoolchildren*. Oxford, Oxford University Press.

Paikeday T 1985 *The Native Speaker is Dead!* Toronto, Paikeday Publishing.

Parekh B 1978 Asian in Britain: problem or opportunity? In *Five Views of Multiracial Britain*. London, Commission for Racial Equality, pp. 36–55.

Parkin D 1977 Emergent and stabilised multilingualism: polyethnic peer groups in urban Kenya. In Giles H (ed.) *Language, Ethnicity and Intergroup Relations*. New York, Academic Press.

Parkin D 1980 The creativity of abuse, *Man* (NS) **15**: 45–64.

Parkin D 1984 Political language, *Annual Review of Anthropology* **13**: 345–65.

Parmar 1982 Gender, race and class: Asian women in resistance. In CCCS, pp. 236–75.

Payne G 1985 Planning activities. In Clarke M M (ed.) *Helping Communication in Early Education*. Department of Education. Birmingham, Birmingham University, Educational Review Occasional Publication No 11

Pearson G 1976 'Paki-bashing' in a north east Lancashire cotton town. In Mungham G and Pearson G *Working Class Youth Culture*. London, Routledge & Kegan Paul.

Penfield J and Ornstein-Galicia J 1985 *Chicano English: An Ethnic Contact Dialect*. Amsterdam, John Benjamins.

Philips S U 1972 Participant structures and communicative competence: Warm Springs children in community and classroom. In Cazden C, John V and Hymes D (eds) *Functions of Language in the Classroom*. New York, Teachers College Press, pp. 370–94.

Philipsen G and Carbaugh D 1986 A bibliography of fieldwork in the ethnography of communication, *Language in Society* **15**: 387–98.

Pica T 1987 Second language acquisition, social interaction and the classroom, *Applied Linguistics* **8** (1): 3–21.

Pollard A 1979 Negotiating deviance and 'getting done' in primary school classrooms. In Barton L and Meighan R (eds) *Schools, Pupils and Deviance*. Driffield, Nafferton, pp. 75–94.

Pollard A 1985 *The Social World of the Primary School*. London, Holt, Rinehart and Winston.

Pomerantz A 1984 Agreeing and disagreeing with assessments: some features of preferred/dispreferred turn shapes. In Atkinson and Heritage (eds), pp. 57–101.

Poplack S 1988 Contrasting patterns of code-switching in two communities. In Heller (ed.), pp. 215–44.

Pryce K 1979 *Endless Pressure*. Harmondsworth, Penguin.

Rampton M B 1983 Some flaws in educational discussion in the English of Asian schoolchildren in Britain, *Journal of Multilingual and Multicultural Development* **4** (1): 15–28.

Rampton M B 1987a Uses of English in a Multilingual British Peer Group. Unpublished PhD Thesis, London, Institute of Education, University of London.

Rampton M B 1987b Stylistic variability and not speaking 'normal' English. In Ellis R (ed.) *Second Language Acquisition in Context*. Oxford, Pergamon, pp. 47–58.

Rampton M B 1988 A non-educational view of ESL in Britain, *Journal of Multilingual & Multicultural Development* 9 (6): 503–29.

Rampton M B 1989 Group affiliation and quantitative sociolinguistics, *York Papers in Linguistics* 13: 279–94.

Rampton M B 1990 Displacing the 'native speaker': expertise, affiliation and inheritance, *ELT Journal* 44 (2): 97–101.

Rampton M B 1991a Interracial Panjabi in a British adolescent peer group, *Language in Society* 20: 391–422.

Rampton M B 1991b Second language learners in a stratified multilingual setting, *Applied Linguistics* 12 (3): 229–48.

Rampton M B 1991c Language education in policy and peer group, *Language and Education* 5 (3): 189–207.

Rampton M B 1992 Scope for 'empowerment' in sociolinguistics? In Cameron D, Frazer E, Harvey P, Rampton B and Richardson K *Researching Language: Issues of Power and Method*. London, Routledge, pp. 29–64.

Rampton M B, forthcoming A sociolinguistic perspective on L2 communication strategies. In Kasper G and Kellerman E (eds).

Rampton B, Bourne J and Cameron D 1989 The Kingman Inquiry: a briefing document, *Linguistics and Politics Newsletter* 5 3–24.

Reid E 1988 Linguistic minorities and language education – the English experience, *Journal of Multilingual and Multicultural Development* 9 (1 and 2): 181–92.

Richards I A 1936 *The Philosophy of Rhetoric*. Oxford, Oxford University Press.

Roberts C, Davies E and Jupp T 1992 *Language and Discrimination*. Longman.

Roberts C and Simonot M 1987 'This is my life': how language acquisition is interactionally accomplished. In Ellis R (ed.) *Second Language Acquisition in Context*. Oxford, Pergamon, pp. 133–48.

Robins D and Cohen P 1978 *Knuckle Sandwich: Growing Up in the Working Class City*. Harmondsworth, Penguin.

Romaine S 1983 Collecting and interpreting self-reported data on the language use of linguistic minorities by means of 'language diaries', *MALS Journal* New series, 8: 3–30.

Romaine S 1984 *The Language of Children and Adolescents*. Oxford, Blackwell.

Romaine S 1988 *Bilingualism*. Oxford, Blackwell.

Rose E, Deakin N, Abrams M, Jackson V, Peston M, Vanags A, Cohen B, Gaitskell J and Ward P 1969 *Colour and Citizenship*. Oxford, Oxford University Press.

Rosen H and Burgess T 1980 *The Languages and Dialects of London Schoolchilden*. London, Ward Lock.

Saville-Troike M 1982 *The Ethnography of Communication*. Oxford, Blackwell.

Said E 1978 *Orientalism*. Harmondsworth, Penguin.

Sapir E 1931 Communication. In *Encyclopaedia of the Social Sciences*. New York, MacMillan. (Reprinted in Mandelbaum D (ed.) 1949 *Edward Sapir: Selected Writings in Language, Culture and Personality*. Berkeley, Cal., California University Press, pp. 104–9.)

Scarcella R and Higa C 1981 Input, negotiation, and age differences in second language acquisition, *Language Learning* 31 (2): 409–35.

Schiffrin D 1977 Opening encounters, *American Sociological Review* 42 (5): 679–91.

Schmidt R 1977 Sociolinguistic variation and language transfer in phonology, *Working Papers in Bilingualism* 12: 79–95.

Schumann J 1978 *The Pidginisation Hypothesis*. Rowley, Newbury House.

Sebba M 1986 London Jamaican and Black London English. In Sutcliffe D, Wong A (eds) *The Language of the Black Experience*. Oxford, Blackwell, pp. 149–67.

Sebba M 1993 *London Jamaican*. London, Longman.

Seidlhofer B, Akoha J, Ardo Z, Simpson J and Widdowson H 1991 Nationalism is an infantile disease (Einstein): What about native-speakerism? *British Association for Applied Linguistics Newsletter* 39: 21–6.

Selinker L and Douglas D 1985 Wrestling with context in interlanguage theory, *Applied Linguistics* 6 (2): 190–204.

Shackle R 1979 Problems of classification in Pakistan Panjab, *Transactions of the Philological Society* 191–210.

Shackle R 1987 Speakers of Indian languages. In Swan M, Smith B (eds) *Learner English*. Cambridge, Cambridge University Press, pp. 170–84.

Singh R, Lele J and Martohardjono G 1988 Communication in a multilingual society: some missed opportunities, *Language in Society* 17 (1): 43–59

Sippy G P 1975 *Sholay*. Bombay.

Sluckin A 1981 *Growing Up in the Playground*. London, Routledge.

Smith G 1979 Attitudes to Language in a Multicultural Community in East London. MPhil Thesis, University College London.

Sperber D 1975 *Rethinking Symbolism*. Cambridge, Cambridge University Press.

Sperber D and Wilson D 1986 *Relevance*. Oxford, Blackwell.

Stewart S 1981 Shouts on the street: Bakhtin's anti-linguistics. In Morson G (ed.) *Bakhtin: Essays and Dialogues on his Work*. Chicago, Chicago University Press, pp. 41–58.

Stølen M 1992 Codeswitching for humour and ethnic identity: written Danish-American occasional songs *Journal of Multilingual and Multicultural Development* **13** (1): 215–28.

Streeck J 1986 Towards reciprocity: politics, rank and gender in the interaction of a group of schoolchildren. In Cook-Gumperz et al. (eds), pp. 295–326.

Sutcliffe D 1982 *British Black English*. Oxford, Blackwell.

Sutcliffe D 1984 British Black English and West Indian Creoles. In Trudgill (ed.), pp. 219–38.

Sutton-Smith B 1971 Children at play, *Natural History* **80**: 54–8.

Sutton-Smith B 1982 A performance theory of peer relations. In Borman K (ed.) *The Social Life of Children in a Changing Society*. Norwood, New Jersey, Ablex, pp. 65–77.

Swigart L 1992 Two codes or one? The insiders' view and the description of codeswitching in Dakar, *Journal of Multilingual and Multicultural Development* **13** (1): 83–102.

Tarone E 1983 On the variability of interlanguage systems, *Applied Linguistics* **4** (2): 142–63.

Taylor J 1976 *The Half-Way Generation*. Windsor, NFER-Nelson.

Taylor M 1981 *Caught Between*. Windsor, NFER-Nelson.

Taylor M and Hegarty S 1985 *The Best of Both Worlds?* Windsor, NFER-Nelson.

Thomas K 1984 Intercultural relations in the classroom. In Craft M (ed.) *Education and Cultural Pluralism*. Lewes, Falmer Press, pp. 57–77.

Thompson J 1984 *Studies in the Theory of Ideology*. Oxford, Polity Press.

Thompson M 1974 The second generation: Punjabi and English, *New Community* 3.(3): 242–8.

Tinkel A 1985 Methodology related to Language Awareness work. In Donmall (ed.), pp. 37–46.

Tinkel A 1991 Language Awareness and the teaching of English language in the upper secondary school. In James and Garrett (eds), pp. 100–6.

Todorov T 1984 *Mikhail Bakhtin: The Dialogical Principle*. Manchester, Manchester University Press.

Tomlinson S 1983 *Ethnic Minorities in British Schools*. London, Heinemann.

Touraine A 1981 *The Voice and the Eye: An Analysis of Social Movements*. Cambridge, Cambridge University Press.

Touraine A 1985 An introduction to the study of social movements, *Social Research* **52** (4): 749–87.

Tourangeau R and Sternberg R 1982 Understanding and appreciating metaphors, *Cognition* **11**: 203–44.

Trosset C 1986 The social identity of Welsh learners, *Language in Society* **15** (2): 165–92.

Troyna B 1978 Race and streaming: a case study, *Educational Review* **30** (1): 59–66

Trudgill P (ed.) 1978 *Sociolinguistic Patterns in British English*. London, Edward Arnold.

Trudgill P (ed.) 1984 *Language in the British Isles*.Cambridge, Cambridge University Press.

Turner G 1983 *The Social World of the Comprehensive School*. London, Croom Helm.

Turner V 1969 *The Ritual Process*. London, Routledge & Kegan Paul.

Turner V 1974 Liminal to liminoid in play, flow and ritual, *Rice University Studies* **60**: 53–92. (Reprinted in *From Ritual to Theatre: the Human Seriousness of Play*. New York, PAJ, pp. 20–60.)

Valdes G 1981 Codeswitching as a deliberate verbal strategy: a micro-analysis of direct and indirect requests among bilingual Chicano speakers. In Duran (ed.), pp. 95–108.

Valdman A 1981 Sociolinguistic aspects of foreigner talk *International Journal of the Sociology of Language* **28**: 41–52

Varonis E and Gass S 1985 Non-native/non-native conversations: a model for the negotiation of meaning, *Applied Linguistics* **6** (1): 71–90.

Verma G K 1985 The role of the media. In DES, pp. 38–45.

Volosinov V [1929] 1973 *Marxism and the Philosophy of Language*. Seminar Press.

Vygotsky L 1962 *Thought and Language*. Cambridge, Mass., MIT Press.

Walvin J 1987 Black caricature: the roots of racialism. In Husband (ed.), pp. 59–72.

Wellek R and Warren A 1949 *A Theory of Literature*. Harmondsworth, Penguin.

Wells J 1982 *Accents of English*, Vols 1–3. Cambridge, Cambridge University Press.

Wertsch J 1991 *Voices of the Mind*. London, Harvester Wheatsheaf.

Wiles S 1981 Language issues in the multicultural school. In Mercer N (ed.) *Language in School and Community*. London, Edward Arnold, pp. 51–76.

Williams R 1973 Base and superstructure in Marxist cultural theory, *New Left Review* **82**:3–16.

Williams R 1977 *Marxism and Literature*. Oxford, Oxford University Press.

Willis P 1977 *Learning to Labour*. Farnborough, Saxon House.

Wong-Fillmore L 1979 Individual differences in second language acquisition. In Fillmore C, Kempler D and Wang W (eds) *Individual Differences in Language Ability and Language Behaviour*. New York, Academic Press, pp. 203–30.

Woodward J et al 1984 Racism in Bradford *The Times Educational Supplement* 4 May.

Woolard K 1988 Codeswitching and comedy in Catalonia. In Heller (ed.), pp. 53–76.

Woolard K 1989 *Double Talk*. Stanford, Stanford University Press.

Wright C 1984 School processes: an ethnographic study. In Eggleston S, Dunn D and Anjali M *The Educational and Vocational Experiences of 15–18 year old Young People of Minority Ethnic Groups*. Keele, Department of Education, University of Keele.

Yule H and Burnell A [1886] 1985 *Hobson Jobson: A Glossary of Anglo Indian Colloquial Words and Phrases*. London, Routledge & Kegan Paul.

General Index

Author Index